Friedrich Albert Lange, Ernest Chester Thomas

The history of materialism and criticism of its present importance

Vol. II

Friedrich Albert Lange, Ernest Chester Thomas

The history of materialism and criticism of its present importance
Vol. II

ISBN/EAN: 9783743355750

Hergestellt in Europa, USA, Kanada, Australien, Japan

Cover: Foto ©Thomas Meinert / pixelio.de

Manufactured and distributed by brebook publishing software (www.brebook.com)

Friedrich Albert Lange, Ernest Chester Thomas

The history of materialism and criticism of its present importance

HISTORY OF MATERIALISM

AND

CRITICISM OF ITS PRESENT IMPORTANCE.

BY

FREDERICK ALBERT LANGE,

LATE PROFESSOR OF PHILOSOPHY IN THE UNIVERSITIES OF ZÜRICH AND MARBURG.

Authorized Translation

BY

ERNEST CHESTER THOMAS,

LATE SCHOLAR OF TRINITY COLLEGE, OXFORD.

IN THREE VOLUMES.

VOL. II.

BOSTON:

HOUGHTON, OSGOOD, & COMPANY.

1880.

TABLE OF CONTENTS.

𝔉irst 𝔅ook—(continued).

HISTORY OF MATERIALISM UNTIL KANT.

FOURTH SECTION.—THE EIGHTEENTH CENTURY.

CHAPTER I.

THE INFLUENCE OF ENGLISH MATERIALISM IN FRANCE AND
GERMANY .   .   .   .   .   .   Pp. 3–48

England the classical land of Materialism, and of the union of religious
faith and Materialism, 3. English Materialists in the eighteenth
century: Hartley, 4; Priestley, 7. Scepticism in France : La Mothe
le Vayer, 9; Pierre Bayle, 10. Beginning of intellectual intercourse between England and France, 11. Voltaire, 12. His activity
in favour of the Newtonian philosophy, 13. His attitude towards
Materialism, 17. Shaftesbury, 19. Diderot, 23 ; his relation to
Materialism, 24. Transition to Robinet and his modification of
Materialism, 29. Intellectual condition of Germany, 32. Influence
of Descartes and Spinoza, 34. Influence of Englishmen, 36. The
'Correspondence on the Nature of the Soul,' 37. Various traces of
Materialism, 47.

CHAPTER II.

DE LA METTRIE   .   .   .   .   .   Pp. 49–91

Rectification of the chronology, 49. Biographical, 54. The 'Natural
History of the Soul,' 56. The hypothesis of Arnobius and Condillac's
Statue, 62. 'L'Homme Machine,' 63. Lamettrie's character, 77.
His theory of morals, 80. His death, 90.

CHAPTER III.

'THE SYSTEM OF NATURE' . . . . Pp. 92–123

The leaders of the literary movement in France, and their relation to Materialism, 92. Cabanis and the materialistic physiology, 93. The System of Nature: general character, 93. Its author, Baron d'Holbach, 94. Holbach's other writings, 95. His ethic, 96. Contents of the work; the anthropological portion and the general foundations of the study of nature, 97. Necessity in the moral world; relations to the French Revolution, 102. 'Order and disorder are not in Nature;' Voltaire's polemic against this principle, 104. Consequences of Materialism through the Association of Ideas, 106. Results for the conception of the æsthetic, 107. Diderot's conception of the Beautiful, 108. The justification of ethical and æsthetic ideas, 109. Holbach's attack upon the Immateriality of the Soul, 111. Remark as to Berkeley, 112. Attempt at a physiological basis for morals, 113. Political passages, 114. The second part of the work: attack upon the idea of God, 115. Religion and morality, 119. General possibility of Atheism, 121. Conclusion of the work, 122.

CHAPTER IV.

THE REACTION AGAINST MATERIALISM IN GERMANY Pp. 124–150

The philosophy of Leibnitz as an attempt to surmount Materialism, 124. Popular effect and true sense of philosophical principles; his doctrine of the Immateriality of the Soul, 127. Optimism and its relation to the mechanical theory, 131. Doctrine of Innate Ideas, 132. Wolff's philosophy and the doctrine of the Simplicity of the Soul, 133. Animal Psychology, 134. Writings against Materialism, 135. The insufficiency of the School-philosophy as against Materialism, 141. Materialism displaced by the ideal effort of the eighteenth century, 142. Reform of the Schools from the beginning of the century, 143. The search for the Ideal, 146. Influence of Spinozism, 147. Goethe's Spinozism and his judgment of the System of Nature, 148.

Second Book.

HISTORY OF MATERIALISM SINCE KANT.

——

FIRST SECTION.—MODERN PHILOSOPHY.

CHAPTER I.

KANT AND MATERIALISM . . . . Pp. 153–234

The Return of German philosophy to Kant. Abiding significance of
Criticism. Reversal of the metaphysical standpoint, 153. Movement and Sensation : the world as phenomenon, 157. Experience as product of Organisation. Kant in his relation to Plato
and Epikuros, 158. Kant in opposition to Subjectivism and to
Scepticism. Impulse from Hume : his standpoint, 159. Kant and
Experience, 163. Analysis of Experience. Synthetic judgments
a priori, 164. The discovery of *a priori* elements, 190. Sensibility
and Understanding, 194. Space and Time as forms of Sensibility.
Whether Sensation cannot measure itself by Sensation. Psychophysics, 198. Apriority of Space and Time equally tenable, 199.
Attitude of Materialism towards the doctrine of Space and Time,
203. The Categories, 204. Hume's attack upon the notion of
Causality, 205. Deduction of the categories, 208. Errors of the
deductive process. Sound Common Sense. The basis of notions
a priori, 209. Various conceptions of the notion of Causality, 211.
Attitude of Empiricists and Materialists to the notion of Causality,
213. The thing-in-itself, 216. The deduction of the Categories and
the origin of ideas, 219. Free will and the moral law, 227. The
intellectual world as ideal, 232.

CHAPTER II.

PHILOSOPHICAL MATERIALISM SINCE KANT . Pp. 235–294

The native lands of modern philosophy turn to practical life, while
metaphysic remains to Germany. The course of intellectual
development in Germany, 235. Causes of the revival of Materialism ; influence of the natural sciences ; Cabanis and the Somatic
method in physiology, 240. Influence of habituation to conflicts of
opinion and freedom of thought, 244. The philosophy of nature,
245. Tendency to Realism since 1830, 245. Feuerbach, 246. Max
Stirner, 256. Decay of poetry ; development of commercial activity
and natural science, 257. Theological criticism and 'Young Ger-

many'; increasing excitement until 1848, 260. The reaction and
material interests ; renewed impulse towards Natural Science, 263.
Beginning of the Materialistic controversy, 263. Büchner and
philosophy, 265. Büchner; impulse from Moleschott; obscurities
and defects of his Materialism, 270. Moleschott; influence of
Hegel and Feuerbach ; Moleschott's unmaterialistic theory of Knowledge, 275. Possibility of Materialism according to Kant. The
categorical imperative : Content thyself with the given world, 282.
Czolbe, 284.

SECOND SECTION.—THE NATURAL SCIENCES.

CHAPTER I.

MATERIALISM AND EXACT RESEARCH   .   .   Pp. 297–350

Materialists and Scientific Specialists; Dilettanteism and Scholasticism
in natural science and philosophy, 297. Scientific and philosophical
modes of thought, 302. The Limits of Natural Knowledge : Du Bois-
Reymond, 308. Misunderstandings of Materialists and theologians,
313. Correction of the consequences of Du Bois-Reymond's hypotheses, 319. The limits of natural knowledge are the limits of knowledge in general, 321. The mechanical cosmology cannot discover
the inmost nature of things, 323. Materialism makes theory into
reality and the immediately given into appearance, 324. Sensation
a more fundamental fact than the mobility of matter, 326. Even
the hypothesis of a sentient matter does not remove all difficulties. The unknown *tertium quid*, 328. Unfair reproaches against
Materialism, 329. Overcoming of Materialism by philosophical and
historical culture, 332. Value of theories, 336. Materialism and
Idealism in scientific research, 337.

CHAPTER II.

FORCE AND MATTER   .   .   .   .   Pp. 351–397

History of the atomic notion. Boyle, 351. Influence of Newton's
law of gravitation, and of Hobbes' relativistic modification of the
atomic notion, 353. Dalton, 354. Richter, 358. Gay-Lussac, 359.
Avogadro's molecular theory. Berzelius. Dulong and Petit,
359. Mitscherlich and Isomorphism. The theory of Types, 361.
Doubts as to theories; stricter distinction between Fact and
Hypothesis, 362. Mathematicians and Physicists. Theory of extensionless atoms, 363. Fechner, 365. Objections to the extensionless
atoms ; W. Weber's idea of an unextended mass, 369. Influence
of modern chemical theories, and of the mechanical theory of heat
upon the notion of an atom, 371. Attempt of the Materialists
to subordinate force to matter; criticism of this attempt, 377. The
molecules become ever better known, the atoms ever more uncertain, 382. The law of the persistence of force, 389. Influence of
this law on the notion of matter. Relativistic definitions of
Thing, Force, and Matter, 391. Fechner's and Zöllner's views.
The problem of force and matter is a problem of the theory of knowledge, 394.

First Book

Continued.

HISTORY OF MATERIALISM
UNTIL KANT.

EIGHTEENTH CENTURY MATERIALISM.

—•—

CHAPTER I.

THE INFLUENCE OF ENGLISH MATERIALISM IN FRANCE AND GERMANY.

ALTHOUGH modern Materialism appeared as a system first in France, yet England was the classic land of materialistic modes of thought. Here the ground had already been prepared by Roger Bacon and Occam; Bacon of Verulam, who lacked almost nothing but a little more consistency and clearness in order to be a Materialist, was wholly the man of his age and nation, and Hobbes, the most consequent of the modern Materialists, is at least as much indebted to English tradition as to the example and precedence of Gassendi. It is true, indeed, that by Newton and Boyle the material world-machine was again provided with a spiritual constructor; but the mechanical and materialistic theory of nature only rooted itself the more firmly the more one could pacify religion by appealing to the Divine inventor of the great machine. This peculiar combination of faith and Materialism [1] has kept its ground in England down to our own days. We need mention only the pious sectarian Faraday, who essentially owes his great

---

[1] Compare what has been said above, vol. i. p. 296 foll. We find as early as Hartley the results of the conservative tendency introduced by Hobbes.

discoveries to the concrete liveliness with which he conceived natural events, and the consistency with which he asserted the mechanical principle through every branch of Physics and Chemistry.

Even in the middle of the eighteenth century, when the French Materialists caused so much perturbation on the Continent, England had Materialists of its own.

The physician David Hartley published in the year 1749 a work in two volumes which made a great sensation. It bore the singular title, " Observations on Man, his Frame, his Duty, and *his Expectations.*"[2] By these were meant chiefly our 'expectations' in the life to come. The book contains a physiological, or one might even call it a psychological section, and a theological section; and it was the latter that caused most excitement. Hartley was a master of theological questions. The son of a clergyman, he would have devoted himself to this profession, but that doubts as to the Thirty-nine Articles drove him into medicine. He did not favour 'Hobbism' in religious matters therefore, or such doubts would scarcely have been entertained. In his work we see where he hesitated; he defends the miracles, asserts the authority of the Bible, deals at great length with the life after death; but he doubts the eternity of punishment! This struck at the roots of hierarchy, and threw the dark shadow of heresy over all the rest of his doctrines.

In the physiological portion of his book, it is true that Hartley undertakes to refer the whole of human thought and sensation to vibrations of the brain, and it cannot be denied that Materialism has drawn plentiful nourishment

---

[2] Hartley, David, Dr.. Observations on Man, his Frame, his Duty, and his Expectations, Lond. 1749, 2 vols. 8vo (6th ed. corr. and revised, Lond. 1834). The preface of the author is dated December 1748. Previously, in the year 1746, there appeared a work by the same author, "De Sensu, Motu et Idearum Generatione," which, however, met with less approval. The statement is inaccurate in Hettner, Literaturgesch. des 18ten Jahrh., i. S. 422, that Priestley issued in the year 1775 a "third and last portion" of the "Observations" under the title "Theory of the Human Mind." Comp. Note 7, *infra.*

from this theory. In Hartley's statement of it, however, it does not offend against orthodoxy. Hartley dutifully divides man into two parts: Body and Soul. The Body is the instrument of the Soul: the brain the instrument of sensation and thought. Other systems also, he remarks, assume that every change of the mind is accompanied by a corresponding change in the body. This system only attempts, supporting itself on the doctrine of the association of ideas, to afford a complete theory of these correlated changes. The doctrine of the association of ideas as the foundation of mental phenomena is, in a germinal form, already to be found in Locke. It was a clergyman, the Rev. Mr. Gay,[3] who was Hartley's immediate predecessor; he had tried to explain all the operations of the soul by the combination of associations, and this psychological basis has continued in England down to our own days without any one's seriously doubting that at the bottom of the association are also fixed antecedent movements in the brain, or, more cautiously expressed, that they are accompanied by corresponding functions of the brain. To this Hartley did nothing but add the physiological theory; but it is precisely this circumstance which made him, despite all his protests, a Materialist. So long, namely, as we speak with a vague generality of the functions of the brain, the mind may be allowed to use its instrument at will without any obvious contradiction. But as soon as we attempt to carry into detail the general idea, it becomes clear that the material brain also is subject to the laws of material nature. The vibrations which appeared to accompany thought so innocently, discover themselves now as products of a mechanism which, set in motion from without, must work according to the laws of the material world.[4] We do not at once get so far as Kant's bold idea

[3] Hartley, as he himself relates in the preface to the "Observations," had been first set thinking by a remark made in conversation by Gay. He then set forth his views in an essay on the principle of virtue, which Law introduced into his English translation of King, "De Origine Mali."

[4] The chief criterion of strict Materialism, as opposed to Hylo-

that a series of actions may, as *phenomenon*, be subject
to an absolute necessity; while the same series may, as
" *Ding-an-sich*," rest upon a foundation of freedom.   The
idea of necessity is inevitably implied in the functions of
the brain, and necessity in the psychological sphere is the
immediate consequence.   Hartley admits this consequence,
but he appears only to have done so after many years' study
of the association theory, and to have adopted it reluc-
tantly.   So that a point which Hobbes dealt with quite
openly and unconcernedly, which Leibniz disposed of
without discovering in it any offence to religion, causes
great difficulties to the 'Materialist' Hartley.   He defends himself by not denying the *practical* freedom of the
will—that is, Responsibility; but he seeks with still greater
zeal to demonstrate that he also admits the practical
eternity of punishment—that is, the extremely long dura-
tion and the intense degree of the punishment, which are
enough to frighten sinners, and to make the salvation promised by the Church appear an infinite blessing.

Hartley's principal book was translated into French and
German, but with a noteworthy difference.   Both trans-
lators consider the book to consist of two heterogeneous
parts, but the German holds the theological portion to be
the most important, and gives only a concise sketch[5] of the
theory of associations.   The French translator confines
himself to the physiological explanation, and leaves the
theology out.[6]   The course taken by the French translator

zoism (comp. Note 1 to First Section,
p. 3 foll.), appears also in Hartley,
and therefore, in spite of his religious views, he may be counted with
the Materialists.

[5] David Hartley's Betrachtungen
über den Menschen, seine Natur,
seine Pflichten und Erwartungen, aus
dem Engl. übersetzt und mit Anmerk-
ungen und Zusätzen begleitet, 2 Bde.
Rostock u. Leipzig, 1772–73.   The
editor and author of the notes and
additions (the translation was made
by the 'Magister' von Spieren), H.

A. Pistorius, dedicates his work to
the well-known free-thinking theologian the Consistorialrath Spalding,
who, on the occasion of a discussion
on the consistency of Determinism
with Christianity, called his attention
to Hartley.

[6] Explication physique des Idées
et des Mouvements tant Volontaires
qu'in Volontaires, trad. de l'Anglais de
M. Hartley par l'Abbé Jurain, Prof.
de Math. à Reims, Reims, 1775; with
a dedication to Buffon.

was also taken by Hartley's somewhat bolder successor, Priestley, who, although himself a theologian, likewise omitted the theological portion in the edition he published of Hartley's book.[7] Priestley was, of course, constantly engaged in controversy, and it cannot be disputed that his 'Materialism' played a great part in the attacks of his opponents; but at the same time we must not overlook that through quite other things he challenged the orthodox or conservative. That he found leisure-time enough in his position as pastor of a dissenting congregation for important scientific investigations is nowadays much more generally known than that he was one of the most fearless and zealous champions of Rationalism. He wrote a work in two volumes on the "Corruptions of Christianity," amongst which he included the doctrine of Christ's divinity; while in another work he taught Natural Religion.[8] Politically as well as theologically a freethinker, he was not sparing in condemnation of the Government, and attacked especially the ecclesiastical institutions and the position of the Establishment. We can easily understand that

[7] Comp. Hartley's Theory of the Human Mind, on the principle of the association of ideas, with Essays relating to the subject of it by Joseph Priestley, Lond. 1775 (2d ed. 1790). Hettner (i. 422) erroneously supposes this to be a third-part of Hartley's book. It is only a selection from the first part, for Priestley omitted even the anatomy for the most part, and chiefly gave the psychological theory of Hartley, together with his own observations on the same subject.

[8] Comp. History of the Corruptions of Christianity, by Joseph Priestley, LL.D., F.R.S., 2 vols. 8vo, Lond. 1782 (translated into German, 2 Bde. Berlin, 1785). Dr. Joseph Priestley, member of the Imperial Academy of St. Petersburg and the Royal Society of London, Institutes of Natural and Revealed Religion: Lond. 1772 (translated into German, with notes, Frankfurt and Leipzig, 1782). The works dealing specially with Materialism, so far as I know, have not been translated into German. Comp. Disquisitions relative to Matter and Spirit, with a History of the Philosophical Doctrine concerning the Origin of the Soul and the Nature of Matter, with its influence on Christianity, especially with respect to the Doctrine of the Preexistence of Christ, Lond. 1777.

The Doctrine of Philosophical Necessity illustrated, with an Answer to the Letters on Materialism, Lond. 1777.

The Letters on Materialism referred to were a controversial publication by Richard Price, who not only attacked Priestley, but appeared in general as the opponent of the Empiricism and Sensationalism then ruling in English philosophy.

such a man must have become the object of persecutions, even though he had never taught that the sensations are functions of the brain.

And here we may point out another very characteristic trait of this English Materialism. The actual head and leader of the English unbelievers at that time was not so much Hartley the Materialist as Hume the Sceptic, a man whose views put an end as well to Materialism as to the dogmatism of religion and metaphysics. Priestley, however, wrote against him from the standpoint of teleology and theism, exactly as the German Rationalists were at the same time writing against Materialism. But Priestley attacked also the " Système de la Nature "—the masterpiece of French Materialism—in which, nevertheless, atheistic zeal very distinctly outweighed the materialistic theory. That he was entirely in earnest in these attacks is shown not only by the tone of the fullest conviction in which, quite in the sense of Boyle, Newton, and Clarke, he regarded the world as the product of a conscious Creator, but quite as much by the recurrent attempt—an attempt which reminds us of Schleiermacher—to win again for religion, by purifying it of superstition, the spirits that had been estranged from it.[9]

Hence it comes, also, that Hartley as well as Priestley was attentively read in Germany, where rationalistic theologians were then very numerous; but it was for their theology rather than their Materialism. In France, on the contrary, where there was no such school of serious and

[9] Comp. Joseph Priestley's Briefe an einen philos. Zweifler in Beziehung auf Hume's Gespräche, das System der Natur und ähnliche Schriften. Aus dem Englischen, Leipz. 1782. (The original Letter to a Philosophical Unbeliever, appeared Bath 1780.) The anonymous translator compared Priestley with *Reimarus* and *Jerusalem*, and remarks correctly enough that Priestley has very often misunderstood Hume ; but this does not lessen the value of his own views. Besides Priestley's first philosophical work, " Examination of Dr. Reid's Inquiry into the Human Mind, Dr. Beattie's Essay on the Nature and Immutability of Truth, and Dr. Oswald's Appeal to Common Sense, Lond. 1774, was so far on the side of Hume, that it undertook a refutation of the philosophy of Common Sense as directed against Hume.

pious Rationalists, it was the Materialism only of these English writers that exercised any influence; but in this point France had at that time no need of further scientific stimulus. Starting from earlier English influences, a spirit had been there developed which boldly strode past any difficulties in the theory, and upon a hastily constructed foundation of scientific facts and theories raised an edifice of the most venturous consequences. De la Mettrie wrote simultaneously with Hartley, and the "System of Nature" found an opponent in Priestley. These two circumstances show clearly enough that Hartley and Priestley are, for the history of Materialism, as a whole, of but slight import- ance, although indeed they are of great interest in connec- tion with the progress of materialistic modes of thought in England.

As the national mind in England showed a tendency to Materialism, so the favourite philosophy of the French, it is quite obvious, was originally Scepticism. The pious Charron and the worldly Montaigne agree in undermining dogmatism, and their work is continued by La Mothe le Vayer and Pierre Bayle, after Gassendi and Descartes had come between to open the way for the mechanical concep- tion of nature. So powerful continued to be the influence of the sceptical tendency in France, that amongst the Materialists of the eighteenth century, even those who are called the most extreme and decided remain widely removed from the systematic finality of a Hobbes, and appear to em- ploy their Materialism only as a means of keeping religious belief in check. Diderot commenced his struggle against the Church under the standard of Scepticism, and even De la Mettrie, who of all the Frenchmen of the eighteenth century attached himself most closely to the dogmatic Materialism of Epikuros, calls himself a Pyrrhonist, and describes Montaigne as the first Frenchman who ventured to think.[10]

[10] Comp. Homme Machine, Œuvres Phil. de M. de la Mettrie, iii. p. 57, and Discours sur le Bonheur (where Montaigne is often quoted), Œuvres, ii. 182.

La Mothe le Vayer was a member of the Council of State under Louis XIV. and tutor of the young prince who became Duke of Orleans. In his "Five Dialogues," indeed, he exalted faith at the expense of theology, and in showing that the imaginary knowledge of the philosophers, like that of the theologians, amounts to nothing, he did not omit to exhibit doubt itself as a preparation for submission to the revealed religion; but the tone of his writings is very different from that of a Pascal, whose original Scepticism was ultimately fused into an intense hatred of the philosophers, and whose reverence for faith was not only honest, but even narrow and fanatical. Hobbes also, as we know, exalted faith that he might attack theology. If La Mothe was no Hobbes, he was certainly no Pascal either.[11] At court he was regarded as an unbeliever, and he maintained his position only by the unexceptionable austerity of his life, by reserve, and calm superiority of culture. The influence of his writings was at least favourable to the cause of enlightenment, and the great consideration which he enjoyed, especially among the upper classes must have very much increased this influence.

Incomparably more important was, of course, the influence of Bayle. Pierre Bayle—who, the child of Protestant parents, was as a young man converted by the Jesuits, but speedily returned to Protestantism—by the severe laws as to mass enforced by Louis XIV. against the Protestants was driven into Holland, which was at that time the favourite asylum of the freethinkers of all nations. Bayle was a Cartesian, but he drew from the main principles of the system other consequences than its author. While Descartes everywhere appeared to maintain the consistency of religion and science, Bayle intentionally pointed out their disagreements. In his famous "Critical and Historical Dictionary," he nowhere, as Voltaire remarks,

---

[11] Hettner, ii. 9, puts La Mothe and Pascal together, which, when we consider the very different characters of these two authors, seems to me not quite right.

in a single line openly attacked Christianity, but he also wrote no line which was not intended to awaken doubt. The contradiction between reason and revelation was apparently decided in favour of the latter, but it was intended that the reader should come to an opposite decision. The influence of this book was as important as that of any book can be. Whilst the mass of various knowledge that was here made most conveniently accessible was calculated to attract the scholar, the herd of superficial readers were fascinated by the piquant and pleasing, if often wilfully offensive, treatment of scientific subjects. "His style," says Hettner,[12] "is of the most dramatic vivacity, and fresh, direct, bold, provoking, and yet ever clear and rapid in the attainment of its aim: while he seems only to be skilfully playing with the subject, he probes and dissects it to its inmost depths." "From Bayle comes the controversial style employed by Voltaire and the French Encyclopædists: even for the literary manner of Lessing, it is not without significance that he studied Bayle much in his youth."

With the death of Louis XIV. (1715) came that remarkable turning-point in modern history, which was as important for the philosophic modes of thought of the educated, as for the social and political fortunes of the nations: the intellectual intercourse between England and France, which developed so suddenly and in such intensity. This transition is pictured by Buckle in his "History of Civilisation" with vivid, perhaps here and there somewhat exaggerated, colours. He doubts whether towards the end of the seventeenth century there were even five persons in France, engaged in literature or science, who were acquainted with the English language.[13] The national vanity had lent to French society a self-sufficiency which despised English culture as barbarous, and the two Revolutions which England had undergone could only increase

---

[12] Comp. the very good characterisation of Bayle and his influence in Hettner, ii. 45–50.

[13] Buckle, History of Civilisation in England, ii. 214.

this contemptuous feeling so long as the brilliance of the
court and the victories of their grand monarch allowed them
to forget at what sacrifice of public happiness this splendour was purchased.   When, however, as the king grew
old, the pressure grew greater and the brilliance fell away,
the more perceptible became the complaints and the griev-
ances of the people, and the thought awoke in all thinking
minds, that the nation with its submission to despotism
had entered upon a path of destruction.   Intercourse with
England was renewed: while in earlier times men like
Bacon and Hobbes had sought to complete their education
in France, the best minds of France now crowded to England,[14] and worked hard to learn English and the literature
of the English.

In the sphere of politics the French took away with
them from England the idea of civil freedom and of the
rights of the individual; but these ideas were combined
with the democratic tendency which awoke in France with
irresistible strength, and which was at root, as De Toqueville[15] has shown, a product of that same monarchical government which found in it its terrible fate.   Similarly in the
sphere of speculation English Materialism combined with
French Scepticism, and the product of this combination
was the radical rejection of Christianity and the Church,
which in England since Newton and Boyle have made
such excellent terms with the mechanical conception of
nature.   Singular and yet quite capable of explanation is
it that the philosophy of Newton should in France be
made to further Atheism, while it had been introduced into
France with the certificate that it was less injurious to
faith than Cartesianism!

It was of course Voltaire who introduced it, one of the
first among those men who furthered the connection of the

---

[14] Comp. the long lists of Frenchmen who visited England and understood English given in Buckle, l. c.,
ii. 215-223.

[15] De Toqueville, L'Ancien Régime
et la Revolution, 1856; [Tr. State of
Society in France before the Revolution, 2d ed. 1873].

French and English intellectual tendencies, and certainly the most influential of the whole series.

Voltaire's prodigious activity is to-day justly placed in a clearer light than was customary in the first half of this century. Englishmen and Germans vie with each other in securing for the great Frenchman, without palliating his defects, the place due to him in the history of our intellectual life.[16] The cause of this temporary depreciation of him Du Bois-Reymond finds, "paradox as it may sound," in the fact "that we are all more or less Voltaireans—Voltaireans without knowing it, and without being called so." "So powerfully has he prevailed, that the ideal advantages for which he struggled a long life through with unwearied zeal, with passionate devotion, with every weapon of the intellect, above all, with his terrible ridicule—toleration, intellectual freedom, respect for man, justice—have become to us as the natural elements of life, as the air, of which we only think when we have it no more—in a word, that what once flowed from Voltaire's pen as a daring speculation is to-day become a commonplace."[17] Even the fact that Voltaire secured recognition for the Newtonian cosmology on the Continent has long been too lightly estimated, as well with regard to his understanding of Newton and the independence of his conduct, as also with respect to the greatness of the difficulties to be surmounted. We need only point out that the "Éléments de la Philosophie de Newton" was not allowed to be printed in France, and that this work also had to seek assistance in the freedom of the Netherlands! We must not, however, suppose that Voltaire employs Newton's cosmology as a weapon to attack Christianity, and that he furnishes it with the caustic Vol-

---

[16] Among the Englishmen we must here especially mention Buckle: among German writers Hettner in the Literg. des 18ten Jahrb.; further, Strauss, Voltaire, 1870, and with especial reference to a particular department, but not without general interest, Du Bois-Reymond's Lecture, Voltaire in s. Bez. zur Naturwissensch., Berlin, 1868.

[17] Du Bois-Reymond, *l. c.*, S. 6.

tairean satire. The work is, on the whole, as seriously and calmly as it is clearly and simply written: indeed, many philosophical questions seem to be treated with a certain timidity, especially where Leibniz, to whose system Voltaire repeatedly refers, is bolder and more consequent than Newton. On occasion of the question whether we must suppose a sufficient reason for God's actions, Voltaire praises Leibniz highly, who answers this question in the affirmative. According to Newton, God has so arranged many things—as, for instance, the movement of the planets from west to east—as they are, simply because he chose to do so without there being any other reason for this than the divine will. Voltaire feels that the arguments which Clarke adduces against Leibniz are not quite satisfactory, and he endeavours to support them with reasons of his own. He is just as vacillating in the question of free-will.[18] Later, of course, we find in Voltaire the concise summing up of a prolix inquiry in Locke — "to be free means to be able to do what we like, not to be able to will as we like ;" and this statement, rightly understood, agrees with Determinism and Leibniz's theory of freedom. In the " Philosophy of Newton," 1738, however, Voltaire shows himself still too much involved in the doctrine of Clarke to attain perfect clearness. He thinks that freedom is perhaps possible to indifference, but is unimportant. The question is not whether I can move the left or right foot without any other cause than my own will, but whether Cartouche and Nadir Schah could have avoided the shed-

---

[18] The views here mentioned are to be found in the Éléments de la Philosophie de Newton, 1738, i. c. 3 and 4, Œuvres compl., 1784, t. 31. Hettner's Litg. ii. 206 ff., has followed in the order of time Voltaire's changes of opinion as to freewill. What is of most importance for us here is to show quite clearly what Voltaire had taught *before the appearance of De la Mettrie;* for in fact the most distinct expressions of Voltaire in this, as in many other questions, are to be found in the "Philosophe Ignorant," which was written in 1767, *twenty years, therefore, after "L'Homme Machine."* Depreciatingly as Voltaire judges the author of "L'Homme Machine," it is nevertheless quite possible that its appearance and its arguments have had some influence upon Voltaire.

ding of blood. Voltaire thinks of course with Locke[19] and Leibniz that they could *not;* but the whole question is how is this *not* to be explained. The Determinist, who seeks responsibility in the character of man, will deny that a persistent will can be formed in him in opposition to the character. If we find an apparent instance, this only proves that in the character of such a man forces still slumbered and could be awakened which we had previously overlooked. But if we will in this way decide any one of the questions relating to the will, the problem of decision in a case of apparently complete indifference—the case of the old scholastic *equilibrium arbitrii*—is by no means so unimportant as Voltaire believes. It is only by getting rid of this phantom that it becomes at all possible to apply scientific principles to the problems of the will.

When such is his attitude with regard to these questions, there is no room whatever to doubt that Voltaire was entirely serious in his approbation of Newton's views as to God or the purpose visible in the universe. How came it, then, that the Newtonian system could nevertheless in France further the cause of Materialism and of Atheism?

We must here never forget that the new cosmology had made the best heads in France reconsider and re-examine with the freshest interest all the questions which had been already raised in the time of Descartes. We have seen the contribution made by Descartes to the mechanical theory, and we shall soon come upon yet further traces of it; but on the whole, the stimulating activity of Cartesianism was already at the outset of the eighteenth century pretty well exhausted. Especially was no further very great influence upon the French schools to be expected from him, since he had been tamed by the Jesuits and clipped—to suit their purposes. It is not a matter of indifference whether a series of great ideas act upon one's contemporaries in their fresh originality, or whether they are transformed into a mere mixture with plentiful addition

[19] Locke, Essay concerning Human Understanding, ii. c. 21, § 20-27.

of traditionary prejudices. Nor, again, is it indifferent with what tone and attitude men's minds receive a new doctrine. Yet we must boldly maintain that, for the complete working out of the cosmology founded by Newton, no more favourable circumstances, no more favourable tone of thought, could be found than those in France in the eighteenth century.

The 'vortices' of Descartes failed to be confirmed by mathematical theory. Mathematics were the sign in which Newton conquered. Du Bois-Reymond very justly remarks that Voltaire's influence upon the elegant world of *Salons* did not contribute less to naturalise the new cosmology. "Only when Fontenelle's 'Mondes' was driven out by the 'Eléments' of Voltaire from the dressing-tables of the ladies, could Newton's victory over Descartes be pronounced in France complete." Even that must not be lacking any more than the satisfaction of the national vanity secured by the Newtonian theory receiving the carefully considered confirmation of a Frenchman ;[20] but at the very foundation of the movement which brought about the great transition, we see the powerful impetus which the mathematical sense of the French received through the influence of Newton. The magnificent phenomena of the seventeenth century were renewed in increased splendour, and to the age of a Pascal and Fermat succeeded with Maupertuis and D'Alembert the long series of French mathematicians of the eighteenth century, until Laplace drew the last consequences of the Newtonian cosmology in discarding even the hypothesis of a creator.

Voltaire himself, despite all his radicalism, did not draw such consequences. Although he was far indeed removed from allowing his masters, Newton and Clarke, to dictate a peace with the Church, he was nevertheless through his life true to the two great principles of their metaphysic. It cannot be denied that the same man who worked with all his might to overthrow ecclesiastical dogma, the author

[20] Comp. Du Bois-Reymond, Voltaire in s. Bez. zur Naturw., S. 10

of the notorious phrase, "écrasez l'infâme," is yet a great supporter of a purified teleology, and that he is perhaps more serious as to the existence of God than any one of the English Deists. To him God is a deliberating artist who has created the world according to reasons of wise purpose. Although later Voltaire undoubtedly went over to a gloomier theory, which preferred to think of the evil in the world, yet nothing remained further from his mind than the assumption of blindly acting natural laws.[21]

Voltaire would not be a Materialist. There is obviously at work in his mind a crude unconscious beginning of the Kantian standpoint, when he constantly comes back to the idea most sharply expressed in the well-known words, "If there were no God, it would be necessary to invent him." We postulate the existence of God as the foundation of moral conduct, teaches Kant. Voltaire thinks that if one were to give Bayle, who held an atheistic state to be possible, five or six hundred peasants to rule, he would immediately have preached the doctrine of a divine retribution. Apart from the playfulness of the remark, it will be found to contain Voltaire's real view that the idea of God is indispensable for the maintenance of virtue and justice.

We can now understand that Voltaire quite seriously opposed the 'System of Nature,' the 'Bible of Atheism,' though not with the mad fanaticism of Rousseau. Much nearer was Voltaire to anthropological Materialism. Here Locke was his guide, who appears to have exercised the utmost influence upon the whole sphere of Voltaire's philosophy. Locke himself, of course, leaves this point undecided. Although he held to the fact that the whole intellectual life of mankind flows from the activity of the senses, yet he leaves it an open question whether it is *matter* that receives the materials provided by the senses, and whether therefore *matter* thinks or not. Against those, however, who kept their feet steadily upon this,

[21] Hettner, ii. 193, shows that Voltaire was first startled out of his earlier optimism by the earthquake of Lisbon in 1755.

that the nature of matter as the extended is inconsistent with the nature of thought, Locke lets fall the somewhat superficial remark that it is godless to maintain that a thinking matter is impossible; for if God had willed it, he might by his omnipotence have created matter capable of thinking. This theological turn of the matter pleased Voltaire, for it promised a desirable support for controversy with the believers. Voltaire thought himself so enthusiastically into this question, that he no longer left it unsettled with Locke, but decided it in the materialistic sense.[22]

" I am body," says he in his London letter on the English, "and I think; more I do not know. Shall I then attribute to an unknown cause what I can so easily attribute to the only fruitful cause I am acquainted with ? In fact, where is the man who, without an absurd godlessness, dare assert that it is impossible for the Creator to endow matter with thought and feeling ? "

Of course we can scarcely claim this expression for the stricter form of Materialism. Voltaire believed that we must have lost all common sense before he could suppose that the mere motion of matter is sufficient to produce feeling and thinking beings. And therefore, not only is a Creator necessary in order to make matter capable of thought, but even the Creator will be unable to produce thought in matter, as was the case with Hobbes, by means of mere motion of matter. It will be a special force that is communicated to matter, and this force will in all probability—according to Voltaire's idea—although it is not motion, yet be able to produce motion (in the voluntary actions). But if the matter is so taken, we are in the sphere of Hylozoism. (Comp. Note I to First Sect., vol. i. p. 3.)

Since we possess the law of the conservation of force, there is in a purely theoretical respect an enormous chasm between strict Materialism and Hylozoism. The former is compatible with that law : the latter not. Kant, indeed, had already declared Hylozoism to be the death of all

[22] Comp. Hettner, ii. 183.

Naturphilosophie,[23] obviously only because it renders the mechanical conception of nature impossible. Nevertheless it would be incorrect to lay too much stress upon this distinction in the case of Voltaire. With him certain conclusions are of more importance than the principles; and practical relations to Christian belief, and to the supremacy of the Church based upon belief, determine his standpoint. His Materialism accordingly grew stronger with the keenness of his attack upon belief. For all that, he had never made up his mind on the question of immortality. He halted between the theoretical reasons which made it improbable, and the practical ones which appeared to recommend it; and here again we find that trait reminding us of Kant, that a doctrine is retained as the presupposition and support of morality which the understanding finds at least incapable of proof.[24]

In moral philosophy also Voltaire likewise followed English suggestions, but his authority on this point was no longer Locke, but his pupil, Lord Shaftesbury, a man especially interesting to us for his deep influence on the leading minds of Germany in the eighteenth century. Locke had combated innate ideas in the sphere of morals also, and had notably popularised the relativity of good and evil as propounded by Hobbes. He gathers materials from all possible books of travel in order to show us how the Mingrelians bury their children alive without any remorse, and how the Tououpinambos believe that they will earn Paradise by revenge and the eating of their enemies.[25] Voltaire also on occasion can employ such things, but they do not in the

---

[23] Kant's Metaphys. Anfangsgr. der Naturwissensch., III. Hauptst. Lehrs. 3 Anm., Werke, Hartenst., iv. 440.

[24] How Voltaire became more aggressive, especially after 1761, is very well shown in Strauss, Voltaire, 1870, S. 188. As to his vacillation with regard to the doctrine of immortality and the features which remind us of Kant, comp. Hettner, ii. 201 ff.; as to the latter in particular, the often-quoted words—" Woe to those who fight each other when swimming, let him who can get to land; but he who says, You swim in vain, for there is no land, dispirits me and robs me of all my strength."

[25] Locke, Essay conc. Human Underst., i. 3, § 9.

least shake his belief in the doctrine that the idea of right and wrong in its innermost being is everywhere one and the same. If this is not born with man as a fully formed idea, he brings at least into the world the predisposition to it. Just as a man is born with legs, although he only later learns to walk, so in the same way he brings with him into the world the organ that is to distinguish right and wrong, and the development of his mind necessarily calls the function of this organ into exercise.[26]

Shaftesbury was a man of idealistic vehemence of enthusiasm, and a poetic conception of the world which, with its pure sense for the beautiful, and its deep comprehension of classical antiquity, were especially adapted to influence Germany, at that time ripening to the richest development of its national literature; at the same time the French drew rich nourishment from him, and by no means positive doctrines only—such as the theory that there lies in every human breast a natural germ of enthusiasm for virtue. And yet we have to learn this doctrine! Locke had indeed looked upon 'Enthusiasm' with no favourable eyes as the source of extravagance and self-exultation, as a noxious product of the overheated brain, and as utterly opposed to all rational thought.[27] And this is entirely in accordance with the hard and sterile prose of his whole manner of thought. Shaftesbury is here better guided by his poetical sense than Locke had been by his understanding. He finds in Art, in the Beautiful, something for which there is no place whatever provided in the psychology of Locke, except along with the calumniated enthusiasm, and yet the value and dignity of which is to him beyond all doubt. But this sheds a bright ray of light upon the whole field, and without denying that enthusiasm often produces extravagance and superstition, Shaftesbury nevertheless finds in it the spring of all that the human mind shows of noblest and greatest. And

---

[26] Comp. Hettner, ii. 210 ff.
[27] Essay conc. Human Underst., iv. c. 19, " Of Enthusiasm."

now we have found the place where morality has its origin. From the same source flows Religion—good of course as well as bad: the comforter of mankind in misfortune, and the fury who kindles the martyr-pile, the purest elevation of the heart to God, and the vilest desecration of the nobility of human nature. As with Hobbes, Religion and Superstition move together, but the wall of distinction between them is no longer the heavy sword of "Leviathan," but—the æsthetic sense. Good-tempered, gay, and cheerful people construct for themselves a noble, exalted, and yet liberal and friendly race of gods; gloomy, morose, and discontented natures produce the gods of hatred and of revenge.

Shaftesbury tries hard to range Christianity on the side of the cheerful and good-tempered religions, but with what great violences to historical Christianity! with what keen censure of ecclesiastical institutions! with what unsparing condemnation of many a tradition prized by believers as sacred and indisputable!

We have an expression of censure from Shaftesbury directed against the attitude towards religion of his master, Locke, whom in all other respects he so highly honoured, though he speaks not so much of Locke personally, but rather includes the whole class of the English Deists, and makes against them a collective accusation of Hobbism. The important point in all this with reference to most English freethinkers is the intimation of their inner aversion from what forms the very essence and spirit of religion. The editor of Locke's works, however, thinks himself entitled to turn this weapon against the enemy; while he defends Locke's orthodoxy, he describes Shaftesbury as a "sneering infidel with regard to revealed religion, and a rank enthusiast in morals." [28]

The man is not wholly wrong, especially if we judge the matter from that clerical standpoint which places the

---

[28] Comp. the Works of John Locke in ten vols., 10th ed., Lond., 1801. Life of the Author, vol. i. p. xxiv. p.

authority of the Church higher than the contents of its doctrines. But we may go much further, and say, Shaftesbury stood at heart nearer to religion generally than Locke, but did not understand the specific spirit of Christianity. His religion was the religion of the happy, who do not find it very difficult to preserve their complacency. His philosophy has been described as aristocratic, but we must add, or rather alter—it is the philosophy of the naive and harmless child placed amidst especially favourable circumstances, who takes his horizon for the horizon of humanity. Christianity was once preached as the religion of the poor and miserable, but through a remarkable dialectic of history it has at the same time become the favourite religion of those who hold poverty and misery to be an everlasting ordinance of God in this life, and who are specially well pleased with this divine arrangement because it is the natural foundation of their own favoured position. To disregard this supposed eternal order may under certain circumstances be equivalent to the sharpest direct attack. We must here again only regard the influence of Shaftesbury upon the minds of men like Lessing, Herder, and Schiller, in order to perceive how slight the step may be from naive optimism to the conscious resolution so to shape the world that it may correspond to this optimism.

It is this that explains that remarkable alliance of extremes against Shaftesbury so admirably shown by his latest biographer;[29] on the one side Mandeville, the author of the "Fable of the Bees," on the other the orthodox. Only we must rightly understand Mandeville in order to find in one and the same person the apologist of vice and the defender of the Capitol of the State Church. When Mandeville maintains against Shaftesbury that true virtue consists in self-conquest and the subjection of the natural

---

[29] Dr. Gideon Spicker, Die Philos. des Grafen von Shaftesbury, Freiburg, 1872, S. 71 ff. With regard to what I have to say of Shaftesbury, I may here, for brevity's sake, once for all refer to this valuable monograph. Comp. further also Hettner, i. 211–214.

inclinations, he does not mean the conquest of his own self and his own inclinations—for if these do not strive after unlimited satisfaction, all commerce and intercourse stands still and the state must perish! He means the selfishness and the appetites of the working-classes, for " Temperate living and constant employment is the direct road for the poor to rational happiness, and to riches and strength for the state." [30]

Whence Voltaire drew his nourishment is easily to be seen if we remember that Shaftesbury attacked not only the stake and hell, miracles and anathema, but also the pulpit and the catechism, and that he considered it his highest distinction to be abused by the clergy ; but it is unmistakable that the positive features also of Shaftesbury's philosophy have not been without their effect upon him, and especially that element in Voltaire's views which we have already pointed out as a prelude to the position taken up by Kant may in its root be traced back to Shaftesbury.

A much more lively influence of course must have been exercised by the positive features of this philosophy upon a man like Diderot. This great leader of the intellectual movement of the eighteenth century was a thoroughly enthusiastic nature. Rosenkranz, who has traced with sure hand the weaknesses of his contradictory character and his unorganised literary activity, brings also into prominence the glowing geniality of his nature in a striking manner. " We can only understand him when we consider that he, like Sokrates, taught rather orally than in writing,

[30] Comp. Karl Marx, On Capital, Hamburg, 1867, S. 602, note 73. When Hettner (i. 213) observes that the question is not whether Mandeville is at one with Christianity in his notion of virtue, but whether he is at one with himself, the answer is very simple. The apologist of vice cannot think of demanding for *all* the virtue of self-denial, but it harmonises admirably with his principles to preach Christianity and Christian virtue *to the* poor. The sermon is apparently of general application ; but he who has the means to indulge his vices knows all the same what he can do, and the stability of society is ensured.

[The quotation in the text is not from Mandeville, as the ambiguity of Marx's note has led Lange to suppose, but from an anonymous "Essay on Trade and Commerce," &c., London, 1770, attributed to J. Cunningham, p. 54.—TR.]

and that in him, as with Sokrates, the process of the times from the Regency to the Revolution fulfilled itself in all the phases of its development. There was in Diderot, as in Sokrates, something demonic. He was then only completely himself when, like Sokrates, he had raised himself up to the ideas of the True, the Good and the Beautiful. Only in this ecstasy, which was, according to his own account, manifested by external signs, and which he first perceived by an agitation in the hair over the middle of the forehead and by a tremor running through all his limbs, did he become the real Diderot, whose enraptured eloquence, like that of Sokrates, carried every listener away." [31]   Such a man could not only grow enthusiastic over Shaftesbury's "Moralists," this "dithyramb to the everlasting beauty which runs through the whole world and combines all apparent dissonances into deep full-toned harmony" (Hettner); but even Richardson's novels, in which the moral tendency is of primitive simplicity, moved him by the liveliness of their treatment into enthusiastic admiration. In all the variations of his constantly changing standpoint he retained the belief in virtue and in its deep foundation in the nature of our souls, a fixed point which he contrived to reconcile with the apparently most contradictory elements of his theoretical speculation.

Diderot is so persistently represented as the head and leader of French Materialism, at least as the first man who carried out the 'Lockian Sensualism' into Materialism, that it will be necessary for us in the next chapter once for all to dispose of the Hegelian passion for construction, which, with its sovereign contempt of all chronology, has nowhere been guilty of so great a confusion as in dealing with the philosophy of the seventeenth and eighteenth centuries. We have only to rest upon the simple facts that Diderot

[31] Rosenkranz, Diderot's Leben und Werke, 2 Bde., Leipz. 1866. The passage quoted is at ii. 410, 411. Although we do not agree with the author as to the position of Diderot in the history of Materialism, we have employed as much as possible this very desirable and valuable contribution to the intellectual movement of the eighteenth century.

was nothing less than a Materialist before the appearance of the "L'Homme Machine," that his Materialism was only developed through his intercourse with the group that gathered around Holbach, and that the writings of other Frenchmen, such as Maupertuis, Robinet, and probably even the abused La Mettrie, exercised a more decisive influence upon him than Diderot on his part exercised upon any noteworthy advocate of Materialism. We say 'decisive' influence with reference to the assumption of a clear theoretical standpoint—for a stimulating influence of the utmost importance was indeed exercised by Diderot, and it lay in the nature of that seething time that all the various revolutionary tendencies reacted upon each other. If Diderot enthusiastically eulogised morality, the thought of attacking the very basis of morality might be awakened in another mind, whilst in both minds there prevailed the same hatred of priestly morality and of the humiliation of mankind by the despotism of the clergy. Voltaire might arouse Atheists with an apology for the existence of God, because he was above all things concerned to deprive the Church of the monopoly of the theistic doctrine which it had so misused and distorted. In this unceasing torrent of assault upon all authority the tone became undoubtedly more and more radical, and its leaders at length seized upon Materialism as well as Atheism to turn it into a weapon against religion. With all this, however, at a very early period of the movement the most theoretically consistent system of Materialism was ready to hand, whilst the leaders of the movement still rested rather upon English Deism or a mixture of Deism and Scepticism.

Diderot's stimulating efficacy was, it is true, thanks to his rare literary talent and his energetic manner, uncommonly great, as well through his independent philosophical writings, as also especially through his indefatigable activity for the great Encyclopædia. It is indeed also true that Diderot has not always in the Encyclopædia expressed his own individual opinion, but it is just as true that at

its commencement he had not yet got as far as Atheism
and Materialism. It is true that great parts of the "Système
de la Nature" came from the pen of Diderot, but it is not
less true that it was not he who carried Holbach with him
to the furthest point, but, on the contrary, Holbach with
his firm will and calm clear persistency attached the
stronger intellect to his path, and won him over to his
ideas.

While La Mettrie (1745) was writing his "Natural History
of the Soul," which scarcely veils its Materialism, Diderot
was still entirely at the standpoint of Lord Shaftesbury.
He toned down in the "Essai sur le Mérite et la Vertu"
the sharpness of the original, and in the notes combated
views which appeared to him to go too far. This may
have been prudent foresight, but his defence of an order
in nature (which he later with Holbach attacked), his
polemic against Atheism, was here as candid as in the
"Pensées Philosophiques," written a year later, in which
he is of opinion, still quite in the sense of the English
teleology derived from Newton, that it is exactly the
scientific research of modern times which has inflicted
the greatest blows upon Atheism and Materialism. The
wonders of the microscope are the true divine miracles.
The wing of a butterfly, the eye of a gnat, are sufficient
to demolish Atheism. At the same time there blows here
quite another atmosphere, and close by the philosophical
annihilation of Atheism burst forth springs of richest
nourishment for social Atheism, if we may thus designate
for the sake of brevity that Atheism which attacks and
rejects the God recognised in the present constitution of
society, in State and Church, in the family and in the
school.

Diderot ostensibly fights only against intolerance, "since
he sees the whimpering dead shut up in hellish prisons,
and hears their sobs, their cries of woe." But this intolerance hangs together with the prevalent conception of
God! "What wrongs have these unhappy souls com-

mitted ?" asks Diderot; "who has condemned them to these torments? The God whom they have offended. Who is then this God? A God of infinite goodness. What! can a God of infinite goodness find any pleasure in bathing himself in tears? These are people of whom we must not say that they fear God, but that they are frightened of him. Considering the picture that is drawn for us of the Supreme Being, of his readiness to anger, or the fury of his vengeance, of the comparatively great number of those whom he allows to perish, as compared with the few to whom he is pleased to stretch forth a saving hand, the most righteous soul must be tempted to wish *that he did not exist.*" [32]

These cutting words, it is certain, acted more energetically on contemporary French society than any passage of " L'Homme Machine," and entirely apart from the speculative theory, any one who finds in Materialism nothing but opposition to religious dogma need not wait for the "Dream of D'Alembert" (1769) in order to designate Diderot as one of the boldest leaders of Materialism. It is no concern of ours, however, to lend our aid to this confusion, however much we are driven by the plan and aim of this work to include, besides the strict Materialism, the consideration of so many related or connected views.

In England the aristocratic Shaftesbury could calmly weigh the God of vengeance in the balances and find him wanting. Even in Germany, although of course much later, could Schiller demand the exclusion from the temples of that God whom nature marks "only on the rack" and who pays himself with the tears of mankind.[33] It was in

[32] Rosenkranz, Diderot, i. S. 39.

[33] Comp. Schiller's Freigeisterei der Leidenschaft, line 75 to end, Werke Hist. Crit. Ausg. iv., Stuttg. 1868, p. 26. That Schiller expresses his own views in these verses, in spite of the note added in "Thalia" (1786, 2 H. p. 59), as well as that at the sacrifice of the inner unity of the poem towards the end he forgets the special occasion and concludes with general ideas on the conception of the Divine Being, scarcely needs further proof. The translator of the " Vrai Sens du Système de la Nature" (under the title " Neunundzwanzig Thesen des Materialismus," Halle, 1873) rightly points out that the lines "Nur auf der Folter

the power of the educated classes to set up a purer conception of God in the place of the one they had over-
thrown.   But to the people, especially the Catholic people
of France, the God of vengeance was also the God of love.
In its religion, heaven and hell, salvation and damna-
tion, were combined in a mystic unity and in all the stereo-
typed definiteness of traditional ideas.   The God here
drawn by Diderot from his shadow side only was *his* God,
the God of his confidence as well as of his fear and his
daily adoration.   This picture might be destroyed as Boni-
face once destroyed the heathen gods, but it was impossible by a stroke of the pen to set the God of Shaftesbury
in its place.   One and the same drop put into different
chemical solutions gives very different precipitates.   Diderot
had actually been long fighting for Atheism whilst he was
still in theory 'demolishing' it.

Under these circumstances a nearer view of the nature
of his Materialism is not of great historical importance,
but for the criticism of Materialism a brief discussion of
his views will not be wholly out of place.   They form,
although they are not very definitely developed, yet in
clearly recognisable features a modification of Materialism
which is new, and in which the chief objection raised
against Atomism from Demokritos to Hobbes is apparently
avoided.

We have often pointed out that ancient Materialism
attributes sensation not to the atoms but to the organisation
of small germs, but that this organisation of germs, according to atomistic principles, can be nothing but a peculiar

---

merkt dich die Natur!" and "Und
diesen Nero beten Geister an!" are
in entire agreement with Chapter xix.
of the "Vrai Sens." But we must not
therefore conclude that Schiller had
read this pamphlet, still less that his
ideas as to the "Système de la Nature"
in its doctrinaire breadth and unima-
ginative prose were very much other
than those of Goethe.   Similar ideas
were found also in Diderot, and in
their germ may be traced back to
Shaftesbury.   That
Schiller was busying himself with
Diderot at the time in which falls
either the production or at least the
inner occasion of this poem, see in
Palleske, Schiller's Leben u. Werke,
5 Aufl. i. S. 535.

arrangement in space of atoms which, taken separately, are incapable of sensation. We have seen how even Gassendi with all his efforts cannot get over this difficulty, and how Hobbes does not improve things with his magic phrase that simply identifies a particular kind of molecular motion with thought. Nothing was left then but to make the experiment of placing sensation as a property of matter in the smallest particles themselves. This was done by Robinet in his book on "Nature" (1761), while La Mettrie in "L'Homme Machine" (1748) still kept to the old Lucretian conception.[34]

Robinet's singular system, rich in fantastic elements and wild hypothesis, has sometimes been regarded as a distortion of Leibniz's "Monadology," sometimes as a prelude to the "Naturphilosophie" of Schelling, sometimes as absolute Materialism. This last view is the only correct one, although it is true that we may read whole sections of the work without knowing on what ground we stand. Robinet attributes to all the smallest particles life and spirit; even the constituent elements of ' unorganic ' nature are living germs, which bear within themselves, only without any *self-consciousness*, the principle of sensation. For the rest, even man knows only—again an important element of the Kantian doctrine—his sensations —not his own essence, nor himself as substance. Robinet, through whole chapters, allows these two principles—the corporeal and the spiritual principle of matter—to act upon each other, as if we were in the sphere of the most unbridled Hylozoism. Suddenly, however, we stumble upon the brief yet very significant explanation that the action of mind upon matter is only a reaction of the material impressions, in which the (subjectively !) voluntary motions of the machine have their origin in nothing else than in the organic (that is here the mechanical) operation

---

[34] Comp. vol. i. p. 266, and the earlier passages there cited ; and further, Note 11. ibid.

of the machine.[35] This principle is then consistently, although without any ostentation, carried through. Thus, for instance, if a sense impression excites the soul to desire something, this cannot be anything else than what acts conditionally through the mechanical influence of the thinking fibres in the brain upon the appetitive fibres, and when I in pursuit of my desire will stretch out my arm, this will is only the inner, subjective side of the strictly mechanical sequence of natural processes which, proceeding from the brain by means of the nerves and muscles, brings the arm into motion.[36]

Kant's charge against Hylozoism, that it is the death-blow to any philosophy of nature, cannot hit this stand-point. The law of the conservation of force, to speak in the language of our time, is applied by Robinet to all the phenomena of man—from the sense impressions right through the brain functions to words and actions. With great acuteness he connects with it the free-will doctrine of Locke and Voltaire : to be free means to be able to do what one will, not to be able to will what one will. The moving of my arm is voluntary because it has followed upon my act of will. Objectively considered, the origin of this act of will is as necessary an event of nature, as its connection with the result. For the subject, however, this natural necessity disappears, and freedom alone is there. The will follows subjectively only motives of a spiritual nature, but these also are in their turn objectively conditioned through necessary processes in the corresponding fibres of the brain.

We see here again indeed how closely consequent Materialism always lies to the limits of all Materialism. A very little doubt in the absolute reality of matter and its motions, and we have the standpoint of Kant, which

Von der Natur, from the French of J. B. Robinet, Frankf. and Leipz., 1764, S. 385 (iv. partie, iiie ch. 1re loi :) "Les determinations d'où proviennent les mouvements volontaires de la ma-chine, ont elles-mêmes leur origine dans le jeu organique de la machine."

[36] Comp. especially *loc. cit.*, Part iv. chap. xxiii.

regards both causal series—that of nature according to external necessity, and that of our empirical consciousness according to freedom and intellectual motives—as mere phenomena of a hidden third series whose true nature remains incognisable by us.

Diderot had been inclined to such a view long before the appearance of Robinet's work. Maupertuis had in the year 1751 in a pseudonymous essay first spoken of sensitive atoms, and Diderot combats this assumption in his "Thoughts on the Explanation of Nature" (1754) after a fashion which allows us to see how clear he is about it: yet at this time Diderot was still in the standpoint of scepticism, and the treatise of Maupertuis appears on the whole to have remained without exerting very much influence.[37]

Diderot did not adopt the views of Robinet without feeling the weak point which still remains even in this modification of Materialism.[38] In "D'Alembert's Dream," the dreamer repeatedly recurs to this point. The matter is simple. We have now indeed sensitive atoms, but how does this sensation sum itself into the unity of consciousness? The difficulty is not a psychological one, for if the sensations commence—no matter how—like tones in a system of harmonious sounds—once to flow into each other, then we may imagine how a sum of elementary sensations may afford the richest and most significant content of consciousness: but how do the sensations effect this transition from atom to atom through void space? The dreaming D'Alembert, that is, Diderot, has nothing to say in answer to this, but to suppose that the sensitive particles act immediately

[37] Comp. Rosenkranz, Diderot, i. 134 ff. The pseudonymous dissertation of Dr. Baumann (Maupertuis) I have not seen, and it may be open to some doubt, according to Diderot and Rosenkranz, whether it does really contain the Materialism of Robinet—that is, the unconditional dependence of the spiritual upon the purely mechanical series of external events—or whether it inculcates Hylozoism—that is, modifications of the natural mechanism by the spiritual content of nature according to other than purely mechanical laws.

[38] Rosenkranz, Diderot, ii. 243 ff., 247 ff.

upon each other, and so form a *continuum.* But this is to be on the point of giving up Atomism, and consequently to give up that form of Materialism which Ueberweg favoured in the esoteric philosophy of his later years.[39]

We turn now, then, to consider the influence of English Materialism upon Germany. But first let us briefly consider what Germany had achieved for itself in this direction. There is indeed extremely little to be found, and the cause is not to be sought so much in the predominance of an enthusiastic Idealism, as in the general decline which had been brought on by the intellectual exhaustion of the country after the great struggles of the Reformation, by its political agitation, and its moral degeneration. While all other nations profited by the fresh breath of nascent intellectual liberty, it appeared as though Germany had fallen a victim in the struggle to obtain it. Nowhere did ossified dogmatism seem narrower than among the German Protestants, and the natural sciences especially had a difficult position.

"The introduction of the improved Gregorian kalendar was opposed by the Protestant clergy merely because this correction had proceeded from the Catholic Church; in the judgment of the Senate of Tübingen of the 24th November 1583, it is said that Christ cannot be at one with Belial and with Antichrist. Keppler, the great reformer of astronomy, was warned by the Consistory in Stuttgart on the 25th September 1612, that he must subdue his too speculative spirit, and govern himself in all things according to the Word of God, and leave the Testament and Church of the Lord Christ untroubled by his unnecessary subtleties, scruples, and glosses."[40]

[39] Fuller details as to the modifications of Materialism will follow in the Second Book. As to Diderot's Materialism, we may here further point out that he nowhere expresses himself as definitely as Robinet does in the passages above quoted. Rosenkranz finds even in the "Dream of D'Alembert" a Dynamism which, if Diderot here expresses his real view, would make even this most advanced production atheistic indeed, but not strictly Materialistic.

[40] Hettner, Literaturg. d. xviii. Jahr., iii. 1, p. 9.

We seem to find an exception in the introduction of Atomism among the German physicists by Sennert, professor at Wittenberg; and yet neither did physics greatly profit by this innovation, nor did it lead to a conception of nature at all inclining to Materialism. Zeller, indeed, says that Atomism "in a shape not essentially differing from the Demokritic" for a long time maintained such importance among the German physicists, that Leibniz could declare that it had not only caused Ramism[41] to be forgotten, but had also inflicted great injury upon the Peripatetic doctrine : but we may very probably conjecture that Leibniz has exaggerated. At least the traces of Atomism in Sennert's "Epitome Naturalis Scientiae" (Wittenberg, 1618) are so insignificant, that the thoroughly Scholastic basis of his views is at all events less disturbed by his Atomistic heresies than by those elements which he borrowed from Paracelsus.[42]

[41] On Petrus Ramus and his followers in Germany, comp. Zeller, Gesch. d. deutschen Phil., pp. 46–49. Ramus borrowed the main features of the doctrine with which he created such a sensation entirely from Vives. Comp. the Art. "Vives" in the Enc. des ges. Erz. u. Unterrichtswesens.

[42] The whole of Sennert's Atomism seems to run into a timid modification of the Aristotelian doctrine of *fusion.* While expressly rejecting the Atomism of Demokritos, Sennert teaches that the elements in themselves do not consist of direct particles, and that a continuum cannot be composed of indivisible elements. (Epitome Nat. Sci., Wittebergae, 1618, p. 63 ff.) On the other hand, indeed, he supposes that in the fusion the matter of the individual elements is first *in fact*—despite their further divisibility — divided into infinite smallest particles, and so primarily forms only a medley. These particles then react with the primary qualities of Aristotle and the School-men, viz., warmth, cold, dryness, and damp, until their qualities are again in a state of equilibrium—upon which the true Scholastic continuum of the mixture again appears (comp. *loc. cit.* pp. 69, foll. p. 225). With this is connected the further hypothesis that by the side of the 'substantial form' of a whole the substantial forms of its parts still retain a certain although subordinate efficiency.

The difference between this doctrine and a genuine Atomism is seen most clearly in Boyle, who, in several of his works, and especially in the "De Origine Formarum," frequently quotes Sennert and controverts his views. One must nowadays be already accurately acquainted with the Scholastic views of nature, in order to find at all the points in which Sennert ventures to deviate from the orthodox path, while Boyle appears in every line as a physicist in the modern sense of the word. Considered in this light, the whole of the excitement which was pro-

While in France Scepticism was by Montaigne, La
Mothe le Vayer, and Bayle, and in England Materialism
and Sensationalism by Bacon, Hobbes, and Locke, were in
a certain sense raised to the rank of national philosophies,
Germany remained the ancestral home of pedantic Scholasticism. The rudeness of the nobility, which Erasmus
had already happily characterised by the nickname of
' Centaurs,' was absolutely opposed to the rise of a complete philosophy on the basis of social culture, such as played
so great a part in England. The restlessly fermenting
element which in France became increasingly active was
not entirely wanting in Germany, but it was diverted by
the predominance of religious views into various curiously
involved, and, at the same time, subterranean paths, and
the confessional schism dissipated the best forces of the
nation in interminable struggles ending in no lasting result.
In the universities an increasingly rude generation took
possession of the chairs and benches. Melanchthon's reaction for the regenerated Aristotelianism led under the
Epigoni to an intolerance reminding us of the dark times
of the Middle Ages. The philosophy of Descartes found
safe shelter scarce anywhere but in the little Duisberg,
which enjoyed a breath of Flemish intellectual freedom and
was protected by the enlightened ruler of Prussia ; and even
that ambiguous fashion of attack under the form of defence, whose importance we have often observed, was still
applied towards the end of the seventeenth century to the
Cartesian doctrine. Nevertheless it gradually made way ;
and towards the end of the century, when the presages of
a better time were announcing themselves in many minds,
we find numerous complaints of the propagation of
' Atheism ' by the Cartesian philosophy. The orthodox
were at no time more ready with the accusation of
Atheism than then: and yet so much is clear, that those
spirits which were struggling for freedom attached them-

duced, according to Leibniz, by Sen-   what even in those days Scholastic
nert's theory, can only convince us   pedantry must still have been.

selves in Germany to a doctrine with which the Jesuits in France had already come to terms.[43]

Thus, then, it came to pass that Spinoza's influence in Germany became sensible almost simultaneously with the deeper hold taken by Cartesianism. The Spinozists form only the extreme Left in this contest against Scholasticism and orthodoxy, and this brings them nearer to Materialism, though only, of course, so far as is permitted by the mystic and pantheistic elements of Spinoza's teaching. The most important of these German Spinozists is Friedrich Wilhelm Stosch, the author of ' Concordia Rationis et Fidei' (1692), which created great excitement and indignation, and the secret possession of which in Berlin was threatened with a penalty of five hundred thalers. Stosch curtly denies not only the immateriality but also the immortality of the soul. "The soul of man consists in the due admixture of the blood and the juices which flow duly through uninjured channels and produce the various voluntary and involuntary actions." " The spirit is the better part of man—with which he thinks. It consists of the brain and its innumerable organs, which are variously modified by the influx or the circulation of a subtle matter, which is likewise variously modified." " It is clear that the soul or the spirit in itself, and of its own nature, is not immortal, and does not exist outside the human body." [44]

[43] On the spread of Cartesianism in Germany and the struggle connected with it, comp. Zeller, Gesch. d. deutschen Phil., pp. 75-77, and Hettner, Literaturg. d. xviii. Jahr., iii. 1, pp. 36-42. Here we find in particular a correct estimate of the meaning of the struggle which was carried on by the Cartesian Balthasar Bekker against the superstitions of the devil, witchcraft, and ghosts.

[44] Further information as to Stosch, as well as Matthias Knuzen and Theodor Ludwig Lau, in Hettner, Literaturg. d. xviii. Jahr., iii. 1, pp. 45-49. We originally intended to devote a special chapter to Spinoza and Spinozism : this notion had, however, to be abandoned in order not to swell the book unduly, and to prevent its varying from its original character. That in general the connection of Spinozism with Materialism is considerably over-estimated (so far as we do not confound Materialism with all kinds of more or less related tendencies) follows from the last chapter of this section, in which it is shown how Spinozism in Germany could unite itself with idealistic elements, which Materialism has never done.

More popular and incisive was the influence of the English, as well as regards the development of the general opposition to ecclesiastical creeds, as in especial the elaboration of Materialistic views. When in 1680 the Chancellor Kortholt at Kiel wrote his book, "De Tribus Impostoribus Magnis," in which he gave an opposite meaning to the old notorious title of a supposititious book, he meant Herbert of Cherbury, Hobbes, and Spinoza as the three great foes of Christian truth.[45]   Thus we find two Englishmen in this trio—one of whom, Hobbes, we have long been acquainted with.   Herbert (*ob.* 1648) is one of the oldest and most influential representatives of "Natural Theology," or rational belief in opposition to revealed dogma.   Of the influence which he as well as Hobbes exercised in Germany, we have clear traces in the "Compendium de Impostura Religionum," published by Genthe, which cannot possibly belong to the sixteenth century.[46]   It is much

[45] Comp. Hettner, Litg., iii. 1, p. 43. On the supposititious book, comp. above, n. 22, vol. i. p. 182.

[46] So it was erroneously assumed in my first ed. after Genthe and Hettner (iii. 1, pp. 8, 35). I have to thank Dr. Weinkauff of Köln, who is thoroughly acquainted with freethinking literature, for a manuscript communication which proves that the "Compendium de Impostura" was in all probability not written until towards the end of the seventeenth century. It is true that the earliest known edition bears the imprint 1598, but this is obviously a fictitious date, and the expert Brunet (Manual du Libraire, Paris, 1864, v. 942) regards the work as a German production of the eighteenth century. It is certain that in 1716 a manuscript of the work was sold at auction in Berlin for eighty thalers. This manuscript, or copies of it, must in all probability have been known to the Chancellor Kortholt, so that it must have been in existence about 1680. All other editions are later, and we have

no certain indication of the earlier existence of the MS. Internal grounds lead us to suppose that it first appeared in the second half of the seventeenth century. The very outset of the book (Esse Deum, eumque colendum esse) seems to contain a clear reference to Herbert of Cherbury; besides, it is impossible, as was noticed by Reimann, not to recognise the influence of Hobbes. The mention of the Brahmans, Vedas, Chinese, and the Great Mogul, betrays a knowledge of the books which opened the study of Hindoo and Chinese literature and mythology, and led to the comparison of religions; namely, the works of Rogerius, "IndischesHeidenthum,"Amsterdam, 1651, German, Nürnberg, 1663; Baldaeus, "Malabar, Coromandel, and Zeylon," Amsterdam, 1672, Dutch and German; and Alexander Ross, "A View of all Religions," Lond., 1653, of which there were three German translations. Moreover the work, although first printed in Germany, appears to be by no means of German origin, for the Gallicism "sortitus est," which is to

more probably a product of that time in which the Chancellor Kortholt endeavoured to turn the enemies' weapons against themselves. How productive that time was in such, for the most part, forgotten freethinking experiments, is shown by the notice that the Chancellor Mosheim (*ob.* 1755) possessed no less than seven manuscripts of this kind, all of which were written in the period after Descartes and Spinoza, and therefore, also, after Herbert and Hobbes.[47]

But the English influence was shown with especial clearness in a little book which belongs completely to the history of Materialism, and which we are glad to discuss here with some fulness, because it has not been properly estimated by the most recent historians of literature, and can scarcely have been very well known to most of them.

This is the " Correspondence on the Nature of the Soul," which in its time caused so much discussion, and which from 1713 appeared in a series of editions, was attacked in replies and reviews, and even induced a professor at Jena to devote a special lecture to the confutation of the tiny book.[48] It consists of three letters, which profess to be written by two different authors, to which a preface of some length is added by a third, who in the edition of 1723 entitles this the fourth edition, and in passing gives expression to the general surprise that the earlier editions had not been confiscated.[49] Weller, in his " Dictionary

be found in the earlier MSS. (so too in Genthe ; corrected in later editions and MSS. into "egressus est "), betrays a French author or a French original.

[47] Comp. Mosheim's Geschichte der Feinde der christl. Religion, edited by Winkler, Dresden, 1783, p. 160.

[48] "Prof. Syrbius zu Jena hat nach des Bücher Saals 28. Ordnung ein Collegium wider den Brieff.-W. v. Wesen d. Secle gehalten und dessen Autori darin seine Abfertigung geben wollen " (Vorrede). Comp. further the German "Acta Eruditorum," x. Theil, No. 7, pp. 862–881 ; Unschuldige Nachrichten, 1 anno 1731, No. 23, p. 155, *et saepe.*

[49] For the first edition of the " History of Materialism," I used a copy from the library at Bonn of the year 1723; at present I avail myself of a copy of the first edition of 1713, obtained from the duplicates of the town library of Zürich. I have for the sake of simplicity left the passages cited verbatim in the text unchanged, so that they represent the edition of 1723 where the contrary is not expressly said. More particular references to the page may be dispensed with in the case of so small a book, yet we have added a more precise indication of the place for all that is taken from the first edition.

of Pseudonyms," names J. C. Westphal, a surgeon in
Delitzch, and J. D. Hocheisel (Hocheisen, attached to the
Philosophical Faculty at Wittenberg ?), as the authors of
this correspondence.   In the last century, strangely
enough, the two theologians Röschel and Bucher were
regarded as the authors, the latter of whom was passionately orthodox, and was certainly not the man to have
entered into correspondence with an 'Atheist'—as at that
time were styled even Cartesians, Spinozists, Deists, and
so on.   Röschel, who was also a physicist, if we rely on
internal grounds, might well have written the second
(anti-materialistic) letter.   But in that case it remains
very doubtful who was the Materialist—the author of the
first and third letter, if not of the whole book.[50]   The
treatise, corresponding to the melancholy time of its production, is written in a horrible style—German inter-
mingled with fragments of Latin and French, and betrays
a witty spirit and thoroughness of thought.   The same
ideas in a classic form and amongst a self-sufficient people
would perhaps have created a sensation like that produced
by the writings of Voltaire ; but the form indicates here the
zero-point of German prose.   The time when it was written
was a time in which all the more eminent freethinkers
drew their wisdom from the Frenchman Bayle, and after
a few eagerly read editions, the voice of the German died
away.   The author was himself quite conscious of this
position of affairs, for he observes : " Dass ich diese Briefe
teutsch concipiret, solches wird man nicht vor übel halten,
weil ich sie nicht Aeternitati gewidmet wissen wollte."
(" That I have written these letters in German will not be
taken amiss, because I have not supposed that they were
written Aeternitati.")   The author had read Hobbes, but,
as he says, " for another purpose ; " of the French illu-
minati he could as yet know nothing.[51]   In 1713, the

[50] In my copy—comp. the previous
note—appears a note from an unknown hand, " Von Hocheisser (*sic*)
und Röschel."

[51] Hobbes, whose influence upon
the whole work cannot be mistaken,
is often quoted ; thus in the "Lusti-
gen Vorrede" of an anonymous writer,

date of the book's appearance, Diderot was born, and Voltaire found his way, as a young man of nineteen, for the first time, because of some satirical poems against the Government, into the Bastille. After the editor in his introduction to the letters has proved the erroneousness of all the earlier philosophies, including the Cartesian, and has shown how physics have recently extorted the first place from metaphysics, he considers the general controversy, whether we shall strike all new ideas to the ground with the old outgrown authority or refute them.

"Etliche * rathen, man solle sich juxta captum vulgi erronei richten und Peter Squentzen mit spielen. Andere aber protestiren Sollenniter, und wollen par tout Märtyrer vor ihre eingebildete Wahrheiten werden. Ich bin zu ungeschickt, das Wagezünglein in dieser Controvers zu sein; doch meinem Bedünken nach schiene es probabel, dass durch tägliche Abmahnung der gemeine Mann allgemach würde klüger werden; denn nicht vi, sed saepe cadendo (Experientia teste) cavat gutta lapidem; dabei ich auch nicht leugnen kann, dass die praejudicia nicht

* [As, it is impossible to reproduce in English the singular style of this early attempt at German prose-writing, it seems better to print the extracts in their original shape, and to give a full analysis in a note.—Tr.]

Some recommend us to range ourselves juxta captum vulgi erronei; while others insist partout upon being martyrs to what they imagine to be truth. I am not clever enough to decide this controversy, but it seems to me probable that the ordinary man would gradually become wiser: at the

as it is expressed in the first edition, p. 11, where we are referred to the "Leviathan" and the Supplement to it; in the first letter, p. 18, in the following words: "Hieraus siehet man, dass die Meinung nicht neu und ungewöhnlich, da sie zumahl viel Engelländer profitiren sollen (von denen ich aber noch keinen, ausser dem Hobbesio, doch in einer andern Intention gelesen habe);" in the second letter, pp. 55, 56; in the third, p. 84. Locke is mentioned in the second letter, p. 58; besides, there is in the third letter, p. 70, the thought, obviously owing its origin to Locke: "Ich hielte es für unchristlich, wenn man Gott nicht so viel zutrauen wollte, dass aus der zusammengefügten Materie unseres Leibes ein dergleichen Effect folgen könnte, der die Menschen von andern Geschöpfen unterschiede." The 'Mechanismus' of the English in general is frequently spoken of. Spinoza is regarded as an Atheist and coupled with Strato of Lampsacus, pp. 42, 50, 76. At p. 44 the "forts esprits" of France are mentioned "nach des Blaiguy relation in Zodiaco Gallico."

nur beim Laico, sondern auch wohl bei den sogenannten
Gelehrten ziemlich schwer wiegen, und sollte es noch
viele Mühe kosten, diese tief eingefressene Wurzel aus
der Leute Köpffen zu graben, weil das Pythagorishe αὐτὸς
ἔφα ein zum Faullentzen herrliches Mittel, ja ein vortrefli-
licher Mantel, womit mancher Philosophus den Ignor-
anten bis auf die Klauen bedecken kann. Sed manum
de tabula. Genug ist's, dass wir in allen unsern Actioni-
bus hessliche, ja sclavische Praejudicia Autoritatis hegen.

"Dass ich aber unter tausenden eines erwehne, so kann
es unsere Seele sein. Was hat das gute Mensch nicht
schon für Fata gehabt, wie offt hat sie müssen in dem
menschlichen Leibe herum marschieren. Und wie viel
wunderliche judicia von ihrem Wesen haben sich in der
Welt ausgebreitet. Bald setzet sie einer in Cerebrum, da
setzen sie ihm viele andere nach. Bald setzet sie einer in
die glandulam pinealem, und dem folgen auch nicht
wenige. Wieder andern scheint dieser Sitz zu enge, und
gar recht. Sie könnte nicht, wie sie, bei einer Kanne
Coffée l'ombre spielen. Darum postieren sie sie in quamvis Corporis partem gantz, und in toto Corpore gantz:
und ob gleich die Vernunft leicht begreifft, dass so viele
Seelen in einem Menschen sein müssten, als Puncta an
ihm sind, so finden sich doch viel Affen, die es auch so
machen, quia αὐτός, ihr seliger Herr Präceptor, der 75
Jahr alt, und 20 Jahr Rector Scholae dignissimus, diss vor
die probabelste Sentenz hielt.

"Noch andre setzen sie ins Hertze und lassensie sich im

same time I see that prejudice is very strong not only with laymen but also
with the so-called learned, and that it will cost much trouble to eradicate it,
since the Pythagorean ipse dixit is an admirable cloak wherewith many a
philosopher can hide his ignorance.

To take one case among a thousand, that of our Soul. What vicissitudes
has this poor creature already endured—wandering all through the human
body. One places it in cerebrum, and has a multitude of followers; another
sets it in the glandulam pinealem, and finds no few supporters. To others
again this seems too narrow an abode, and they make it exist wholly in
quamvis corporis partem, and wholly in toto corpore: and although reason
says that there must then be as many souls in a man's body as there are
points in it, yet there are many apes ready to follow their worthy Herr

Blute herum schwemmen; bei andern muss sie ins Ventriculum kriechen; ja bei einem andern muss sie gar ein barmhertziger Thürhüter des unruhigen Hinter-Castells abgeben, wie die Aspectio der Bücher sattsam zeiget.

"Noch thümmer aber ist's wenn sie von dem Wesen der Seele reden; ich mag nicht sagen, was ich vor Gedanken habe, wenn ich die unreiffe Geburt beym Herrn Comenio, salvo honore, Orbe picto aus lauter Puncten bestehend sehe, ich danke Gott, dass ich nicht mit spiele, und so viel Unrath im Leibe habe."

Dr. Aristotle himself would in the "examen rigorosum Baccalaureale" not know how his Entelechy was to be explained, and Hermolaus Barbarus would not know whether to translate his rectihabea by a Berlin night lantern or a Leipzig watchman's rattle. Others, who will not pollute their consciences by the use of the heathen word ἐντελέχεια, make the soul, in order that they may say something, a "qualitas occulta." "Weil * nun ihre Seele eine qualitas occulta, so wollen wir ihnen selbe occultam lassen, weil ihre Definition nicht zu verachten, massen sie die Kraft hat, sich selbst zu refutieren.

"Wir wenden uns vielmehr zu denen die Christlicher zu reden und mit der Bibel einzustimmen gedenken. Bei diesen geistreichen Leuten nun heisst die Seele ein Geist. Das heisst, die Seele heisst etwas, was wir nicht wissen, oder was vielleicht nichts ist?"

Professor, who is seventy-five years old, and has for twenty years been Rector Scholae dignissimus.

Others again place it in the heart, and make it circulate with the blood: others pin it into the ventriculum ; another even makes it a pitiful door-keeper in the unruly.

Still worse is it when they speak of the return of the soul: I could rather not say what I think of the abortion of Comenius, and I thank God that I have, at least, had nothing so absurd about me.

* As their soul is a qualitas occulta, we will leave it occultam, for their definition is not to be despised since it has strength enough to refute itself.

We turn rather to those who think that they are better Christians, and are in agreement with the Bible. These clever people call the soul a spirit. That is to say, the soul is Something that we do not know, or that perhaps is nothing at all.

The materialistic author of the first letter gives us a circumstantial account of how he came upon his train of thought. Because he saw that the physiologists, and with them the philosophers, thrust the more complicated functions of man upon the soul, as though one need not hesitate to credit it with every capability, he began in order to get behind the nature of such functions to compare the actions of animals with those of men. "Da nun,"* he says, "die Aehnlichkeit in denen affectionibus animalium et brutorum etliche neue Philosophos auf die Meinung gebracht, dass die bruta gleichfalls eine animam immaterialem hätten, so gerieth ich auf den Gedanken, dass, da die neuen Philosophen zu diesem Entschluss gekommen sind, die alten aber ohne dergleichen Seele die actiones brutorum expliciret hätten, ob es nicht auch angehen könnte, dass man die actiones hominis ohne einige Seele zu werke richten könne." He shows then that at bottom scarcely any of the ancient philosophers held the soul for an immaterial substance in our sense: the forma of the Aristotelian philosophy being defined by Melanchthon quite rightly as ipsam rei exaedificationem, which Cicero conceived as a continual motion (ἐνδελέχεια), "which motion follows from the organisation of the body, and is thus an essential part hominis viventis, and separated, not realiter, but only in mente concipientis." Even the Bible, the Christian fathers, and various sects are adduced. Among others a thesis of the Anabaptists printed at Cracow in 1568: "We deny that any soul continues to exist after death." His own views are of the following nature :—

The functions of the soul, insight and will, which are usually called inorganic (that is not organic), are based upon sensation. The "processus intelligendi" is as fol-

* As the similarity in the affectionibus animalium et brutorum led some modern Philosophos to the opinion that the bruta also have an animam immaterialem, so I came upon the idea, whether as the old philosophers had explained the actiones brutorum without any soul, it might not be possible *to set going the actiones hominis without any soul.*

lows: "Wenn das organum sensus, sonderlich visus und auditus auf das objectum gerichtet wird, so geschehen unterschiedne Bewegungen in denen fibris cerebri"— (when the sense organ, especially that of sight or hearing, is directed to the object, there occur various movements in the fibris cerebri), which all have their termination in a sense organ. This motion in the brain is identical with that in which rays fall upon the table of a camera obscura and form a certain picture, since indeed that picture is in reality not upon the table but is caused in the eye. Now as the fibres of the retina are excited, this motion is continued in the brain and forms there the idea. The combination of these ideas, however, is brought about by motion of the fine brain fibres, in the same way in which a word is formed through the movements of the tongue. And this origin of the ideas validates the principle: nihil est in intellectu, quod non prius fuerit in sensu. A man would know nothing if his brain fibres were not properly stimulated by the senses. And this occurs through education, practice, and habituation. As the man in his external members exhibits a certain similarity with his parents, we must imagine a like condition with regard to the internal parts.

The author, who often makes himself unreservedly merry over the Theologian, yet, for all his completely materialistic notions of man, takes care not to come into too sharp conflict with Theology. He absolutely refrains himself, therefore, from speculations on the universe and its relation to God. As he openly enough rejects in various places the notion of an immaterial substance, it involves a contradiction that he did not provide for an extension of his principle to the whole of nature. But whether this be a real inconsistency, or whether he is acting on the principle of *gutta cavat lapidem,* we do not know. In his theological views he nominally follows the English Cudworth—that is, he supposes that at the day of judgment there will be a resurrection of the soul together with the body, in order to accommodate himself to the Church's faith. And so he explains God to be the contriver of a perfect construction of the brain in the first man, that through the Fall was injured just as when one loses his memory through an illness.

The decision of the will in action always follows the stronger motive, and the doctrine of the freedom of the will is entirely useless. The motives influencing the will may be reduced to the passions and the law. We might perhaps suppose that so many movements in the brain must necessarily lead to confusion, but let us only reflect how many aether rays must intersect each other in order to convey the image of things to us, and how, nevertheless, the proper rays always find each other. If our tongues can pronounce innumerable words and form innumerable expressions, why may not the brain fibres produce still more movements? That everything depends upon these, we see in particular from the case of delirium. So long as the blood is agitated, and the fibres accordingly are moved unequally and confusedly, the delirium persists; if, however, such a confused movement arises without fever, then madness is developed. That delusions can, in fact, be introduced through the blood, is proved by hydrophobia, the bite of the tarantula, and so on.

Another kind of mental disease is *ignorance,* which must be cured by education, teaching, and discipline. " This education and teaching is the right soul of man. which constitutes him a reasonable creature " (p. 25, 1st edition). In another place (p. 39) the writer suggests that those who distinguish three parts in man, namely, Spirit, Soul, and Body, would do best, if by 'spirit' they were to understand the education that is received, but by 'soul' the aptudinem omnium membrorum corporis nostri, especially fibrarum cerebri, in a word, facultatem.

At some length the author attempts to effect a reconciliation with the Bible, although the affectation of orthodoxy is often enough interrupted by malicious and ironical remarks. The theory underlying this first letter leans indeed strongly on the side of that ancient materialistic turn of the Aristotelian theory, which makes the form a property of the matter. And accordingly the author is fond of quoting Strato and Dikaearchos, although it be with a protest against their Atheism; but he is especially delighted with Melanchthon's definition of the soul, and repeatedly recurs to it. The explanation of the soul or the spirit, as the result of education, is in one place (p. 35 of the first edition) expressly referred to Averroes and Themistius; but it is easily seen that the Platonising Pantheism of Averroes is here transformed into Materialism. With Averroes, it is true, the immortal reason is in all men one and the same substance, and is identical with the objective content of knowledge; but this identification of the mind and of its content rests upon the doctrine of the identity of thought with real being, which, as divine and constitutive reason, has · its real existence outside the individual, and only shines in upon the individual like a ray of light from heaven. But in the present case the education is a material influence of spoken words upon the brain. This, in fact, does not look like an unintentional ' dilution ' of the Aristotelian theory, but like a conscious modification of it in a materialistic sense.

In the third letter the author expresses himself as follows :—" Dass* ich die Animam hominis vor ein materielles Wesen hätte halten sollen, darzu habe ich niemalen können gebracht werden, ob ich gleich viele Disputes deswegen mit angehöret. Ich konnte niemahls begreiffen, was vor Vortheil die Physic in hac materia durch Annehmung dieser Opinion hätte ; am allerwenigsten aber wolte es sich in meinem Kopfe reimen, dass da gleichwohl die an-

---

* I have never been induced to hold the soul to be a material thing, in spite of much controversy. I could never understand what advantage there was to physical science in holding this opinion ; least of all could I understand why, when the other animals are so constructed that we attribute the effects we see in their case to the matter adapted by God to the purpose, man alone may not boast of this distinction, but must be considered quite iners, mortuus, inefficax, and so on; so that it is necessary to *insert some-*

dern Geschöpfe also erschaffen, dass man den Effect, den sie von sich spüren lassen ihrer von Gott darzu adaptirten Materie zuschreibet, der Mensch allein dieser Wohlthat sich nicht zu rühmen, sondern ganz iners, mortuus, inefficax u. s. f. sey, und dass man noch nöthig habe, etwas in den Menschen hinein zu stecken, welches nicht nur die Actiones, die den Menschen von andern Geschöpfen unterscheiden, zu verrichten capable wäre, sondern auch sogar das Leben mittheilen müsste."

Nevertheless, the author thinks it advisable to defend himself against the reproach that he is a 'Mechanicus,' *i.c.*, a Materialist. "Ich rede von keinem andern Mechanismo oder Dispositione materiae, als demjenigen, der die formas Peripateticorum einführet; und zwar, damit es nicht scheinet, als wenn ich eine neue Philosophie aushecken wollte, so will ich mich hier lieber des Praejudicii autoritatis beschuldigen lassen, und bekennen, dass mich Melanchthon (!) dazu· bewogen hat, welcher sich des Wortes exaedificationis materiae (zur Erklärung der Form, d. h. für den Menschen der Seele) bedienet." Now, when we come to consider more clearly the Aristotelian standpoint, it is very easy to see that the expression 'exaedificatio materiae,' or more exactly 'ipsius rei exaedificatio,' leaves it still quite undetermined whether the formative force comes from the material, or whether it must be attributed to the form as a special, higher, and self-existent principle, that might in that case be very well designated " soul." Here the writer has, it is obvious, wished either to intrench himself behind the authority of Melanchthon, or to imitate the theologians; perhaps both. That he is not quite serious in his whole Peripatetic position seems to be shown by the

thing into the man that may be able merely to supply those actions that distinguish man from other creatures, but even to supply him with life. . . . I speak of no other mechanism or disposition of matter than that which introduces the formas Peripateticorum ; and, in fact, that I may not seem to be introducing a new philosophy, I will rather incur the blame of the Praejudicii autoritatis, and admit that I have followed Melanchthon, who avails himself of the phrase Exaedificatio materiae (for the explanation of the form, that is, the man of the soul).

difficulties that he immediately afterwards finds in the explanation of the forms, and which finally drive him to take refuge in these "Atomis Democriti," which he regards as preserving the forms of all material bodies.[52] A similar hide-and-seek procedure seems also to consist in this, that the ostensible opponent of Materialism in the second letter attempts to convict the writer of the first of atheistic conclusions. It is not impossible that this is a mere ruse in the manner of Bayle, in order to guide the reader towards these conclusions; and this, again, would be another argument that the whole work proceeded from one and the same pen.

The remarkable treatise which we have just discussed the more deserved attention in that it by no means stands alone as a monument of German intellectual struggle, and as a proof that modern Materialism (apart from Gassendi) is older in Germany than in France. Who knows anything now of the honest doctor, Pancratius Wolff, who as early as 1697, as he says himself, in his " Cogitationibus Medico-Legalibus," submitted to the judgment and opinion of the learned world, "that the thoughts are not actiones of the immaterial Soul, but are Mechanismi of the human Body, and in specie of the Brain." In 1726 Wolff, who in the meantime can have had anything but a very plea-

---

[52] The word 'not' had here fallen out in the first edition. Meantime, on a repeated perusal of the "confidential correspondence," I have changed my opinion, and think now that the author, in his philosophical as well as his theological orthodoxy, plays a double game, since on the one hand he guards himself in all events, and on the other he is obviously jesting. It is possible, indeed, that we have here an *extension* of the fusion (mentioned by Zeller after Leibniz) of Atomism, with a modification of the doctrine of the 'forma substantialis' (comp. above, Note 42); yet still as nothing but a general foundation upon which the author moves with great subjective freedom. Moreover, that the atoms as 'conservatores specierum' —that is, preservers of the *forms* and the *species*—are not Demokritean, but Epikurean, must be sufficiently clear from our account in the First Section, since Epikuros connects the maintenance of definite forms of nature with the *finite* number of the different kinds of atom. Here, indeed, as often, Demokritos was probably followed instead of Epikuros, not only because in him is found the fundamental idea of Atomism, but also because his name was less of a stumbling-block.

sant time of it, published a pamphlet, in which he sets out his old view, " freed from all the unchristian conclusions that thereby the special providence of God, the liberum Arbitrium, and all morality, were denied." Wolff had attained his views through his own observations in the delirium of fever, and so in much the same way as De la Mettrie.

Even the celebrated Leipzig professor of medicine, Michael Ettmüller, is said to have " established a material soul," yet in such a way that its immortality was by no means denied. Ettmüller was the head of the iatrochemical school, and this circumstance alone will scarcely allow us to consider him as a Materialist in our sense of the term. It is clear, however, that medical men as early as the end of the seventeenth and beginning of the eighteenth century, long before the spread of French Materialism, were beginning to emancipate themselves from the theological and Aristotelian notions as to the soul, and to follow their own ideas. It is certain that much was condemned as Materialism by the champions of the orthodox view that cannot be so included. On the other side, however, we must not fail to observe that a distinct course of development leads medicine and the natural sciences towards consistent Materialism, and therefore these transitional standpoints also deserve the most careful consideration in a history of Materialism. But at present there are still everywhere lacking the necessary materials.[53]

[53] Here one sees how the fact that historical treatises rest upon original authorities is nevertheless no guarantee for the correct, or even the complete, characterisation of an epoch. It only too easily becomes a habit to take always the same once-cited authorities, and what has once been forgotten becomes more and more thoroughly forgotten. A valuable protection against this one-sidedness is provided, so far as they extend, by periodicals. I remember that I first stumbled upon the "Confidential Correspondence," as well as upon Pancratius Wolff, while I was searching for reviews and other traces of the influence of "L'Homme Machine" in Germany. Generally speaking, indeed, in the history of German intellectual life, the period from about 1680–1740 seems still to contain many important gaps.

CHAPTER II.

DE LA METTRIE.

JULIEN OFFRAY DE LA METTRIE, or simply Lamettrie, as it is commonly written, is one of the most abused, but one of the least read, authors in the history of literature—an author known even superficially to but few of those who thought proper to abuse him when it suited them. This traditional treatment dates even from the circles of his contemporaries, not to say of those who shared his opinions. Lamettrie was the scapegoat of French Materialism in the eighteenth century. Whoever came into unfriendly contact with Materialism attacked him as its extremest representative; and even those who approached to Materialism in their own views, protected their own backs against the worst reproaches by giving Lamettrie a kick. And this was the more convenient, as Lamettrie was not only the extremest of the French Materialists, but was the first also in point of time. The scandal was therefore doubly great, and for several decades men could with virtuous indignation condemn this sinner, while they were gradually absorbing his ideas; later, too, they could with impunity sell as their own manufacture what they had learned from Lamettrie—because they had separated themselves from him with a unanimity and an energy that quite set at fault the judgment of their contemporaries.

Let us first of all bring order into the chronology! Hegel's initiative in the history of philosophy we have to thank for the inheritance of his innumerable arbitrarinesses. Of 'mistakes,' at least in the majority of cases, there can be no suggestion; for Hegel, as everybody knows, constructed the true succession of the notions out of the principle, and washed his hands in innocency if Nature had committed the oversight of letting a man or a book come into the world some years too early or too late. His school has followed him in this; and even men who no longer approve of this violent procedure yet remain under the influence of its consequences. Thus we are indebted, for example, to Zeller for the conscious elimination of nearly all these contempts of chronology from the history of Greek philosophy; and in his 'History of German Philosophy since Leibniz,' there is everywhere conspicuous the effort to do justice to the actual course of things. But where he refers incidentally to the French Materialism, this appears nevertheless, in spite of all the cautiousness of the expression, simply as a consequence of the 'Sensationalism' which Condillac developed from the Lockean 'Empiricism.' But Zeller points out at least in passing that Lamettrie drew this consequence even *before the middle* of the century.[54] The usual plan is this,

[54] Comp. Zeller, Gesch. d. deutschen Philos. seit Leibnitz, München, 1873, S. 304 and 396 ff. Expressions like: "Ebensowenig thut Condillac *schon* den Schritt vom Sensualismus zum Materialismus;" "Weiter ging Helvetius, . . . bei ihm hat der Sensualismus *schon* eine unverkennbare Neigung zum Materialismus" (S. 397); and again: "*Noch stärker* tritt diese Denkweise bei einem *Lamettrie*, einem Diderot und Holbach hervor," will involuntarily be understood by the reader as referring to a chronological series, and thus, at least with regard to Lamettrie, an erroneous conception is immediately given of his position in the history of philosophy.   For the rest, the whole of Hegel's view of this succession is, even from the standpoint of logical consequence, totally false.

In France, the advance from Condillac to Holbach is simply explained by this, that Materialism, as the *more popular* standpoint, afforded a more effective weapon against religious belief. It was not *because* philosophy advanced from Sensationalism to Materialism that France became revolutionary, but because France (through deeper causes) became revolutionary, the philosophers of the Opposition ever seized upon *simpler* (*more primitive*) standpoints; and Naigeon, who abridges the writings of Holbach and Diderot, is at last the true man of the time. In the unhampered theoretical development Empiricism (*e.g.,* Bacon) leads first to Materialism (Hobbes), this to Sensationalism (Locke), and from this are developed Idealism (Berkeley), and Scepticism or Criticism (Hume and Kant). This

that Hobbes, one of the most influential and original of modern thinkers, is entirely passed over, is referred to the history of political science, or is regarded as a mere echo of Bacon. Then Locke, who popularises 'Hobbism' for his own age, and rounds off his corners, appears as the original progenitor of a double line of development, an English and a French one. In this latter there succeed each other on the string of the system Voltaire, Condillac, the Encyclopædists, Helvetius, and finally Lamettrie and Holbach. This order of succession has become so familiar, that Kuno Fischer once indeed, in passing, makes Lamettrie a disciple of Holbach! [55] This kind of thing extends its influence far beyond the limits of the history of philosophy. Hettner forgets his own chronological data when he maintains that Lamettrie, instigated chiefly by Diderot's 'Pensées Philosophiques,' wrote in 1745 the 'Histoire Naturelle de l'Ame,' and in 1748 'L'Homme Machine;' and in Schlosser's 'History of the World' we may read that Lamettrie was a very ignorant man, who had the impudence to pass off the discoveries and observations of others as his own.[56] Only that in nearly every case where we find a striking similarity of ideas between Lamettrie and any famous contemporary of his, the former had an indisputable priority!

will hold still more decidedly for the future, since even the men of science have accustomed themselves to see that the senses give us only a 'Welt als Vorstellung.' Nevertheless this order of succession may at any moment be disturbed by the practical influence above mentioned; and in the greatest revolutions, of whose inner causes, buried deep in 'consciousness,' we as yet know scarcely anything but the *œconomic* side, even Materialism is at last not sufficiently popular and trenchant, and myth appears against myth, creed against creed.

[55] Kuno Fischer, Franz Baco von Verulam, Leipzig, 1856, S. 426, E. T., p. 453: "It was Condillac who systematically carried out the principles of Locke, . . . leaving only one result possible—Materialism in its most naked form. Condillac was followed by the Encyclopædists; and his Materialism was further elaborated by the Holbachians, represented by Lamettrie and the 'Système de la Nature.'"

[56] Hettner, ii. S. 388 (instead of 1748, the date of 'L'Homme Machine' is given erroneously as 1746). Schlosser's Weltgesch. f. d. deutsche Volk, xvi. (1854), S. 145.

Lamettrie was, in point of age, to begin with, one of the oldest among the authors of the French Illumination. Except Montesquieu and Voltaire, who belong to an earlier generation, nearly all are younger than he. Buffon, Lamettrie, Rousseau, Diderot, Helvetius, Condillac, D'Alembert, follow each other in this order, and at brief intervals, from 1707 to 1717; Holbach was not born till 1723. When the last-named gathered together in his hospitable house that circle of able free-thinkers which now always passes under his name, Lamettrie had long ceased to be numbered with the living. Moreover, as an *author*, especially with regard to the questions with which we are concerned, Lamettrie stands at the commencement of the whole series. Buffon began the publication of his great work on natural history in the year 1749, with the first three volumes; but it was only in the fourth volume that he unfolded the idea of the unity of principle in the multiplicity of organisms, an idea which occurs again in Maupertuis in an anonymous work in 1751, in Diderot in the 'Pensées sur l'Interprétation de la Nature,' 1754,[57] while we find it developed with great clearness and distinctness by Lamettrie as early as the 'L'Homme Plante' in 1748. Lamettrie was led to write this treatise by Linné's just published pioneering work on the classification of plants (1747), just as we find in all his writings constant traces of the zealous following up of the newest scientific investigations. Lamettrie cites Linné; none of the later writers think it necessary to cite Lamettrie, although there can be no doubt that they had read him. Whoever swims with the stream of tradition and neglects the chronology, will of course represent the 'ignorant' Lamettrie as decking himself with borrowed plumes !

Rosenkranz, in his work on Diderot,* gives incidentally what is in the main a correct account of the life and writings of Lamettrie. He mentions even the 'Natural History of

---

[57] Comp. Rosenkranz, Diderot, i. S. 136.   * Rosenkranz, ii. 65 ff.

the Soul' of the year 1745. This does not prevent him, however, from declaring the Lockean Sensationalism, "as it was introduced by Condillac from Paris into France," to be "the starting-point of the principles of French Materialism;" and then immediately follows the statement that Condillac's first work appeared in 1746. The starting-point, therefore, appears later than the last consequence; for in the 'Natural History of the Soul,' the Materialism is covered only by a very transparent veil. In the same work we find an idea which in all probability afforded the suggestion for Condillac's sensitive statue.

So much for the present as tribute to truth! That the true connection could so long be misrepresented is, next to the influence of Hegel and his school, chiefly to be attributed to the resentment excited by Lamettrie's attack upon the Christian morality. People forgot, in consequence, his theoretical writings; and the calmest and most serious of them, including the 'Natural History of the Soul,' were most completely forgotten. Many of the censures passed upon Lamettrie, as man and author, applied strictly only to his ethical writings. Those forgotten books are by no means so empty and superficial as is commonly imagined; but it is true that Lamettrie, especially in the last years of his life, made the struggle against the fetters of morality a very special subject of his efforts. This circumstance, combined with the provoking deliberateness with which, even in the title of his chief work, he represents man as a 'machine,' has probably chiefly contributed to make a bugbear of the name of Lamettrie, in whom the most tolerant writers will recognise no favourable trait, and whose relation to Frederick the Great is considered as particularly scandalous. And yet Lamettrie, in spite of his cynical treatise on lust, and in spite of his death through immoderate indulgence in a pasty, was, as we shall see, a nobler nature than Voltaire and Rousseau; much weaker, it is true indeed, than these ambiguous heroes, whose fermenting influence moved the whole eighteenth century, while Lamettrie's activity remained limited to a much narrower sphere.

Lamettrie might then, perhaps, be called the Aristippos of modern Materialism; but the lust which he represents as the end of life is related to Aristippos's ideal, as is a statue of Poussin to the Venus de Medici. His most notorious productions have neither great sensuous energy nor seductive fervour, and appear as if artificially manufactured in pursuance of a once-adopted principle. Frederick the Great ascribes to him, certainly not wholly without ground, an imperturbable natural gaiety, and eulogises him as a pure soul and an honourable character. Nevertheless the reproach of frivolousness will always cling to this character. As a friend, he may have been obliging and self-sacrificing; as an enemy, he was, as Albrecht von Haller in particular had to experience, malicious and low in the choice of his means.[58]

Lamettrie was born at St. Malo, the 25th December 1709.[59] His father carried on a business that placed him in a position to give his son a good education. Upon finishing his preparatory studies, this son so distinguished himself that he carried off all the prizes. His talents were especially rhetorical and poetical. He was passionately fond of polite literature; but his father reflected that a clergyman makes a much better living than a poet, and he destined him for the service of the Church. He was sent to Paris, where he studied logic under a Jansenist professor, and so thoroughly studied himself into his teacher's views, that he himself became a zealous Jansenist. He is even said to have written a book which gained the approbation of this party. Whether he also adopted the mystical asceticism, and inclination to pietistic mortifica-

---

[58] Comp. Zimmermann, Leben des Herrn von Haller, Zurich, 1855, S. 226 ff.

[59] In the biographical details we follow, here and there literally, the Éloge of M. De la Mettrie, composed by Frederick the Great, in the Histoire de l'Academie Royale des Sciences et Belles Lettres, Année 1750, Berlin, 1752, 4to, pp. 3–8.

tion, by which the Jansenists were distinguished, we are not told. At all events, this tendency cannot have lasted, in his case, for any considerable time.

While on a visit to his native town of St. Malo, a doctor of the place excited in him a taste for the study of medicine, and he succeeded in persuading his father "that a good prescription is still more profitable than an absolution." With great zeal the young Lamettrie threw himself into physics and anatomy, graduated at Rheims, and practised as a doctor for some time, until, in the year 1733, attracted by the fame of the great Boerhaave, he went to Leyden to resume his studies.

There was at that time collected round Boerhaave, although he had already ceased to lecture, a distinguished school of zealous young doctors. The University of Leyden formed at that time a centre of medical studies, such as perhaps has never been seen again. Around Boerhaave himself flocked his disciples with an unbounded reverence. This man's great reputation had acquired him considerable riches, amidst which he lived so plainly and simply that only his great benevolence and liberality gave evidence of them. In addition to his eminent gifts as a teacher, he was eulogised in particular for his character, and indeed his piety, although he had at one time incurred the imputation of atheism, and had scarcely ever changed his theoretical views. For Boerhaave too, like Lamettrie, had begun with the theological career, which he had been compelled to abandon because of his unconcealed adhesion to the philosophy of Spinoza; for Spinozism was to the theologians the same thing as Atheism.

The serious and thoroughly solid spirit of the great master, in devoting itself to medicine, had been far from seeking to enter into controversy with the representatives of other principles on the ground of his naturalistic philosophy. He was contented with his work and activity; but at the same time his whole influence cannot but have favoured the spread of materialistic views among his pupils.

France was at that time, in comparison with England, the Netherlands, and Germany, decidedly backward in medicine. Lamettrie therefore undertook a series of translations of Boerhaave's works, in order to prepare the way for a better system; some writings of his own followed, and he was speedily entangled in bitter animosities with the ignorant authorities of Paris. Meanwhile he was practising with great success in his native town, unremittingly engaged at the same time with medical literature. The positive spirit of his teacher did not soon relax; and although his sanguine restlessness had already brought medical controversies enough upon him, yet he still left philosophy at rest.

In the year 1742 he went to Paris, and by means of influential recommendations he received there a position as surgeon to the Guard. In this capacity he made a campaign in Germany, and this campaign determined his whole future course. For he was seized by a violent fever, and used this opportunity in order to institute observations upon himself as to the influence of quickened circulation upon thought. He came to the conclusion that thought is nothing but a consequence of the organisation of our mechanism. Filled with this idea, he tried during his convalescence to explain the mental functions by the help of anatomy, and he had his conjectures printed under the title of a ' Natural History of the Soul.' The regimental chaplain sounded the alarm, and soon a universal cry of indignation was raised against him. His books were recognised as heretical, and he could no longer continue to be surgeon of the Guard. Unhappily, he had allowed himself, about the same time, in order to help a friend who wished to be made surgeon to the King, to be persuaded into writing a satire on his rivals, the foremost Paris practitioners. Aristocratic friends advised him to avoid the universal cry for vengeance, and he fled in the year 1746 to Leyden. Here he wrote immediately a new satire upon the charlatanism and ignorance of doctors, and soon afterwards (1748) appeared also his 'Homme Machine.'[60]

The 'Natural History of the Soul'[61] begins by showing that as yet no philosopher, from Aristotle down to Malebranche, had been able to account for the nature of the soul. The nature of the soul of man and of the animals will always remain as unknown as the nature of matter and of bodies. Soul without body is like matter without any form : it cannot be conceived. Soul and body have been formed together, and in the same instant. He who wishes to learn the qualities of the soul must previously study those of the body, whose active principle the soul is.

Our consideration of the subject leads to this conclusion, that there is no safer guide than the senses—"they are my philosophers." However much we may revile them, we must always come back to them if we wish seriously to discover the truth. Let us therefore inquire fairly and impartially what our senses can discover in matter, in bodies, and especially in organisms, but without seeing anything that is not there! Matter is in itself passive : it has only a power of inertia. Wherever, then, we see motion,

[60] In the first edition the date of publication of 'Homme Machine' was given as 1747 (end), following Zimmerman, Leben des Herrn von Haller, S. 226. Quérard, 'France Littéraire' (the fullest and most accurate, although still not complete, enumeration of Lamettrie's works), gives the year 1748. For the rest, Lamettrie, according to the Éloge of Frederick the Great, went to Berlin as early as February 1748.

[61] In Lamettrie's philosophical works, under the altered title, 'Traité de l'Ame.' That this work is identical with the 'Histoire Naturelle' is shown *inter alia* by an observation of the author's, chap. xv. of the Histoire, vi. of the Traité : "On parlait beaucoup à Paris, quand j'y publiai la première édition de cet ouvrage, d'une fille sauvage," &c. (I may take this opportunity of observing that in the indication of the chapters, as generally in the division of the parts of the work, a great confusion prevails in the editions. Of the four editions which I have before me, the earliest (Amsterdam, 1752, 12mo) marks this section as 'Histoire, vi.,' which is probably correct. Then there follows after chap. xv. an Appendix of seven sections, of which the first six are marked as 'Histoire i., ii.,' and so on ; the seventh, containing the 'Belle Conjecture d'Arnobe,' is marked as § vii. So also in the edition of Amsterdam, 1764, 12mo. On the other hand, the editions of Berlin, 1774, 8vo, and Amsterdam, 1774, 12mo, make chap. vi. follow here, while the order of the chapters requires the number xvi.).

we must refer it to a moving principle. If, then, we find in the body a moving principle which makes the heart beat, the nerves feel, and the brain think, we will call this the soul.

So far the standpoint taken by Lamettrie seems empirical indeed, but not quite materialistic. In what follows, however, very subtly, and with constant reference to Scholastic and Cartesian principles, he gradually passes over into Materialism. Lamettrie explains the nature of matter, its relation to form, to extension, its passive qualities, and finally its capacity for motion and for sensation, apparently in agreement with the most generally accepted notions of the schools, which he very vaguely attributes to the philosophers of antiquity, as though these had been in the main agreed. He calls attention to the strict distinction made by the ancients between substance and matter, in order the more surely to sweep this distinction away. He talks of the forms through which the otherwise passive matter first receives its determination and its motion, in order indirectly to make these forms mere qualities of matter, which are inalienably attached to matter, and are inseparable from its existence.

The main object in all this, as it had already been in Stratonism, is the setting aside of the ‘Primum Movens Immobile,’ the Aristotelian extramundane, world-moving God. Matter only becomes a definite substance through form, but whence does it receive the form? From another substance, which is also material in its nature. This again from another, and so on to infinity, that is, we know the form only in its combination with matter. In this indissoluble union of form and matter things react and form each other, and so is it also with motion. Only the abstract, separately conceived matter is that passive thing: the concrete, actual matter is never without motion, as it is never without form; it is, then, in truth identical with substance. Where we do not perceive motion it is yet potentially present, just as matter also potentially (" *en puissance* ") contains all forms in itself. There is not the slightest reason for assuming that there is an agent outside the material world. Such a being would not even be an ' ens rationis ' (*être de raison*). Descartes' assumption that God is the only cause of motion has, in philosophy, which requires evidence, absolutely no meaning: it is only a hypothesis which he has formed after the light of faith. Immediately after this comes the proof that matter possesses also the capacity of *sensation*. The method here adopted is, that this view is shown to be the original and natural one, and thus all that is needed is to demonstrate the errors of the moderns, especially of Descartes, who had controverted it. The relation of man to the brute, the weakest point of the Cartesian philosophy, naturally comes to the front. Very ingeniously Lamettrie observes that at bottom I am immediately certain only of my own feeling. That other men also feel, I conclude with very much stronger conviction from the expression of their feelings in gestures and cries than from their articulate speech. That energetic language of the emotions is, however, the same in the animals as in men, and it carries with it much stronger proof than all the sophisms of Descartes. If an argument is sought in the difference of external conformation, on the other hand comparative anatomy shows us that the internal organisation of man and of the animals offers a perfect analogy.   If it remains for the present incomprehensible how the capability of feeling can be an attribute of matter, it is with this, as with a thousand other puzzles, in which, according to an idea of Leibniz, instead of the thing itself we see only the veil that hides it.   It is uncertain whether matter *in itself* has the capability of feeling, or whether it attains this only in the form of organisms; but even in this case sensation, like motion, must at all events *potentially* belong to all matter. So thought the ancients, whose philosophy is preferred by all capable minds to the inadequate attempts of the moderns.

After this Lamettrie passes to the doctrine of substantial forms, and here again he still moves in the sphere of

traditional notions.   He examines the view that in reality
it is the forms that actualise things, because these things
without form, that is, without qualitative determination,
are not what they are.   By substantial forms were understood those forms that determine the essential qualities of
bodies ; by accidental forms those that determine accidental
modifications.   In living bodies the ancient philosophers
distinguished several forms : the vegetative soul, the sensitive, and, in the case of man, the rational soul.[62]

All feelings come to us through the senses, and these
are connected with the brain, the seat of sensation, by
means of the nerves.   In the nerve-tubes, then, flows a
fluid, the '*esprit animal*,' life-spirit, whose existence Lamettrie regards as established by experiments.   There
arises, then, no sensation without a change being produced in its organ by which the animal spirits are affected,
and then these conduct the sensation to the soul.   The
soul does not feel in the places where it supposes that it
feels, but it refers its sensations, according to their nature,
to some point outside itself.   And yet we cannot know
whether the substance of the organs does not also feel;
but this can only be known to the substance itself, and not
to the whole creature.[63]   Whether the soul occupies only a

[62] Here follows, moreover, at the end of the seventh chapter, a passage which very characteristically anticipates the standpoint of the 'Homme Machine,' unless, that is to say, it belongs perhaps to the later recension of the 'Hist. Nat.,' and was added therefore after the completion of the 'Homme Machine.' Lamettrie says that before he discusses the vegetative soul, he must answer an objection. He had been asked how he could maintain the absurdity of the Cartesian view ·that *animals* are mere *machines*, while he himself denied the existence in animals of any principle other than matter. Lamettrie answers in a word ; because Descartes denies all feeling to his machines. The application to man is obvious. Lamettrie does not reject the notion of the *mechanical* nature of the machine, but that of its *incapability of sensation*.   We see here again clearly enough in how close relation Descartes stands to Materialism.

[63] Observe the cautiousness and acuteness with which the "ignorant and superficial" Lamettrie here goes to work. He would certainly never have made the mistake of Moleschott mentioned in the first edition, S. 440, in dealing with the case of Jobert de Lamballes. If head and spinal cord are separated, we must, according to Lamettrie, ask the spinal end whether it has any feeling, and not the head.   We may here point out also that Lamettrie anticipates the standpoint of Robinet as at least conceivable.

particular point or a circuit we do not know, but as all nerves do not meet in one point in the brain, the former supposition is improbable. All knowledge is in the soul only at the moment in which it is affected by it; all preservation of it is to be resolved into organic conditions.

Thus the 'Natural History of the Soul,' starting from ordinary notions, gradually leads us on into Materialism, and at length, after a series of chapters, it is concluded *that that, then, which feels must also be material.* How this comes about Lamettrie too does not know; but why should we (according to Locke) limit the omnipotence of the Creator because of our ignorance? Memory, imagination, passions, and so on, are then explained in a thoroughly materialistic way.

The very much shorter section on the rational soul discusses freedom, reflection, judgment, and so on, with the same strong leaning to Materialism and the same reticence of results, until at length there follows a chapter over which is written, " That religious faith alone can confirm our belief as to the existence of a rational soul." But the object of this very chapter is to show how metaphysics and religion came to adopt the notion of a soul, and it concludes by saying that true philosophy freely confesses that the incomparable being which is dignified with the beautiful name of the soul is unknown to her. And mention is also made of Voltaire's phrase, 'I am body, and I think;' and Lamettrie refers with pleasure to the way in which Voltaire scoffs at the Scholastic proof for the proposition that no matter can think.

Not without interest is the last chapter,[64] which bears the title, " Narratives which prove that all Ideas are derived from the Senses." The deaf mute of Chartres, who suddenly recovered his hearing and learned to talk, and who was then found to have no religious idea of any kind, although from his youth upward he had been trained to all kinds of religious ceremonies and gestures; the blind man

[64] Chap. xv. inclusive of the Appendix; comp. Note 62.

of Cheselden, who, after the operation of couching, at first saw only a coloured light, without being able to distinguish a sphere from a cube ; Amman's method of teaching the deaf and dumb, are all adduced and discussed, not without care and circumspection. Without any attempt at criticism, as was then the custom, he introduces again a series of stories of men who had become wild, and describes the orang-outang, according to very much exaggerated accounts, as of almost human conformation. Everywhere the consequence is drawn that only the education he receives through the senses makes man man, and gives him what we call the soul, while no development of the mind from within outwards ever takes place.

As the author of the Correspondence on the Nature of the Soul cannot help dragging Melanchthon into his system, so Lamettrie goes back to the father of the Church, Arnobius, from whose book, ' Adversus Gentes,' he borrows a hypothesis, which possibly became the original of the statue-man which plays its part in Diderot, Buffon, and particularly in Condillac.

Let us suppose that in a feebly illuminated subterranean chamber, from which all sounds and sense-impressions are far removed, a new-born child is scantily nourished by a naked and ever-silent nurse, and so is reared up without any knowledge at all of the world or of human life until the age of twenty, thirty, or even forty years. Then let this being leave his solitude. And now let him be asked what thoughts he has had in his solitude, and how he has been nourished and brought up. He will make no answer; he will not even know that the sound addressed to him has any meaning. Where now is that immortal particle of deity ? Where is the soul that enters the body so well taught and enlightened ?[65]

[65] Comp. the very interesting passage in Arnobius, Adversus Nationes, I. c. 20 ff. (p. 150 ff. ed. Hildebrand, Halis Sax., 1844), where in fact, with the view of controverting the Platonic doctrine of the soul, this hypothesis is carried out and discussed in great detail. Lamettrie's account of the passage in Arnobius is considerably abbreviated, and in the text only the main ideas are briefly stated.

Like Condillac's statue, then, this creature, which has only the shape and the physical organisation of a man, must be supposed to have received feelings through the use of the senses that gradually arrange themselves, and education must do what else is necessary to give him the soul, the capacity for which is only dormant in his physical organisation. Although Cabanis, as pupil of Condillac, rightly rejected this unnatural hypothesis, we must nevertheless concede to it a certain justification as compared with the extremely weak foundation of the Cartesian doctrine of innate ideas.

In conclusion, Lamettrie lays down the principles, " No senses, no ideas." " The fewer senses, the fewer ideas." " Little education, few ideas." " No sense-impressions, no ideas." So he very gradually attains his aim, and finally concludes : " The soul, then, depends essentially upon the organs of the body, with which it is formed, grows, decreases : ' Ergo participem leti quoque convenit esse.'"

In very different fashion does the book set to work that already in its very title declares that *man is a machine.* While the ' Natural History of the Soul ' was cautious, cunningly arranged, and only gradually surprising us with its results, here, on the contrary, the final conclusion is expressed at the outset of the work. While the ' Natural History of the Soul ' allied itself with the whole Aristotelian metaphysics only in order to prove by degrees that the soul is but an empty form, into which we may pour a materialistic content, here we no longer deal in all those fine distinctions. On the question of substantial forms Lamettrie controverts himself ; scarcely because he had essentially changed his opinion, but because by this means he hoped to protect his name, which he tried to hide as much as possible, the more effectually from his persecutors. In the form also of the two works there is an essential difference. While the ' Natural History of the Soul ' follows a regular division into chapters and sections, the ' Man as Machine ' runs on in unbroken flow of speech.

Equipped in all the adornments of rhetorical prose, this work seeks to persuade as much as to prove : it is written with a conscious intention that it may find an easy reception and rapid circulation among the educated classes ; a polemical treatise intended to prepare the way for a theory, not to establish a discovery. For all this, Lamettrie did not omit to support himself on a broad scientific basis. Facts and hypotheses, arguments and declamations, all are assembled in order to serve this same object.

Whether it was with the view of gaining more acceptance for his work, or the better to conceal himself, Lamettrie added to it a Dedication to Albrecht von Haller. This dedication, which Haller disavowed, led to the mixing up with the scientific question of a personal difference between these men. Nevertheless Lamettrie had this dedication, which he regarded as a masterpiece of his prose, printed still in the later editions of the book. The dedication consists of an impassioned eulogy of the delights of the Arts and Sciences.

The work itself begins with the statement that it must not suffice for a wise man to *study* nature and truth : he must dare, for the good of the few who can and will think, to *spread* them ; the great mass of people is incapable of rising to the truth. All the systems of philosophers reduce themselves, with reference to the human soul, to two ; the older system is Materialism, the second is Spiritualism. When we ask, with Locke, whether matter can think, that is just as if we were to ask whether matter can show the time. It will depend upon whether it can of its own nature.[66]

---

[66] The very acute remark of Lamettrie against Locke (indirectly also against Voltaire) runs thus: "Les métaphysiciens qui ont insinué que la matière pourroit bien avoir la faculté de penser, n'ont pas déshonoré leur raison. Pourquoi ? c'est qu'ils ont un avantage (car ici c'en est un) de s'être mal exprimés. En effet, demander si la matière peut penser, sans la considérer autrement qu'en elle même, c'est demander, si la matière peut marquer les heures. On voit d'avance, que nous éviterons cet écueil, où M. Locke a eu le malheur d'échouer" (Homme Machine,

Leibniz has in his 'Monads' set up an unintelligible hypothesis. "He has spiritualised matter, instead of materialising the soul."

Descartes has made the same mistake, and set up two substances, as though he had seen and counted them.

The most cautious have said that the soul can only discover itself through the light of faith. But if they reserve to themselves, as rational beings, the right to inquire what the Scriptures mean by the word 'spirit,' by which they designate the human soul, they become inconsistent with the theologians, as the theologians do amongst themselves. For if there is a God, he is just as much the author of nature as of revelation; he has given us the one in order to explain the other, and reason in order to bring them into harmony. The two cannot contradict each other, unless God is to be a deceiver. If, then, there is a revelation, it must not contradict nature. As an example of a frivolous objection against this line of thought, Lamettrie quotes the words of the Abbé Pluche,[67] who in his 'Spectacle de la Nature' had observed, with reference to Locke: "It is astonishing that a man who degrades our soul so far that he considers it a *soul of dirt*, ventures to make Reason the supreme judge in the mysteries of the faith; for what singular idea of Christianity should we have if we were to follow his Reason?" Against this childish

---

pp. 1, 2, ed. Amsterd. 1744). Lamettrie no doubt means to say that if we consider matter only in itself, without regarding also the relation of force and matter [the German *Materie* includes both Force and Matter, that is, *Kraft* and *Stoff*—Tr.], we may just as well answer the famous question of Locke with a Yes as with a No, and in neither case with any decisive result. The matter of the clock can show the hour or not, according as we speak of an active or a passive capacity. So too the material brain could in a certain sense think, in so far as it is actuated by the soul as an instrument for the expression of thoughts. The real question is this, whether the power of thinking, which we may at all events *in thought* separate from matter, is in truth a necessary outcome of it or not. This question Locke has evaded.

[67] 'Le Spectacle de la Nature, ou Entretiens sur l'Histoire Naturelle et les Sciences,' Paris, 1732 ff., 9 vols., second edition, La Haye, 1743, 8 vols., appeared anonymously; the author is, according to Quérard (agreeing with Lamettrie, who mentions him by name), the Abbé Pluche.

kind of controversy, which even in our own day is unfortunately often directed against Materialism, Lamettrie wages quite justifiable warfare. The merit of Reason does not depend upon the word 'immateriality,' but upon her achievements. If a "soul of dirt" were to discover in a moment the relations and the due succession of an immeasurable number of ideas, then it would obviously be preferable to a dull, simple soul, though it were made of the most precious materials. It is unphilosophical to blush with Pliny over the pitiableness of our origin. For what here appears so vulgar is just the most precious thing, upon which nature has bestowed the greatest art. Even though man sprang from a much lower source, he would none the less be the noblest of beings. If the soul is pure, noble, and elevated, then it is a beautiful soul, and it honours him who is endowed with it. And as to the second remark of M. Pluche, we might just as well say, "We must not believe in Torricelli's experiment, for if we were to banish the 'horror vacui,' what a singular kind of philosophy should we have." (This illustration would be better stated thus: We must never judge of nature by experiments, for if we were to follow Torricelli's experiment, what a singular idea we should obtain of the 'horror vacui.')

Experiment and *observation*, says Lamettrie, must be our only guides: we find them in medical men who have been philosophers, and not in philosophers who have been no medical men. Doctors alone, who calmly observe the soul in its greatness as in its misery, are here entitled to speak. What can the others have to say, and especially the theologians? Is it not ridiculous to hear how they decide without shame on a question which they were never in a position to understand, from which they have, on the contrary, been constantly diverted by obscure studies, which have led them to a thousand prejudices— in a word, to fanaticism, which then still further contributes to their ignorance of the mechanism of the body?

Here, however, Lamettrie himself is already guilty of a *petitio principii*, such as he has just rightly reproached his opponents with. Even the theologians have occasion to acquire a practical experience of the human soul, and the difference therefore in the value of this experience can only be a difference of the method and of the categories under which the experience is brought.

Man is, as Lamettrie goes on to explain, a machine so constructed that it is impossible to form *a priori* a correct idea of it. We must admire the great minds that have vainly attempted this, a Descartes, Malebranche, Leibniz, and Wolff, even in their unavailing efforts, but must pursue an entirely different path from theirs; only *a posteriori*, starting from experience and from the study of the bodily organs, can we attain, if not to certainty, at least to the highest degree of probability. The various temperaments, resting upon physical causes, determine the character of the man. In diseases, the soul is at one time obscured; in another, we might say that it doubled itself; and again, it is distracted into imbecility. The convalescence of a fool makes a man of sense. The greatest genius often becomes a fool, and away goes all the admirable learning that has been acquired by so much labour. One patient asks if his leg is in his bed, another thinks that he still has the arm that has been amputated. The one cries like a child at the approach of death, the other jests at it. What would have sufficed in the case of Julius Cæsar, of Seneca, of Petronius, to turn their fearlessness into timidity or into braggartry? An obstruction in the spleen, the liver, or the vena portæ. For the imagination is intimately connected with these viscera, and from them arise all the curious phenomena of hypochondria and hysteria. What are we to say of those who believe themselves transformed into were-wolves and vampires, or who think that their noses or other limbs are of glass? Lamettrie then passes on to the effects of sleep; opium, wine, and coffee are described in their effects upon the soul. An army to which strong drinks are given charges boldly upon the enemy, from which it would have fled after drinking water; a good meal exercises an enlivening influence.

The English nation, which eats half-raw and bloody meat, appears to derive its fierceness from such nourishment, which can be counteracted by education only. This begets in the soul pride, hatred, contempt of other nations, unlearnedness, and other defects of character, just as a coarse diet renders the mind heavy and sluggish.   Hunger and continence, climate, and so on, are all traced in their influences. Physiognomy and comparative anatomy contribute their aid. If we do not find degeneration of the brain in all diseases of the mind, there are conditions of congestion or other changes in the smallest parts which occasion the disturbance.[68] "A mere nothing, a little fibre, some trifling thing that the most subtle anatomy cannot discover, would have made two idiots out of Erasmus and Fontenelle."

It is a curious idea of Lamettrie's, again, that the experiment might perhaps be successfully made of getting an ape to speak, and in this way of bringing a portion of the animal world into the sphere of human education. He compares the ape with a deaf mute; and as he is particularly enthusiastic for the recently invented method of Ammann for the education of the deaf and dumb, he is anxious to have a large and particularly clever ape in order to make experiments upon it.[69]

---

[68] In the whole treatment of the relation between the brain and the intellectual functions there is a striking similarity between Lamettrie and modern Materialism. He treats the matter with some fulness, while in the text only the chief points are briefly noticed. In particular, Lamettrie (the "ignorant") studied industriously Willis's epoch-making book on the Anatomy of the Brain, and took from it all that could serve his purpose. And accordingly he recognises the importance of the cerebral convolutions, the difference in the relative development of the various parts of the brain in the higher and lower animals, and so on.

[69] The detailed discussion of this problem is at pp. 22 ff. of the edition of Amsterdam, 1774.   Of Ammann's method Lamettrie gives a most minute account in the 'Histoire Natur. de l'Ame'—a proof of his serious treatment of this subject.

What was man, asks Lamettrie, before the invention of words and the knowledge of language? An animal after his kind, with much less instinct than the others, and distinguished from them by nothing but his physiognomy and Leibniz's intuitive knowledge. The most excellent and better-organised specimens invented signs and taught the others, exactly as when we break in animals.

As in a violin-string the striking of a piano produces a vibration and a sound, just so the strings of man's brain, when struck by sensations of sound, produced words. But as soon as the signs of various things are given, the brain by a similar necessity begins to compare them and to note their relations, just as the properly organised eye must see. The similarity of various objects leads to their being classed together, and hence arises counting. All our ideas are closely connected with the representation of the corresponding words or signs. Everything that passes in the soul may be referred to activity of the imagination.

Whoever, then, has the most imagination must be considered the greatest mind. Whether nature took more pains to form a Newton or a Corneille, an Aristotle or a Sophokles, cannot be determined, but we may certainly say that both kinds of talent indicate merely different directions in the use of the imagination. If it is said, then, that any one has much imagination but little judgment, we only mean by this that his imagination has been too exclusively directed to the reproduction of sensations instead of to their comparison.

The chief excellence of man is his organisation. It is accordingly unnatural to suppress a moderate pride in real excellences, and all excellences, wherever they may come from, deserve to be esteemed; we must only know how to value them properly. Genius, beauty, wealth, nobility, although children of chance, have their value just as much as skill, knowledge, and virtue.

When it is said that man is distinguished from the animals by a natural law which teaches him to distinguish good and evil, this also is a delusion. The same law is found among the animals. We know, for example, that we feel remorse after bad conduct: that other men feel the same, we must take their word for, or we must infer it from certain signs which we find in like cases in ourselves; but these very signs we see also in the animals. If a dog has bitten his master, who was teasing him, we see him immediately sad, downcast, and ashamed; by a crestfallen and crouching mien he confesses his guilt. History affords us the famous instance of that lion who would not tear his benefactor, and who displayed his gratitude amidst bloodthirsty men. From all this it is concluded that men are made of the same materials as the animals.

The moral law is, in fact, still present even in those persons who, from a morbid impulse, steal, murder, or in fierce hunger devour their dearest relatives. These unhappy creatures, who are sufficiently punished by their remorse, should be handed over to the doctors, instead of being burned or buried alive, as has been the practice. To do good involves such pleasure, that to be wicked is in itself a sufficient punishment.   At this point of the argument an idea is introduced, which strictly perhaps does not belong here, but which belongs as essentially to Lamettrie's whole mode of thought as it on the other hand strikingly reminds us of Rousseau. We are all created to be *happy*, but it does not lie in our original destiny to be *learned;* perhaps we have become so only through a kind of *misuse of our talents.*   Here, again, let us not forget to bestow a glance upon the chronology! The 'Homme Machine' was written in 1747, and published at the beginning of 1748. The Academy of Dijon announced in 1749 the famous thesis for the solution of which Rousseau received their prize in 1750. This small circumstance will, however, after previous experiences, scarcely prevent Lamettrie from being reproached with having decked himself in Rousseau's plumes!

The essence of the natural moral law—he then goes on —lies in the doctrine, Not to do to others what we would not that they should do to us. Perhaps, however, there lies at the bottom of this law merely a wholesome fear, and we respect the purse and the life of our fellow-man only that we may keep our own possessions safely; just as the 'Ixions of Christianity' love God and embrace so many a chimerical virtue merely because they are in fear of hell. The weapons of fanaticism can destroy those who teach these truths, but will never destroy the truths themselves.

The existence of a Supreme Being Lamettrie will not doubt; all probability speaks for it; but this Existence no more proves the necessity of worship than any other existence: it is a theoretical truth without any use in practice; and as it has been shown by innumerable examples that religion does not bring morality with it, so we may conclude that even Atheism does not exclude it.

For our peace of mind it is indifferent to know whether there is a God or not, whether he created matter, or whether it is eternal. What folly to trouble ourselves about things the knowledge of which is impossible, and which, even if we knew them, would not make us a bit happier!

People refer me to the writings of famous apologists; but what do they contain except tedious repetitions, which serve rather to confirm Atheism than to undermine it. The greatest weight is laid by the opponents of Atheism on the design in the world. Here Lamettrie refers to Diderot, who, in his 'Pensées Philosophiques,'[70] then not

[70] In the first edition it was here wrongly supposed that Lamettrie agreed with Diderot, whereas he attacks him as a Deist and Teleologist, and laughs at his 'Universum,' with the weight of which he proposes to "crush" the Atheist. On the other hand, I may point out that Diderot follows up this passage, which Rosenkranz too (i. 40) adduces to prove Diderot's Deism, with a chapter (xxi.) of quite opposite tendency. Diderot here combats the argument for Teleology (recently reproduced by Von Hartmann) from the mathematical improbability of adaptations as a mere special case of purposeless combinations of causes. Diderot's criticism

long published, had maintained that one could slay the Atheist with a butterfly's wing or with the eye of a gnat, while one had the weight of the universe with which to crush him. Lamettrie observes, on the other hand, that we are not sufficiently acquainted with the causes which operate in nature to be able to deny that she produces everything out of herself. The polyp cut up by Trembley [71] had in itself the causes of its reproduction. Only ignorance of natural forces has made us take refuge in a God, who, according to certain people (he means himself in the 'Natural History of the Soul'), is not even an 'ens rationis.' To destroy chance is no proof of the existence of God, because there may very well be something which is neither chance nor God, and which brings forth things as they are—namely, Nature. The 'weight of the universe' will therefore frighten no true Atheist, to say nothing of 'crushing' him; and all these thousand-times repeated proofs for a Creator are sufficient only for people of

fundamentally upsets this specious argument, if not with the completeness and clearness exhibited by the principles of Laplace. It is an interesting question whether Diderot in this chapter did not intend to destroy, in the case of those who *understood*, the whole effect of the previous one, while to the mass of readers he appeared to pose in an attitude of devout Deism. But we may also suppose—and this seems to be the right view—that premises naturally leading to entirely opposite conclusions lay as clearly side by side in Diderot's mind as they have found expression in the successive chapters of his work. But any one who wishes to show that Diderot was even then inclined to Atheism must rest chiefly upon this chapter. Lamettrie, indeed, who cared little for mathematics, seems not to have observed the importance of this chapter, which Rosenkranz also has overlooked. He calls the 'Pensées Philosophiques' a "sublime ouvrage, qui ne convaincra pas un athée," but he nowhere regards Diderot's refutation of Atheism as a furtive recommendation of it. And thus we must reduce to a minimum Diderot's influence upon Lamettrie. We have shown that 'L'Homme Machine' was already in principle contained in the 'Histoire Naturelle' (1745). Comp. Œuvres de Diderot, i. 110 ff., Par. 1818, Pensées Phil., cc. xx., xxi.; Rosenkranz, Diderot, i. 40 ff.; Œuvres Phil. de. M. de la Mettrie, Amsterd. 1747, iii. 54, Berlin, 1747, i. 327.

[71] Here, again, we find how Lamettrie eagerly followed the newest inquiries in the sphere of the natural sciences, and brought them into connection with his speculations. Trembley's most important publications upon Polyps fall in the years 1744-47.

hasty judgment,—proofs to which the students of nature can oppose an equal weight of contrary arguments.

"Thus is it with the arguments for and against," concludes Lamettrie; "I embrace neither side." We see, however, clearly enough which side he embraces. For he goes on to say, further, that he had communicated all this to a friend, a 'sceptic (pyrrhonien),' as he was; a man of great merit, and worthy of a better lot. His friend had said that it was certainly very unphilosophical to trouble one's self about things which we can nevertheless not make out; *the world, however, would never be happy unless it was atheistic.* And these were the 'abominable' man's reasons: "If Atheism were universally disseminated, all the branches of religion would be torn up by the roots. Then there would be no more theological wars: there would no longer be soldiers of religion, that terrible kind of soldier. Nature, which had been infected by the consecrated poison, would win back her rights and her purity. Deaf to all other voices, men would follow their own individual impulses, and these impulses alone can lead them to happiness along the pleasant path of virtue."

Lamettrie's friend has only forgotten that even religion itself, quite apart from any revelation, must be reckoned among the natural impulses of man, and if this impulse leads to all unhappiness, it is not easy to see how all the other impulses, since they have the same natural origin, are to lead to happiness. Here, again, it is not a consistent, but an inconsistent, carrying out of the system that leads to the destructive consequences. Immortality, again, is treated by Lamettrie in a similar way to the idea of God, yet he is obviously glad to maintain it to be possible. Even the insect caterpillar, he supposes, has probably never really known it was to develop again into a butterfly; we know only a small part of nature, and as the matter of which we are made is eternal, we do not know what may yet come of it. Our happiness here depends upon our ignorance. He who thus thinks will be wise and just, tranquil as to his lot, and consequently happy. He will await death without fearing it, and also without demanding it.

Here it cannot be doubted that it is this negative side of the conclusion for which Lamettrie cares, and to which he inclines in his indirect way. He declares the idea of an immortal machine to involve no contradiction whatever; but this is not to gain immortality, but to establish in every way the machine hypothesis. In what way Lamettrie can have possibly conceived that his machine could be immortal, we indeed cannot discover: except the comparison with the caterpillar, there is no suggestion whatever made, and there was probably none intended to be made.

The life principle Lamettrie not only does not find in the soul (which is with him only the material consciousness); he does not find it in the whole, but in the separate parts. Each tiny fibre of the organised body is stirred by a principle inhabiting it. For this he adduces the following grounds:

1. The flesh of animals continues to palpitate after death, and the longer in proportion to the coldness of the animal's nature (tortoises, lizards, snakes).

2. Muscles separated from the body contract when they are excited.

3. The intestines retain for a long period their peristaltic action.

4. The injection of warm water reanimates the heart and the muscles (according to Cowper).

5. The heart of the frog moves for more than an hour after its separation from the body.

6. Similar observations have been made, according to Bacon, in the case of a man.

7. Experiments upon the hearts of fowls, pigeons, dogs, rabbits. The amputated paws of the mole still move.

8. Caterpillars, worms, spiders, flies, snakes exhibit the same phenomenon. In warm water the movement of the separated parts is increased ("à cause du feu qu'elle contient").

9. An intoxicated soldier beheaded a turkey-cock with his sabre. The creature halted, moved on, and finally ran. When it ran up against a wall, it turned round, beat its wings as it continued to run, and finally fell down (own observation).

10. Dissected polyps reproduce themselves in eight days into as many animals as there were portions made.

Man stands in the same relation to the animals as one of Huyghens' astronomical clocks to a common timepiece. As Vaucanson used more wheels for his flute-player than for his duck, so the driving-works of a man are more complicated than those of the animals. For a speaker Vaucanson would require still more wheels, and even such a machine can no longer be considered an impossibility.

It certainly must not be supposed that by a speaker Lamettrie had meant here a rational man; yet we see how delighted he is to compare the masterpieces of Vaucanson, which are so characteristic of their age, with his human machine.[72]

Lamettrie, moreover, in thus carrying out to extremities the principle of mechanism in human nature, is controverting himself, since he makes it matter of reproach to the author of the 'Natural History of the Soul' that he had retained the unintelligible doctrine of 'substantial forms.' But from what has been already said, it will be

---

[72] As to the mechanical automata of Vaucanson, and the still more ingenious ones of the two Drozs, father and son, comp. Helmholtz, 'Ueber die Wechselwirkung der Naturkräfte, Vortrag vom 7 Febr. 1854,' where the connection of these attempts, which to us seem mere child's play, with the progress of mechanics and with the expectations of what was to be achieved by them, is very justly demonstrated. Vaucanson may in a certain sense be called a forerunner of Lamettrie in the idea of the 'Homme Machine.' The two Drozs, with their still greater achievements (the Writing Boy and the Piano-playing Girl), were as yet unknown to Lamettrie. Vaucanson's Flute-player was first exhibited at Paris in 1738.

[73] The first edition of the 'Natural History of the Soul' professed to be a translation from the English of Mr. Sharp (thus given in Quérard, 'France Littéraire') or Charp (so written in the 'Homme Machine,' where "le prétendu M. Charp" is attacked, in the editions of the Œuvres Philosophiques of 1764 Amsterdam, 1774 Amsterdam, and 1774 Berlin).

evident that there is here no change of opinion, but merely an artifice adopted partly to help his anonymity, but partly also that he may, while starting from two opposite sides, yet work up to the same point. To make it more than clear, however, we will point out yet another passage from the fifth chapter of the 'Natural History of the Soul,' in which it is expressly said that the forms arise out of the pressure of the particles of one body upon the particles of another, which means simply this, that it is the forms of Atomism which are here concealed beneath the mask of the 'substantial forms' of the Scholastics.

Upon this same occasion, also, the tables are suddenly turned with regard to Descartes. However wrong he may have been in other respects, it is here said, this single fact would still make him a great philosopher, that he had declared the animals to be machines. The application of this to man is so obvious, the analogy is so striking and overwhelming, that every one must see it, and the theologians were the only people who did not detect the poison lurking in the bait which Descartes induced them to swallow.

Lamettric concludes his work with some considerations on the conclusiveness and certainty of the conclusions he had built up on the foundation of experience, as compared with the childish exertions of the theologians and metaphysicians.

"This is my system; nay, if I am not mistaken, this is the truth. It is short and simple; let him who can refute it do so!"

The scandal which this work produced was great, but not unintelligible; and just as rapid was its diffusion. In Germany, where every educated person was acquainted with French, there appeared no translation, but the original was read the more eagerly, and in the course of the next few years it was reviewed in all the more important periodicals, and immediately called forth a torrent of refutations. No one declared himself freely and openly in favour of Lamettrie; but the moderate tone, as compared with our contemporary controversy, and the calm and thorough criticism of many of these replies, show the more plainly that the general feeling did not regard this Materialism as being so absolutely monstrous as it is in our own day declared to be. In England there appeared soon after the publication of the original a translation, which attributed the book to the Marquis d'Argens, an amiable freethinker, also one of the intimates of Frederick the Great; but the real author could not long remain concealed.[74]

It made Lamettrie's case decidedly worse that he had already published a professedly philosophical work on 'Volupté,' a production followed later by others of the same kind. In the 'L'Homme Machine' also, sexual matters, even where they have no strict relevancy to the argument, are here and there discussed with a certain deliberate license. We have no wish either to overlook here the influence of his age and nationality, or even to deny a certain lamentable personal weakness, but we must insist upon this, that Lamettrie believed that his system required him to justify sensual pleasure, and that because he had conceived these ideas, so therefore he expressed them. In the preface to the collective edition of his philo-

---

[74] In the review of the 'L'Homme Machine' in Windheim's Götting. Phil. Bibliothek, i. Bd., Hannover, 1849, S. 197 ff., it is said: "We will only add further, that this work has already been published in London by Owen, under the following title : 'Man a Machine; translated of the French of the Marquis d'Argens,' and that the author has very much copied the 'Histoire de l'Ame,' which was published in the year 1745, and which also defends Materialism." Lamettrie's plagiarisms from himself may therefore, as we can see from this instance, have very probably contributed to gain him the reputation of decking himself with other people's plumes. The French original contained an advertisement of the publisher, Elie Luzak (reprinted in the edition of Berlin, 1774, written, we may conjecture, by Lamettrie, who published later the reply, 'L'Homme plus que Machine,' under the same name), in which it is stated that the manuscript had been sent to him from Berlin by an unknown hand, with the request that six copies of the work might be sent to the Marquis d'Argens, but that he was convinced that this address was a mere mystification.

sophical writings he confesses this principle : " So write as if thou wert alone in the universe, and hadst nothing to fear from the jealousy and prejudices of men, or—thou wilt fail of thy end."

Perhaps Lamettrie has tried to wash himself too white when in this defence, written with all the powers of his rhetoric, he distinguishes between his life and his writings; but at all events, we know of nothing to justify the tradition that he was a " licentious profligate, who sees in Materialism only the justification of his own debauchery." The question we have to consider is not whether Lamettrie, like so many authors of his own times, led a profligate and frivolous life—although even for this there are scarcely satisfactory proofs—but rather whether his literary activity had its foundation in personal depravity, or whether he was possessed by an idea of real importance and value as a transitional stage, and devoted his life to its exposition. We understand the resentment of his contemporaries, but we are nevertheless convinced that posterity must pass a much more favourable judgment upon this man, unless he alone is to be denied the justice otherwise generally accorded.

A young man who, after passing brilliantly through his course of study, has already acquired a successful practice, does not give this up in order to carry his studies deeper in a special home of science, unless there is in him a living ardour in the pursuit of truth. The satirist of medicine knew only too well that charlatanism in medicine was better paid than rational treatment. He knew that it would cost a struggle to secure the entrance into France of the principles of a Boerhaave and a Sydenham. Why did he undertake this struggle, instead of insinuating himself into the confidence of the ruling authorities ? Was it only his natural love of gain that impelled him to this ? Why then, in addition to satire, the toilsome and time-engrossing labour of translations and excerpts ? Money to so clever and skilful a man could undoubtedly come better and more easily by medical practice. Or was it perhaps that Lamettrie by his medical writings tried to drown the voice of his conscience? The whole idea of a personal justification is as alien as possible to his nature. Before whom was he to justify himself? Before the people—that he, in common with most of these French philosophers, regarded as an indifferent rabble, who are not yet ripe for free thought? Before his own circle, in which, with rare exceptions, he found only people who loved the debaucheries of sensuality as much as he did, and who only took care not to write books about it? Or, finally, to himself? In the whole range of his writings we find only cheerful contentment and self-sufficiency, without any trace of that dialèctic of the passions which is developed in a lacerated spirit. Lamettrie may be called shameless and frivolous, and these are serious charges, but they are not in the least decisive of the whole significance of a character. We are not aware of any special enormities of his. He neither sent his children to the Foundling, like Rousseau, nor betrayed two girls, like Swift; he was not convicted of corruption, like Bacon, nor does the suspicion of forgery rest upon his name, as upon Voltaire's. In his writings, indeed, crime is excused as a disease, but nowhere is it, as in Mandeville's notorious 'Fable of the Bees,' recommended.[75] Lamettrie was fully

[75] It is only when we regard particular passages in Lamettrie, apart from their context, that he seems to recommend vice; while in Mandeville vice is justified by the chain of his ideas, by the fundamental idea of a philosophy expressed in few lines, but very definite, and in our own days very widely spread, though without any ostentation. The strongest thing that Lamettrie has said in this direction is no doubt the passage in the 'Discours sur le Bonheur,' p. 176 ff., which may be thus summarised: 'If nature has made you a hog, go wallow in the mire like the swine; for you are capable of no higher happiness, and your remorse would only poison the only happiness of which you are capable, without benefiting anybody.' But the very condition is that one shall be a hog in human form—not a very inviting supposition. With this compare the following passage taken by Hettner (Literaturg., i. 20) from the Moral of the 'Fable of the Bees:' "Then leave Complaints: Fools only strive To make a Great, an Honest Hive. T'enjoy the World's Conveniences, Be fam'd in War, yet live in Ease Without great Vices, is a vain Eutopia seated in the Brain.

justified in his attack upon the unfeeling cruelty of the administration of justice, and when he proposes to substitute the physician for the clergyman and the judge, we may find in this an error, but no extenuation of crime; for nobody finds anything desirable in disease. It is, in fact, surprising, considering the intense indignation with which Lamettrie was everywhere regarded, that not one single positive accusation has been brought against his life. All the declamations over the wickedness of this man, whom we certainly do not propose to reckon amongst the most virtuous of men, are simply abstracted from his own writings, and these writings, with all their one-sided rhetoric and idle ridicule, nevertheless contain a very considerable core of sound thinking.

Lamettrie's theory of morals, as it is laid down especially in the 'Discours sur le Bonheur,' contains all the essential principles of the doctrine of self-love as a virtue, as it was later systematically developed by Holbach and Volney. The foundation consists of the subversion of absolute morality and the substitution of a relative morality, founded upon society and the state, as it is seen in Hobbes and Locke. With this Lamettrie combines his own peculiar doctrine of pleasure, which was again stripped away by his French successors, and replaced by the vaguer idea of self-love. A further element peculiar to him is the

---

Fraud, Luxury, and Pride must live, whilst we the Benefits receive. . . . So Vice is beneficial found, . . . As necessary to the State, As Hunger is to make 'em eat." I remember reading an attempt, in a since extinct periodical ('Internationale Revue,' Wien, Hilberg's Verlag), to defend Mandeville, with express reference to this passage of my work. The method of defence is to summarise the 'Fable of the Bees,' and to point out that there is nothing here that could excite any particular surprise nowadays. But this I have never said. On the contrary, I am of opinion that the theory of the extreme Manchester school, and the practical morality of its founders, as well as of other very respectable circles of contemporary society, are in no merely accidental agreement with Mandeville's 'Fable,' but historically and logically spring from the same source. And in so far as it is shown that Mandeville, in representing a great historical idea, is at least raised above any personal and individual complacency towards vice, I have nothing to object. All I maintain is this : Mandeville recommended vice, Lamettrie did not.

great importance which he attaches to *education* in relation to morality, and the polemic which he combines with it against *remorse.*

In view of the singular caricatures which are still constantly served up as accounts of Lamettrie's moral doctrine, we will not omit to describe very briefly the most essential features of his system.

Man's happiness rests upon the feeling of pleasure, which in its quality is in coarse and delicate, brief and lasting pleasure everywhere the same. As we are merely bodies, consequently the highest intellectual delights are also in substance bodily pleasure, although in point of value the feelings of pleasure are very different. Sensuous pleasure is intense but brief, the happiness which flows from the harmonious concord of our whole nature is calm but lasting. The same unity in variety which reigns through all nature is found also in this sphere, and every kind of pleasure and happiness must therefore in principle be regarded as equally justified, although noble and cultured natures have other joys than low and vulgar ones. This difference is secondary, and simply considered in its essence, pleasure comes not only to the ignorant man as well as to the educated, but also to the wicked no less than to the good man (compare Schiller: " Alle Guten, alle Bösen folgen ihrer Rosenspur ").

Sensation is an essential, culture only an accidental, property of man ; the main question therefore is, whether man can be happy under all circumstances, that is, whether his happiness is based upon sensation and not upon culture. This is proved by the vast mass of the uncultivated who feel themselves happy in their ignorance, and who even in death console themselves by chimerical expectations which are a benefit to them.

Reflection may heighten pleasure, but cannot afford it. He who is happy through it has a higher happiness, but more frequently it destroys happiness. One man feels himself happy owing to his natural disposition, another enjoys wealth, fame, affection, and yet feels himself un-happy, because he is unquiet, impatient, jealous, and a slave of his passions. The intoxication of opium produces by physical means a happier frame of mind than any philo-sophical treatise. How happy a man would be who all through his life could enjoy such a frame of mind as this intoxication transiently procures him! The happiness of a dream, yes, even of a happy delusion, is therefore to be regarded as a real happiness, especially as our waking state is often not much more than a dream. Intellect, know-ledge, and reason are often useless to secure happiness, sometimes even injurious. They are a superfluous adorn-ment with which the soul can dispense, and the great mass of mankind, who actually do dispense with them, are not thereby shut out from happiness. The sensuousness of happiness is rather the great means by which nature has given to all men the same right and the same claim to contentment, and has rendered existence pleasant for them all alike.

About up to this point (about one-sixth of the whole) Hettner, judging from his report,* appears to have exa-mined the 'Discours sur le Bonheur,' although, indeed, even here not without destroying the logical connection of the ideas. But so far we have only the groundwork of this ethical system, and it is quite worth while to see what theory of virtue is erected upon this foundation. But first another word about the foundation.

It will be seen already, from what we have said above, that Lamettrie only gives the first place to sensual plea-sure because it is universal. What we understand by intellectual enjoyment is not denied in its objective nature, still less so in its value for the individual, nor in the individual ranked lower than sensual pleasure, but it is simply subsumed under the universal nature of the latter; it is treated as a special case, which in the general consideration of principles cannot have the same import-

* Literaturg. des 18ten Jahrh., ii. S. 388 ff.

ance as the universal principle itself, but the relatively higher value of which is nowhere controverted.   Let us compare with this a saying of Kant's : " We may, then, as it seems to me, very well concede to Epikuros that all pleasure, if it is occasioned by notions which awake æsthetic ideas, is *animal*, that is, corporeal sensation, without thereby doing the least violence to the *intellectual* feeling of respect for moral ideas, which is not pleasure, but a self-esteem (of humanity in us) that raises us above the need of it,—aye, or even to the less noble feeling of *taste*." [76] Here we have justification and criticism together.   Lamettrie's ethic is objectionable because it is a system of hedonism, not because it analyses even such enjoyments as are produced by means of ideas into sensual pleasure.

Lamettrie, next of all, explains more exactly the relation of happiness and culture, and finds that reason is not in itself hostile to happiness, but only through the prejudices that attach themselves to thought. When freed from these, and based upon experience and observation, even reason is rather a support of our happiness. It is a good guide if it will permit itself to be guided by nature. The cultivated man enjoys a higher happiness than the ignorant.[77]   Here, too, we have the first reason for the importance of education.   The natural organisation is indeed the first and most important source of our happiness, but education is the second, and is also of the utmost importance.   It may by its advantages compensate for the defects of our organisation : its first and highest aim, however, is to tranquillise the soul by the truth.   It will hardly be necessary to add that Lamettrie here, like Lucretius, has chiefly in his mind the subversion of belief in immortality. He takes especial pains to show that Seneca[78] and Descartes

---

[76] Kant's Kritik d. Urtheilskraft, § 54; v. S. 346, ed. Hartenstein.

[77] "Toutes choses égales, n'est-il pas vrai, que le savant avec plus de lumières, sera plus heureux que l'ignorant?" pp. 112, 113, ed. Amsterdam, 1774.

[78] The 'Discours sur le Bonheur' or 'Anti-Sénèque' served originally as introduction to a translation made by Lamettrie of Seneca's treatise 'De Vita Beata.'   Ou the fondness of the French for Seneca, comp. Rosenkranz, Diderot, ii. S. 352 ff.

were at bottom of the same opinion. The latter especially is here again warmly eulogised ; what he dared not teach, because of the theologians, who sought to corrupt him, he has at least so prepared that lesser but bolder minds after him could not but discover the consequences of themselves.

In order now from this eudæmonistic foundation to reach the notion of virtue, Lamettrie employs the state and society—in a way, however, differing essentially from Hobbes.[79] He agrees with Hobbes in holding that there is no such thing as virtue in an absolute sense, that anything can be called good or bad only relatively—in relation, in fact, to society. Instead of the absolute command by the will of ' Leviathan,' however, we have the free judgment of the individual as to the good and evil of society. The distinction between legality and morality, which in Hobbes wholly disappears, here again asserts itself; although here, too, law and virtue so far flow from the same spring that they are both in a sense political institutions. Law is there to frighten and restrain the bad ; the ideas of virtue and merit are the inducements to the good to dedicate their powers to the common weal.

Here we find in the way in which Lamettrie describes the furtherance of the common weal through the sense of honour, the complete germ of the moral theory that was later so thoroughly worked out by Helvetius. The most important principle, too, upon which Materialism can depend, the principle of sympathy, is mentioned, although only incidentally. " We are enriched in a manner by the good that we do, we participate in the joy that we confer." The relation to the individual prevents Lamettrie from recognising in its full extent the general truth that he now

---

[79] Towards the end of the work, S. 188, ed. Amsterdam, 1774, Lamettrie asserts that he has borrowed nothing whether from Hobbes nor from Milord S—— (Shaftesbury?); he has created everything out of nature. It is clear, however, that assuming the *bona fides* of the declaration, the influence of these predecessors upon the development of his modes of thought is in no way redargued.

touches on. How incomparably purer and more beautiful is the expression of Volney later in the ' Catechism of the French Citizen.' Nature, it is there said, has organised man for society. " In giving him sensations, she so organised him that the sensations of others are mirrored in him, and awaken answering sensations of pleasure, of pain, of sympathy, that make the charm and indissoluble bond of society." Of course the ' charm ' here, too, is not lacking as a bond between sympathy and that principle of self-love which the whole series of the French moralists from Lamettrie onwards consider indispensable   With bold sophistry Lamettrie derives even the contempt of vanity, in which he finds the height of virtue, from vanity. Even happiness, he teaches, must come from ourselves, not from others. It is a great thing when we have at our command the hundred-voiced goddess to bid her be silent, and to be one's-self one's own glory. He who knows that he outweighs in credit all his native town loses no glory by dispensing with the approbation of his fellow-citizens, and contenting himself with his own self-approval.

The source from which the virtues are derived is, we see, not the purest; but still the virtues are there and are recognised, and we have no reason for supposing that Lamettrie was not quite serious. But how stands it with his notorious defence or even recommendation of the vices ?

Lamettrie explains quite correctly from his standpoint that the whole distinction between the good and the bad consists in this, that with the former public outweigh private interests, while the contrary is the case with the latter. Both are subject to necessity. From this Lamettrie thinks it must follow that repentance is to be wholly condemned, since it only disturbs the man's peace of mind without influencing his conduct.

It is interesting to observe how here, in the worst point of his system, there has obviously crept in an inconsistency with his own principles, and that, too, the point where the charges against his personal character find most support.

Let us, in order that we may present neither too unfavourable nor too favourable a picture of him, show how it was that he came to direct this attack upon remorse. The starting-point was obviously the observation that, as a consequence of our bringing up, regret and remorse often move us in regard to things which the philosopher cannot consider blameworthy. In this we refer at first, of course, to the whole attitude of the individual with regard to religion and the Church, but also and especially to the presumably harmless sensual pleasures, particularly those of sexual love. Now in this very sphere there was lacking in the French writers of that era, with Lamettrie at the head of them, any finer sense of discrimination, because in the only society that they knew the blessings of a stricter family life, and the greater purity of manners inseparable from it, were already long lost and almost forgotten. The eccentric notion of a systematic reward of virtue and bravery by intimacy with the most beautiful women, which is recommended by Helvetius, is preluded by Lamettrie in the complaint that virtue is deprived of part of its natural reward by inexpedient and unjustifiable scruples; and the universal application of this principle rests upon his designation of remorse as the rights of an earlier moral stage, which has now, however, no longer a meaning for us.

Here, however, Lamettrie clearly forgets that he has expressly attributed to education the highest importance for the individual as well as for society, and this in two ways. Primarily education serves, as we pointed out above, the improvement of the individual's own organisation. But next Lamettrie also admits the right of society, for the sake of the common weal, to promote by education the extension of those ideas which lead the individual to serve the community, and in its service to find his happiness, even at a sacrifice to himself.

As, now, the good man is fully justified in rooting out those stings of conscience that are due to a defective education which unjustly condemns sensuous enjoyments, so the bad man, to whom Lamettrie would always allow so much happiness as is possible for him, is invited to rid himself of any remorse whatever, because he could not act otherwise than he does, and because avenging justice will, with or without his remorse, sooner or later overtake him.

There is here obviously not only the error of the absolute division of men into 'good' and 'bad,' which overlooks the infinite varieties in the psychological combinations of good and bad motives, but, moreover, psychological causality with regard to remorse of the bad is abandoned, while it is assumed in the case of the good. If it may happen that these latter abstain from harmless enjoyments through the remains of their acquired morality, it must manifestly be possible also that the bad may abstain from bad actions through the like remains of acquired sentiments. It is evident also that the regret felt in the first case may become a restraining motive in the second case; but this Lamettrie must deny or overlook in order to reach his radical rejection of all regret.

A better result of his system is his demand that punishments shall be humane and as mild as possible. Society must for its own preservation prosecute the bad, but it must not inflict upon them greater evil than this object requires. Finally, we may observe that Lamettrie tries to give greater completeness to his system by maintaining that pleasure makes man gay, cheerful, and amiable, and is therefore in itself a real bond of society, while self-denial makes the character hard, intolerant, and unsociable.

Judge this system of morals as we like, we cannot deny that it is thought out and rich in ideas whose importance is sufficiently shown by the fact that they later appear in other thinkers in broad and systematic development, and powerfully excite the interest of their generation. How far men like Holbach, Helvetius, and Volney were conscious of drawing upon Lamettrie we cannot inquire. It is very certain that they all read him, and that they all believed themselves far above him.   And in fact, many of these ideas lie so much in the character of the time, that we may credit Lamettrie with priority, but not so certainly with originality.   How much of such things circulates from mouth to mouth before any one ventures to write it down and have it printed!   How much conceals itself in works of the most different kinds in some ambiguous phrase, in hypothetical shape, apparently thrown out in a jest, where we should never have thought of looking for it. Montaigne especially is for French literature an almost inexhaustible treasure of daring ideas, and Lamettrie shows by his citations that he had read him industriously.   If we add to him Bayle and Voltaire, of whom the latter indeed only began to show his radical leanings after Lamettrie's appearance, we shall easily see that it would require a special study of the question to establish everywhere what is reminiscence and what is Lamettrie's own idea. So much, however, we may conscientiously assert, that scarcely a single author of this period tries less than he to deck himself with borrowed plumes.   Seldom as we find *exact* citations in him, just as frequently do we find that he indicates his predecessor, at least by a word, by an allusion ; perhaps concerned rather to find sharers of his views where he stands alone than conversely to exhibit himself as original where he is not so.

An author, moreover, like Lamettrie, must easily have chanced upon the most heterodox ideas, as he not merely does not shrink from heterodox ideas and expressions shocking to ordinary minds, but actually seeks for them.   In this respect we cannot find a greater opposition than there is between the outspokenness of Montaigne and that of Lamettrie.   Montaigne seems to us, even in his boldest ideas, almost always *naïf*, and therefore amiable.   He gossips away like a man who has not the remotest intention of shocking any one, and from whom there suddenly slips an expression the force of which he seems himself not to perceive, while it startles or astonishes the reader as soon as he

realises it and dwells upon it. Lamettrie is never *naïf.*
Studied seeking for effect is his worst error, but it is also
the error which has most avenged itself, because it makes
it so easy for his opponents to misrepresent his real idea.
Even apparent contradictions in his statements may be
very frequently explained (apart from the deliberate
attacks upon himself to veil his personality) from the
exaggerated expression of a contradiction which must not
be understood as denial, but only as partial limitation.

The same character makes those productions of Lamettrie so specially repulsive in which he has attempted a
sort of poetical exaltation of sexual pleasure. Schiller
says as to the licenses of poetry in respect of the laws of
decorum, "Only *nature* can justify them," and "Only
beautiful nature can justify them." In both respects the
mere application of this standard to Lamettrie's 'Volupté'
and 'L'Art de Jouir' most conclusively condemns them as
literary products. Ueberweg says with justice of these
works that they attempt to justify sensual enjoyment in
a manner of artificial exaggeration much more than of
frivolousness. Whether a man is to be more sharply condemned who deliberately invents such things from principle than when they flow naturally from his pen, we
leave undetermined.

At all events, we need not take it so ill of Frederick the
Great that he showed so much interest in Lamettrie, and
when he was forbidden to stay in Holland invited him to
Berlin, where he became reader to the King, was admitted
to the Academy, and resumed his medical practice. "The
reputation of his philosophy and his misfortunes," says the
King in his 'Éloge,' "were sufficient to secure M. Lamettrie
an asylum in Prussia." So that he accepted the 'L'Homme
Machine' and the 'Histoire Naturelle de l'Ame' as philosophy. When later he spoke disparagingly of Lamettrie's
productions, he was doubtless thinking rather of the works
we have just been discussing. Of his personal character
the King always spoke very favourably, not only in this

official 'Éloge,' but also in private conversation.   And this is the more important as Lamettrie, it is well known, took many liberties at court, and behaved with much nonchalance in the King's society.

It is chiefly by his death that Lamettrie has injured his own cause.   If modern Materialism had only had such representatives as Gassendi, Hobbes, Toland, Diderot, Grimm, and Holbach, those fanatics who are so fond of basing their judgments upon passing individualities would have lost an admirable opportunity of condemning Materialism.   Scarcely had Lamettrie enjoyed for a few years his new prosperity at the court of Frederick the Great, when the French ambassador Tirconnel, whom Lamettrie had recovered from a severe illness, gave a feast to celebrate his recovery, which was fatal to his imprudent doctor.   It is said that to exhibit his power of gluttony, and perhaps also of his robust constitution, he devoured the whole of a pâté aux truffes, after which he became unwell immediately, and died in the ambassador's house in the delirium of a violent fever.   This circumstance caused the greater sensation as just then the euthanasia of the Atheists was a much-debated question.   In 1712 a French work had appeared, attributed chiefly to Deslandes, which contained a list of the distinguished men who have died with a jest upon their lips.   In 1747 it had been translated into German, and was still fresh in the public recollection.   In spite of its defects, it had a certain importance, through its opposition to the orthodox doctrine that recognises only a death of despair or one of reconciliation with the Church.   Just as people were always discussing whether an Atheist could lead a moral life, and so (according to Bayle's hypothesis) whether a community of Atheists is possible, it was also a topic of controversy whether an Atheist can die in peace.   In defiance of logic, which attaches much greater importance to a single negative instance, in the forming of a universal proposition, than to a whole series of positive instances, vulgar prejudice in such cases regards a single case that favours its own view more than all that are against it. But Lamettrie's death in a delirious state after the devouring of a large pâté aux truffes is an object that so completely fills the fanatic's narrow horizon as to leave room for no other idea. And yet the whole sensational story as to its chief point—the real cause of death—is by no means free from doubt. Frederick the Great says in his funeral oration : " Lamettrie died in the house of Milord Tirconnel, the French plenipotentiary, whom he had restored to life. It seems that the disease, knowing with whom it had to deal, was cunning enough to attack him first by the brain, in order to destroy him the more surely. A violent fever with fierce delirium came on. The invalid was obliged to have recourse to the science of his colleagues, but he failed to find the succour that his own skill had so often afforded as well to himself as to the public." The King tells indeed a very different story in a confidential letter to his sister, the Markgräfin von Bayreuth.[81] There he mentions that Lamettrie had contracted an indigestion by devouring a pheasant pasty. But as the proximate cause of death the King seems to regard a blooding which Lamettrie prescribed for himself, in order to prove to the German physicians, with whom he was at variance on this point, the utility of bleeding in such a case.

[81] This letter, in which occurs also the unfavourable judgment of Lamettrie as an author mentioned above ("Il était gai, bon diable, bon medecin et tres mauvais auteur ; mes en ne lisant pas ses livres il y avait moyen d'en être tres content "), is dated the 21st Nov. 1751 ; an extract is to be found in the Nouv. Bibliogr. Générale s. v. Lamettrie.

CHAPTER III

IF it lay within our plan to trace through all their wind-
ings the individual ramifications of materialistic thought,
to test the greater or less consistency of the thinkers and
writers who sometimes merely upon occasion favour Materialism, sometimes in a gradual development approach
nearer and nearer to it, sometimes finally betray, only, as it
were, against their will, distinctly materialistic sentiments,
no epoch would offer us such plentiful material as the
second half of the eighteenth century, and no land would
occupy a larger space in our history than France.   There
is, first of all, Diderot, the man of fire and genius, who is
so often called the head and leader of the Materialists, while
he really not only needed a long course of development before he reached what can be properly called a materialistic
standpoint, but even to the last moment remained in a
state of ferment which never allowed him to perfect and
elucidate his views.   This noble nature, which comprised
in itself all the virtues and all the faults of the Idealist,
especially zeal for human welfare, self-sacrificing friend-
ship, and unfaltering faith in the good, the beautiful, the
true, and in the perfectibility of the world, was driven, as
we have seen, by the tendency of the times and against
his will, as it were, towards Materialism.   Diderot's friend
and colleague, D'Alembert, on the other hand, was already
far beyond Materialism, " feeling himself tempted to believe that everything we see is but an illusion of the
senses, that there is nothing without us corresponding to

what we believe we see." He might have become for France what Kant became for the world, if he could have held fast to this idea, and had raised himself but a little above the level of a sceptical fit. As it was, however, he did not even become the 'Protagoras' of his time, as Voltaire's jest would have made him. The cautious and reserved Buffon, the discreet and diplomatic Grimm, the vain and superficial Helvetius—all these men approach to Materialism without exhibiting the fixity of principle and the logical carrying out of a great idea which distinguish Lamettrie in spite of his frivolity of phrase. We ought, indeed, to mention Buffon as a zoologist, and especially deal with Cabanis, the father of the materialistic physiology, but that our plan requires us at once to take up the decisive points, and to reserve a glance at the special sciences, until we have exhibited the history of the fundamental problems. And so we are justified in lightly passing over the period between the appearance of the 'L'Homme Machine' and of the 'Système de la Nature,' rich field as it presents to the historian of literature, and coming at once to the work which has often been designated as the Code or the Bible of all Materialism.

The 'System of Nature,' with its frank, straightforward speech, its almost German march of ideas, and its doctrinaire prolixity, suddenly and clearly exhibited the result of all the brilliant ideas with which the age was then fermenting, and this result in its rigid absoluteness repelled even those who had most contributed to bring it about. Lamettrie had chiefly frightened Germany. The 'System of Nature' frightened France. If in Germany this result was aided by the frivolity which is repugnant to the German's inmost soul, in France the didactic seriousness of the book had doubtless its share in the irritation which it encountered. A great difference was made by the time of their appearance as compared with the intellectual condition of the two nations. France was approaching the Revolution, while Germany was about to enter on the classic era of its literature and philosophy. In the 'Système de la Nature' we feel already the cutting blast of the Revolution.

It was in the year 1770 that the work appeared under the title 'Système de la Nature, ou les Lois du Monde physique et du Monde moral,' nominally in London, but really at Amsterdam. It bore the name of Mirabaud, then ten years dead, and even gave a short sketch of the life and writings of this man, who had been secretary of the French Academy. Nobody believed in his authorship, but singularly no one divined the true origin of the book, although it had proceeded from the very heart of the materialistic camp, and was, in fact, but one link in the long chain of the literary productions of an original and important personage.

Paul Heinrich Dietrich von Holbach, a rich German baron, born at Heidelsheim in the Palatinate in 1723, came to Paris early in his youth, and, like his countryman Grimm, whose intimate friend he was, became naturalised into French life. If we consider the influence exercised by these men in their circle, and compare with them the characters of the gay and brilliant society that gathered round Holbach's hospitable hearth, we easily see that we must attribute to these two Germans a decisive part in the philosophical questions that were here discussed. Quiet, inflexible, impassive, like self-absorbed helmsmen, they sit among this whirlpool of eddying talent. With the function of observers they unite, each in his own way, a far-reaching influence that is the more irresistible because it is so imperceptible. Holbach especially seemed little more than the always good-natured and generous *maître d'hotel* to the society of philosophers, whose humour and friendliness charmed everybody, whose benevolence, whose domestic and social virtues, whose modest and simple feeling in the midst of affluence, were the more admired because every kind of talent about him met with the fullest recognition, without Holbach's claiming any other part than that of an amiable host. This very modesty it is that is the real cause why people found it so difficult to consider Holbach himself as the author of the book which had set the learned world in commotion. Even after it had long been certain that the book must have proceeded from his immediate circle, it was still attributed now to the mathematician Lagrange, who had been tutor in Holbach's family, now to Diderot, and again to a systematic collaboration of several minds. There is now, however, no room to doubt that Holbach is the real author, although particular sections were contributed to by Lagrange, the specialist, Diderot, the master of style, and Naigeon, a literary assistant of Diderot and Holbach.[82] Not only was Holbach the actual author of the whole, but his was the systematic head that controlled the work and gave it its tendency. And he did not merely bring its tendency to the work, but had at his command a rich store of scientific knowledge. He had particularly studied chemistry, and had written articles on it for the ' Encyclopédie,' and translated several chemical works from the German. " It was with his learning," writes Grimm, " as with his wealth. No one would ever have suspected it if he could have concealed it without lessening his own satisfaction, and especially that of his friends."

Holbach's other writings,[83] which are numerous, treat for the most part the same questions as the 'System of Nature,'—partly as in his 'Le Bon Sens, ou Idées Naturelles opposées aux Idées Surnaturelles,' 1772, in a popular shape, with the express object of influencing the masses. Even Holbach's political views were clearer and more definite than those of most of his French contemporaries, though he does not pronounce for any particular form of government. He does not share the vague enthusiasm for English institutions which rest upon so much that it is

[82] Comp. Hettner, ii. 364. On Naigeon, the ' Parson of Atheism,' comp. Rosenkranz, Diderot, ii. 288 ff.

[83] Comp. Rosenkranz, Diderot, ii. 78 ff.

impossible to impart. With calm and passionless force
he develops the right of nations to decide for themselves,
the duty of all authorities to submit to this right, and to
serve the destinies of the nations, the criminality of all
pretensions against the sovereignty of the people, and the
nullity of all treaties, laws, and formalities that seek to
maintain such criminal pretensions on the part of individuals. The right of the people to revolution in desperate
circumstances is to him an axiom; and here he hit the nail
upon the head.

Holbach's morality is serious and pure, though he never
gets beyond the notion of happiness. It lacks the in-
wardness and the poetic breath that animates Epikuros's
theory of the harmony of the soul, yet it makes a great
effort to surmount the standpoint of the individual, and
to establish virtue upon the interests of the state and of
society. What we are inclined to regard as a frivolous
feature in the 'System of Nature' is not so much a superficial
trifling with morality—which would be real frivolity—as
the complete ignoring of the moral and ideal value of
traditional institutions, especially of the Church and belief
in revelation. While this is, in the first place, a result of
the lack of historical sense in the eighteenth century, it is
doubly intelligible in a nation which, like the French in
these times, possesses no genuine poetry; for from this vital
source it is that everything flows that has a deep-seated
principle of life and action in the nature of man, without
waiting for any justification from reason. Thus it is that
in Goethe's celebrated judgment on the 'System of Nature'
the profoundest criticism, fused with the greatest injustice
in the *naïf* self-consciousness of the poet's own activity,
exhibits the sublime opposition of the young intellectual
life of Germany to the apparent "decrepitude" of France.

The 'System of Nature' falls into two parts, of which the
first contains the general foundations and the anthropology; the second, so far as this expression may be used,
the theology. Already in the preface it is evident that

the real starting-point of the author is the effort to secure the happiness of mankind.

"Man is unhappy," the preface begins, "merely because he misunderstands nature. His mind is so infected by prejudices that one must almost believe him to be for ever doomed to error; the chains of illusion in which he is so entangled from childhood have so grown upon him, that he can only with the utmost trouble be again set free from them. Unhappily he struggles to rise above the visible world, and painful experiences constantly remind him of the futility of his attempts. Man disdained the study of nature to pursue after phantoms, that, like will-o'-the-wisps, dazzled him and drew him from the plain path of truth, away from which he cannot attain happiness. It is therefore time to seek in nature remedies against the evils into which fanaticism has plunged us. There is but one truth, and it can never harm us. To error are due the grievous fetters by which tyrants and priests everywhere succeed in enchaining the nations: from error arose the bondage to which the nations are subject; from error the terrors of religion, which brought about that men mouldered in fear, or fanatically throttled each other for chimeras. From error arose deep-rooted hatred and cruel persecutions; the continual bloodshed and the horrid tragedies of which earth must be made the theatre to serve the interests of heaven.

"Let us try, therefore, to banish the mists of prejudice, and to inspire man with courage and respect for his reason! If there is any one who cannot dispense with these delusions, let him at least allow others to form their own ideas in their own way, and let him be convinced that, for the inhabitants of earth, the important thing is to be just, benevolent, and peaceful."

Five chapters discuss the general principles of his view of nature. Nature, motion, matter, the regularity of events, and the nature of order and chance, are the subjects with which Holbach connects his fundamental propositions.

Among these chapters, it is the last especially which, by its absolute elimination of the last relic of theology, for ever separated the Deists from the Materialists, and which in particular stirred up Voltaire to violent attacks upon the 'System of Nature.'

Nature is the great whole of which man is part and by which he is influenced. The beings that we place outside nature have always been creatures of imagination, of whose character we can form an idea as little as of their abiding-place and modes of action. There does not and cannot exist anything beyond the sphere that includes all creatures. Man is a physical being, and his moral existence is only a special aspect of his physical nature, a particular mode of action due to his peculiar organisation.

Everything that the human mind has devised for the improvement of our condition is but a consequence of the reaction between his impulses and the nature that environs him. Even the animal proceeds from simple needs and forms to ever more complicated ones; and so also the plant. Imperceptibly the aloe grows through a series of years, until it at last produces the flowers that are the harbingers of its speedy death. Man, as a physical being, acts according to visible sensuous influences; as a moral being, according to influences which our prejudices will not permit us to recognise. Education is development; as, indeed, Cicero had already said—"Est autem virtus nihil aliud quam in se perfecta et ad summum perducta natura." All our inadequate ideas are due to want of experience, and every error involves injury. From defective knowledge of nature man has imagined deities that became the one object of his hopes and fears, without thinking that nature knows neither hate nor love, and works on and on, producing now weal now woe, according to invariable laws. The world shows us everywhere nothing but matter and motion. It is an endless chain of causes and effects; the most various elements are continually reacting on each other, and their different qualities and combinations constitute for us the nature of individual things. Nature in the wider sense, then, is the combination of the different elements in individual things in general; in the narrower sense, the nature of a thing is the sum of its properties and modes of action. If, then, we say that nature produces an effect, we must not personify nature as an abstraction, but we mean only that the effect in question is a necessary result of the properties of some one of the things forming the great whole that we see.

In the theory of motion Holbach keeps close to the basis laid down by Toland in the essay we have mentioned already. He defines motion, indeed, badly,[84] but he treats it comprehensively and thoroughly, though without entering upon mathematical theories, just as in the whole work, agreeably to his practical aim, the positive and special treatment gives place to general and abstract considerations.

Everything is, in virtue of its peculiar nature, capable of certain movements. Thus our senses are capable of receiving impressions from certain objects. Of no body can we know anything unless it directly or indirectly produces a modification in us. Every movement that we perceive either removes a whole body to another place, or it takes place amongst the smallest particles of this body, and produces perturbations or changes that are perceptible to us only through the changed properties of the body. Movements of this kind are at the bottom of the growth of plants and animals and the intellectual activity of man.

The movements are called communicated if they are forced upon a body from without; spontaneous, if the

[84] The definition (chap. ii.) runs: "Le mouvement est un effort par lequel un corps change ou tend à changer de place." In this definition the identity of motion with the 'nisus' or 'conatus' of the theorists of the time, which Holbach tries to demonstrate in the course of the chapter, is already presupposed, which leads to the positing of a higher idea ("effort"), that at bottom includes the notion of motion, and moreover has an anthropomorphic tinge, from which the simpler idea of motion is free. Comp. the following note.

cause of movement is in the body itself. Amongst the latter are reckoned, in the case of man, walking, speech, thought, although we may find, on closer examination, that, strictly considered, there are no spontaneous movements. The human will is determined by external causes.

The communication of movement from one body to another is regulated by necessary laws. Everything in the universe is constantly in motion, and all rest is only apparent.[85] Even what physicists have called 'nisus' can only be explained by movement. If a stone weighing 500 pounds rests upon the earth, it is pressing every instant with its whole weight, and receives a corresponding pressure from the earth. One need only lay one's hand between them to discover that the stone shows sufficient force to crush it, in spite of its apparent rest. Action is never without reaction. The so-called dead forces and the living ones are therefore of the same kind, and only show themselves under different circumstances. Even the most durable bodies are subject to continual changes. Matter and motion are eternal, and creation out of nothing is an empty phrase. To go back to the origin of things is only to postpone our difficulties, and to withdraw them from the test of sense.

As to matter, Holbach is not a strict Atomist. He assumes, indeed, elementary particles, but declares the nature of the elements to be unknown. We know only some of their properties. All modifications of matter are a consequence of motion; this transforms the shape of things, dissolves their constituent parts, and forces them

---

[85] In this passage (p. 17 ff. of the edition, London, 1780) the author quotes Toland's 'Letters to Serena,' though he does not apply in all its precision Toland's theory of motion. Toland shows that 'rest' must not only be always understood relatively, but also that it is at bottom only a special case of motion, since just as much activity and passivity are involved when a body in the conflict of forces maintains its place for some time, as when it changes its place. Holbach only approaches to this end indirectly, and nowhere exactly hits the decisive point ; whether because he had not conceived Toland's view in all its precision, or because he considered his own mode of treatment to be more popular.

to contribute to the development or conservation of things of quite different nature.

Between what are called the three kingdoms of nature there exists a continual exchange and circulation of material particles. The animal acquires new strength by the consumption of plants or of other animals; air, water, earth, and fire aid in its maintenance. But the same elements, under other forms of combination, become the cause of its dissolution; and immediately the same constituents are worked into new formations, or cause fresh destruction.

This is the invariable course of nature; this is the everlasting cycle that must be described by all existence. It is thus that motion originates the parts of the universe, maintains them for a time, and destroys them gradually, the one by means of the other; while the sum of existence remains always the same. Nature, in its combining activity, creates suns which become the centre of as many systems; she creates the planets which gravitate by their own nature, and describe their orbits round the sun. Very gradually motion changes the one and the other, and she will perhaps some day scatter again the particles out of which she formed the wondrous masses, of which man in his short span of life gets only a passing glimpse.[86]

While, however, Holbach thus in general principles is quite at one with our modern Materialism, he stands (and this is a proof how far these abstractions lay from the true path of natural science) in his views as to the changes of matter still quite on the old ground. With him fire is still the life-principle of things. As with Epikuros, as with Lucretius and Gassendi, so with him the fiery particles are in play in all the events of life, and, now visible, now concealed beneath the rest of matter, produce numerous phenomena. Four years after the 'System of Nature' appeared Priestley discovered oxygen, and while Holbach was still writing or discussing his principles with his

[86] Vol. i. ch. iii. p. 39, ed. 1780.

friends, Lavoisier was already working at that magnificent series of experiments to which we are indebted for the true theory of combustion, and at the same time for an entirely new foundation for that science of which Holbach too was a student. But the latter was content, like Epikuros, with the logical and moral results of previous inquiry, while the former was inspired by a scientic idea to which he dedicated his life.

In treating of the regularity of events, Holbach goes back to the fundamental forces of nature. Attraction and repulsion are the forces from which all combination and separation in bodies proceed; they are related to each other, as Empedokles had seen, like love and hate in the moral world. Even this combination and separation are regulated by absolute laws. Many bodies, which by themselves admit of no combination, may be brought to it by the mediation of other bodies. To be is only to move in a particular manner; to endure means to communicate or receive such movements as condition the continuance of individual existence. A stone resists decomposition merely by the cohesion of its particles; organised beings by complicated means. The impulse of self-preservation is called in physics durability, in morality self-love.

Between cause and effect rules necessity in the moral as in the physical world. The particles of dust and water in a tempest or a whirlwind move by the same necessity as an individual in the stormy movements of a revolution.[87]

Holbach died the 21st June 1789, a few days after the deputies of the 'Tiers État' had constituted themselves a National Assembly. The Revolution, which drove his friend Grimm back to Germany, and often enough involved Lagrange in danger of his life, was on the point of being realised when he departed who had so powerfully prepared the way for it by teaching that it must be regarded as a natural and necessary event.

[87] Vol. i. ch. iv. p. 52, ed. 1780.

Of especial importance is, finally, the chapter on Order, against which Voltaire directed his first bitter attack.[88] Voltaire is here, as so often, the representative of the ordinary common sense, which, with its inarticulate prejudices and vulgar declamation, is absolutely valueless as compared with even the lowest form of philosophical thought. Nevertheless it will serve our purpose for once to balance arguments and counter-arguments, in order to show that to get beyond Materialism far other means are needed than those that were at the disposal even of the acute and skilful Voltaire.

Originally, says the 'System of Nature,' the word order meant merely the way in which we easily embrace in its individual relations a whole whose forms of existence and operation offer a certain correspondence with our own. (We note the familiar anachronism which regards the *stricter* conception as the *original* one, though in reality it is only later developed.) Man has proceeded to impose his own peculiar mode of thought upon the external world. But since in the world everything is equally necessary, there cannot in nature be any possible distinction between order and disorder. Both conceptions belong only to our reason; and, as with all metaphysical notions, there is nothing corresponding to them outside ourselves. If, nevertheless, we wish to apply these notions to nature, we can only mean by order the regular succession of phenomena which is the result of invariable natural laws; while disorder remains a relative notion, embracing only those phenomena by which an individual thing is disturbed as to the form of its existence, although there is no disturbance at all, looking from the standpoint of the great whole. There is in nature no such thing as order or disorder. We find order in everything that is conformable to our

---

[88] Comp. the article 'Dieu, Dieux,' in the 'Dict. Philos.,' reprinted in the collected edition of Voltaire, and, under the title 'Sentiment de Vol- taire sur le Système de la Nature,' with a different arrangement of the sections, in the 1780 edition of the 'Système de la Nature.'

nature; disorder in all that is contrary to it. The immediate result of this view is that there can be no such things in nature as miracles. In exactly the same way we create within ourselves the notion of an intelligence acting with purpose, and its antithesis, the notion of chance. The whole can have no purpose, because outside it there is nothing at which it could aim. We regard as intelligent such causes as operate after our manner, and consider the operation of others as a play of blind chance. And yet the word chance has a meaning only as opposed to that intelligence the idea of which we have drawn from ourselves. But there are really no blindly operating causes, but we are ourselves blind, since we misunderstand the forces and laws of nature, whose effects we attribute to chance.

Here we find the 'System of Nature' quite in the paths prepared by Hobbes with his vigorous Nominalism. It is obvious that the notions of Good and Bad, although Holbach has forborne to develop them, must also be regarded as merely relative and subjective, like those of order and disorder, intelligence and chance. From this there is no retreat is possible; for the demonstration of the relativity of these notions and their foundation in human nature remains the irrevocable first step to a purified and thorough science; the way of advance is of course still open. It is by way of the doctrine of the origin of these ideas in the human organisation that the path lies that leads us beyond the limits of Materialism: on the other hand, the positions of the 'System of Nature' stand immovably firm against any opposition based upon vulgar prejudices. We attribute to chance those effects whose connection with their causes we cannot see; order and disorder are not in nature.

What is Voltaire's answer to this? Let us hear him. We will take the liberty of answering him in the name of Holbach.

"What! in the physical world is a child born blind or without legs, an abortion, not against the nature of the race? Is it not the usual regularity of nature that consti-

tutes order, and its irregularity that constitutes disorder?
Is not a child to whom nature has given hunger but closed
its œsophagus a violent disorder and a fatal irregularity?
Evacuations are necessary, and yet the proper channels
often lack an opening, so that surgical aid is necessary.
This disorder has doubtless its cause: there is no effect
without cause; but still this effect is a great violation of
order."

It cannot, indeed, be denied that, to our common unscientific modes of thought, an abortion does violence to the
nature of the race; but what else is this 'nature of the
race' than an empirical human idea, that for objective
nature has no binding force, and indeed no meaning? It
is not enough to admit that the effect which, in its intimate relations to our own sensations, appears a disorder
has a cause; we must also admit that this cause stands in
a necessary and immutable connection with all the other
causes in the universe; and that the one great whole, in
the same way and by the same laws, in most cases produces the complete organisation, and in some cases the
incomplete. But looked at in connection with the great
whole—and this is what Voltaire should have done if he
wished not to be unjust—it is impossible to regard as disorder what is merely a result of its eternal order, that is,
of its regular course; while the 'System of Nature' never
denied that such phenomena present to sensitive, sympa-
thising men the appearance of frightful irregularity. So
that Voltaire has proved nothing but what was conceded
from the first, and has not so much as touched the core of
the question. But let us see whether he proves more in
the case of the moral world.

"The murder of a friend, of a brother, is that not a
frightful disorder in the moral sphere? The calumnies of
Garasse, of Tellier, of Doucin against the Jansenists, those
of the Jansenists against the Jesuits; the trickeries of
Patouillet and Paulian, are they not small disorders?
The Bartholomew Massacre, the butcheries in Ireland,

&c., &c., are they not accursed disorders? These trans-
gressions have their causes in the passions, but their effect
is abominable: the cause is fatal; this cause makes us
shudder."

Murder is indeed a thing at which man shudders, and
which he regards as a frightful violation of moral order.
And yet we may reach the view that these complications
and passions in which crime originate are only necessary
aspects of human impulses and activities, as shadows are
inseparable from light. We shall be absolutely obliged to
admit this necessity as soon as we cease to play with the
idea of cause, and seriously admit that even human actions
to each other and to the sum of nature stand in a complete and effectual causal relation. For then we shall find
here, too, as well as in the physical sphere, a common
foundation—nature itself—indissolubly bound together by
a causal connection in all its parts, which acts according to
eternal laws, and produces in the same order virtue as well
as crime, and as well horror of crime as the conviction that
the idea associated with this horror, of a violation of order,
is a merely one-sided and inadequate human conception.

"We have only to show the origin of this disorder,
which actually exists."

The origin lies in human conceptions; there indeed the
idea of disorder exists, but Voltaire has proved nothing
more. But the inaccurate and illogical human understanding, even though it be that of the ablest of men, has
at all times confounded its own empirical conceptions
with the nature of things in themselves, and will probably
continue to do so.

Without entering here into a deeper criticism of Holbach's standpoint—a criticism which will indicate itself
in the course of our work—we will only point out that
the Materialists, in their victorious demonstration of the
uniformity of nature, confine themselves to this range of
ideas with a one-sidedness that seriously hinders the due
appreciation of the intellectual life, in so far as merely

human ideas play a legitimate part in it. Because the critical understanding refuses the title of objectivity claimed for the ideas of teleology, of intelligence in nature, of order and disorder, and so on, it too easily results that the value of these ideas to mankind is too much depreciated, even when they are not wholly rejected. Holbach, it is true, recognises a certain justification for these ideas: man may avail himself of them if he is not enslaved to them, and if he knows that he has to do, not with objective things, but with inadequate conceptions of them. But that such ideas, although in no way answering to the things in themselves, must in extensive spheres of life not only be suffered as convenient and harmless habits of childhood, but that they belong in spite of, nay, perhaps, *because* of, their birth in the mind of man to the noblest treasures of mankind, and can afford him a felicity which nothing can replace, these are considerations far removed from the Materialist; and they are indeed removed from him, not because they would be inconsistent with his system, but because the modes of thought engendered in him through struggle and labour carry him away from this aspect of human life.

And from this too it results that Materialism is not only more dangerous in a struggle with religion than other weapons, but that it shows itself more or less hostile also to poetry and to art, which have, however, the advantage, that in them the free creativeness of the human mind as opposed to reality is openly conceded, while in the dogmas of religion and the architectural constructions of metaphysic it is intimately associated with false pretensions to objective truth.

There are therefore deeper aspects of the relation of religion and metaphysic to Materialism which will later display themselves. Meanwhile let us take a side glance at the subject of art in relation to the chapter on order and disorder.

If order and disorder do not exist in nature, then also

the antithesis of the Beautiful and the Ugly rests merely upon human ideas. The circumstance that this thought is always present to the Materialist easily estranges him to some extent from the sphere of the Beautiful ; the Good is nearer him, the True nearest of all. If, then, a Materialist undertake the function of judge in art, he will necessarily be more inclined than another critic to emphasise natural truth in art, but to ignore and depreciate the ideal and the strictly beautiful, especially when they conflict with natural truth. Thus, then, we find also Holbach almost without sense for poetry and art ; at least he betrays none in his writings. Diderot, however, who took up art criticism at first against his will, but later with extraordinary zeal, exhibits in a surprising way the influence of Materialism upon the appreciation of the Beautiful.

His "Essay on Painting" is, with Goethe's masterly remarks, in everybody's hands. With what tenacity Goethe insists upon the ideal aim of art, while Diderot obstinately seeks to make the idea of the consistency of nature the principle of the fine arts ! There are no such things as order and disorder in nature. From nature's standpoint (if only our eye could trace out the subtle features of a logical whole), is not the figure of a hunchback as good as that of a Venus ? Is not our idea of beauty at bottom a mere human limitation ? In developing more and more widely this thought, Materialism diminishes our pure joy in beauty and the sublime influence of the ideal.

The fact that Diderot was by natural disposition an Idealist, and that we accordingly find in him expressions of the distinctest Idealism, only shows more clearly the influence of the Materialistic ideas, which again against his will carry him away. Diderot goes so far as to deny that the ideal, 'the true contour,' can be found by an empirical combination of the most beautiful parts that nature presents. It springs from the mind of the great artist as an archetype of the really beautiful, from which nature always and in all parts is removed by the pressure of necessity. This thesis is as true as the assertion that nature in the structure of a hunchback or a blind woman follows out to the very toes the consequences of the defect once given, with a delicacy that the greatest artist could not attain. But what is not true is the combination of these two propositions by the remark that we should need no ideal, that we should find the highest satisfaction in the immediate copying of nature, if we were only in a condition to penetrate the whole system in its logical connection.[89] It is true that, if we push the matter to extremities, it may be asked, whether for *absolute* knowledge—that sees in a fragment its relations to the whole, and for which therefore every intuition is an intuition of the universe—whether for such knowledge there can be any beauty at all apart from reality? But Diderot does not look at it in this way. His proposition must admit of a practical application for the artist and art critic. It must also be maintained, then, that the deviations from the 'true contour' of the ideal are admissible—nay, as compared with the merely normal, constitute the true ideal—so far as we succeed in bringing them out, at least in sentiment, in their unity and consistency. But then the ideal loses its independence. The beautiful is subordinated to the true, and thus loses its own special significance.

If we wish to avoid this mistake, we must above all regard ethical and æsthetic ideas as themselves necessary

---

[89] Essai sur la Peinture, i. : "Si les causes et les effets nous étaient évidents, nous n'aurions rien de mieux à faire que de représenter les êtres tels qu'ils sont. Plus l'imitation serait parfaite et analogue aux causes, plus nous en serions satisfaits." Œuvres Compl. de Diderot, iv. 1 part., p. 479 (Paris, 1818). Rosenkranz, to whom we are indebted for his energetic reference to Diderot's Idealism (comp. especially Diderot, ii. 132 ff., the passages taken from the Letter to Grimm on the *Salon* of 1767, Œuvres, iv. 1, p. 170 ff.), has not sufficiently weighed this important passage in his account of the argument of the 'Essai sur la Peinture' (Diderot, ii. 137). There is no course open but either to suppose Diderot to be here contradicting himself, or to combine the superiority of natural truth to beauty here taught with the theory of the 'true contour' in the mode adopted in the text.

products of the general forces of nature, developed according to eternal laws in the special province of the human
spirit. Human speculations and endeavours beget the idea
of order as they beget the idea of beauty. Then comes
the philosophy of nature and destroys it; but from the
hidden depths of the soul it ever springs forth again. In
this struggle of the creative and the critical faculty, there
is nothing more unnatural than in any other contest of
the forces of nature, or in that war of extermination between living creatures battling with one another for existence. We must, indeed, from the most abstract standpoint,
deny that there is error any more than disorder. Error,
too, arises from the strictly ordered reaction between the
individual with his organs and the impressions of the
external world. Error is, like better knowledge, only a
mode or fashion in which the things of the external world
project themselves, as it were, in man's consciousness. Is
there any absolute knowledge of things in themselves?
Man at least does not seem to possess it. If, however,
there exists a higher knowledge answering to his nature,
as compared with which ordinary error—though it too is a
mode of knowledge depending upon law—may yet be described merely as error, that is, as a condemnable deviation
from this higher mode of knowledge; in that case will there
not also be an order based upon the nature of man that
deserves something better than to be placed upon one and
the same level with its opposite disorder, that is, just those
kinds of order that deviate and are entirely opposed to
human nature?

Although the style of the 'System of Nature' is prolix
and full of repetitions, yet it contains many discussions
that partly deserve notice for their vigour and soundness,
but partly are particularly suited to exhibit in a clear light
the narrow limits in which the materialistic philosophy
moves.

While Lamettrie took a malicious delight in giving
himself out as a Cartesian, and affirming, perhaps in good

faith, that Descartes had explained man on mechanical principles, and had only attached a soul to the machine to please the parsons, Holbach, on the contrary, makes Descartes chiefly responsible for the dogma of the spirituality of the soul. "Although even before him the soul had been conceived to be spiritual, yet he is the first who laid down the principle that the thinking nature must be distinct from matter, and from this concludes that the thinking element in us is a spirit, that is, a simple and indivisible substance. Would it not be more natural to conclude: Because man, a material being, does actually think, it follows that matter is capable of thinking? Leibniz comes off no better with his pre-established harmony, or even Malebranche, the inventor of Occasionalism. Holbach does not take the trouble to refute these men thoroughly; he is content with pointing out continually the absurdity of their principles. From his point of view, not unreasonably; for if one fails to appreciate the effort of these men to shape the ideas that lived in them, if one submits their systems to a strict logical examination, then, in truth, no expression of contempt can be strong enough to characterise the shallowness and frivolity with which these much-admired philosophers laid the foundations of their systems upon absolute nothingness. Holbach sees everywhere only the influence of theology, and ignores the metaphysical instinct, which seems to lie quite as deep in our nature as, for instance, the feeling for architecture. "It must not surprise us," thinks Holbach, "to see the ingenious and unsatisfying hypotheses in which the deepest thinkers of modern times, driven by theological prejudices, are obliged to take refuge whenever they attempt to reconcile the spiritual nature of the soul with the physical influence of material things upon this immaterial substance, and to explain the reaction of the soul upon these things, as well as generally its union with the body." Only a single spiritualist offers him any difficulty, and here we recognise the fundamental problem to which our whole investigation is bringing us. It is Berkeley, who, as a bishop of the Church of England, was certainly led by theological prejudices more than Descartes and Leibniz, and yet who reached a philosophy more logical, and in principle further from ecclesiastical dogma, than both of them.

"What shall we say of a Berkeley, who tries hard to convince us that everything in the world is but a chimerical illusion, and that the whole universe exists only in ourselves and in our imagination, and who makes the existence of everything doubtful by the help of sophistries that are insoluble for all those who maintain the spirituality of the soul?" How those who are not keen to maintain an immaterial soul are to dispose of Berkeley, Holbach has forgotten to set forth; and in a note he confesses that this, the most extravagant of systems, is almost the most difficult to refute.[90] Materialism obstinately takes the phenomenal world for the world of realities. What weapons has it against him who attacks this main standpoint? Are things as they seem? *Are* they at all? These are questions that continually recur in the history of philosophy, and to which only the present can give a half-satisfactory answer—an answer, indeed, which adopts neither extreme.

Holbach devoted special and obviously conscientious pains to the foundations of Ethic. We shall, indeed, find hardly a single idea that had not already made itself heard in Lamettrie; but what in him is casual, carelessly thrown out and mixed with frivolous remarks, meets us in Holbach purified, methodised, and systematically developed, with rigid avoidance of all that is mean and vulgar. Like

[90] Syst. de la Nat., i. c. x. p. 158 ff., ed. 1780. We may point out here, in view of the recent very extravagant over-estimate of Berkeley, that the "irrefutableness" of his system only extends so far as it denies the existence of a physical world different from our ideas. The conclusion that there is a spiritual, incorporeal, and active substance which is the cause of our ideas, is as full of flat and palpable absurdities as any metaphysical system whatever.

Epikuros, Holbach made durable felicity, and not transient pleasure, the aim of human effort. The 'System of Nature' contains also an attempt to base morality upon physiology, and in connection with this an energetic assertion of the civic virtues.

"If we were to consult experience instead of prejudice, medicine could solve for morality the riddle of the human heart, and we might be assured that sometimes she would cure the mind by curing the body." It was only twenty years later that the noble Pinel, a physician of Condillac's school, founded the modern 'psychiatry,' which by degrees brought us, to the great alleviation of the most terrible of human sufferings, to tend the insane with benevolence, and to recognise insanity in a large proportion of criminals. "The dogma of the immortality of the soul has made morality into a science of conjectures, which teaches us nothing at all of the true means to influence mankind. If, aided by experience, we knew the elements that formed the basis of the temperament of an individual, or of the majority of the individuals in a nation, we should know what is suited to them—what laws are necessary, and what institutions useful for them. In a word, morality and politics might derive advantages from Materialism that the dogma of an immaterial soul can never give them, and which it prevents us even from thinking of."[91] This idea of Holbach's has still its future before it; only that probably, to begin with, statistics will do more for morals than physiology.

All the moral and intellectual faculties are derived by Holbach from our sensibility to the impressions made by the external world. "A sensitive soul is nothing but a human brain so constituted that it easily receives the motions communicated to it. Thus we call him sensitive who is moved to tears by the sight of an unhappy creature, or the account of a terrible accident, or the mere idea of an afflicting scene." Here Holbach stood at the very threshold

[91] L, c. ix.; ed. 1780. i., p. 124.

of a materialistic moral philosophy, in which we are still
lacking, and whose development we must desire, even
though we have no idea of remaining at the materialistic
standpoint.   What is needed is to find the principle that
will carry us beyond Egoism.   Pity, indeed, is not enough;
but if we include sympathetic pleasure, and extend our
view so as to take in all the natural sympathy felt by all the
finer organisation with the beings whose likeness to himself he recognises, we have then already a foundation upon
which we may at all events build up something like a
proof that the virtues also find their way insensibly into
man through eyes and ears.   Without venturing, with
Kant, upon the decisive step that inverts all the relations
of experience to man and his ideas, we might yet find a
solid basis for this ethical theory, by showing how, through
the mediation of the senses, there is gradually formed
in the lapse of thousands of years a community amongst
mankind, resting upon this fact, that every individual
shares in the fortunes of the race through the harmony,
or want of harmony, in his own sensations and ideas.

Instead of following out this natural succession of ideas,
Holbach, after some discussions reminding us strongly of
Helvetius on the nature of mind (*esprit*) and of imagination, proceeds to deduce morality from the purely rational
recognition of the means to happiness—a proceeding
which reflects the unhistorical and generalising spirit of
the previous century.

The political passages of the work are undoubtedly
more important than is commonly supposed.   They are
so distinctly marked by a firm, complete, and thoroughly
radical theory—they conceal, often beneath the appearance
of a magnanimous objectivity or philosophical resignation,
such an embittered hatred of the existing order, that they
must have exercised a profounder influence than long
tirades of brilliant and passionate rhetoric.   They would
doubtless have been more regarded if they were not brief
and scattered.

"As government only derive its powers from society, and is established only for its good, it is evident that society may revoke this power when its interests demand, may change the form of government, extend or limit the power intrusted to its leaders, over whom it retains a supreme authority, by the immutable law of nature that subordinates the part to the whole." This passage, from the (ninth) chapter on the foundations of morality and politics, gives the general rule: does not the following passage from the (eleventh) chapter on the freedom of the will contain a clear indication of its applicability to the present? "We only see so many crimes on earth, because everything conspires to make men criminal and vicious. Their religions, their governments, their education, the examples before their eyes, all drive them irresistibly to evil: in vain, then, does morality preach virtue which would only be a painful sacrifice of happiness in societies where vice and crime are perpetually crowned, honoured, and rewarded, and where the most frightful disorders are only punished in those who are too weak to have the right to commit them with impunity. Society chastises in the small the excesses that it respects in the great, and often is unjust enough to condemn to death those whom the prejudices that it maintains have rendered criminal."

What distinguishes the 'System of Nature' from most materialistic writings is the outspokenness with which the whole second part of the book, which is still stronger than the first, in fourteen elaborate chapters combats the idea of God in every possible shape. Almost all the materialistic literature, ancient and modern, had ventured upon this conclusion either timidly or not at all. Even Lucretius, who holds the deliverance of mankind from the fetters of religion to be the most important basis of moral regeneration, at least allows certain phantom deities to lead an enigmatical existence in the interspaces of the universe. Hobbes, who certainly came very near in theory to open Atheism, would in an atheistic state have had any citizen hung who taught the existence of God; but in England he recognised all the articles of the Anglican Church. Lamettrie, who spoke out indeed, but not without circumlocution and equivocation, devoted all his efforts to anthropological Materialism only: Holbach is the first who appears to regard the cosmological doctrines as most important. If you look into the matter, it is true that Holbach, like Epikuros, seems to be led chiefly by practical considerations. Regarding religion as the chief source of all human corruption, he tries to eradicate all foundation for this morbid tendency of mankind, and therefore pursues the deistic and pantheistic ideas of God, that were yet so dear to his age, with no less zeal than the ideas of the Church. This circumstance it is, no doubt, that made such violent enemies of the 'System of Nature,' even amongst the freethinkers.

At the same time, it must be admitted that the chapters directed against the existence of God are for the most part excessively tedious. The logical constructions that are supposed to represent proofs for the existence of God are so utterly vague and misty, that the question of their acceptance or rejection is only a matter of more or less self-deception. The man who clings to the proofs only gives a scholastic expression to his inclination to believe in a God. This inclination itself, long before Kant struck out this method of basing the notion of God, was always merely an outflow of moral activity, or of the life of the emotions, but not of theoretical philosophy. The scholastic fondness for idle disputation may indeed find satisfaction in the discussion of such propositions as these: 'The self-existent being must be infinite and omnipresent,' or, 'The necessarily existent being must necessarily be but one;' but it is impossible to find in such vague conceptions any starting-point for a serious investigation worthy of the human mind. What can we say, then, when a man like Holbach devotes nearly fifty pages of his work merely to Clarke's proof for the existence of God—a proof that deals throughout in propositions to which, from first to last, it is impossible to attach a definite sense? With touching conscientiousness, the 'System of Nature' tries to fill the cask of the Danaides. Proposition after proposition is pitilessly taken up and dissected, only to return continually to the same simple principles, that no reason can be found for believing in a God, and that matter has existed from all eternity.

Holbach, indeed, knew quite well that he was combating, not an argument, but hardly the shadow of an argument. He shows in one place that Clarke's own definition of Nothing absolutely coincides with his definition of the idea of God, which contains only negative predicates. In another place he remarks, that it is commonly said that our senses show us only the rind of things; but that in the case of God they don't show us even that. But the following observation is specially to the point :—

"Dr. Clarke tells us it is enough that the attributes of God are possible, and so that we cannot prove the contrary. Singular logic! Theology in that case would be the only science in which we may conclude that a thing *is* because it is possible."

Might it not have occurred to Holbach here how it is possible that people of passably healthy brain, and who are not particularly vicious, can content themselves with assertions so completely built in the air? Might this not have led him to the view that the self-delusion of man in religious doctrines is, after all, something different from ordinary delusions? In external nature Holbach could not see even the rind of a God. But what if these very baseless proofs are a fragile rind, beneath which lurks an idea of God more deeply founded upon the faculties of the human spirit? But for this he would have needed at the same time a juster appreciation of religion in regard to its value as a moral and civilising element; and this is what has least to be expected from the ground out of which grew the 'System of Nature.'

How blunt is the attitude of the 'System of Nature' towards the idea of God is best shown by the chapter on Pantheism (Part. ii. c. iv.). If we remember that for a long time Spinozist and Materialist were considered synonymous, and that both views were frequently included under the term Naturalism, and, in fact, that we frequently find a pantheistic turn in men who are reckoned the leaders of Materialism, we may be surprised at the zeal shown by Holbach to banish the very name of a God, even though it be regarded as identical with nature, from the sphere of human thought. And yet Holbach, from his own point of view, by no means goes too far. It is precisely the mystical tendency in man's nature that he regards as the disease that causes the greatest evils that afflict humanity. And in truth, as soon as an idea of God is given at all, however it is based and carefully defined, the human heart will seize upon it, will give it poetic shape and personification, and will dedicate to it some kind of worship and adoration, the influence of which will henceforth be almost entirely independent of the logical and metaphysical origin of the idea. If this tendency to religion, which continually breaks through the limits of logic, is of less value even than poetry; nay, if it is rather absolutely hurtful, then indeed we must get rid of the very name of a God, and in this elimination only lies the keystone of a philosophy truly representing nature. Even then, however, we must charge Holbach with a slight rhetorical weakness, that might perhaps have dangerous consequences, when he talks of the true cultus of nature and of her altars!

Yet how often extremes meet! The same chapter in which Holbach summons his readers to free humanity for ever from the phantom of the Deity, and to abolish even his name, contains a passage that represents the tendency of man to the supernatural as so universal, so deeply rooted, so irresistible, that it is impossible to regard it as a passing disease of human nature; but we must actually suppose a fall of man (in the reverse sense) in order to avoid the conclusion that this tendency to the supernatural is just as natural to man as the love of music and of beautiful colours and forms, and that a struggle against the natural law that makes this so is absolutely inconceivable.

"Thus men ever prefer the marvellous to the simple, what they do not understand to what they can understand. They despise familiar things, and only value those they are not able to appreciate. Though of these they have only vague ideas, they conclude that they possess something important, supernatural, divine. In a word, they need the stimulus of the mysterious in order to excite their imagination, to occupy their mind, and sate their curiosity, which is never keener than when it is engaged upon riddles that it is impossible to answer."

In a note to this passage it is pointed out that several nations have gone over from an intelligible deity, the sun, to an unintelligible one. Why? Because the most hidden, most mysterious, unknown God is always more pleasing to the imagination than a visible being. All religions, therefore, employ mysteries, and—in this lies the secret of priest-craft. Again, the priests are suddenly made responsible, though it would have been more reasonable to conclude that this class in the beginning sprang naturally from the popular need of mystery, and that, in spite of increasing intelligence, it cannot raise the people to purer views, just because this natural impulse to the mysterious remains too powerful. So we see that here, too, in this most radical attack upon all prejudices, a very important part is played by prejudice itself.

The same thing appears again especially in the chapters devoted to the relation between Religion and Morality. Far from adopting a merely critical treatment, and combating the prejudices that make religion the only basis of moral conduct, the 'System of Nature' goes on to show the moral hurtfulness of the positive religions, and especially of Christianity. Here, it is true, dogma and history alike afford him numerous instances, but the treatment is nevertheless essentially superficial. Thus, for instance, it is treated as morally hurtful that religion promises pardon to the bad, while it overwhelms the good by the superfluity of its demands. The former, therefore, are encouraged, the latter disheartened. But what reaction this weakening of the old antithesis of 'the good' and 'the bad' must have exercised upon humanity in the course of thousands of years the 'System of Nature' has not taken into consideration. And yet a genuine system of nature ought to show us how false is this sharp antithesis, and how it leads to the deeper depression of poverty, to the degradation of weakness, to the mistreatment of disease, while the equalisation of faults, as it has been laid down by Christianity, coincides exactly with the principles to which the exact study of nature, and especially the abolition of the idea of free-will, must lead us. The 'good,' that is, the fortunate, have always tyrannised over the unfortunate. Indeed, in this matter, medieval Christianity is in the same position as Paganism, and it is only the enlightenment of modern days that has brought a distinct improvement. The historical inquirer will have to ask himself seriously, whether the principles of Christianity, after struggling for thousands of years in a mythical form against the brutality of men, are not at length exercising most influence in the moment when their form may disappear, because men have become riper for pure ideas. As to religious forms in themselves, especially as to that tendency of the mind to worship and ceremony, or to emotional processes that unsettle and disorganise, which has been so often confounded with religion, it may be seriously questioned whether the resulting feebleness and sensuousness, combined with the suppression of guiding sense and with the corruption of the natural conscience, are not often exceedingly pernicious to individuals as well as to populations. At least the histories of lunatic asylums, the annals of criminal law, and the statistics of morality supply us with facts that may perhaps be some day collected into practical demonstration. Holbach knows little of this. He goes to work not empirically, but deductively, and all his theories as to the effect of religious views presuppose an adjustment of dogmas by mere reason. The result is, of course, that the results of his discussion remain extremely inadequate.

Much more pertinent and profound are the chapters in which he proves the existence of Atheists, and that Atheism is compatible with morality. Here he relies upon Bayle, who was the first to maintain expressly that the actions of man spring not from their general ideas, but from their passions and impulses.

Not without interest, 'finally, is the treatment of the question whether a whole people can profess Atheism. We have repeatedly pointed out the democratic tendency of French Materialism, as opposed to the influence of this philosophy in England Holbach is certainly not less revolutionary than Lamettrie and Diderot; how comes it, then, that the man who took so much pains to be popular, by whom, in an excerpt from his chief work, Atheism was "accommodated to chambermaids and hairdressers," as Grimm put it, nevertheless declares quite plainly that "these ideas are not suited for the mass of the people"? Holbach, who, because of his radicalism, was as good as shut out from the brilliant circles of the Parisian aristocracy, does not share the uncertainty of many writers of that age, who work with all their might to overturn the existing order, and yet play the part of aristocrats, despise the stupid peasants, and are ready to invent a God for them if need be, in order that a bugbear may not be lacking to keep them in awe. Holbach starts from the principle that the truth can never be injurious. He derives this from the wider proposition that theoretical principles, even though they may be wrong, can never be dangerous. Even the errors of religion receive their sting only through the passions that unite with them and the secular power that despotically maintains them. The most extreme opinions can exist side by side if no attempt be made to secure by violent means exclusive dominance for any of them. Atheism, however, which bases itself upon the knowledge of natural laws, cannot become universal simply because the great mass of mankind have neither time nor inclination to attain to an entirely new set of ideas by means of this serious study. The 'System of Nature' is, however, far from leaving religion to the mass of mankind as a substitute for philosophy. As it demands absolute freedom of thought and entire indifference on the part of the state, it proposes to leave the souls of men to a natural course of development. Let them believe what they will and learn what they can! The fruits of philosophical inquiry will sooner or later benefit all, just as is already the case with the results of the natural sciences. The new ideas will, indeed, experience violent opposition, but men will gradually learn by experience that they bring only blessings. But in their propagation we must not limit our view to the present; we must embrace the future and all mankind. Time and the progress of ages will one day enlighten even those princes who now so obstinately oppose truth, justice, and the liberty of man.

The same spirit animates the final chapter of the whole work, in which we seem to trace the inspired pen of Diderot. This 'Sketch of the Code of Nature' is no dry and arid catechism, such as the French Revolution created on Holbach's principles, but rather a rhetorical showpiece, in many respects one may say a masterpiece. In a long passage Nature appears discoursing, as in Lucretius. She invites mankind to obey her laws, to enjoy the happiness that is allotted them, to serve virtue, to disdain vice, though not to hate the vicious, but rather to pity them as unfortunate. Nature has her apostles, who are unremittingly engaged in promoting the happiness of the human race. Even though their efforts do not succeed, they will at least have the satisfaction of having ventured the attempt.

Nature and her daughters, Virtue, Reason, and Truth, are finally invoked as the only deities, to whom alone belong incense and adoration. Thus by a poetic impulse the 'System of Nature,' after having destroyed all religions, becomes itself a religion. May this religion also some day produce an ambitious priesthood ? Is the tendency of man to mysticism so great that the principles of the work which rejects even Pantheism, in order to eradicate even the name of the Deity, may become the dogmas of a new church, which will succeed in skilfully mingling the intelligible with the unintelligible, and creating ceremonies and forms of worship ?

Where does nature produce the unnatural ? How can the eternal necessity that governs all development produce perversity and wrongness ? Upon what rests our hope of a better time ? What shall restore nature to her rights if there is nowhere anything but nature ? These are questions to which the 'System of Nature' gives us no sufficient answer. We have attained to the perfection of Materialism, but also to its limits. What the 'System of Nature' gives us in strict co-ordination, recent times have again scattered and dispersed in many ways. New motives, new points of view have been attained in plenty; but the circle of fundamental problems has remained invariably the same,—the same as, in truth, it already was in Epikuros and Lucretius.

CHAPTER IV.

REACTION AGAINST MATERIALISM IN GERMANY.

WE have seen how early Materialism took root in Germany; but it was in Germany also that a very important reaction against this tendency appeared, extending through a great part of the eighteenth century, which we must not omit to consider. At the very beginning of the century the philosophy of Leibniz became popular, the essential features of which result in a splendid effort to get rid of Materialism at a single stroke. None can fail to recognise the relationship of the monads with the atoms of the physicists.[92] The expression 'principia rerum' or 'elementa rerum,' applied by Leibniz to the atoms, would equally well stand for a wider notion which should include the atoms and the monads. It is true that Leibniz's monads are the primary existence, the true elements of things in his metaphysical world, and it has long been admitted that the God adopted into his system as the 'sufficient cause of the monads' plays at least as unnecessary a part as do the gods of Epikuros with their shadowy existence in the interspaces of the worlds.[93] Leibniz, a

[92] Zeller, Gesch. d. deutschen Phil., München, 1873, explains (p. 99 ff.) the influence of Atomism upon Leibniz, and then observes: "He now turns from the atoms to the substantial forms of Aristotle, in order to produce his atoms from both;" and loc. cit., p. 107, "in the place of material atoms appear intellectual individuals, in the place of physical 'metaphysical points.'" Leibniz himself calls the monads "formelle Atome." Cf. Kuno Fischer, Gesch. d. n. Phil., ii. 2d ed., p. 319 ff.

[93] That the view of the incompatibility of Leibniz's theology with the philosophical principles of his system was very widely spread (and not expressed by Erdmann alone, cf. Schilling, Beitr. zur Gesch. d. Mat., S. 23)

diplomatist and a universal genius, and yet a man, as

is expressly shown by Kuno Fischer (Gesch. d. neueren Phil., ii. 2 Aufl., S. 627 ff.), who at the same time strongly combats the view. His proof to the contrary rests upon the necessity of a supreme monad, which is consequently named the 'absolute' or 'God.' It is admitted that the system presupposes a supreme monad, but not that this monad, so far as it is really conceived in accordance with the principles of the system, can take the position of a God maintaining and governing the world. The monads are developed by a strict necessity, according to the forces inherent in them. None of them can, either in the sense of ordinary causality or in that of pre-established harmony, become the productive cause of the rest. Even the pre-established harmony does not produce the monads, but only determines their condition, in precisely the same way as, in the system of Materialism, the universal laws of motion determine the condition, that is, the relations in space, of the atoms. And it is easy to see that it is a mere logical consequence of Leibniz's Determinism to break off here the causal series, instead of setting up another 'sufficient reason' for the monads and the pre-established harmony, which reason has no other purpose than just to be this sufficient reason. Newton at least gave his God some driving and cobbling tools; a reason that has no object but to be the reason of the ultimate reason of the world is as superfluous as the tortoise that supports the earth, and immediately suggests the further question, What, then, is the sufficient reason of this God? Kuno Fischer tries to escape this inevitable consequence by deriving, not the condition of the monads from the pre-established harmony, but this latter from the monads. "Sie folgt nothwendig aus den Monaden, weil sie ursprünglich darin liegt" (*l. c.*, S.

629). This is a simple inversion of the identical proposition; the pre-established harmony is the pre-determined order in the condition of the monads. This affords not the least ground for the necessity of deriving all the other monads from the most perfect. The fact that this affords the *explanation* of the condition of the rest (in itself not an incontestable proposition) does not make it the real cause, and, even if this were so, there might result indeed, in a certain sense, an 'extra-mundane' God, but not one that could be of use to religious Theism. Zeller has rightly observed (Gesh. d. deutschen Phil., S. 176 ff.), "It would not be very difficult to show that the Leibnizian, like all theological Determinism, if logically developed, would carry us beyond the theistic standpoint of its author, and would compel us to find in God not the creator only, but the substance of all finite beings." And this not difficult demonstration is a part of the necessary criticism of the system of Leibniz, all the more because a mind like Leibniz's must itself have made this discovery even after Descartes, Hobbes, and Spinoza. The one point that seems necessarily to connect God with the universe is the doctrine of the choice of the 'best' world from an infinite number of possible worlds. But here we may refer to the thorough treatment of the matter, with reference to the sources, in Baumann, Die Lehren von Raum Zeit u. Mathematik, Berl. 1869, ii. 280 ff., where it is shown that we may conceive the eternal essences of things, in whose nature God can alter nothing, just as well as eternal forces, by whose actual strife is attained that minimum of reciprocal constraint which Leibniz brings about by the (necessary!) choice of God. The logical consequences of his mathematical conception of the world lead to the eternal predestination of all things

Lichtenberg [94] happily says, who "had little stability," could with equal facility plunge into the abysses of the most profound speculations, or in the shallow water of everyday discussion avoid the rocks which practical life throws in the steady thinker's way. It will be vain to attempt to explain the contradictions of his system merely from the desultory form of his occasional productions, as though that great genius had preserved in his own mind a perfectly clear system, as though he had only by chance omitted to give us an explanation which would supply us at once with a key to all the puzzles of his writings. These contradictions are there; they are indeed proofs of weaknesses of character, but we must not forget that these are but the shadows in the picture of a truly great man. [95]   Leibniz, who

" by simple fact." "Everything ends in bare, naked matter of fact; the dependence of things upon God is an empty shadow " (S. 285).

[94] It by no means follows from the logical superfluity of the idea of God in Leibniz's metaphysical system that Leibniz could have subjectively dispensed with it, and the nature of the subject renders it difficult to find conclusive evidence. Nor is it always easy to discriminate between religious needs (which Zeller, S. 103, supposes in Leibniz), and the need of living in peace with the religious sentiments of one's surroundings. At the same time, we do not wish to put Leibniz in this matter on exactly the same level with Descartes. Not only does much in the latter seem to be simply cunning calculation, that in the case of Leibniz leaves the impression rather of the sympathetic compliance of a tender spirit, but we can detect in the latter a certain leaning to Mysticism that is quite wanting in Descartes (Zeller, S. 103). And in this there is not any psychological inconsistency with the clear and rigid Determinism of his system, nor yet an argument for the sincerity of his theological juggleries. The saying of Lichtenberg referred to in the text

(in the ' Observations on Man ' in the First Part of the ' Vermischte Schriften ') is in full: " Leibniz has defended the Christian religion. To conclude at once from this, as the theologians do, that he was a good Christian, shows very little knowledge of the world. The vanity of handling a subject better than its professors is, with a man like Leibniz, who had little solidity, a much more likely impulse to do so than religion. Let us look a little more closely into our own hearts, and we shall learn how little can be affirmed of others. Nay, I even venture to say that sometimes we believe that we believe something, and yet do not believe it. Nothing is more unsearchable than the system of our springs of action."

[95] A good characterisation of Leibniz, with special reference to the influences that determined his theology, is given by Biedermann, Deutschland im 18. Jahrh., II. Band. 5 Abschnitt; comp. especially S. 242 ff. Biedermann is quite right when he regards as inadequate Lessing's well-known defence of Leibniz's position. Lessing talks of esoteric and exoteric doctrines, in a way, however, which seems to us to be itself somewhat esoteric.

introduced Toland to his royal friend the Princess Sophie Charlotte, must have himself known that the shifting and ambiguous foundations of his Theodicy could form but a weak protection against Materialism—to the true thinker none at all. Serena can have as little derived from this work any real satisfaction as she had derived serious anxiety from Bayle's Dictionary and Toland's Letters. For us only the doctrine of monads and the pre-established harmony possess importance. There is more philosophical weight in these two notions than in many a prolix system. But to show their importance we need only explain them.

We have repeatedly seen how difficult, how impossible even, it must ever be for Materialism, so far as it adopts the notions of atoms, to account for the *locality* of sensations, and generally for the facts of consciousness (cf. vol. i. p. 267). Do they consist in the combination of atoms? Then they exist in an abstraction, and are, objectively speaking, nowhere. Are they in the motion? That would be the same thing. We only regard the moved atom itself as the seat of the sensation. How, then, does sensation result in consciousness? Where is this consciousness? In an individual atom, or again in abstractions—or in void space, which then would be no longer void, but filled with a strictly immaterial substance.

To explain the mutual influence of the atoms there is no principle available but that of impact. An infinite succession of such impacts could produce sensation in the atom acted upon. This seems at least as likely as that the vibration of a string or of a part of the atmosphere should produce a sound. But where is the sound? In truth, so far as we become conscious of it, in the hypothetical central atom: that is an illustration does not help us. We are no further than we were before. We lack in the atom the combining principle which transforms a multiplicity of collisions into the unity of sensation. We are ever faced by the same difficulty. We may think of the atom as we will—as composed of dead or mobile particles, of sub-atoms,

as capable of 'inner conditions' or not: to the question
where and how the collisions pass from their manifoldness
into the unity of feeling, there is not only no answer
ready, but so soon as we go to the root of the matter, so far
from being obvious, it ceases to be even conceivable. Only
when we remove, as it were, the eye of our understanding
will it seem natural that such a combination of collisions
can result in the production of sensations, just as several
points, when we carry back the bodily eye, flow together
into one.   Is it that the intelligibility of things lies in
this, that we make only a moderate use of our understanding, as the Scottish Common-sense philosophers?   That
would be no *rôle* for a Leibniz!   We see him in face of
the difficulty : impact, as Epikuros had proposed ; or action
at a distance, as the successors of Newton ; or perhaps no
action at all.

That is the *salto mortale* to the pre-established harmony.
Whether Leibniz reached his doctrine through other similar
views, or at a leap, or as ever, we will not ask.   But here
is the point that lends its importance to this doctrine
and it is this very point which makes it also so important
in the history of Materialism.   The mutual interaction of
the atoms as producing sensations in one or several of
them is unthinkable, and therefore we must not adopt it.
The atom produces its own sensations from itself: it is a
monad developing itself in accordance with its own internal laws of life.   The monad has no windows.   Nothing
goes out of it, nothing comes into it.   The outer world is
its idea, and this idea arises within it.   Every monad is a
world to itself: no one is like another.   The one is rich
in ideas, the other is poor.   The ideas, however, of all
the monads consist in an eternal system, in a complete
harmony, which was ordained before the beginning of
time, and which constantly persists through the continuous vicissitudes in all the monads.   Every monad represents to itself confusedly or clearly the whole universe,
the whole sum of all that happens, and the sum of all

monads is the universe. The monads of inorganic nature have only ideas which completely neutralise themselves as those of a man in dreamless sleep. Higher stand the monads of the organic world: the lower animals consist of dreaming monads; in the higher animals appear sensation and memory; in man we have thought.

Thus we begin from a starting-point based upon reason, and, by means of a vivid imaginative process, find ourselves in the poetry of notions. Whence did Leibniz know, if the monads all produce ideas from themselves, that there are other monads besides his own Ego? Here he has to meet the same difficulty as Berkeley, who reached the same point by the path of Sensationalism which we here attain by means of Atomism. Berkeley also regarded the whole world as idea, a standpoint which Holbach could not refute. Cartesianism had already led certain of its continuators to doubt whether, besides their own being, which produces action and passion, pleasure and pain, strength and weakness, as its own ideas from itself, anything exists in the whole wide world.[96] Many will believe that such a theory can easily be refuted by a douche or a Seidlitz powder with a moderate diet; but nothing will prevent the thinker who has reached this standpoint from holding that powder, doctor, his own body, and, in brief, the whole universe, are but an idea of his own, and that outside this nothing exists. Even if such a one wishes to believe that there are other beings—which will always be admitted as conceivable—we are still far from showing the necessity of pre-established harmony. The ideal worlds of these beings might be in most flagrant contradiction: no one would observe it. And yet the thought which Leibniz made the basis of his philosophy has a rare sublimity, nobleness, and beauty. It may be indeed that the æsthetic, the practical, even in that philosophy whose

[96] Cp. i. sec. 2, vol. i. p. 242, and Note 63, ibid. Hennings, in the Gesch. von. d. Seelen der Menschen u. Thiere, Halle, 1774, p. 145, makes the supporters of this opinion a special class of Idealists, whom he designates as 'Egoists,' in opposition to the 'Pluralists.'

end is knowledge, have a more real importance than we are accustomed to suppose.

The monads, with their pre-established harmony, reveal to us the true nature of things as little as the atoms and the laws of nature. They afford, however, a pure and self-contained conception of the world, like Materialism, and do not contain more inconsistencies than this system. But what especially secured the popularity of the Leibnizian system is the ductile looseness of its notions, and the circumstance that its radical consequences were much better masked than those of Materialism. In this respect nothing is more useful than a thoroughgoing abstraction. The tyro who shudders at the thought that the ancestors of the human race might once have been compared with the apes of to-day, comfortably swallows down the monad theory, which declares the human soul to be essentially like all the beings of the universe, down to the most despised mote, which all mirror the universe in themselves, are all small divinities to themselves, and bear within them the same content of ideas, only in various arrangement and development. We do not immediately observe that the ape monads are also included in the series, that they are as immortal as the human monads, and that they may yet perchance, in the course of development, attain to a beautifully ordered content of ideas. If, on the other hand, the Materialist boldly sets the ape at man's side, compares him to a deaf mute, and proposes to educate and train him like a Christian, then we hear the creature gnash its teeth, we see its wild grimaces and obscene gestures, we feel with infinite repugnance the meanness and repulsiveness of the creature, alike in its form and character; and the most convincing arguments, although each of them has a fatal defect, flow together in abundance in order to demonstrate, so clearly that every one may see it, how absurd, inconceivable, and unreasonable such a theory is.

As in this case abstraction does its work, so it does in

all other points. The theologian can on occasion make
an admirable use of the idea of an eternal, sublime, divine
harmony in all that takes place. That the laws of nature
are pure appearance, are but an inferior kind of knowledge
possessed by the empirical understanding, suits him admirably, whilst the consequences of this theory, so soon
as they are inconsistent with the circle of his doctrines,
may easily be disregarded. They are indeed present only
in the germ of the notion, and nothing disturbs a man to
whom contradictions of all kinds are as his daily bread,
except what is apprehensible by the senses. Thus, then,
even the establishing of the immateriality and simplicity
of the soul was a splendid field for the philosophic grave-
diggers, whose special function it is to cover a great idea
with the refuse and rubbish of commonplace ideas, and so
to render it harmless. That this was an immateriality
which for ever dislodged by a bold push the old opposition of spirit and matter more effectually than Materialism could—this troubled nobody. Immateriality, this
great, this sublime thought, had been proved by the great
Leibniz! How contemptuously could one look down on
the folly of those who held the soul to be material, and
did such ignoble violence to their consciousness!

It was very much the same with the much-extolled
and much-abused Optimism of Leibniz's system. Viewed
in the light of reason, and tested by its real presuppositions
and consequences, this Optimism is nothing but the application of a mechanical principle to the foundation of the
facts of the world. God, in choosing the best of possible
worlds, does nothing that would not be quite mechanically
produced if we suppose the 'essences' of things to act
upon each other. In all this God proceeds like a mathematician in solving a problem,[97] and he must so proceed

[97] Very pertinently says Du Bois-
Reymond, Leibnitz'sche Gedanken
in der Modernen Naturwissenschaft
(Zwei Festreden, Berl. 1871), S. 17:—
"As is well known, the theory of the
maxima and minima of functions was
indebted to him for the greatest progress, through the discovery of the
method of tangents. Well, he conceives God in the creation of the

because his perfect intelligence is bound to the principle
of sufficient reason. The place occupied in a system of
self-moving particles by the 'principle of least resistance'
is in the divine creation taken by the principle of the
least evil. In the result, it all comes to the same thing
as if we were to deduce the development of the universe
from the mechanical presuppositions of a Laplace and a
Darwin. The world may indeed be utterly bad, and yet
it is all the time the best of possible worlds. But all this
by no means prevents the popular adaptation of Optimism
from speaking of the wisdom and goodness of the Creator,
as though there were, in fact, no evil in the world at all
which is not introduced by our wickedness and our un-
reason. God is in the system powerless; but in the popular
interpretation of the ideas thus established, his omnipotence appears in the most splendid light.

So it is also with the doctrine of innate ideas. Locke
had shaken this doctrine; Leibniz restored it, and the
Materialists, with Lamettrie at their head, laugh at Leibniz
in consequence. Which is right in this point? Leibniz
teaches that all thoughts proceed from the spirit itself,
that there is no influence whatever exerted from the outside upon the spirit. It is difficult to find a satisfactory
objection to this view. But we see at once that there
is a complete contrast between the innate ideas of the
Scholastics and the Cartesians. With the latter it
amounts to this, that we take certain universal conceptions, to which is also usually added the notion of a most

world like a mathematician who, is
solving a minimum problem, or rather,
in our modern phraseology, a problem in the calculus of variations—
the question being to determine,
among an infinite number of possible
worlds, that for which the sum of
necessary evil is a minimum." That,
however, God has to deal in this
with *given* factors (the possibilities
or the 'essences') has been most
clearly pointed out by Baumann
(Lehren v. Raum, Zeit und Mathematik, ii. S. 127-129). It is, of
course, understood that God's perfect intelligence follows undeviatingly
the same rules that our reason recognises as the most correct (Baumann, *l. c.*, 115); that is, the activity
of God effects that everything is fulfilled according to the laws of mathematics and mechanics. See above,
Note 93.

perfect being, and prefer them to all other ideas as regards the witness of their origin, assigning to them a higher degree of credibility. Well then, as in the case of Leibniz *all* ideas are innate, the distinction between empirical and what is called original knowledge completely disappears. Locke holds that the soul is, to begin with, entirely empty ; according to Leibniz it contains the universal. Locke makes all knowledge whatever come from outside ; Leibniz has it that none so comes. The result of these extremes, as so often happens, is pretty much the same. Suppose we concede to Leibniz that what we call external experience is, in fact, internal development, then Leibniz must, on the other hand, admit that, besides knowledge drawn from experience, there is no specific knowledge. So that Leibniz has in reality only saved the appearance of innate ideas. His whole system must always be reduced to a single great idea—an idea which cannot be proved, although it is also true that, from the standpoint of Materialism, it cannot be refuted, and which takes its start from an obvious insufficiency of Materialism.

If in Leibniz German profoundness reacted against Materialism, it was German pedantry that did so in those who repeated him. The bad habit of setting up definitions out of which nothing essential results was deeply rooted in the nation. It envelops still, like rank weeds, the whole system of Kant, and only now is the fresher spirit brought by the development of our poetry, of the positive sciences, and of our practical efforts, gradually freeing us by a process not yet completed from the nets of the metaphysical. The most influential of the followers of Leibniz was a wide-awake, free-thinking man, but an extremely mediocre philosopher, Professor Christian Wolff, who invented a new Scholasticism, which contrived to assimilate the old to an astonishing extent. Whilst Leibniz produced all his profound ideas in a scattered way, and as it were, incidentally, everything with Wolff was formula and system. All keenness disappeared from the thoughts, whilst their expression became ever more precise. Wolff gave to the doctrine of pre-established harmony only a corner in his system, and reduced the theory of monads to the old scholastic principle that the soul is a simple incorporeal substance.

This simplicity of the soul, which was exalted to a metaphysical dogma, plays the most important part in the struggle against Materialism. The whole of the great parallel between monads and atoms, harmony and the law of nature, in which the extremes are so sharply opposed and yet so nearly related to each other, shrivels away into certain axioms of the so-called ' rational psychology '—a scholastic discipline of Wolff's invention. Wolff was quite justified in protesting when his less keenly thinking pupil Bilfinger introduced the term ' Leibniz-Wolffian philosophy.' Bilfinger, a man who is several times quoted with respect by Holbach in the ' Système de la Nature,' certainly understood Leibniz quite differently. He got so far in psychology as to give up the old method of self-observation, and to introduce the method of the natural sciences. In terms, at all events, Wolff endeavoured after the same goal in his empirical psychology which he allowed to exist by the side of the rational system; in reality, of course, this empiricism was very slight, although the tendency at least in these and the natural reaction from the wearying struggles for the existence of the soul brought about the leaning which runs through the whole eighteenth century to gather together as many positive facts as possible as to the life of the soul. Lacking as these inquiries were for the most part in keen criticism and steady method, we must yet recognise an essential feature of method in their founding above all things animal psychology. The old controversy between the supporters of Rorarius and Descartes had never been laid to rest, and now came Leibniz, who, by the doctrine of monads, made at once the distinction between all souls a mere question of degree. Occasion enough for renewed comparison! Men compared, tested, collected anecdotes, and under the influence of the well-meaning and sympathetic tendency which distinguishes the culture of the last century, and especially the rationalistic element, it became more and more common to recognise very nearly related creatures in the higher animals.

This movement in favour of a universal and comparative psychology embracing both man and beast might in itself have come very opportunely for Materialism; but the honourable consistency of the Germans held fast as long as was at all possible to *religious* ideas, and they could not at all accustom themselves to the manner of the English and French, who simply ignored the connection between belief and knowledge. There was no way open but to declare the souls of the animals to be not only immaterial, like those of men, but to be immortal also. Leibniz had pitched the tune for the doctrine of the immortality of animals. He was followed as early as 1713 by the Englishman, Jenkin Thomasius, in an Essay on the Soul of Animals, dedicated to the German Parliament, and Professor Baier wrote a preface to this work, which expresses itself, however, somewhat ambiguously as to this question of immortality.[98] In the year 1742 appeared a whole society of friends of animals, who continued to publish for a number of years collected essays on questions of animal psychology, necessarily all in the Leibnizian sense.[99]

[98] In the first edition, Baier and Thomasius were incorrectly called "medical men of the University of Nürnberg." Jenkin Thomasius is an English physician, who was at that time living in Germany, and had probably become connected with the University of Altdorf. At all events, Professor Baier concludes his preface with the words, "Cujus proinde laborem et studia, Academiae nostrae quam maxime probata, cunctis bonarum literarum fautoribus meliorem in modum commendo." The Baier, however, who wrote this is not the physician Johann Jacob Baier, then living in Nürnberg, but the theologian Johann Wilhelm. A brief extract from the work, which appeared at the University press of Kohlesius in 1713, is in Scheitlin's Thierseelenkunde, Stuttg. u. Tüb., 1840, i. 184 ff.

[99] I have not been able to find fuller details as to this society in my preparations for the first edition, and refer therefore for proofs to Grässe's Bibl. Psychologica, Leipz., 1845,

The most famous of these was the production of Professor
G. F. Meier, ' Versuch eines neuen Lehrgebäudes von dem
Seelen der Thiere,' which appeared in 1749 at Halle.
Meier did not content himself with maintaining that animals have souls, but went so far as to propose the hypothesis that these souls go through various stages, and finally
reach the degree of *spirits*, that is, will stand on the same
level with man.

The author of this work had already made himself a
name, indeed, by his attack upon Materialism.   As early as
1743 he published his 'Beweis, dass keine Materie denken
könne' (Proof that no matter is capable of thought), which
appeared rewritten in 1751.   It is far from possessing as
much originality as the Animal Psychology.   It revolves
merely in the circle of the Wolffian definitions.   About
the same time the Königsberg professor Martin Knutzen
made an attempt upon the great question of the day, whether matter can think.   Knutzen, who numbered Immanuel
Kant among his most zealous pupils, supports himself
freely upon Wolff, and supplies not only a metaphysical
framework, but also very felicitous examples and historical
material testifying to wide reading.   And yet here, too,
keenness is wanting to the proof itself, and there is no
doubt that writings like these, proceeding from the most
learned professors against a doctrine decried as quite
untenable, as frivolous, paradoxical, and absurd, must
have greatly contributed to shake the reputation of metaphysic to its foundations.[100]

where, under the name of Winkler,
the titles of the treatises are referred
to.   One of them (in the year 1743)
discusses the question, 'Whether
the Souls of Animals die with their
Bodies.'   In Henning's Gesch. v. d.
Seelen der Menschen u. Thiere, Halle,
1774, the title of the collective essays
is somewhat more fully given than in
Grässe.   It runs, "Philosophische
Untersuchungen von dem Seyn und
Wesen der Seelen der Thiere, von
einigen Liebhabern der Weltweisheit
in sechs verschiedenen Abhandlungen
ausgeführt und mit einer Vorrede
von der Einrichtung der Gesellschaft
dieser Personen an's Licht gestellt von
Johann Heinrich Winkler, der griech.
und lateinischen Sprache Professorn
zu Leipzig: Leipz. 1745."
    [100] Further information as to Knut-
zen's work may be found in Jürgen
Bona Meyer, Kant's Psychologie, Berlin, 1870, S. 225 ff.   Meyer proposed

Through these and similar writings, (wholly disregarding Reimann's 'Historia Atheismi' (1725), and similar works of a more general character), the materialistic question was powerfully raised in Germany, when suddenly the 'Homme Machine' fell upon the literary arena like a bomb hurled from an unknown hand. Of course the self-confident school of philosophy did not long neglect to show its superiority to this object of annoyance. While men were still disputing whether the Marquis d'Argens, whether Maupertuis, or some personal enemy of Von Haller's, had written the book, there appeared a flood of criticisms and polemical writings.

Of the German replies we shall here mention but a few. A Magister Frantzen attempted to prove against the 'Homme Machine,' by the usual arguments, the sacredness of the whole Bible, and the credibility of all the narratives of the Old and New Testaments. He might have directed himself to a better address, but he proved this at least, that at that time even an orthodox theologian could attack a Lamettrie without getting into a passion.[101]

More interesting is the production of a famous Breslau physician called Tralles. He, an inordinate admirer of Von Haller, whom he calls the twofold Apollo (in medicine and poetry), must be distinguished from the well-known physicist Tralles, who lived considerably later, but, on the other hand, may be one and the same with the follower of Haller, who is mentioned by Gesenius as the author of an 'incredibly pitiful' didactic poem on the 'Riesengebirge.'

---

to inquire whence Kant derived his idea of the 'rational psychology.' That serves as a basis for the refutation contained in the 'Kritik.' The result is, that in all probability these words are the most important: "Knutzen's Philos. Abhandl. von der immater. Natur · der Seele, darinnen theils überhaupt erwiesen wird, dass die Materie nicht denken könne, und dass die Seele unkörperlich sei, theils die vornehmsten Einwürfe der Materialisten deutlich beantwortet werden, 1774; Reimarus, Vornehmste Wahrheiten der natürl. Religion, 1774; und Mendelssohn's Phädon, 1767." Knutzen deduces the nature of the soul from the unity of self-consciousness; precisely the point against which Kant later directed all the vigour of his criticism.

[101] Frantzen, Widerlegung des 'L'Homme Machine:' Leipz. 1749. The book contains 320 pages.

He wrote a stout book in Latin against the 'Homme Machine,' and dedicated it to Von Haller, probably to console him for Lamettrie's perfidious dedication.[102]

Tralles starts from the point that the 'Homme Machine' wants to persuade the world that all doctors are necessarily Materialists. He struggles to maintain the honour of religion and the innocence of medical science. It is characteristic of the *naïveté* of his standpoint that he draws for the grounds of his refutations upon all the four principal sciences, whose weight of proof he seems to regard as being co-ordinate, if indeed it is not graduated according to the precedence of the faculties. In all the main points the current proofs drawn from the Wolffian philosophy meet us everywhere here also.

All that Lamettrie wants to conclude from the influence of the temperaments, from the effects of sleep, opium-taking, fever, hunger, drunkenness, pregnancy, blood-letting, climate, and so on, is simply disposed of by saying that all these observations only go to show a certain correspondence between body and soul. The propositions as to the teachableness of animals occasion the obvious remark that no one would question the right of the 'Homme Machine' to the sceptre in the new monkey-kingdom that was to be founded. Speaking animals do not belong to the best world, or otherwise we should have had them long ago.[103] But even supposing that the animals could talk, they would certainly not learn geometry. Mere external movement can never become internal sensation. Our thoughts, which are bound up with nerve changes, yet proceed from nothing but the divine will. The 'Homme Machine' ought rather to study Wolff's psychology, in

---

[102] The title of his work runs, "De machina et Anima humana prorsus a se invicem distinctis, commentatio, libello latere amantis autoris Gallico 'homo machina' inscripto opposita et ad illustrissimum virum Albertum Haller, Phil. et Med. Doct. exarata a D. Balthas. Ludovico Tralles, Medico Vratisl.: Lipsiae et Vratislaviae apud Michael Hubertum, 1749."

[103] It need scarcely be pointed out that Leibniz's theory of the actual world as the best, rightly understood, excludes no kind of development.

order to improve his erroneous ideas of the power of imagination.

More subtly and skilfully, but by no means more thoroughly than Tralles, goes Professor Hollman to work, who attacked the anonymous author anonymously, the satirist satirically, the Frenchman in fluent French, which of course, therefore, brought no result in the deepening of knowledge.[104] The 'Lettre d'un Anonyme' found especial approbation through the humorous fiction that there was really a 'man machine' who could not think otherwise, and was incapable of comprehending anything higher. This assumption gives occasion to a series of witty turns, and spares the letter-writer the trouble of proof. What, however, incensed Lamettrie more than all the jesting was the expression of a conjecture that the 'Homme Machine' was a plagiarism from the 'Confidential Correspondence.'

Towards the end of the anonymous letter a prosaic fanaticism became increasingly apparent. Spinozism especially has to bear the brunt. "The Spinozist is in my eyes a pitiful and deluded creature, whom one must commiserate, and if he is not beyond assistance, attempt to help by two or three not too profound remarks from the 'Theory of Reason,' and a clear explanation of what 'one' is, and 'many,' and what a substance is. He who has clear ideas of these, freed from all prejudices, will be ashamed that the deluded notions of the Spinozists have even for a quarter of an hour disturbed him."

Scarcely a generation later and Lessing had uttered the ἓν καὶ πᾶν, and Jacobi declared war upon reason itself, because he supposed that it must inevitably lead to Spinozism any one who follows it alone.

[104] Hollman, a teacher of wide but ephemeral reputation, was at that time (since 1737) professor in Göttingen. According to Zimmermann, Leben des Herrn von Haller, Hollmann is the writer of the letter ('Lettre d'un Anonyme pour servir de Critique ou de refutation au livre intitulé L'Homme Machine'), which first appeared in German in the Göttingen journals, and was then translated at Berlin. So that the merits of the French style would not belong to Hollmann.

If, in the midst of this storm against the 'Homme Machine,' the connection between general psychology and the reaction against Materialism for some time disappeared from sight, yet later it became once more conspicuous. Reimarus, the well-known author of the Wolfenbüttel Fragments, was a pronounced Deist and a zealous partisan of theology, and therefore a thoroughgoing enemy of Materialism. His 'Considerations on the Art Instincts of Animals,' which, starting from the year 1760, passed through several editions, serve him to demonstrate everywhere the design in creation and the traces of a creator. So that it is in the two leaders of German Rationalism, Wolff, who was threatened by the King of Prussia with the cord for his teaching, and Reimarus, whose 'Fragments' involved their editor, Lessing,* in such violent controversies, that we find the most energetic representatives of the reaction against Materialism.   Henning's 'History of the Souls of Men and Animals' (1774), a work of little acuteness but of great erudition, which by its numerous quotations affords an excellent view of the controversies of the time, may be regarded as almost from beginning to end an attempt to refute Materialism.

The son of the Reimarus of the 'Fragments,' who continued his father's inquiries in animal psychology, a skilful doctor and a freethinker, published later, in the 'Göttingische Magazin für Wissenschaften und Literatur,' a series of 'Considerations on the impossibility of corporeal recollections, and of a material imagination,' essays that we may consider as the most solid work produced by the eighteenth century reaction against Materialism.   But in the very next year after these essays there appeared in Königsberg a work that must not be looked at from the narrow standpoint of this reaction, and yet whose decisive influence put an end for a time to Materialism together

---

* [See Mr. Sime's valuable 'Life of Lessing,' the fruit of many years' study and research : 2 vols. 1877.]

with the old metaphysic, to all those who stood on the heights of science.

One circumstance, however, that helped to bring about so thorough a reform of philosophy was, above all, the defeat that Materialism had inflicted upon the old metaphysic. In spite of all refutations upon special points, Materialism lived on, and gained ground, all the more perhaps because it was not a narrow and exclusive system. Men like Forster, like Lichtenberg, leaned strongly to this philosophy, and even religious minds and enthusiastic natures, like Herder and Lavater, borrowed important elements from Materialism. Especially materialistic modes of thought very quietly gained ground in the positive sciences, so that the physician Reimarus could not unfairly begin his 'Considerations' with the remark that recently the operations of thought in many, and indeed in nearly all, writings on the subject had been treated as corporeal. This was written by a keen-sighted opponent of Materialism in 1780, after philosophy had vainly broken so many lances against it. The truth was, that all the Scholastic philosphy of the time could supply no sufficient counterpoise to Materialism. The point on which Leibniz had really outbid Materialism in consistency was not forgotten, indeed, but had lost its force. The impossibility of the transition of an external, multiple movement into an internal unity, into sensation and thought, is indeed upon occasion pointed out by nearly every opponent of Materialism; but the point is lost in a wilderness of other and quite worthless arguments, or stands in abstract nakedness before the rich colours of the Materialistic argument. In treating the positive principle of the simplicity of the soul quite dogmatically, and so exciting the liveliest controversy, the strongest argument was actually made the weakest. The monad theory is justified merely as a development of Atomism, the pre-established harmony only as a necessary transformation of the idea of necessity in nature. When deduced from pure notions, and so directly opposed to Materialism, these important ideas lose all their force.

On the other hand, Materialism too was utterly incompetent to fill the gap and make itself the dominant system. We should be very far wrong if we saw in this only the influence of university traditions and of the ruling powers in State and Church. This influence could not long have maintained itself against a living and general conviction. Much rather were men thoroughly weary of the everlasting monotony of materialistic dogmatism, and longed for revival through life, through poetry, through the positive sciences.

The whole intellectual impulse of the eighteenth century was unfavourable to Materialism. It was marked by an ideal character that became clear and obvious only after the middle of the century, but that was already contained in the first beginnings of the movement. If, indeed, we start from the end of the century, it may appear as though it was only in the brilliant epoch of Schiller and Goethe that the ideal effort of the nation rose above the barren poverty of the rationalistic era, and above the prosaic pursuit of utility; but if we follow the various confluent tendencies to their sources, we shall find a very different picture. From the end of the seventeenth century, it was observed by thorough, clear-sighted men in Germany how far they were behind other nations. A struggle for freedom, intellectual progress, and national independence began in the most various spheres in various shapes, appearing here and there in isolated efforts, until there resulted a general and profound movement of men's minds. The Rationalists at the beginning of the eighteenth century were for the most part very different from that insipid Berlin society with which Goethe and Schiller were at strife. Mysticism and Rationalism became allies in the battle against the ossified orthodoxy in which men were beginning to recognise the fetters of the spirit and the hindrance of progress. Since Arnold's important ' History of the Church and of Heretics'(1699), the recognition of the rights of the suppressed persons and parties in history had become a valuable aid to free thought.[105]   This ideal starting-point is very characteristic of the German Rationalistic movement.   While Hobbes admitted the right of the prince to erect a general superstition into a religion by his sovereign command, while Voltaire wished to retain the belief in God in order that the peasants might pay their rents and obey their superiors, in Germany we are met with the remark that truth dwells with the persecuted, the oppressed, and the calumniated, and that every church in possession of power, of dignity, and endowments is by this very circumstance inclined to persecute and to suppress the truth.

Even the direction of the mind towards utility gained in Germany an ideal character.   Here no great industrial movement was developed as in England, no towns sprang up out of the ground, riches did not heap themselves up in the hands of capitalists; poor preachers and teachers asked what could help the people, and set to work to found new schools and introduce new branches into existing schools, to advance the technical education of the honest burghers, and in the country advance agriculture, to promote intellectual activity as well as energy in one's calling, and to enlist labour in the service of virtue.   But even the opposite tendency to the beautiful and sublime was prepared long before the beginning of the classic age of literature, and here too it was the schools that in their sphere fostered and developed the beginnings of this upward movement.   The very time at which the dominance of Latin in the universities was broken down brought about the revival of classical education.   This stood in that melancholy period, during which Latin was learned for the sake of theology, and theology for the sake of Latin,[106] in

---

[105] Comp. Biedermann, Deutschland im 18. Jahrh., Leipz. 1858, ii. 392 ff.

[106] Comp. Justi, Winkelmann, i. 25. At p. 23 ff. are interesting details on the condition of the schools towards

a surprisingly degraded state through nearly all Germany. The classical were replaced by modern Latin authors on Christian subjects. Greek was not studied at all, or confined to the New Testament and a collection of moral aphorisms; the poets, who were deservedly put in the front rank by the great humanists, and who in England, to the great benefit of the national culture, had gained a safe position of esteem, had in Germany almost utterly disappeared from the school programmes. Even in the universities there was little humanistic culture to be found, and Greek literature was completely neglected. From this time until the brilliant period of German philology, from Friedrich August Wolf, progress was made, not by a sudden spring, nor by a revelation from without, but by a painful struggle from step to step, and in the train of that great movement that may be described as the second renascence in Germany. Gervinus jests at " the antiquarian scholars, the collectors of materials, the most prosaic of men," who towards the end of the seventeenth and beginning of the eighteenth century everywhere began " in their leisure hours to write poetry instead of going out

the close of the seventeenth century. We will only add that Winkelmann's teacher, Tappert, though he knew little Greek, yet obviously belonged to the reformers who, on the one hand, provided for the needs of life by introducing new branches of study, and put an end to the exclusive use of Latin; while, on the other, they sought even in Latin to assert the humanistic tendency in opposition to the old pedantry of the seventeenth century. It is not mere chance that men fell back on many points in gymnasial government in the beginning of the eighteenth century, upon the traditions of Sturm, and therefore, e.g., the zeal in the imitation of Cicero at this period must not be regarded as mere traditional veneration of Latin, but as a newly awakening sense of elegance and beauty in language

As more important illustrations of scholastic reform in this sense we will mention only the activity of the Nuremberg inspector Feuerlein (comp. Von Raumer, Gesch. d. Päd., 3te Aufl., ii. 101, &c., where indeed too little stress is laid on Feuerlein's efforts to improve the quality of Latin and Greek teaching, besides his efforts in favour of German and positive science. The well-known polyhistor Morhof exercised much influence on Feuerlein), and the learned rector Köhler at Ansbach, from whose school came J. M. Gesner, who established the reforms here mentioned by his 'Institutiones Rei Scholasticae' (1715), and his 'Greek Chrestomathy' (1731). Comp. Sauppe, Weimarische Schulreden, viii., Joh. M. Gesner (Weimar, 1856.)

to walk;" but he overlooks that these same learned authors of mediocre verses were quietly introducing another spirit into the schools. What they lacked in inspiration must be supplied by zeal and purpose, until a generation arose developed under the passionate stimulus of youth. In almost all the notable poets of the pre-classical period, like Uz, Gleim, Hagedorn, and so on, we may detect the influence of the school.[107] Here they were making German verses, there reading Greek authors; but the spirit in which both were done was the same; and the most influential reviver of classical education in the Gymnasia, Johann Mathias Gesner, was at the same time a friend of practical studies and a zealous promoter of the study of German. Not in vain had Leibniz and Thomasius shown the advantages that other nations were deriving from the study of their mother tongue.[108] What Thomasius had been obliged to assert by violent struggles, the use of German in academical lectures and in the handling of the sciences, became gradually triumphant in the eighteenth century, and even the conservative Wolff by his use of German in philosophical writings helped to develop the growing enthusiasm for national life.

Strangely enough, it was men without any poetic gifts who had to prepare the way for the outburst of poetry— scholars of pedantic character and corrupt taste who must lead the way to the models of noble simplicity and free humanity.[109] The forgotten news of the splendour of the

[107] Uz, whom his contemporaries later admired as the German Horace, was educated at the Gymnasium in Ausbach, from which J. M. Gesner came (see the previous note). Gleim came from Wernigerode, where indeed they were still backward as to Greek, but wrote Latin and German verses all the more zealously (comp. Pröhle, Gleim auf der Schule, Progr., Berlin, 1857). In Halle, where these young men formed the Anakreontic Society, they began by reading Anakreon in the original. The two Hagedorns, poet and art connoisseur, came from Hamburg, where the famous polyhistor Joh. Alb. Fabricius wrote good books, and at the same time "bad versicles" (Gervinus).

[108] On Thomasius and his influence comp. especially Biedermann, Deutschl. im 18. Jahrh., ii. 358 ff.

[109] A specially characteristic instance of this is afforded by Professor Damm in Berlin (admirably portrayed by Justi, Winkelmann, i. 34 ff.), whose influence was very important in the spread of Greek, and especially of Homer.

old classical literature led men's minds towards an ideal of beauty, of which neither the seekers nor the guides had a clear idea, until daylight came with the achievements of Winckelmann and Lessing. The idea by education and science to come nearer to the Greeks appears here and there as early as the eighteenth century, and gains strength with every decade, until at length, by the profound inquiries of Schiller, the spheres of the ancient and the modern were rationally separated, while the supremacy of Greek art, within certain limits, was the more firmly established.

Search for the ideal runs through the whole century. Although they could not yet think of competing with the most advanced nations in power and wealth, in political dignity, and in the magnitude of material undertakings, at least they tried to surpass them in the highest and noblest of efforts. In this sense Klopstock announced the rivalry of the German with the British muse, when there was as yet little to be said for the pretensions of the former; and Lessing. burst asunder with his powerful criticism the fetters of all false authorities and defective models, in order to smooth the way to the highest achievements, without troubling himself as to who would walk in it.

In this sense, moreover, foreign influences were not passively adopted, but were transformed. We have seen how English Materialism early took root in Germany, but could not gain the upper hand. Instead of Hobbes's hypocritical theology, men demanded a real God, and an idea on which to base the universe. Nor could the leaders of German Rationalism content themselves with the way in which Newton and Boyle, by the side of a great and magnificent order of the universe, kept the patchwork of miracles. With the Deists they were more in harmony; but above all Shaftesbury gained a great influence, who unites with the abstract clearness of his system a poetical force of imagination and a love for the ideal, by which mere reason is balanced, so that, without any criticism, the

services of the Kantian philosophy in securing peace between the heart and the understanding were anticipated.
So that it was for the most part in Shaftesbury's sense
that the doctrine of the perfection of the world was understood, even when one ostensibly rested on Leibniz. The
text is taken from Leibniz, the interpretation from Shaftesbury; and instead of the mechanism of the uncreated
essences, appeared, as in Schiller's youthful philosophy,
the hymn to the beauty of the universe, in which evil
contributes to the harmony of the whole, like shadows in
painting, like discords in music.

With this circle of thoughts and feelings, Spinozism is
much more consonant than Materialism; nay, perhaps
nothing could more clearly show the difference between
the two tendencies than the influence which Spinoza
exercised upon the leading minds of the eighteenth century.
In this we must not, of course, forget that no single one
of these men was a Spinozist in the strict sense of the
word. They kept to a few main ideas: to the unity of all
that exists, the regularity of all that happens, the identity
of spirit and nature. They cared very little for the form
of the system and the connection of the individual principles; and if it is asserted that Spinozism is the necessary
result of natural thought, this involves no admission of
the correctness of its proofs in their mathematical form,
but the totality of this philosophy, as opposed to the traditional Christian and Scholastic philosophy, is recognised
as the aim of all speculation. Thus the acute Lichtenberg
said: "If the world continues to exist for countless numbers of years, the universal religion will be a purified
Spinozism. Reason left to itself leads to nothing else, and
it is impossible that it should." [110] Here Spinozism, the
purification of which doubtless involves the rejection of
the mathematical formulæ that contain so many fallacies,
is estimated, not as a final system of theoretical philosophy, but as a religion; and in this Lichtenberg, who,

[110] Lichtenberg's Vermischte Schriften herausgegeben von Kries, ii. 27.

with all his leaning to theoretical Materialism, had a strong religious element, was entirely in earnest. No one would find the religion of the future in the theoretically more logical, and in details the more correct, system of Hobbes. In the 'Deus sive Natura' of Spinoza the God is not lost behind matter. He is present and lives, as the inner side of the same great whole that to our senses appears as nature.

Goethe also protested against our conceiving the God of Spinoza as an abstract idea—that is, as a cipher—while he is rather the most real and active unit, that says to itself: "I am that I am, and in all the forms in which I may appear shall be what I shall be."[111] Decidedly as Goethe turned away from the Newtonian God, who "from outside only impels" the world, he as decidedly held fast to the divinity of the one inward essence, which appears to its own phenomena, to men, only as the world, while in its true nature it is exalted above any conception of one of its creatures.   Still in his later years Goethe took refuge in the Ethics of Spinoza if any unsympathetic theory had affected him unpleasantly, and he calls it his pure, deep, innate, and habitual mode of thinking, which "had taught him inevitably to see God in nature, nature in God."[112]

As everybody knows, Goethe has also let us know the impression made by the 'System of Nature' upon the youthful poet. The judgment which he formed of it, although very far from doing justice to Holbach, so strikingly exhibits the antithesis between two utterly opposite intellectual movements, that we may in fact let Goethe speak here as representative of the aspiring German youth of that period: ".We could not understand how such a book could be dangerous. It appeared to us so dark, so Cim-

---

[111] Comp. Goethe's letter, published by Anton Dohrn (in Westermann's Monatshefte), reprinted in Bergmann's Philosophische Monatshefte, iv. S. 516 (Mar. 1870).

[112] In the Annalen, 1811, on occasion of Jacobi's book, 'Von den göttlichen Dingen.'

merian, so death-like, that we could scarcely find patience to endure its presence." [113]

The further remarks which Goethe there makes in the spirit of his youthful modes of thought are not of any great importance, except in so far as they also show that the book appeared to him and his young companions "as the very quintessence of senility, as unsavoury, nay, absurd." They demanded a full, entire life, such as a theoretical and polemical work neither could nor ought to give: they were unwilling to dispense, even in a work of Rationalism, with that satisfaction of the spirit which is really to be found only in the sphere of imagination. They did not reflect that, even if the universe were also the supreme work of art, yet an analysis of its elements would always have to be something else than the enjoyment of the whole in the contemplation of its magnificence. What becomes of the beauty of the 'Iliad' if it is resolved into its letters and spelt? and the very task undertaken by Holbach was to break up the most necessary knowledge into its letters, according to his notions. No wonder that Goethe concludes his judgment with the following remark: "How hollow and empty did we feel in this melancholy, atheistical half-night, in which earth vanished with all its creatures, heaven with all its stars! There was to be a matter in motion from all eternity, and by this motion, right and left, and in every direction, without anything further, it was to produce the infinite phenomena of existence. Even all this we should have allowed to pass, if the author, out of his moved matter, had really built up the world before our eyes. But he seemed to know as little about nature as we did; for having set up some general ideas, he quits them at once for the sake of changing that which appears as higher than nature, or as a higher nature within nature, into material heavy nature, which is moved, indeed, but without direction or form— and thus he fancies he has gained a great deal."

[113] Wahrheit und Dichtung, Buch xi.

These youths, moreover, could of course make no use of the proofs of the Scholastic philosophy 'that no matter can think.' Goethe says: "If, after all, this book did us any mischief, it was this, that we took a hearty dislike to all philosophy, and especially metaphysics, and remained in that dislike; while, on the other hand, we threw ourselves into living knowledge—experience, action, and poetising—with all the more liveliness and passion."

Second Book.

HISTORY OF MATERIALISM
SINCE KANT.

MODERN PHILOSOPHY.

———•———

CHAPTER I.

KANT AND MATERIALISM.

THE pre-eminent position which we have assigned to Kant by the very division of our work stands already in much less need of justification, or even of explanation, than when the first edition appeared, almost eight years ago. It is true, indeed, that the retreat of our philosophical Romanticism in Germany had been settled long before. As a routed army looks around it for a firm point where it may hope to collect again into order, so there was heard everywhere in philosophic circles the cry, 'Retreat upon Kant!' Only more recently, however, has this retreat upon Kant become a reality, and it is found that at bottom the standpoint of the great Königsberg philosopher could never have been properly described as obsolete; nay, that we have every reason to plunge into the depths of the Kantian system with the most serious efforts, such as have hitherto been spent upon scarcely any other philosopher than Aristotle.

Misapprehensions and impetuous productiveness have combined in an intellectually active age to break through the strict barriers which Kant had imposed upon speculation. The reaction which succeeded the metaphysical intoxication contributed the more to the return to the prematurely abandoned position, as men found themselves again confronted by the Materialism which at the appearance of Kant had disappeared, and left scarcely a wrack behind.   At present we have not only a young school of Kantians in the narrower and wider sense,[1] but those also who wish to try other paths see themselves compelled first to reckon with Kant, and to offer a special justification for departing from his ways.   Even the factitious and exaggerated enthusiasm for Schopenhauer's philosophy partly owed its origin to a related tendency, while in many cases it formed for more logical minds a transition to Kant.   But a special emphasis must here be laid on the friendly attitude of men of science, who, so far as Materialism failed to satisfy them, have inclined for the

---

[1] Otto Liebmann here specially deserves mention, who, in his work 'Kant und die Epigonen' (1865), expressed it as his conviction: "Es muss auf Kant zurückgegangen werden" (S. 215).   Jürgen Bona Meyer, who as early as 1856 contributed to the then raging 'Controversy on Body and Soul,' one of the best elucidations from the Kantian standpoint, has in 'Kant's Psychologie' (1870) similarly expressed himself as to Kant's importance for present philosophy (Einl., S. 1–3). But of the utmost importance is especially 'Kant's Theorie der Erfahrung von Dr. Hermann Cohen,' Berlin, 1871, because here for the first time the whole energy of a special effort was employed to master thoroughly the terminology of Kant, and so, under the guidance of the most accurate fixing of his ideas, to penetrate deeper into the philosopher's meaning; the indispensable necessity of which had just been made clear to everybody by the singular controversy between Trendelenburg and Kuno Fischer. That the thoroughness with which Dr. Cohen went to work has not been without result will perhaps be evident from our present account of Kant's philosophy in its relation to Materialism.   The changes made since the first edition are due to a renewed examination of the whole Kantian system, occasioned chiefly by Dr. Cohen's book.   A very careful treatise, resting upon an accurate and independent investigation, is the essay contained in the 'Altpreuss. Monatsschrift,' Bd. vii. (reprinted, Königsb. 1870), of Dr. Emil Arnoldt, 'Kant's transscendentale Idealität des Raumes und der Zeit: Für Kant, gegen Trendelenburg.'   A thorough understanding of the main point in the Kantian philosophy is shown also by Carl Twesten in his book published in 1863: 'Schiller in seinem Verhältniss zur Wissenschaft.'   This work is of later origin than the recently published posthumous historico-philosophical work of Twesten, in which he declares himself a Positivist.   If we compare what Twesten says at p. 2 of the essay on Schiller, we are forced to the conclusion that Kant had displaced Comte in Twesten's case.

most part to a way of thinking which, in very essential points, agrees with that of Kant.

And it is, in fact, by no means strictly orthodox Kantianism upon which we must have laid distinctive stress; least of all that dogmatic turn with which Schleiden thought he could crush Materialism when he compared Kant, Fries, and Apelt with Keppler, Newton, and Laplace, and maintained that by their labours the ideas 'Soul, Freedom, God,' were as firmly established as the laws of the stellar world.[2] Such dogmatism is entirely foreign to the spirit of the 'Critick of Reason,' although Kant personally attached great value to his having withdrawn these very ideas from the controversy of the schools, by relegating them, as utterly incapable as well of positive as negative proof, to the sphere of practical philosophy. But the whole of the practical philosophy is the variable and perishable part of Kant's philosophy, powerful as were its effects upon his contemporaries. Only its site is imperishable, not the edifice that the master has erected on this site. Even the demonstration of this site, as of a free ground for the building of ethical systems, can scarcely be numbered among the permanent elements of the system, and therefore, if we are speaking of the salvation of moral ideas, nothing is more unsuitable than to compare Kant with Keppler, to say nothing of Newton and Laplace. Much rather must we seek for the whole importance of the great reform which Kant inaugurated in his criticism of the *theoretical* reason; here lies, in fact, even for ethic, the lasting importance of the critical philosophy, which not only aided the development of a particular system of ethical ideas, but, if properly carried on, is capable of affording similar aid to the changing requirements of various epochs of culture.

Kant himself was very far from comparing himself with

[2] Comp. Dr. M. J. Schleiden, 'Ueber den Materialismus der neueren deutschen Naturwissenschaft, sein Wesen und seine Geschichte,' Leipzig, 1863. A sharp but not unfair review of this work appeared anonymously under the title, 'M. J. Schleiden über den Materialismus,' Dorpat, 1864.

Keppler; but he made another comparison, that is more significant and appropriate. He compared his achievement to that of Copernicus. But this achievement consisted in this, that he reversed the previous standpoint of metaphysic. Copernicus dared, " by a paradoxical but yet true method," to seek the observed motions, not in the heavenly bodies, but in their observers. Not less " paradoxical" must it appear to the sluggish mind of man when Kant lightly and certainly overturns our collective experience, with all the historical and exact sciences, by the simple assumption that our notions do not regulate themselves according to things, but things according to our notions.[3] It follows immediately from this that the objects of experience altogether are only *our* objects; that the whole objective world is, in a word, not absolute objectivity, but only objectivity for man and any similarly organised beings, while behind the phenomenal world, the absolute nature of things, the ' thing-in-itself,' is veiled in impenetrable darkness.

For a moment we will deal with this idea. How Kant carried it out does not for the moment concern us; but we must all the more closely consider the question how the position of Materialism is affected by this new standpoint.

The end of the First Book showed us the German school philosophy entangled in a serious controversy with Materialism. The favourite image of the hydra, from which two new heads always spring forth when the demigod has struck off one, is anything but suitable to the drama which is unfolded to the unprejudiced spectator of these struggles. Materialism does indeed receive each time a

---

[3] Comp. the preface to the second edition of the ' Kritik.' Kant indeed lets it here appear (note to p. xxii., Hartenst., iii. 20 ff.) that in thoroughgoing criticism he claims the rôle of a Newton, by whose theory had been *proved* what Copernicus in his opinion (comp. as to this vol. i. p. 230) had only proposed as " hypothesis." But for the purpose of gaining a first view of the nature of the Kantian reform, the comparison with Copernicus made in the preface is more important.

blow that it cannot parry; it is ever the same carte that always strikes home, however clumsily it may often be dealt. *Consciousness* cannot be explained out of material movements. However conclusively it is shown that it is entirely dependent upon material changes, the relation of *external movement* to *sensation* remains inconceivable, and the more light is thrown upon it only a more glaring contradiction is revealed. But next we observe that all the systems that are brought to oppose Materialism, whether they are called after Descartes, Spinoza, Leibniz, Wolff, or after our old friend Aristotle, contain precisely the same contradiction, besides, it may be, a dozen worse ones. When we come to reckon with Materialism, everything comes to light. We here leave entirely out of view what advantages the other systems may perhaps possess in their profoundness, in their relations with art, religion, and poetry, in brilliant divinations and stimulating play of mind. In such treasures Materialism is poor; but it is just as poor in those gross fallacies or hair-splitting sophisms which help the other systems to their so-called truths. In the contest with Materialism, where what is wanted is proof or refutation, all the advantages of profoundness can give no help, and the hidden contradictions are brought to light.

We have, however, made the acquaintance in many forms of a principle against which Materialism has no weapons, and which, in fact, leads us on beyond this way of thinking to a higher view of things. At the very outset of our task we were met by this principle when we saw Protagoras pass beyond Demokritos. And again, in the last era which we treated, we find two men differing in nationality, modes of thought, calling, faith, and character, who nevertheless both abandoned the foundation of Materialism upon the same point—Berkeley the bishop, and D'Alembert the mathematician. The former looked upon the whole world of phenomena as one great delusion of the senses; the latter doubted whether there exists outside us anything corresponding to what we suppose we see. We have seen how angry Holbach grows over Berkeley without being able to refute him.

There is one province of exact physical inquiry that prevents contemporary Materialists from perversely turning away from the doubt as to the reality of the phenomenal world, that is the physiology of the sense-organs. The astonishing progress made in this field, of which we must later speak again, seems expressly calculated to confirm the Pythagorean proposition that man is the measure of things. When it has once been demonstrated that the quality of our sense-perceptions is entirely conditioned by the constitution of our organs, we can no longer dismiss with the predicate " Irrefutable but absurd " even the hypothesis that the whole system also, into which we bring our sense-perceptions—in a word, our whole experience—is conditioned by an intellectual organisation which compels us to feel as we do feel, to think as we do think, while to another organisation the very same objects may appear quite different, and the thing in itself cannot be pictured by any finite being.

In fact, the idea that the phenomenal world is only the distorted copy of another world of real objects runs through the whole history of human thought. Among the thinkers of ancient India, as well as among the Greeks, is found in many forms the same fundamental idea, which, in the shape given to it by Kant, is now suddenly compared to the achievement of Copernicus. Plato believed in a world of ideas, the eternal and perfect types of earthly phenomena. Kant calls him the foremost philosopher of the intellectual, and Epikuros, on the other hand, the foremost philosopher of the sensible. How much, however, Kant's relation to Materialism differs from that of Plato is clear from the fact that Kant devotes a special eulogy to Epikuros, because in his conclusions he has never transcended the limits of experience, while, *e.g.*, Locke, " after having derived all the conceptions and principles of the mind from experience, goes so far in the employment of these conceptions and principles as to maintain that we can prove the existence of God and the immortality of the soul —both of them objects lying beyond the limits of possible experience—with the same force of demonstration as any mathematical proposition." [4]

On the other hand, Kant differed no less decidedly from those philosophers who content themselves with proving that the phenomenal world is a product of our ideas. Protagoras made himself at home in this phenomenal world. He completely gave up the idea of an absolute truth, and based his whole system on the proposition that that is true for the man which seems to him true, and that good which seems to him good. The object of Berkeley, in his contest against the phenomenal world, was to get fresh air for distressed faith, and his philosophy stops where his real aim appears. The sceptics entirely content themselves with shattering all fancied truth, and doubt not only the world of ideas and the phenomenal world, but, in fact, the unconditional validity of the laws of thought. And yet it was a sceptic who, by a violent shock, threw our Kant out of the paths of German Scholasticism, and brought him into that direction in which, after thinking and labouring for years, he reached the goal announced in his immortal ' Critick of Pure Reason.' If we wish to get a clear grasp of Kant's fundamental idea, without analysing the whole structure of his system, our way leads through David Hume.

Hume is fully entitled to rank with the series of English thinkers denoted by the names of Bacon, Hobbes, and Locke; nay, it is a question whether the first place among them all is not due to him. Sprung from a noble Scotch family, he was born at Edinburgh in 1711. As early as 1738 appeared his work upon ' Human Nature,' written during a visit to France in complete and studious leisure.

---

[4] Comp. Krit. d. r. Vern., transcend. MethodenL., 4 Hptst. ; Hart. iii. 561 ; E. T. Meiklejohn, p. 516.

Only fourteen years later did he devote himself to those historical studies to which he owes a great part of his fame. After various occupations, he became at length Secretary of Embassy in Paris; finally, Under Secretary of State. To us Germans, who, by a philosopher, through involuntary association of ideas, understand a professor standing with raised finger before his chair, it must necessarily appear striking that among the English philosophers there have been so many statesmen; nay, what is almost more remarkable, that in England the statesmen are sometimes philosophers.

Hume, in his way of thinking, stands as close to Materialism as a so decided sceptic ever can. He stands on the ground prepared by Hobbes and Locke. He sometimes explained the origin of error, without, however, attaching much value to the hypothesis, by means of a faulty conduction in the brain, in which he imagines all notions to be localised. For that weak point of Materialism which the Materialists themselves know not how to protect, Hume has found a sufficient defence. In admitting that the transition from movement in space to perception and thought is inexplicable, he points out that this inexplicableness is by no means peculiar to this problem. He shows that exactly the same contradiction attaches to all relations of cause and effect. "Place one body of a pound weight on one end of a lever, and another body of the same weight on another end, you will never find in these bodies any principle of motion dependent on their distances from the centre, more than of thought and perception." [5]

Our modern mechanical science would perhaps object to this; but let us remember that all the progress of science has not solved, but only pushed further back, the difficulty to which Hume refers. If we consider two ultimate molecules of matter, or two heavenly bodies, when the motion of the one influences that of the other,

[5] The philosophical works of Hume, Edinb., 1826, i. 315.

we shall be able to account admirably for all the rest, but the relation of the attractive power which brings about the connection to the bodies themselves is concealed under the incomprehensibleness of every single change in nature. It is true that we have not in this way explained the passage of movement in space into thought, but we have shown that this inexplicableness can form no argument against the dependence of thought upon motion in space. The price paid by Materialism for this defence is, indeed, not less than that which the Devil in the legend demands for his aid. The whole cause of Materialism is for ever lost by the admission of the inexplicableness of all natural occurrences. If Materialism quietly acquiesces in this inexplicableness, it ceases to be a philosophical principle; it may, however, continue to exist as maxim of scientific research. This is, in fact, the position of most of our modern 'Materialists.' They are essentially sceptics; they no longer believe that matter, as it appears to our senses, contains the last solution of all the riddles of nature; but they proceed in principle as if it were so, and wait until from the positive sciences themselves the necessity arises to adopt other views.

Still more striking, perhaps, is Hume's kinship with Materialism in his keen polemic against the doctrine of personal identity, of the unity of consciousness, and the simplicity and immateriality of the soul.

"There are some philosophers who imagine we are every moment intimately conscious of what we call our *self* (in German philosophy, 'das Ich'); that we feel its existence and its continuance in existence, and are certain, beyond the evidence of a demonstration, both of its perfect identity and simplicity. . . .

"Unluckily all these positive assertions are contrary to that very experience which is pleaded for them; nor have we any idea of *self*, after the manner it is here explained. . . . For my part, when I enter most intimately into what I call *myself*, I always stumble on some particular perception or other, of heat or cold, light or shade, love or hatred, pain or pleasure. I never can catch *myself* at any time without a perception, and never can observe anything but the perception. When my perceptions are removed for any time, as by sound sleep, so long am I insensible of *myself*, and may truly be said not to exist." If any one has a different notion of *himself*, Hume cannot reason with him. "He may, perhaps, perceive something simple and continued, which he calls *himself*, though I am certain there is no such principle in me.   But setting aside some metaphysicians of this kind, I may venture to affirm of the rest of mankind that they are nothing but a bundle or collection of different perceptions, which succeed each other with an inconceivable rapidity." [6]

The delicate irony which is here directed against the metaphysicians elsewhere hits the theologians. That Hume's views are quite inconsistent with the immortality of the soul in the theological sense need not be said. Nevertheless, he sometimes amuses himself by the malicious observation that all the arguments for the immortality of the soul would have just as much force on his view as on the ordinary assumption of the simplicity and identity of the soul.

That this was the man who produced so profound an impression upon Kant, whom Kant never names but with the utmost respect, must at once place Kant's relation to Materialism in a light other than that in which we are usually willing to regard it. Decided as Kant is in his opposition to Materialism, still this great mind cannot possibly be numbered with those who base their capacity for philosophy upon a measureless contempt for Materialism.

"Physical science will never discover to us the internal constitution of things, which is not phenomenon, yet can serve as the ultimate ground of explanation of phenomena; but it does not require this for its physical expla-

[6] *Loc. cit.*, p. 319, ff.

nations. Nay, even if such grounds should be offered from other sources (for instance, the influence of immaterial entities), they must be rejected, and not used in the course of its explanations; for these explanations must only be grounded upon that which, as an object of sense, can belong to experience, and be brought into connection with our real perceptions, according to the laws of experience." [7]

Kant, in a word, fully recognises two ways of thinking —Materialism and Scepticism—as legitimate steps towards his critical philosophy; both he regards as errors, but errors that were necessary to the development of knowledge. He admits that the former, by reason of its intelligibleness, may become dangerous for the mass of people, while the latter, by reason of its difficulty, will remain confined to the schools; but as to a purely scientific judgment, both he regards as equally respectable, while, however, the preference belongs to Scepticism. There is no philosophical system to which Kant did not occupy a more negative attitude than to these two. The ordinary Idealism, in particular, stands in the sharpest opposition to Kant's 'transcendental' Idealism. In so far as it attempts to prove that the phenomenal world does not show things to us as they are in themselves, Kant agrees with it. As soon, however, as the Idealist will teach us something as to the world of pure things, or even set this knowledge in the position of the empirical sciences, he cannot have a more irreconcilable opponent than Kant.

A hasty reviewer had found "higher Idealism" in Kant's 'Critick.' This appeared to Kant much as if he had been charged with "higher absurdity," so entirely was he misunderstood. We must admire the moderation, and at the same time the keenness, of the great thinker when he replies by setting down two propositions, whch even to

[7] Prolegomena zu jeder künftigen Metaphysik, Riga, 1783, S. 167, Hart. iv. 101. [I have followed Mr. Mahaffy in his translation of the Prolegomena, Kant's Crit. Phil. for Eng. Readers, iii. 154, with one or two changes. The accidental omission of the word 'not' in Mr. Mahaffy's version makes nonsense of the passage.--TR.]

the blindest must throw a gleam of light into the essence of the Critical Philosophy. " The proposition of all genuine Idealists, from the Eleatic school to Bishop Berkeley, is contained in this formula: 'All cognition by sense and experience is nothing but mere appearance, and truth is in the ideas of the pure understanding and of pure reason only.' The principle which throughout governs and determines my Idealism is, 'All cognition of things from pure understanding, or pure reason only, is nothing but appearance, and truth is in experience only.'"[8]

The purest empiricist cannot express himself more plainly; but how do we reconcile with this so unequivocal proposition the singular phrase that things range themselves according to our ideas?

There can obviously be here no question of the actually formed ideas of a speculating individual. In a certain sense, indeed, to the incarnate Hegelian or Aristotelian things range themselves according to his ideas. He lives in the world of his mental cobwebs, and contrives to make everything harmonise with them. Before a thing can have really become a thing to *him*, it must have modelled itself upon his ideas. But all things are not so yielding, and experience plays such philosophers the awkwardest tricks. Remember Cremonini, who took care not to look through a telescope for fear of stumbling on the rebellious satellites of Jupiter! Kant, who finds all truth in experience, cannot thus have understood the correspondence of things with our ideas. The influence of 'our ideas,' according to Kant's understanding of the matter, must rather be such that it expresses itself in the most general and invariable features of experience in things that are absolutely free from the caprice of the individual. The riddle will then be solved by an analysis of experience, in which we have to demonstrate an intellectual factor due not to things but to ourselves.

All judgments are, according to Kant, either analytical

or synthetical. Analytical judgments assert in the predicate nothing but what was already involved in the notion of the subject. If I say, All bodies are extended in this proposition, I have not increased my knowledge of bodies; for I cannot posit the notion of bodies at all without already including the notion of extension. The judgment only resolves the subject into its constituents in order to emphasise one of them by means of the predicate, and so to bring it more fully into consciousness. Synthetic judgments, on the contrary, increase our knowledge of the subject. If I say, All heavenly bodies gravitate, I suppose a quality to be connected with all heavenly bodies which is not already involved in the mere idea of heavenly bodies.

We see, then, that it is the synthetic judgments by which only our knowledge is really extended, while the analytic serve as a means to make things clear and to refute errors; for a judgment that says nothing in the predicate but what was already involved in the subject can, at the most, only remind me of knowledge that I already possessed, or bring out particularly points that otherwise I should overlook; but it can teach me nothing really new. And yet there exists an entire science, perhaps the most important of all, in which we may doubt whether its judgments are synthetic or analytic: it is mathematics.

Before we discuss this important question, we must first briefly refer to what is a judgment *a priori* and a judgment *a posteriori*. The latter draws its validity from experience, the former not. An *a priori* judgment may indeed be based indirectly upon experience,—not, however, as a judgment, but only in so far as its elements are concepts drawn from experience. Thus, for example, the whole sum of true analytic propositions are also *a priori* valid; since, in order to develop the predicate from the idea of the subject, I do not need the help of experience. The subject itself, however, may even in this case indicate an object that I have only become acquainted with through experience. Thus, for example, the idea of ice is an idea of experience. The proposition, Ice is a solid body, is however, analytical, because the predicate was already contained in the idea I formed of the subject.

Synthetic judgments are with Kant the field of investigation. Are they all *a posteriori*, that is, deduced from experience, or are there also some that are not indebted to experience for their validity? Are there any synthetic judgments *a priori?* Metaphysic pretends to extend our knowledge without needing the aid of experience. But is this possible? Can there be any metaphysic at all? How are, quite generally speaking, synthetic propositions *a priori* possible?

Let us wait an instant. Answers such as, ' By revelation;' ' By inspiration of genius;' ' By the soul's recollection of a world of ideas in which it had once its home;' ' By the development of innate ideas, which unconsciously slumber in man from his birth;'—such answers need no refutation merely because metaphysic, as a matter of fact, has till now fumbled about in bewilderment. If it could be shown that from the bases of such doctrines a real science proceeds, which develops itself with sure footing, instead of having ever to begin again, we might perhaps content ourselves with the lack of a further foundation, just as in mathematics we have been content to abide by the indemonstrableness of the axioms; but all further extension of metaphysic is vain as long as it is not certain whether its structure can have a foundation at all.

Sceptics and Empiricists will make common cause, and will dispose of the question with a simple No! If they succeed in proving this, they may in intimate alliance for ever dominate the field of philosophy. With dogmatic Materialism, too, all would be over, since it builds its theories upon the axiom of the intelligibility of the world, and overlooks that this axiom is at bottom only the principle of order in phenomena; but Materialism may resign its claims to have demonstrated the ultimate causes of all phenomena. It will then, indeed, resign too its original character, but in alliance with Scepticism and formal Empiricism it threatens all the more to swallow up all other philosophic efforts. To meet them Kant brings forward a formidable ally—Mathematics.

Hume, who doubted every judgment that went beyond experience, was not quite clear whether, for example, two straight lines meeting in an exceedingly small angle might not have a segment of a certain extent in common, instead of cutting each other in one point only as mathematics require. Still Hume conceded the pre-eminent conclusiveness of mathematics, and thought he could trace it to this, that all mathematical judgments rest only upon the principle of contradiction — in other words, that they are entirely analytical. Kant maintains, on the contrary, that all mathematical judgments are synthetical, and therefore, of course, synthetical judgments *a priori*, since mathematical propositions need no confirmation by experience.

Unless we are to misunderstand Kant completely, we must here strictly distinguish between intuition and experience. An intuition, that, for instance, of a series of triangles with continually obtuser angles at the apex, and continually broader base, is indeed also an experience; but the experience here is merely the circumstance that I see before me this particular series of triangles. If I now gather from the intuition of these triangles by the aid of imagination, which conceives an extension of the base to infinity, the proposition that the sum of the angles—whose constant relation was previously demonstrated—is equal to two right angles, this proposition is by no means a judgment of experience. My experience consists merely in the fact that I have seen these triangles, and have found in them what I must recognise as universally true. The judgment of experience as such can at any time be refuted by a new experience. Men had observed the fixed stars to be motionless, as far as could be seen, for hundreds of years, and from this concluded that they are immovable.

This was a judgment of experience; it could be amended, and was amended, by more exact observations and calculations. Similar examples are afforded on every hand by the history of science. We are chiefly indebted to the pre-eminent logical talent of the French that to-day the exact sciences in all matters of experience no longer assert any absolute truths, but only relative ones; that we are always reminded of the conditions of the knowledge that has been gained, and the accuracy of all theories is based upon a reservation for increasing insight. This is not the case with mathematical propositions; they all alike involve, whether they are mere inferences or fundamental theories, the consciousness of absolute necessity. This consciousness, however, is not automatic; the propositions of mathematics, even the axioms, must no doubt once have been *discovered*. They must be ascertained either by the exercise of reflection and intuition, or by the rapid and happy combination of both. This discovery, however, essentially rests upon an accurate application of the mind to the problem. And therefore it is that mathematical principles are as easy to communicate to a learner as they are difficult to discover. The man who scans the heavenly spaces day and night until he has found a new comet may be likened to him who endeavours to win a new side for mathematical intuition. But just as the telescope may be so directed that any one with sound eyes must see the comet, so the new mathematical principle can be so exhibited that every one must recognise its truth who is capable at all of proper intuition, whether by means of a described figure or of a merely mental picture. The circumstance that mathematical truths are often sought and found with difficulty has accordingly nothing to do with what Kant calls their *a priority*. By this we must rather understand that the mathematical principles, as soon as they are ascertained by intuition, are immediately combined with the consciousness of their universality and necessity. Thus, for example, in order to show that 7 and

5 produce the sum 12, I shall employ intuition, and take a collection of dots, strokes, small objects, and so on. The experience in this case only amounts to this, that these particular dots, strokes, and so on have led me upon this occasion to this particular sum. If I am to learn by *experience* that it is always so, then I must *repeat* this experience until, through habit and association, the conviction is established in me, or I must institute systematic experiments to see whether, perhaps, in the case of bodies very different in kind, or irregularly arranged, or under other special circumstances, a different result may unexpectedly be given. This rapid and unconditional generalisation of what has once been seen cannot, moreover, be simply explained by the obvious similarity of all numerical relations. If the propositions of algebra and arithmetic are propositions of experience, then the conviction of the independence of all numerical relations of the constitution and arrangement of the bodies numbered would be the *very last* thing to occur to us, since all induction gives the more general propositions later than the particular ones. The proposition that the numerical relations are independent of the nature of the things numbered is rather itself *a prioristic.* That it is also synthetic may be easily shown. We might easily take away its synthetic nature by taking it up into the definition of what we would call numbers. Then we should straightway have a self-contained algebra, of which, however, we should not at all know whether it may be applied to objects or not. But every one knows that our conviction of the truth of algebra and arithmetic includes also the conviction of their applicability to all objects that we can meet with. The circumstance that the objects of nature, where we have to do, not with the numbering of separate bodies or parts, but with measuring and weighing, can never correspond to exactly determined numbers, that they are altogether incommensurable, does not alter this in the least. Numbers are, to any desired extent of accuracy, applicable to any kind of object. We are

convinced that an iron rod constantly subject to the effects of varying temperature in an infinitely small space of time has an infinitely exact and definite measure, although we can never have the means for completely ascertaining this measure. The circumstance that we only gain this conviction as a result of a mathematical and physical training does not lessen its *a priority*. We have to do in regard to knowledge *a priori*, according to Kant's incomparable definition, neither with innate ideas lying ready in the soul, nor with inorganic inspirations or incomprehensible revelations. Knowledge *a priori* develops itself in man just as much in accordance with law and from out of his nature as knowledge from experience. It is characterised simply by this, that it is combined with the consciousness of universality and necessity, and therefore as to its validity is independent of experience.

Here, of course, we have at once a point that, even to this time, is still subject to the most violent attacks. On the one hand, the *a priority* of mathematical knowledge is attacked, and, on the other, the synthetic nature of mathematical judgments is denied. The conception of mathematics is so important for the foundation of the Kantian philosophy, that we cannot avoid here an examination of both these points.

As to the *a priority* of mathematics, the liveliest controversy took place in England, where the influence of Hume has been most profoundly operative. Whewell, the meritorious philosopher and historian of Induction, maintained the doctrine of the *a priority* of mathematics, and of the origin of the necessity that we attach to mathematical propositions from a really *a priori* element—the *conditions* or the *form* of our knowledge. He was opposed by the astronomer Herschel and by John Stuart Mill, who agrees with Herschel in nearly all points.[9]

[9] The controversy of the English philosophers on this subject began by Whewell's attack in his ' Mechanical Euclid ' on the view maintained by Dugald Stewart, that the fundamental doctrines of geometry are built upon hypothesis. An article written by Herschel in the ' Edinburgh Re-

The doctrine of these Empiricists is simply the following : Strict necessity rules in mathematics only so far as it rests upon definitions and upon inferences from these definitions. The so-called axioms are for the most part only definitions, or may be resolved into definitions. The rest, especially the fundamental propositions of Euklid's geometry, that two straight lines cannot enclose a space, and that two parallel lines produced to infinity never meet—these, the only real axioms, are nothing but generalisations from experience, the results of an induction. They lack, accordingly, that strict necessity that is peculiar to the definitions (in the Kantian sense, one might say, to all analytical judgments). Their necessity in our consciousness is merely subjective, and can be psychologically explained. It arises in the same way as we often attribute necessity to propositions that are not even true, or declare something to be unintelligible and inconceivable that we ourselves perhaps some time ago held to be true. Even though the mathematical axioms are thus entirely due to the association of ideas, and, psychologically considered, have no better origin than many an error, it does not, of course, follow from this that we must fear that they may some day be refuted ; but it does follow that we have no other source for the certainty that we attribute to them than for our empirical knowledge generally, that appears to us probable, certain, or absolutely necessary, according to the strength of the induction from which it results.

view' defended Stewart's view. Whewell answered in his 'Philosophy of the Inductive Sciences' (London, 1840), i. 79 ff., in the section 'The Philosophy of the Pure Sciences,' which contains a special chapter (ch. v. p. 98 ff.) in answer to Herschel's objections. Herschel continued the controversy in a review in 1841 of Whewell's principal books ('History of the Inductive Sciences' and 'Philosophy of the Inductive Sciences') in the July number of the 'Quarterly Review.' Upon this Mill took up the contest in his 'Logic' (1843), and continued it in his later editions after Whewell had answered him in a special publication ('On Induction, with especial reference to Mr. Mill's System of Logic'). We have used the third edition of the original and the third edition of Schiel's translation (after the fifth of the original), Braunschw. 1868 ; besides Whewell's 'Philosophy of the Inductive Sciences.'

On this view, then, there are indeed synthetical judgments in mathematics, but they are not *a priori;* there are judgments *a priori,* but these are only the analytical, or, as Mill calls them, identical, judgments.

As applied to the objects of experience, all judgments on this view are only hypothetically valid. Nature nowhere supplies us with the pure forms of geometry, and no algebraic formula will ever represent the measure of a magnitude or of a force with absolute accuracy. We can only say, therefore, that *if* and *so far as,* for example, a planetary orbit corresponds to the line assumed by us, and called an ellipse, does it necessarily possess all those qualities that we deduce from this notion ? But of none of these properties can we say in any but a hypothetical sense that it belongs to the planet's orbit; nay, even the actual course of the planet will never completely correspond to our theories.

This is the kernel of the doctrine; as to the polemic against Whewell, it is not perfectly fair and unprejudiced, although the long-continued controversy was on the whole very courteously conducted. Mill, who generally represents an opponent's views very candidly and clearly, does not always quote quite accurately, and puts many expressions of his opponent into an unjustifiable connection.[10]

[10] It is a great defect, to begin with, that Mill seldom in his very lengthy polemic gives Whewell's views exactly in his own words and in their true connection, but always slips in ideas in which the point at issue represents itself from his own standpoint. We will give a couple of instances of the resulting misrepresentations, quoting the original. In Bk. II. ch. v. § 4 (3d ed. i. 258): "It is not necessary to show that the truths which we call axioms are originally *suggested* by observation, and that we should never have known that two straight lines cannot enclose a space if we had never seen a straight line; thus much being admitted by Dr. Whewell, and by all in recent times who have taken his view of the subject. But they contend that it is not experience which *proves* the axiom; but that its truth is perceived *a priori* by the constitution of the mind itself, from the first moment when the meaning of the proposition is apprehended; and without any necessity for verifying it by repeated trials, as is requisite in the case of truths really ascertained by observation." The italicised words 'suggest' and 'prove' do not occur in Whewell in this sense and connection. This whole opposition of suggestion and proof supposes the superficial treatment of the Empiricists, to whom

The reason of this striking circumstance lies in this, that Mill has always before his eyes the phantom of the old innate ideas, and of the Platonic revelations from a super-sensible world—the phantom that has so long played its part in metaphysic, and whose connection with confusions of the worst kind is well calculated to irritate a sober and unmystical opponent. It is the same reason that misled Ueber-

'experience' is something final, almost like a personal being opposed to the passive spirit. According to Whewell, in every act of knowledge a formal, active, and subjective element that he calls "idea" (in Kant the "Form") co-operates with a material, passive, and objective element, the "sensation" (in Kant's language "Empfindung" or "das mannigfaltige der Empfindung"). It is obvious that in the first recognition of an axiomatic truth *both elements co-operate*, as, in fact, like form and matter in an ivory spear they can only be separated in thought. Thus, too, there can be no question of an admission that experience without that formal element could suggest the axiom; still more merely from the fact that this first becomes active in combination with an external objective element. Just as little can insight into the truth of the axiom be separated as the demonstrative element from the sensible. When we speak, then, of the "constitution of the mind," this must not Platonically be referred to an 'intellectual intuition,' but to the form of the same sensibility, by which we receive from without impressions at all, and consequently experience. Very unequivocally says Whewell on this point ('Philos. of the Induct. Sciences,' i. 92): "The axioms require not to be granted, but to be seen. If any one were to assent to them without seeing them to be true, his assent would be of no avail for purposes of reasoning; for he would be also unable to see in what cases they might be applied." Again, in the same chap., § 5, "In-

tuition is 'imaginary looking' [with reference to Hist. Sci. Ideas, i. 140]; but experience must be real looking: if we see a property of straight lines to be true by merely fancying ourselves to be looking at them, the ground of our belief cannot be the senses or experience; it must be something mental." By this passage, in which Mill professes to give Whewell's view, Dr. Cohen has obviously been misled in ' Kant's Theorie der Erfahrung,' S. 96 (in a passage, I may add, that states Mill's relation to Kant with admirable clearness), into attributing to Whewell a doctrine related to the Leibnizian conception, which Mill would rightly object to. It is nothing of the sort; the expression "something mental" is simply introduced by Mill into Whewell; and then, too, the 'imaginary looking' must not be unduly pressed as an imaginary seeing, but simply as a seeing in thought. Whewell has no idea in the passage referred to of laying special weight upon the difference of seeing in imagination from actual seeing; nay, he expressly says, "If we arrange fifteen things in five rows of three, it is seen by looking, or by imaginary looking, which is intuition, that they may also be taken as three rows of five." Thus he expressly attributes the same value to actual seeing and to seeing in imagination for the process of knowledge. Whewell is therefore, in this point at least, an orthodox Kantian, which we are the more pleased to point out, as we failed to recognise this in the first edition, being also misled by Mill.

weg, in our own country, into bitter injustice towards the
Kantian system, in which we were asked to find latent
behind the "*a priori*" the whole apparatus of supernatural
revelations.   Kant's *a priori* is entirely different from that
of the old metaphysic, and his whole conception of these
questions stands indeed most distinctly opposed to the way
in which Leibniz sets the truths of reason above the
teachings of experience.   We will speedily show how the
Empiricism of Mill must be dealt with in a strictly Kantian
sense; before that we will point out its weak points as
they became apparent in the debate between Mill and
Whewell.

The most obvious difficulty meets us at once in the axioms
of geometry.   Our conviction that two straight lines, if continued to infinity, cannot enclose a space, must be looked
upon as an induction from experience, and yet of this,
in the ordinary sense of the term, we can have no experience.   Mill here admits that imaginary intuition must be
substituted for actual intuition, but believes none the less
that the proof is still inductive; that is to say, we may
substitute observation of the image in our mind for
observation of the external reality, because we know that
our images faithfully represent the reality.   But how do
we know this?   By experience?   But then we only know
that this correspondence exists with regard to finite distances.

A second difficulty consists in this, that the doctrine of
the merely hypothetical validity of mathematics is insuffi-
ciently established.   Whewell points out that the hypotheses of natural science are never *necessary*.   They are
more or less probable, but can always be replaced by
others.   But the propositions of mathematics are necessary, and therefore not absolutely hypothetical.   Mill
answers this with the apparently conclusive remark that
necessary hypotheses are still hypotheses. Suppose that
we see ourselves obliged, by the constitution of our mind,
to assume that there are circles, right angles, and so on, is

not this assumption still only hypothetical, since we do not know whether there are anywhere in nature circles, right angles, &c., exactly conformable to our definitions? On the other hand, however, we may remark that it would be very absurd to let so important a question degenerate into a hollow dispute as to words. If there is a kind of hypotheses distinguished from all others by the necessity of their origination in our minds, we gain nothing by the general observation that they are still but hypotheses; what we must rather seek to discover is the real explanation of their special character. With regard, moreover, to the relations of the material world to our mathematical conceptions, we may add another important observation; and this is, that it is by no means correct to say that we make the hypothesis that there are bodies or things conformable to the definitions of mathematics. The mathematician develops his propositions by the aid of intuition through figures, without any reference to bodies, but is convinced at the same time that he can never anywhere meet with an object in experience inconsistent with these propositions. An external thing may not completely answer to any mathematical form: then we presuppose that its actual form is an extremely composite and perhaps variable thing, so that our simple mathematical intuitions cannot exhaust its whole nature. At the same time, however, we presuppose that it is determined in each infinitesimal portion of time with complete accuracy by the same mathematical laws of which we have mastered only the first elements.

Finally, we come to the kernel of the controversy: the notion of the necessity of mathematical judgments and its origin. Here Mill feels particularly strong in the historical demonstration that the human mind has often held as quite inconceivable what has afterwards been proved to be true, or, conversely, has held as necessary what has later been recognised as gross error. But it is just this that is the weakest point in all Empiricism; that is to say, as soon as it is shown that our consciousness of the *neces-sity* of certain knowledge hangs together with our view of the notion of the knowing faculty, we have then finally decided on the main point against one-sided Empiricism, however wrong we may be in drawing a conclusion from this nature of the knowing faculty.

A simple illustration may make this clear. Suppose I see that contrasted colours gain a special brilliancy, this is at first an induction from repeated experience. I may conjecture that it will always be so, but I cannot know this. A new and unexpected observation may cancel my calculation, and oblige me to see a new and wider pro-position cover the common elements of the phenomena. But now suppose I discover that the explanation of my observation lies in the constitution of my eye, then I shall immediately conclude that the observation must in all cases be the same. In order to examine the matter quite thoroughly, let us now assume that there is again some mistake; that, for instance, it is not the contrast in itself, but only some cause *usually* found in combination with contrast, that produces the effect in question. Then I may be obliged, just as in the first instance, to alter my judgment, although in the first case it was assertory, but in the second apodeictic. I might, in fact, before I had ever discovered the inaccuracy of my physiological hypo-theses, have been obliged by a fact of experience to give up my supposed necessary judgment. What, then, does this prove? At all events, not that my hypothesis of necessity arises from experience; for I might have found it before any special·experience at·all. If I know, for example, that a telescope has spots on its glass, I know before I have tried that these spots *must* appear upon any object at which I direct the telescope. Suppose, now, I take the telescope, direct it upon the landscape, and see— no spots! What then? Materially my judgment was false, but the form of necessity entirely corresponded with the position. I knew the reason of the universality of the expected phenomenon, and this is precisely what justifies me in adopting the apodeictic form as regards every particular falling within this case. Perhaps now I have confounded the spotted telescope with a clear one lying near it, or what I took to be a spot in the glass was a shadow, a spot in my own eye, or something else; in short, I have made a mistake, and yet I was quite right, so far as I could make a judgment at all, in giving my judgment an apodeictic form.

The highest degree of universality in our knowledge then clearly belongs to the knowledge that is conditioned by the nature of our knowing faculty, and in this sense alone are we justified in talking of inconceivable or of necessary things. But here we must point out, before distinguishing more strictly, that there is room not only for error, but for obvious misuse of the word. Men stand, as Mill has very rightly shown, so much under the influence of habit, that in order to strengthen a familiar notion, or to refute what seems an unnatural theory, they are only too apt to attribute things to the thinking faculty that are clearly mere subjects of experience. Where, however, we might really assume that the knowing faculty is concerned, as in the instance of the Newtonian laws, by which we declare *actio in distans* to be absurd, we can even then, it is true, be refuted by experience, whether because we have really mistaken the nature of the thinking faculty, or whether we have only, in an inference from it, overlooked an accompanying circumstance.

Mill, then, would believe that he has entirely gained his case, because he has shown that the proof of the truth of the assertion lies in experience; but we have not yet got so far. We are rather concerned with the origin of the apodeictic form of the predication. This is justified as soon as I gather my predication, not from the single observation, but from a universal source, and a source recognised to be universal.

We will now try, so far as it is possible at this stage, to

exhibit Kant's standpoint as clearly as possible. Let us go back to the axioms of Euklid. According to Mill, the proof of the proposition that two straight lines cannot enclose a space lies in experience; that is, it is an induction from experience in combination with imaginary intuition. From the Kantian standpoint very little objection can be made to this. That imaginary intuition should be reckoned as part of experience could at most afford a discussion as to words; that the view of the truth of the proposition is gained from sensuous intuition, and so in a sense arises inductively, is not Kantian in expression, but is, in fact, quite in harmony with Kant's notions.[11] The only difference is that Kant begins where Mill stops. Mill thinks that the matter is now fully explained: with Kant the real problem begins here. The problem is this: How is experience at all possible. We have not here to deal with the solution of this problem, but only to show that it exists—that there is here yet another question that empiricism cannot answer. And for this we use the proof that the consciousness of the necessity, of the absolute universality of the principle is there, and that this consciousness does not spring from experience, although it is first developed together with experience, or upon occasion of experience.

Here we recall the question: How do we know that our mental pictures of two straight lines are just the same as real lines?[12] The Kantian answer is: Because we ourselves cause this agreement; not, indeed, by an act of our individual will, but by the very nature of our mind, that must combine with the external impression in all our intuitions. Intuition in space, with all the fundamental

[11] Cp. Cohen, 'Kant's Theorie,' S. 95, where, upon Mill's proposition that the axiom that two straight lines cannot enclose a space is "an induction from the evidence of our senses," it is curtly observed, "This is thoroughly Kantian."

[12] Cohen, 'Kant's Theorie,' S. 6, observes: "But if we now ask, Whence do we 'know' and how can we know that the real lines are *exactly* like the imaginary lines? Mill answers that, in fact, there is no other certainty in mathematics. But this is to take back his account of mathematical evidence."

properties inherent in it, is a product of our mind in the act of experience; and for this very reason it is equally and necessarily inherent in every possible experience, as well as in every mental intuition. But this is to anticipate. Let the answer be what it may; for the present it is enough to have shown that we need an answer to this question. Even the question whether this judgment of necessity is strictly correct, and whence it arises, does not come yet. We shall see further on that this is not a psychological but a "transcendental" question, and we will try to explain this expression of Kant's. At present we are concerned with the existence of a judgment of necessity, and with the origin of this consciousness of necessity from another source than the merely passive part of experience.

We now proceed, then, to the attacks that are directed, not against the *a priori*, but the synthetic nature of mathematical judgments. Here the main attack is directed, not as before, against the conception of ideas of magnitude, but those of number, although, of course, the geometrical axioms also must be divested of their synthetic character, if the principle is to be consistently carried out. The latest notable advocate of this view, R. Zimmermann,[13] has written an essay 'On Kant's Mathematical Prejudice and its Consequences.' It would, indeed, be better to talk of Leibniz's mathematical prejudice, meaning by this the doctrine that from any simple propositions a whole science full of unforeseen results in detail can be developed by analysis! The strict deductions of Euklid especially have resulted in the obscuration of the synthetic factor in geometry by mere syllogising. Here we were supposed to have a science that develops all its results from the simplest beginnings merely by the aid of the principle of contradiction. To this error was due the prejudice that such a creation from nothing is possible by the mere magic of formal logic; for, in fact, what is wanted

[13] Sitzungsber. .der Wiener Akademie, phil.-hist. Klasse, 67 Bd. 1871, S. 7 ff.

is a standpoint that admits the *a priori*, but must gain all its results analytically, and that is much concerned either to dispense with the axioms altogether or to resolve them into identical propositions.[14]

All such attempts bring us back at last to certain general notions of the nature of space, and these notions are, without the corresponding intuition, empty words. But that it is the general nature of space, as it is known in intuition, out of which the axioms flow, by no means refutes Kant's doctrine, but rather confirms and extends it. It is, moreover, a great mistake to suppose that the few principles that are premised as axioms, or even as a description of the general nature of space, exhaust the synthetic portions of geometry. Every construction that is employed for the purpose of a demonstration is of a synthetic nature; and it is at the same time quite wrong to admit with Ueberweg the synthetic nature of these factors, but to deny them all importance for the proof.[15] Ueberweg thinks that to the discoverer of mathematical principles mathematical 'tact' and an 'eye' for constructions may, indeed, be of special importance, but that for the scientific rigour of development this geometrical 'eye' possesses no more importance than tact in the selection of

---

[14] And therefore even Leibniz occupied himself with the reduction of atoms to certain general principles. Comp. his Essay 'In Euklidis πρῶτα,' in Leibn. Math. Schriften, hg. v. Gerhardt, 2 Abth. 1 Bd., quoted in Ueberweg's quite relevant review of Delboeuf's 'Prolégomènes philosophiques de la géométrie,' Liége, 1860, in the 37th vol. of the 'Zeitschr. f. Philos. u. phil. Kritik.' Ueberweg tries here, as he had tried before in 1851 (Leipziger Archiv für Philol. u. Pädog., Bd. vii. 1), in an essay on the Principles of Geometry, to show that the apodeictic character of mathematics is quite consistent with its origin from empirically acquired axioms. The attempts of Ueberweg,

as well as those of Delboeuf and others, show that we may perhaps develop the general properties of space more rationally than was the case with Euklid, but that it is impossible to reduce them to ideas that would be intelligible without intuition.

[15] Ueberweg's 'System of Logic,' E. T., p. 346: "The force of the proof does not lie in the construction, but in the application, which it renders possible, of propositions previously proved, and, in the last instance, of axioms and definitions to the proposition to be proved, and this application is in its essence a syllogistic procedure. The construction is only the way of learning, not the way of knowing; the scaffolding, not the foundation."

appropriate premises in other deductions. But this is entirely to pass over the decisive point, namely, that we must *see* the construction, or represent it to ourselves in imagination, in order to conceive its possibility at all. This indispensableness of intuition extends, in fact, to the definitions, which here are by no means always purely analytical propositions. When, for instance, we define a plane surface as a superficies (Legendre), in which the straight line between any two points in it lies wholly in that superficies, we do not even know without the aid of intuition that we can unite all the points in a superficies by straight lines at all. We may try to combine syllogistically the bare definition of a superficies with the definition of a straight line without using any kind of intuition to help us; we shall not attain our end. Let us further consider any of the numerous demonstrations in which a property of the figures is demonstrated by superposition, in order to effect our object by an argument *ad absurdum*. Here we have to do, not, as Ueberweg thinks, merely with the choice of premisses, in order to effect our demonstration by the pure use of syllogism. We shall always make one of the premisses possible at all only by the help of an intuition—by covering with one figure the other! It does not, therefore, influence the main question whether, with Zimmermann, we declare the proposition that the straight line is the shortest way between two points to be analytic. This happens to be the very instance chosen by Kant to show the opposite. Kant finds nothing in his definition of the straight line out of which to get the notion of shortest distance.[16] Conceding that we can bring this idea into the definition, and thus make the proposition analytical, then there immediately emerge again other predications as to the nature of the straight line, which are, indeed, very 'evident,' but

[16] The proposition declared by Zimmermann (*loc. cit.*, S. 18) to be "thoroughly analytical" is circumstantially demonstrated by Ueberweg in the essay of 1851, quoted in Note 14: two different ways of getting free from the synthesis *a priori!*

only on the basis of intuition. Legendre, who also endeavoured to reduce the definitions as much as possible, has chosen such a definition ; but immediately after it follows the addition : it is evident that if two portions of two straight lines coincide, these coincide also in their whole extent. But whence comes the evidence ? From intuition !

No one, in fact, has yet succeeded, even in appearance or as an experiment, in entirely discarding the synthetic element from geometry ; and Ueberweg, who has given unusual attention to this subject, saw himself therefore forced to the standpoint of Mill, who admits the synthetic element in geometry, but explains it from experience. Beneke, to whom Ueberweg, next to Mill, most attached himself, explains the universality of the synthetic geometrical propositions by the rapid comparison of an infinite number of cases. Because of the constant relation in which the different figures stand to one another (*e.g.*, an angle in a triangle varying through all degrees from o up to two right angles), this glance occupies an almost inappreciable time. No doubt, psychologically considered, there is some truth in this. But it will be gathered from the remarks on the first objection that it is a mere misunderstanding of the Kantian doctrine to suppose that it is thereby refuted.

Much stronger, as we have said, is the attack upon the synthetic nature of arithmetical propositions. Zimmermann maintains that the judgment $7 + 5 = 12$, which Kant calls synthetical, is not only analytical, but even identical. He will admit that in order to combine 7 and 5 we must go beyond the notion of 7, as well as beyond that of 5, but we do not as yet receive the judgment, but merely the notion of the subject $7 + 5$. But with this the predicate 12 is absolutely identical.

Pity that Zimmermann is not right ! The teachers in our national schools could then save themselves the trouble of teaching Addition. When they had taught Numeration all would be done.   As soon as the child had acquired on its fingers or the board an intuition of 5 or of 7, and had besides learned that the number which follows 11 is called 12, it must at once be clear to him than 7 and 5 make 12, for the notions are identical!   Against this there is a plausible objection, viz., that it is not enough to know that 11 and 1 are 12 in order to have the notion of 12.   This notion would include in itself, in its complete development, the knowledge of all its modes of origin from $11 + 1$, $10 + 2$, $9 + 3$, &c.   This requirement may have a meaning for the mathematician, who develops the theory of numbers from an abstract principle, although we see that the same requirement is applicable to the origin of the 12 from its factors and any other kind of operation.   Moreover, we might conceive a method of teaching arithmetic that should, at least, work through all the modes of origin, from the four rules in every single number proceeding from 1, on the same principle that we now go through these operations within the limit of 1 to 100 before proceeding to the larger numbers.   In that case Numeration, Addition, Subtraction, Multiplication, and Division would be learned at the same time, and thus from the first a more adequate notion of figures would be acquired.   As opposed to such possibilities, however, the proposition of Kant is justified by the simple fact that we do not proceed in this manner; [17]

---

[17] How little Kant here deserves the reproach of superficiality, covertly insinuated in Zimmermann's account of his doctrine, may be shown by the single observation, not noticed by Zimmermann, in which Kant guards against the confusion of the *combination* of 7 and 5 with the *addition* of them. There is, in fact, already contained in the notion of addition the adding of the units of the five to the series of those of the seven; so that, in fact, beginning with 8, we make five additions of one each time to the series of numbers, just the problem that children at school have painfully to learn when they have already learned to count. By "union of $7 + 5$," then, Kant means, not that union which arises by going back to the sum of the units and counting them anew, but merely the combination of the already counted group 7 with the also counted group 5. More than this does not lie in the notion of union, nor in the original force of the sign +. But as we use this at the same time as sign of the operation of addition, Kant saw himself obliged expressly to guard against the misapprehension into which Zimmermann has fallen. Comp. Krit.

that as a matter of fact we prefer first to form the ideas of number, and then afterwards learn as something new what greater number arises if I resolve two smaller numbers into their units, and begin again to count them altogether.

It might still be objected that the learning of Addition is only an exercise in the use of words and signs to express a given number in the simplest way; that the mere idea of the number 12 is perfectly given by every single

---

d. r. Vern. Elementarl., 2 Th., 1 Abth., 2 B., 2 Hptst., 3 Abschn., Hartenst. iv. 157, E. T. Meiklejohn, p. 124.

If we say that Kant's principle would be justified by the mere fact that "we do not usually proceed so," we apply also, it is true, that the difference between analytic and synthetic judgments is merely *relative*, and so that the same judgment, according to the mental constitution and the ideas of the thinking subject, may be analytic or synthetic. Yet by no scientific treatment of the idea of number can we do away with the synthetic element of arithmetic; we can only bring it to another place, and more or less reduce it. So far, at all events, Kant is wrong in believing that there are innumerable such synthetic propositions in arithmetic (which therefore he calls not axioms but number formulæ). Their number depends rather from the system of numeration, since the synthesis of three tens and two tens is precisely the same function as the synthesis of three pebbles and two pebbles. Kant, indeed, maintained (Introd. to 2d ed., v. 1) that in the case of *larger* numbers their synthetic nature becomes specially prominent, as here we like to turn and vary the ideas as we will; without calling in intuition we should never find the sum by the mere dissection of the ideas. To this doctrine Hankel (Vorles. über die complexen Zahlen, 1 Thl., Leipz., 1867, S. 53), opposes the exact opposite. On our five fingers we may very well show $2.2 = 4$, but it would be quite impossible to prove in that way $1000.1000 = 1,000,000$. The latter view is undoubtedly correct, while as to the negative portion of Kant's assertion, it very much depends upon what we mean by the idea of a number. In reality operations with larger numbers are deduced neither directly from the idea nor directly from intuition, but are carried on throughout upon that system of subdivision into partial operations which is at the foundation of the systems of number, and which in the Arabic system of ciphers also has found its completely corresponding expression in writing. In ordinary life we confine ourselves almost wholly to the intuition of these *signs*, and that in the successive stages of the partial operations. That the intuition of the sign also is an intuition that can represent the intuition of *things* has been very well shown by Mill (Logic, B. ii. c. vi. § 2). The succession of partial operations we usually take up quite mechanically, but the rules of this mechanism are reduced scientifically by the aid of the *a priori* (according to Mill the 'inductive') principle, that equals added to equals make equals. With the aid of the same principle science can reduce the synthetic elements of arithmetic to a minimum, but can never entirely get

mode of its origin, whether it be by $1 + 1 + 1$, &c., or $6 + 5$, or perhaps by $9 + 3$. Even this will not hold; for we receive every idea of number originally as the sensuously determined picture of a group of objects, whether they are only our fingers or the knobs and balls of a calculating machine. Here we may adduce the modes and expressions used in counting by primitive peoples and early culture as satisfactory evidence for the synthetic nature of

---

rid of them; and it holds, in fact, here too, as in Geometry, that not only in the first rudiments, but also in the progress of the science from time to time (here in this case of the transition to a new kind of operations) we cannot dispense with synthetic principles, acquired by the aid of intuition.   Let me also add here that Sigwart too, in his Logic (Tübingen, 1873), too late to be noticed in the text, insists on the *relativity* of the distinction between Kant's analytic and synthetic judgments (S. 106 f.). Moreover, that the whole distinction, from a logical standpoint, is of very doubtful value, may be conceded without prejudice to the object served by the distinction in the 'Critick.' But when Sigwart maintains that all individual judgments of perception, as 'this rose is yellow,' 'this fluid is sour,' are analytic, then the definition of the analytical that underlies this view is of still more doubtful value than that of Kant. The judgment, 'this fluid is sour,' cannot be separated from the synthesis of ideas which Sigwart (S. 110) makes to precede as a separate act, without losing all definite signification. The judgment, 'this rose is yellow,' is logically almost as equivocal as the circumstances under which we can suppose it to be spoken. Even the judgment, 'the accused is guilty,' in the mouth of the witness (S. 103 Anm.) cannot be regarded as analytic, since the idea of the 'accused' is given to the speaker by the court, and he does not enounce his proposition in order to analyse this idea for himself, but in order to produce the synthesis of the ideas of the subject and the predicate in the judges or jury. It will, indeed, be quite useless to attempt to classify the infinite variety of the psychological contents of one and the same expression of language under other than merely relatively valid concepts. For the appreciation of the Kantian division, and the consequences based upon it, the question is unimportant, as Kant beyond doubt places the genesis of the judgment of experience in the moment of perception, even though the *spoken* judgment follows a moment later. So it is also in the judgment $7 + 5 = 12$, which, according to Kant, we must regard as arising in the moment that the addition of the units reaches 12, and the synthesis (recognised by Sigwart also as necessary) of the ideas is thus completed; while, on the contrary, Sigwart makes this psychical act of the synthesis of the ideas precede, and then makes an (according to *his* definition, S. 101) analytic judgment (*i.e.*, one resolving the synthesis of ideas that has been reached once more into subject and predicate) follow a separate act. Even if we adopt Sigwart's definition, the essential part of Kant's assertion therefore remains, and must then only be referred no longer to the judgment, but to the psychical act of synthesis in the perception that makes the judgment possible.

ideas of number. And we find everywhere at the foundation the sensuous picture of the group or of the arrangement of the fingers used to represent the number.[18] As
soon, moreover, as we start with Mill from the principle
that all numbers are "numbers of something," and that
the objects, the number of which is in question, produce
by their quantity a definite impression upon the senses,
we cannot doubt the synthetic nature of an operation
that combines, whether in reality or in idea, two such
groups of similar objects. And therefore, true to his principle, Mill shows too that it is a fact attained by experience that three objects arranged in a particular form still
make the same total, if we put one of them a little on one
side, so that now the total appears divided into two portions, as $2 + 1$.[19] How little Kant rejects this kind of "experience" is shown by the fact that, for the demonstration
of the proposition $7 + 5 = 12$, he uses *intuition* through the
five fingers, or even through points. Kant has only looked
somewhat deeper into the "remarkable peculiarity," noted
by Mill also, of propositions concerning numbers, "that

[18] Comp. Tylor, 'Primitive Culture,'
ch. vii., 'The Art of Counting.' It
is here shown that men counted on
their fingers before they invented
words for the numbers. Thus an
Indian tribe on the Orinoco indicates
the number 5 by 'a whole hand;' 6
is expressed by a term which means
'one of the other hand;' for 10 they
say 'both hands.' Then comes the
toes: so that 'a whole foot' means
15, and 'one to the other foot' 16;
'one Indian,' 20; 'one to the hands
of the other Indian,' 21, and so on.
A translation of the Bible into a
Melanesian language renders the number 38 (John v. 5) by 'one man and
both sides five and three.' How
easily the signs and expressions thus
arising fuse with the idea of the thing
counted is shown especially by a
striking grammatical construction in
the Zulu language. Here the word
'forefinger.' or 'pointer' (of the
second hand, in which counting begins with the thumb), makes the
number 7. Consequently the sentence, 'there were seven horses,'
is expressed by 'the horses have
pointed.' When then, later, numerals
were invented independently of finger-
counting, the number was expressed
by qualities of the objects from which
the name was borrowed; *e.g.*, 'moon,'
or 'earth' (because there is only 1) for
1, 'eye,' 'wing,' 'arm,' for 2. Characteristic, again, is a way of counting
among the Letts: "They throw crabs
and little fish, three at a time, in
counting them, and therefore the
word *mettens*, 'a throw,' has come
to mean 3; while flounders being
fastened in lots of thirty, the word
kahlis, or 'cord,' becomes a term to
express this number" (i., p. 233).
[19] Comp. Mill, System of Logic.
B. ii. c. vi. § 2; and iii. xxiv. 5.

they are propositions concerning all things whatever, all objects, all existences of every kind, known to our experience," and that demonstration as to a single kind of objects is enough to convince us that it must be so with every possible kind of object. This, however, belongs to the previous objection: here we are concerned only with the synthetic nature of ideas of number, and here Mill seems in essentials to be of one mind with Kant.[20]

[20] We ought to notice here the effort of the mathematicians to free themselves entirely from the "limits of intuition," and to establish, apparently, a purely intellectual, intuitionless mathematic. So long as these efforts confine themselves to the sphere of the mathematical specialist, and avoid coming to any settlement with philosophical questions, it is not easy to know how far we have to face a conscious opposition to the Kantian view, or merely another mode of expression. In a certain sense, indeed, ordinary analytical geometry emancipates itself from intuition—that is, it sets in the place of geometrical intuition the incomparably simpler intuition of arithmetical and algebraical relations of magnitude. Recently, however, the thing has been carried much further, and the boundary between mere technical and mathematical assumptions and philosophical assertions seems to have been often passed, without any thorough understanding having been come to as to the point in question. Thus Hankel especially, in the work quoted in Note 17, has several times openly asserted that his "general doctrine of forms" is to set forth a mathematic purely intellectual, and freed from all intuition, "in which not quantities or their pictures, figures, are connected, but intellectual objects, things of thought, to which actual objects or the relations of each *may*, but not *must*, correspond." The universal formal relations, that form the subject of this mathematic, he calls also 'transcendental' or 'potential,' in so far as they involve the possibility of actual relations (i. S. 9 f.). Hankel protests expressly against this purely formal mathematic being regarded merely as a generalisation of ordinary arithmetic: it is "an entirely new science," the rules of which are "not proved, but only exemplified," by the ordinary arithmetic. But the 'exemplification' is just the intuitional proof for the synthetic basis of this new science, which can then, indeed, carry out the deductive method by means of its things of thought, just as algebra does by means of universal signs of number, and arithmetic by means of actual figures. In fact, one need with Hankel, as with Grassmann, the true inventor of this universal theory of form (comp. his thoroughly philosophical 'Lineale Ausdehnungslehre,' Leipz., 1844, and the larger and more strictly mathematical 'Ausdehnungslehre,' Berl., 1862), only examine more closely any one of the universal notions employed in order to discover at once the factor of intuition. How, for instance, can we know that words like 'connection,' 'permutation,' &c., mean anything unless we call in the help of the intuition of connected and permuted objects, even if there be only the letters *a*, *b*, and *b*, *a*? Something, too, may well depend upon this, that the "purely formal mathematic" has, in fact, been developed through the principle of generalisation, like the majority of the most

What the one-sided Empiricists do not observe is, that experience is no open door through which external things, as they are, can wander in to us, but a process by which the appearance of things arises within us. That in this process all the properties of these 'things' come from without, and the man who receives them has nothing to do, contradicts all the analogy of nature in the case of any development of a new thing from the co-operation of two others. Though the 'Critick of Pure Reason' may go much beyond the picture of a combination of two forces in a resultant third force, yet there can be no doubt that this picture may serve to give us a first idea of the matter. That *our* things are different from things *in themselves* may be made plain to us, therefore, even by the simple opposition between a tone and the vibrations of the string that occasions it. Inquiry recognises, indeed, yet other phenomena in these vibrations, and at length, attaining its goal, removes the 'thing in itself' into the unattainable sphere of a mere thing of thought; but the justification of criticism and the meaning of its first preparatory steps we may very well realise to ourselves through this opposition between the tone and what occasions it from without. What in us, whether we conceive it physiologically or psychologically, makes the vibration of the string become a tone is the *a priori* in this event of experience. If we had no sense but hearing, then all experience would consist of sounds; and however much all the rest of knowledge might then follow from experience, yet the nature of this experi-

---

important advances made by mathematic in modern times. It loses no importance on this account; and we must not consider it impossible that, by the same principle and in the same path, starting from mathematic, a new light may be won for logic also. We shall mention again below the inquiries of Riemann and Helmholtz, which border on the transcental (in a philosophical sense). Here let us only observe that, as against them, J. C. Becker has maintained the importance of intuition in the Kantian sense, with thorough knowledge of the subject, in his 'Abhandlungen aus dem Grenzgebiete für Mathematik u. der Philosophie,' Zurich, 1870, and in the 'Zeitschr. für Mathem. u. Physik,' u. 17 Jahrg., S. 314 ff.; 'Ueber die neuesten Untersuchungen in Betreff unserer Anschauungen vom Raume.'

ence would be entirely determined by the nature of our hearing, and we could say, not with probability, but with demonstrative certainty, that all phenomena must consist of sound. We must not overlook, therefore, that the origin of experience differs entirely from a conclusion from experience. The fact that we have experience at all is, however, determined by the organisation of our thinking,[21] and this organisation exists *before experience.* It leads us to distinguish individual marks in things, and to conceive in succession what is in nature inseparably fused and simultaneous, and to lay down this conception in propositions with subject and predicate. This is all not only *before* experience, but it is the condition of experience. Nothing else than to seek out these first conditions of all experience in thinking and in sense is the immediate aim of the ' Critick of Pure Reason.' Kant showed first of all, in the instance of mathematics, that our thought is actually in possession of certain knowledge *a priori*, and that even the common understanding is never without such know-

[21] In the first edition the phrase here was 'faculty of thought' (Denk-vermögens), when this expression was used in that generality with which Kant frequently speaks of the faculties of the soul ; so that, without any reference to a particular psychological theory, the mere possibility of the function in question is understood by it. We have preferred to remove even this reminiscence of the Scholastic view of the psychological. For the rest, we may observe here that the well-known polemic of Herbart against the theory of the faculties of the soul only touches a certain popular, although widely - spread, modification of it. The true scholastic theory was never any other than this, that in all psychical acts the same one and only soul is engaged, and that the 'faculty' is not a separate organ, but only the (objectively conceived) possibility of this particular activity. Thus the matter still stands with Wolff, as soon as we keep to his definitions, and not to the explanations which are very often based upon the popular notion of faculties, on the analogy of bodily organs. Kant went still further in his abstraction from the psychological, since he could not, of course, presuppose any one unified soul-essence at all. With him, therefore, the faculty of the soul is throughout merely the possibility of the function of an unknown subject, and he obviously only clung to the theory of faculties because he believed that in it he really possessed a tabular view and classification of phenomena that might be of use. The consequences of this classification, at the same time, carried him often far from his goal. Why we have not retained the by no means strictly Kantian expression, 'organisation,' or its synonym, 'disposition,' will be explained further on.

ledge. Proceeding from this, he seeks to show that not only in mathematics, but in every act of knowledge, *a priori* elements co-operate, which throughout condition our experience.

But how are these elements to be discovered ? Here is a dark point in the Kantian system, which the most careful inquiry into the exact meaning of the great thinker will hardly ever be able to dispose of. At the same time, we may with the utmost certainty refute a widely spread misapprehension in connection with this question. The following dilemma has been thought justifiable : either the *a priori* elements of thought are themselves deduced from an *a priori* valid principle, or they are sought out empirically. Such a principle is not to be found in Kant, and the empirical process can afford no strictly necessary results ; and hence the whole transcendental philosophy of Kant is in the most favourable view nothing but a section of empirical psychology. It has even been maintained that apodeictically valid propositions must also be deduced apodeictically, and therefore from an *a priori* valid principle.[22] As though the question were to prove these propositions ! Kant is only concerned to *discover* them, and for this he has no other clue than the question, What must I

---

[22] So especially Kuno Fischer and Zimmermann, partly agreeing with him, in the essay mentioned above (Note 13), on 'Kant's Mathematical Prejudice,' S. 24-28. J. B. Meyer, in 'Kant's Psychologie,' S. 129 ff., has very well described the discovery of the *a priori* by means of steadfast reflection. Comp. also Cohen, 'Kant's Theorie der Erfahrung,' S. 105-107. Cohen condemns the proposition of J. B. Meyer : "On this point Kant has never expressed himself clearly, that we do not acquire the *a priori* forms of experience, but yet do attain the consciousness of this possession by reflection upon experience." In this form the objection to Kant seems, of course, unjustifiable ; but we must, on the other hand, insist that Kant has not sufficiently considered that reflection or experience is also an inductive process, and cannot be anything else. The universality and necessity of mathematical principles is, it is true, not gathered from experience (of mathematical objects), but discovered by reflection. This reflection, however, cannot take place at all without experience—not of the objects of mathematics, but of mathematic as object. But from this it follows that the pretension to the entire discovery of everything *a priori* is untenable ; and Kant makes this pretension, supporting himself, of course, not upon an *a priori* deduction of the *a priori*, but upon a supposed indisputable classification of what is given in logic and psychology.

presuppose in order to explain the fact of experience? The psychological side of the question is not only not the chief point with him, but he obviously tries to avoid it, since he puts his question so generally that the answer is equally consistent with the most various psychological theories.[23]   Deduction from a metaphysical principle, such as was undertaken by his successors from Fichte on, could be no part of Kant's purpose, if only because this would have already presupposed the metaphysical method, the rights and the limits of which he proposes to investigate. There thus remained to him only the mode of ordinary reflection, methodical indeed, but starting from facts. That Kant consciously trod this path seems sufficiently proved, but so much is clear that he must have deceived himself as to the consequences of this procedure; otherwise he could not have so sharply emphasised the absolute sureness of his procedure, and so contemptuously rejected all mere probability, as he has repeatedly done.[24]   This was

[23] The greatest portion of all the obscurities of the 'Critick' flow from the single circumstance that Kant undertakes what is, on the whole, a psychological investigation without any special psychological presuppositions. What seems to the beginner an often uselessly involved expression has its reason always in this fact, that Kant endeavours to carry on his inquiry into the necessary conditions of all experience with such generality, that it fits equally well with any assumption as to the transcendental nature of the soul, or, more correctly, without presupposing anything whatever as to the nature of the soul, nay, without even assuming a soul at all as a separate entity independent of the body.

[24] In the preface to the first edition (1781) Kant says: "As regards certitude, I have fully convinced myself that in this sphere of thought opinion is perfectly inadmissible, and that everything that bears the least semblance of an hypothesis must be ex-

cluded, as of no value in such discussions.   For it is a necessary condition of every cognition that is to be established upon *a priori* grounds that it shall be held to be absolutely necessary; much more is this the case with an attempt to determine all pure *a priori* cognition, and to furnish the standard—and consequently an example—of all apodcictic (philosophical) certitude." This *rôle* might very well be applied in favour of the (otherwise quite unreliable) interpretation of Kuno Fischer (comp. Note 22), if it were not that we can see from the same preface that Kant had then in view only the general deduction of the categories as a presupposition of all experience (S. 92 ff. of the first edition), and that, on the other hand, he was entangled in the prejudice that "the common logic" supplied an example that "all its simple actions may be fully and systematically enumerated," so that the supposed certitude here in the discovery of the complete table of categories is not the

an effect of the metaphysical school in which Kant had grown up, and the over-estimate of the value of the preparations that he thought he would find for his purpose, especially in the traditional logic, seems to have strengthened him in it. He failed to see that his method for the discovery of the *a priori* in reality could be nothing but the method of induction.

It may, indeed, seem very obvious that the rudiments of our knowledge *a priori* must be also discovered *a priori* by pure deduction from necessary concepts; and yet this assumption is erroneous. We must distinguish between a necessary proposition and the proof of a necessary proposition. Nothing is more easily conceivable than that the *a priori* propositions are only to be discovered by the road of experience; indeed, that the border between really necessary knowledge and between mere assumptions from which we might with increasing experience emancipate ourselves is a vanishing one. As in the case of the nebulæ of the starry heaven there is the utmost probability that some of them really consist of nebulous masses, while the telescope resolves them, one after the other, into a cluster of single stars: so there is nothing to be said against it

certitude of a deduction from principles *a priori*, but the certitude of a complete view of what is supposed to be given. Even the strong passage in the 'Prolegomena,' 1783, S. 195 ff., where Kant deprecates "trifling about probability and conjecture," and declares that " Everything that is to be cognised *a priori* is thereby announced as apodeictically certain, and must therefore be proved in this way," does not mean that even the existence of such knowledge must be deduced from a principle *a priori*. The content rather of this knowledge is *a priori* certain; but its existence, according to Kant, is inferred by sure inferences, according to the law of contradiction from an inwardly perceived fact. We must, moreover, expressly observe here, that this explanation is only abstracted from Kant's actual procedure, and that we have, in fact, no unequivocal proof that Kant was quite clear as to the methodical foundations of his great undertaking. It is rather not at all improbable that Kant in this point had not yet got sufficiently beyond the views of his 1763 essay, 'Ueber die Evidenz in Metaphysischen Wissenschaften,' although they are entirely incompatible with the standpoint of the 'Critick.' If we have, therefore, in this point also, from a balance of reasons, modified the view taken in our first edition of Kant's procedure, yet we cannot but point out that passages like those above quoted, and many similar ones, must have thrown a strong weight into the opposite scale.

when we, in a long series of Kant's fundamental ideas and
highest principles, destroy the appearance of *a priori* knowledge, and nevertheless hold fast to this, that there are
actually fundamental ideas and principles, which are present in our mind before all experience, and by which even
experience is psychologically obliged to order itself. Mill has
at all events the merit of having shown that a great number
of propositions have been looked upon as *a priori* that have
later turned out to be false. Defective as his attempt is
to derive mathematical principles from experience, that
service remains undiminished. It is certain that the consciousness of the universality and necessity of a proposition can deceive; only, of course, this does not prove that
such propositions are then always derived only from experience. Mill himself talks, although not quite in the
right sense, of errors *a priori;* and there are, in fact, many
of them. It is with *erroneous a priori* knowledge not
otherwise than with *a priori* knowledge *generally.* It is
for the most part not an unconsciously acquired result of
experience, but a proposition whose necessity is given
before any experience by the physico-psychological
organisation[25] of man, and which therefore appears imme-

[25] The expression 'the physico-
psychical organisation' is perhaps
not happily chosen; but it is an attempt to indicate the idea that the
physical organisation, as *phenomenon*,
is at the same time the psychical
one. This goes, indeed, beyond Kant,
but not so far as might at first sight
be supposed, and in a point that can
be defended; while, at the same
time, the modification gives a very
intelligible and easily conceivable
notion, instead of the scarcely com-
prehensible Kantian idea of transcendental presuppositions of experience.
The whole difference lies in this, that
Kant, for the wholly incomprehensible notion that lies in the thing-in-
itself at the bottom of the synthetic
judgment *a priori*, substitutes the
notions as something unattainable by
us, and that he speaks of these notions, the categories, as if they were
the *origin* of the *a priori,* though
they are at most only its simplest expression. If we wish to denote the
true cause of the *a priori,* we cannot
speak at all of the 'thing-in-itself,'
for the idea of the cause does not
reach to this (or, what is the same
thing, a judgment in relation to this
has no other significance than as a
rounding off of our circle of ideas).
For the 'thing-in-itself' we must
substitute the phenomenon. Even the
notion is only phenomenon; but when
we put it in the place of the *cause of
the notion,* or regard it as it were
within the phenomenal as ultimate
cause, we fall into a Platonism which
is a much more dangerous deviation
from the critical principles than the

diately upon the earliest experience, without the intervention of induction; which nevertheless, with the same necessity, by means of deeper-lying *a priori* notions, is upset as soon as a certain series of experiences has given the preponderance to these deeper-lying notions.

The metaphysician, then, must be able to distinguish the *a priori* ideas that are permanent and essentially rooted in human nature from those that are perishable, and correspond only to a particular stage of development, although both kinds of *a priori* knowledge are bound up in the same way with the consciousness of necessity. For this, however, he cannot employ again an *a priori* principle, and therefore also not the so-called pure thought, just because it is doubtful whether the foundations of this have permanent worth or not. We are therefore confined in the searching and testing of the universal propositions which do not arise

choice of the expression, 'organisation.' In a word, by the absolute and obviously well-considered rejection of the notion of organisation, that must have been very near to him, Kant avoids the mere appearance of Materialism, to fall a prey to an Idealism that he ha shimself elsewhere rejected. If we attempt to escape this dilemma, the whole 'Critick of Reason' resolves itself into a mere tautology, to the effect that the synthesis *a priori* has its. cause in the synthesis *a priori*. If we admit, on the other hand, the notion of organisation, not only does the tautology disappear (which, however, affords the simplest, though the most incorrect, interpretation of the 'Critick of Reason'), but also the obligation to hypostasise the categories Platonically. In return, as we have said, there remains the *appearance* of Materialism; but this appearance every consequent interpretation of the theoretical part of the Kantian philosophy must take upon itself.

Where the difficulties lay, and how near the notion of organisation must have been to the transcendental inquiry, is best shown by Reinhold's 'Theorie des menschl. Vorstellungs-vermögens' (Prag u. Jena, 1789), as is well known, an attempt to solve the problem of the 'Critick' in a new way. Here the 'Theorie des Vorstellungsvermögens überhaupt' begins at once with a definition of it by the 'conditions' of ideation; in this avoidance of all special metaphysical and psychological—but also in the inclination to tautology—it is genuinely Kantian. There ensues a long exposition (S. 195-199), turning chiefly upon an attempt to show that we may not introduce the organisation into the explanation of the faculty of ideation, because philosophers are not agreed whether this faculty is based in mere organisation (Materialists), or in a simple substance without any organisation, or in some kind of co-operation of these factors. We see, then, clearly that what is here spoken of is the organisation as thing-in-itself, as otherwise it could not be placed in a line with the pure transcendental monads and other inventions of metaphysic. If, on the other hand, we take the organisation from experience merely to the ordinary means of science; we can only set up probable propositions, whether the ideas and forms of thought that we must now, without any proof, assume as true, arise from the permanent nature of man or not; whether, in other words, they are the true root-ideas of all human knowledge, or whether they will turn out some day to be mere " delusions *a priori.*"

Let us go back now to Kant's decisive question, How are synthetic judgments *a priori* possible ? and the answer is, Because in all knowledge is contained a factor which springs not from external influences, but from the nature of the knowing subject, and which for this very reason is not accidental, like external impressions, but necessary, and is constant in all our experience.   It is, then, our business to discover this factor, and Kant hopes to

as phenomenon, and therefore with the proviso that it may be phenomenon of an unknown thing-in-itself, not only does the Materialism disappear, but also all right ceases to co-ordinate this view with the inventions of metaphysicians. These, then, may continue to assume that at the bottom of this organisation there is nothing further (Materialism), or the activity of a monad (Leibnizian Idealism), or something absolutely unknown (Criticism). As phenomenon, however, the organisation is *given,* while everything else is but cobwebs of the brain. But, for this very reason, it seems to me a necessity to bring this one thing that is given, in which all the peculiarities of human nature, so far as we know them, run on the thread of causal relation, into connection also with the faculty of ideation, or with the cause of the synthesis *a priori.* We must not then, however, as Otto Liebmann, for instance, does, talk of the organisation of the *mind,* for this is transcendental, and therefore co-ordinated with other transcendental assumptions. We must rather understand by organisation simply, or physico-psychical organisation, what to our external sense appears to be that part of the physical organisation which stands in the most immediate causal relation with the psychical functions, while we may hypothetically assume that at the basis of this phenomenon there lies a purely spiritual relation of the things in themselves, or even the activity of a spiritual substance. Rightly to appreciate Kant's attitude to this conception of the cause of the *a priori,* we must consider, besides many equally important but less distinct passages, especially the conclusion of the ' Critick ' of the Second Paralogism of the Transcendental Psychology, in the first edition (1781), S. 359 u. f.   "In this way, what in one respect is called corporeal would in the other be at the same time a thinking being, whose thoughts indeed we cannot, but the signs of them as phenomenon we can, perceive. Thereby would fall away the expression that only souls (as particular kinds of substances) think ; we should rather have to say, as we commonly do, that men think, *i.e.,* that that which, as external phenomenon, is extended, is internally (in itself) a subject which is not compound but simple, and thinks."

attain his object by regarding one by one the chief functions of the mind in cognition, without troubling himself
with their psychological connection, in order to see what
a priori elements occur in them. For this purpose he assumes two main sources of human knowledge—sense and
understanding. With profound insight he observes that
both perhaps spring from a common, unknown root. This
conjecture may now be considered as already confirmed;
not by Herbart's psychology nor Hegel's ' phenomenology
of spirit,' but by certain experiments in the physiology of
the sense-organs which irrefutably prove that, even in the
apparently quite immediate sense-impressions, processes
co-operate which, through the elimination or completion of
certain logical connecting links, strikingly correspond to
the conclusions, true or false, of conscious thought.

Kant has not rightly estimated the value of the idea
that sense and understanding. perhaps spring from a common root, for the purposes of his ' Critick of Pure Reason,'
although the question must have presented itself whether
the true solution of the transcendental problem is not to
be sought precisely in the unity of sense and thought.
He teaches, indeed, also that both factors must co-operate
in knowledge, but even in the way of conceiving this
co-operation he betrays a considerable remnant of that
Platonising doctrine of a pure thought, free from all
elements of sense, which ran through the whole traditional
metaphysic, and at last found an expression that leavens
the whole system of Leibniz, and dominates the views of
the school of Wolff. According to Leibniz, only pure reflection is able to conceive things clearly and in their essence,
while the knowledge of the senses is not an equally
valid source of knowledge of another kind, but something
absolutely inferior; it is confused knowledge, and therefore an obscure and troubled analogon of that which pure
thought furnishes in the highest perfection. What Kant
establishes by way of reform against radically false views
is amongst his best work; what he retains of the old

modes of thought belongs to the worst weaknesses of his system.

His merit is that he has raised sense to the level of a source of knowledge equally valid as understanding; his weakness, that he allowed to continue at all an understanding free from all influence of the senses. Excellent is his doctrine that all thought must ultimately fall back upon intuition, that without intuition no object of our knowledge can be given us at all; inadequate, on the other hand, is the view that, in fact, mere intuition, without any co-operation of thought, affords no knowledge at all, while mere thought, without intuition, still leaves *the form* of thought.[26]

His method of discovering by the isolation of sense what *a priori* elements are contained in it may, at all events, awake justifiable hesitation, because it rests upon a fiction whose methodical success there is nothing to guarantee. In no act of knowledge can isolated sense be observed, as it were, in its function. Kant, however, assumes that this may happen, and the result of this assumption is the prin-

---

[26] It is of course still a problem of the future to show that there is no such thing as ' pure thought ' in the sense of the metaphysicians, from whom Kant in this point cannot be excepted. Kant leaves the senses purely passive; accordingly the active understanding, in order to produce merely a picture in space of sensuous objects, must create the unity of the manifold. In this absolutely necessary and subjective act of synthesis, however, there is involved nothing of what we otherwise call ' understanding.' Only on the artificially imported supposition that all spontaneity belongs to ' thought,' all receptivity to sense, can the synthesis of *impressions to things* be at all connected with the understanding. When we find, however, that the synthesis of the impressions in the thing presupposes the category of substance, we must ask, As category? and the answer can only be in the negative. Rather is the sensuous synthesis of the impressions the foundation out of which a category of substance is first developed. A complete proof of the original sensuousness of all thought would here lead us too far. Let it only be remarked, that even the apodeictic character of logic must be referred entirely to sense-pictures of ideas, and that the much despised asses' bridges of logical circles (or lines, angles, &c.), far from being a merely didactic importation (Nebenwerk), rather contain in themselves the foundation of the apodeictic character of logical rules. The proof of this I have been in the habit of giving in my Logic Lectures for some years, and hope, if I am permitted to work some years longer, to be able to submit it to a wider audience.

ciple that the *a priori* element in intuition must be the form of the phenomena, the matter of which is given by sensation. This necessary and universal form of all phenomena, however, is for the external sense Space, for the internal Time.

The proof is not without several defects; especially the limitation of the *a priori* to space and time is not convincing. We might still ask whether motion ought not to be added : we can perhaps show that several categories are in truth not pure ideas of the understanding, but intuitions; as, for instance, that of a persistent substratum in change. Even the qualities of sense impressions, as colour, tone, and so on, do not deserve perhaps to be so utterly rejected as something individual, as a subjective thing out of which no *a priori* principles can flow, and which therefore can found no objectivity. Above all, however, is the principle doubtful by which Kant proposes to show that the regulative form must be *a priori;* the principle, namely, that sensation cannot again regulate itself upon other sensations. Among the scanty beginnings of a future scientific psychology appears a principle which teaches us that—within ordinary limits—sensation increases with the logarithm of the corresponding stimulus; the formula $x = \log. y$, which Fechner has made the basis of his 'Psychophysics,' as the 'law of Weber.' It is not improbable that this law has its ground in consciousness itself, and not in those psycho-physical processes that lie between the external (physical) stimulus and the act of consciousness.[27] We may therefore without violence (names must be subordinate !) distinguish between

[27] Recent inquiries seem, indeed, to show the contrary, but the matter still needs confirmation. The result of inquiries by Dewar and M'Kendrick as to change in the electromotor power of the optic nerve by the influence of light on the retina is, that the change is not proportional to the quantity of light, but to the logarithm of the quotient, from which it is concluded that the psycho-physical law of Fechner does not originate from consciousness, but from the anatomical structure and the physiological qualities of the organ itself. Cf. 'Nature,' No. 193 (10th July 1873), tr. in 'Naturforscher'), vi., No. 37 (13th September 1873).

the quantum of sensation (y) forcing itself upon consciousness and the quantum taken up by consciousness (x). This being presupposed, the mathematical formulas to which we are led by exact inquiry express at bottom nothing else than that the quantum of sensation forcing its way every instant is the unity by which consciousness measures on each occasion the degree of the increase to be taken up.

As sensation may very well measure itself by other sensation in point of intensity, so it may order itself in the representation of juxtaposition according to the already existing sensations. Numerous facts show that sensations do not group themselves according to a ready-made form, the idea of space, but, on the contrary, the idea of space is itself determined by our sensations. A composite line consisting of numerous sensible particles is, to the immediate consciousness, always longer than a mathematically equally long line, which offers no special supports for the exciting of sensations. For this very reason, indeed, our ordinary ideas of space are utterly unmathematical, and an inexhaustible source of subtle illusions, because our sensations find no ready-made system of co-ordinates in the mind to which they could surely arrange themselves, but because such a system develops itself, in some unknown way and with great imperfection, only from the natural competition of sensations.

For all that, the thought that Space and Time are forms which the human mind lends to the objects of experience is by no means such as to be rejected straight away. It is just as bold and magnificent as the hypothesis that all the phenomena of a so-called physical world, together with the space in which they are disposed, are only ideas of a purely intellectual nature. But while this *material* Idealism always leads into bottomless speculations, Kant, with his formal Idealism, opens only a glance into the depths of metaphysic, without losing the connection with the sciences of ·experience. For, according to Kant, those forms of our knowledge that exist prior to experience are only through experience able to afford us knowledge, while beyond the sphere of our experience they lose all significance of any kind. The doctrine of 'innate ideas' is nowhere more completely refuted than here; for while, according to the old metaphysic, innate ideas are, as it were, witnesses from a supra-sensuous world, and able, indeed absolutely adapted, to be applied to supra-sensuous things, according to Kant the *a prioristic* elements of knowledge serve exclusively for the use of experience. By them all our experience is determined, and by them we know all necessary relations of the objects of our experience; but just because of their nature, as form of all human experience, every attempt to apply the like forms to supra-sensuous things is vain. It is true indeed that the question here easily arises, What is all the knowledge of experience if we only find the laws created by ourselves again in these things, which are no longer things at all, but only 'phenomena'? Whither leads all our knowledge if we must represent to ourselves the *absolutely* existing things, the 'things-in-themselves,' without space and time, and therefore in a manner quite inconceivable to us? To these questions let us for the present only put this question in reply: Who, then, says that we are to occupy ourselves at all with the, to us, inconceivable 'things-in-themselves'? Are not the natural sciences in every case what they are, and do they not accomplish what they accomplish, quite independently of the ideas as to the ultimate grounds of all nature to which we are ourselves conducted by philosophical criticism?

Looking at things from this side, then, we have no occasion to reject without examination the doctrine of the *a priority* of space and time. But even the doubts that we have raised as to the psychological origin of the idea of space are by no means sufficient to bid us reject it.

Nor does our view of the origin of ideas of space from sensation dispose of the question. It is a very different thing whether the ideas of space are regarded in their development, or whether the question is put how it comes that we conceive at all in forms of space, *i.e.*, that our sensations in their co-operation produce the idea of a co-existence measurable in three dimensions, to which then, as it were as a fourth dimension of all existence, the idea of time associates itself. Even if space and time are not ready-made forms, which have only to fill themselves with matter through our intercourse with things, yet they may be forms that, through organic conditions, which might be wanting in other things, necessarily develop themselves out of our mechanism of sensation. Indeed, in this more strictly limited sense it could hardly be possible to doubt the *a priority* of space and time, and the question will much rather turn upon what Kant calls the 'transcendental ideality' of space and time, *i.e.*, upon the question whether space and time *beyond* our experience have no further significance. This is what Kant undoubtedly supposes. Space and time have reality, according to him, for the sphere of human experience, in so far as they are necessary forms of our sensible intuition; outside it they are, like all ideas that stray beyond the sphere of experience, mere delusions.

Here now the thing lies obviously so, that the psychological arrangement by virtue of which we are compelled to intuite things in forms of space and time is at all events given before all experience; and so far as the very first sensation of an external thing must be connected with an idea of space, however vague, so far is space an *a priori* given mode of sensible intuition. But that there exist 'things-in-themselves,' which have a spaceless and timeless existence, Kant could never prove to us out of his principles, for that would be a transcendental, even though negative, knowledge of the properties of the 'thing-in-itself,' and such a knowledge is, on Kant's own theory, entirely impossible. This, besides, is not Kant's view: it is enough for him to have shown that space and time have absolute validity for all experience, only because they lie as forms of experience in the subject, and cannot therefore extend their validity beyond the sphere of their function. Nothing, on the other hand, hinders us, if we wish to tread this doubtful province, from conjecturing that their sphere extends further than the limit of our ideas.[28]   Kant himself, in fact, occasionally expresses the conjecture that " all finite thinking beings must necessarily (*i.e.*, according to a general principle unknown to us) in this respect (in the mode of intuition in space and time) agree with man." [29]

[28] I need not say that there is here no idea of adopting Trendelenburg's 'Lückentheorie,' for Trendelenburg not only requires space to be at once subjective and objective, but he proclaims also a causal connection between the two, and believes that Kant has overlooked such a possibility, whereas Kant expressly bases the universality and necessity of space and time, and therefore his " empirical realism," upon the fact that these forms are only and *exclusively* subjective. See the careful treatise of Dr. Emil Arnoldt, ' Kant's Transcendentale Idealität des Raumes u. der Zeit,' Königsberg, 1870 (reprinted from the 'Altpreuss. Monatsschrift.,' Bd. vii.), as well as Dr. Cohen ('Kant's Theorie der Erfahrung,' v. S. 62–79.)   In order to prevent misunderstanding, however, to these statements, which, in the strict connection of the system, are entirely right, we must add the remark that Kant could never have wished to prove that things-in-themselves are without time and space; the whole standpoint of the 'Critick' makes it impossible. He is quite content to have shown that space and time (of which we only know anything at all by the means of our *ideas*) beyond experience have absolutely no significance. If Kant, instead of the stricter phrase that our idea of space "has no meaning," sometimes shortly says, " Space is nothing," yet this is always to be taken in the same sense : *our* space, and we know no other. Of other beings (cf.

the next note), we may well conjecture that they also have ideas of space, but of spatiality (Räumlichkeit), as property of things in themselves, we cannot even understand the possibility. So far and no further goes the denial. If any one now by means of a *conjecture*, which is absolutely outside the system, will assume that extension in three dimensions belongs to things in themselves, Kant will never make him another reproach than that he is dreaming. There can be no question of a demonstrated impossibility of objective *space in this sense ;* we can only maintain that any extension of the properties of the space *we know* to this *imaginary* space (comp., *e.g.*, infinity) is unjustified, and thus in fact the imaginary notion would become a mere empty phrase.

[29] Cf. 2te Ausg., S. 72, at the end of the General Remarks on Transcendental Æsthetic (iii. 79 Hart., E.T. Meiklej. 43) : " It is, moreover, not necessary that we should limit the mode of intuition in space and time to the sensuous faculty of man. It may well be that all finite thinking beings must necessarily in this respect agree with man (though as to this we cannot decide), but sensibility does not on account of this universality cease to be sensibility," &c.   In the sequel the oft-recurring suggestion is made, of course again outside the system, that another mode of apprehension, namely, 'intellectual intuition,' seems to belong wholly to the Supreme Being (God). This phantom of an intellec-

But this means, in other words: It may be that all knowledge of objects is necessarily like ours; any purely problematical divine mode of knowledge, however, excepted.
On the other hand, we may also admit that, *e.g.*, we can
conceive creatures that by virtue of their organisation are
not at all in a position to measure space by three dimensions, that perhaps conceive it only in two dimensions,
perhaps in no clear dimensions at all. In accordance with
this we cannot again deny the possibility of a conception
that rests upon *more* perfect ideas of space than our own.

Even if, furthermore, it must be true that all things in
the universe are in interaction, and everything hangs immutably together according to fixed laws, yet Schiller's
poetic saying, 'Und in dem Heute wandelt schon das
Morgen,' would be, in the strictest sense of the word, a
metaphysical truth, and it must be possible to conceive
intelligences that apprehend *simultaneously* what to us
stands as a succession in time. It is indeed certain that
we can know nothing of all this, and that sound philosophy
will only concern itself with such questions when it is
important to refute the dogmatic assertion of the absolute
objectivity of our ideas of space by the setting up of opposed
possibilities. Kant is, at any rate, so far justified as the
principle of intuition in space and time *a priori* is in us,
and it was a service to all time that he should, in this first
great example, show that what we possess *a priori*, just
because it arises out of the disposition of our mind, beyond
our experience has no longer any claim to validity.

As to Materialism, this treats time and space as it treats
at bottom the whole sensible world, simply as objective.
The deviations from this standpoint, such as we find, *e.g.*,
in Moleschott, are deviations from the system of Material-

tual intuition, moreover, in another
place plays a considerable part in the
system: in the arbitrary assumption
explained in note 25, that only our
thought can be active, and our sense
can be only passive. It may be
said in passing, that we may find, too,
in the passage of Kant above quoted,
a very clear instance of a *problematical necessity*, a combination in which
Professor Schilling, 'Beitr. zur Gesch.
u. Kr. d. Mat.,' Leipz., 1867, found
an "obvious logical contradiction,"
which may be just mentioned to
show how heedlessly logic may be
handled.

ism.   Precisely with regard to space and time does Materialism feel safest as against Kant's criticism ; for here we
have not only the consciousness that we cannot imagine
to ourselves an end of space and time, or an intuition
entirely free of space and time, but even in the highest
abstraction of thought, that entirely renounces an impossible picturableness, it will ever remain probable that, at
most, there may exist among different physically organised
beings, different degrees of the comprehension of space and
time, but that these forms themselves, in their inmost
nature, must belong to every possible conception, just
because they are grounded in the nature of things.   Kant,
while he wished to accomplish more, has at least actually
accomplished the lesser task.   He established the doubt
whether space and time have any meaning at all outside
the experience of thinking, finite beings ; and while he
was far removed from leaving these limits and straying
away with metaphysical speculations into the pathless
beyond of 'absolute existence,' he has more effectually
shattered the primitive *naïveté* of that belief in the senses
which underlies Materialism, than any system of material
Idealism could ever do.   For while the latter serves up its
ideas as reality and truth, the logical conscience of the
sober thinker awakes, and we are then only too ready with
the poetic phantasies of such speculation to reject also the
reasons that are rightly alleged against the absolute reality
of the sense-world as we represent it to ourselves.

As Kant, with regard to sensibility, established space
and time as forms of intuition *a priori,* so in the sphere of
reason he thought he had demonstrated the categories as
the *a priori* given primary ideas.   This demonstration,
inadequate as it is, cost him much thought.   By means of
a single one of these ideas, the idea of causality, against
which Hume had directed the solvent of his scepticism,
Kant to a certain extent attained to his whole philosophy;
and it was probably the supposed discovery of the complete table of the categories that decided Kant to appear

as the reformer of philosophy, after he had already gained no slight reputation as a philosopher of the Wolffian school, and especially as a thorough master of mathematics and natural science. Yet as to the inner history of this important change let us hear Kant's own words. The idea of causality has such especial import for the criticism of Materialism, that the most important section in the history of this idea may well deserve a place in the history of Materialism. In the preface to his Prolegomena,[30] Kant declares that since the origin of metaphysic, no event had come to pass that might have been more decisive of its fate than the attack of Hume, if only he had found a more receptive public. Then follows a long and extremely noteworthy passage, which we quote at length: "Hume started chiefly from a single but important concept in metaphysic—that of Cause and Effect (including the deduced notions of action and power). He calls on reason, which pretends to have generated this notion from itself, to answer him, with what right it thinks anything to be so constituted that, if granted, something else must necessarily be granted thereby; for this is the meaning of the concept of cause. He demonstrated irresistibly that it was perfectly impossible for reason to think such a combination by means of concepts and *a priori*—a combination that contains necessity. We cannot at all see why, in consequence of the existence of one thing, another must necessarily exist, or how the concept of such a combination can arise *a priori*. Hence he inferred that reason was altogether deluded by this concept, which it considered erroneously as one of its children, whereas in reality the concept was nothing but the bastard offspring of the imagination, impregnated by experience, and so bringing certain representations under the law of association. The subjective necessity, that is, the custom which so arises, is then substituted for an objective necessity from real

[30] Proleg. zu einer jeden zukünft. Metaphysik, Riga, 1788, S. 8-15, Hart. iv. 5-9, Mahaffy, iii. 4-10.

knowledge. Hence he inferred that the reason had no power to think such combinations, even generally, because its concepts would then be mere inventions, and all its pretended *a priori* cognitions nothing but common experiences marked with a false stamp. In plain language, there is not, and cannot be, any such thing as metaphysic at all.

" This conclusion, however hasty and mistaken, was at least founded upon investigation, and the investigation deserved to have suggested to the brighter spirits of his day a combined attempt at a happy solution of the problem proposed by him, if such solution were possible. Thus a complete reform of the science must have resulted.

" But the perpetual hard fate of metaphysic would not allow him to be understood. We cannot, without a certain sense of pain, consider how utterly his opponents, Reid, Oswald, Beattie, and even Priestley, missed the point of the problem. For while they were ever assuming as conceded what he doubted, and demonstrating with eagerness, and often with arrogance, what he never thought of disputing, they so overlooked his indication towards a better state of things, that everything remained undisturbed in its old condition.

" The question was not, whether the concept of cause was right, useful, and even indispensable, with regard to our knowledge of nature, for this Hume had never doubted. But the question to which Hume expected an answer was this, whether that concept could be thought by the reason *a priori*, and whether it consequently possessed an inner truth, independently of all experience, and therefore applied more widely than to the mere objects of experience. It was surely a question concerning the *origin*, not concerning the *indispensable use*, of the concept. Had the former question been determined, the conditions of the use and valid application of the concept would have been given *ipso facto*.

" But the opponents of the great thinker should have

probed very deeply into the nature of the reason, so far as it concerns pure thinking, if they would satisfy the conditions of the problem—a task which did not suit them. They therefore discovered a more convenient means of putting on a bold face without any proper insight into the question, by appealing to the *common sense of mankind.* It is indeed a great gift of God to possess right or (as they now call it) plain common sense. But this common sense must be shown practically, by well-considered and reasonable thoughts and words, not by appealing to it as an oracle when you can advance nothing rational in justification of yourself. To appeal to common sense when insight and science fail, and no sooner, this is one of the subtile discoveries of modern times, by means of which the most vapid babbler can safely enter the lists with the most thoroughgoing thinker, and hold his own. But as long as a particle of insight remains, no one would think of having recourse to this subterfuge. For what is it but an appeal to the opinion of the multitude, of whose applause the philosopher is ashamed, while the popular and superficial man glories and confides in it? I should think Hume might fairly have laid as much claim to sound sense as Beattie, and besides to a critical understanding (such as the latter did not possess), which keeps common sense within such bounds as to prevent it from speculating, or, if it does speculate, keeps it from wishing to decide when it cannot satisfy itself concerning its own principles. By this means alone can common sense remain sound sense. Chisels and hammers may suffice to work a piece of wood, but for steel-engraving we require a special instrument. Thus common sense and speculative understanding are each serviceable in their own way, the former in judgments which apply immediately to experience, the latter when we judge universally from mere concepts, as in metaphysic, where that which calls itself (often *per antiphrasin*) sound common sense has no right to judge at all.

"I honestly confess the suggestion of David Hume was

the very thing which, many years ago, first interrupted my dogmatic slumber, and gave my investigations in the field of speculative philosophy quite a new direction. I was far from following him in all his conclusions, which only resulted from his regarding, not the whole of his problem, but a part, which by itself can give us no information. If we start from a well-founded, but undeveloped, thought, which another has bequeathed to us, we may well hope, by continued reflection, to advance farther than the acute man to whom we owe the first spark of light.

" I therefore first tried whether Hume's objection could not be put into a general form, and soon found that the concept of the connection of cause and effect was by no means the only one by which the understanding thinks the connection of things *a priori*, but rather that metaphysic consists altogether of such connections. I sought to make certain of their number, and when I had succeeded in this to my expectation, by starting from a single principle, I proceeded to the deduction of these concepts, which I was now certain were not deduced from experience, as Hume had apprehended, but sprang from the pure understanding. This deduction, which seemed impossible to my acute predecessor, which had never even occurred to any one else, though they were all using the concepts unsuspiciously without questioning the basis of their objective validity,—this deduction was the most difficult task ever undertaken in aid of metaphysic. More especially no existing metaphysic could assist me in the least, because this deduction must prove the very possibility of metaphysic. But as soon as I had succeeded in solving Hume's problem, not merely in a particular case, but with respect to the whole faculty of pure reason, I could proceed safely, though slowly, to determine the whole sphere of pure reason completely and from general principles, in its limits as well as in its contents. This was what metaphysic required in order to construct its system safely."

In these words of Kant we have before us, in a single view, the influence of Hume upon German philosophy, the development of the table of Categories, and with it of the whole Critick of Reason, the true root-idea, and the explanation of all the errors of our Reformer of philosophy. This latter lies open before us in the confusion of the methodical and scientific handling of the laws of thought with so-called speculation that deduces from general conceptions.

The illustration of the engraving tool is better than its application. It is not a completely different starting-point of thought and an opposite method that guarantee its success to philosophical criticism, but solely and simply greater accuracy and precision in the handling of the general laws of thought. Metaphysic as *criticism of ideas* must go to work still more carefully and precisely than the philological criticism of a traditional text, than the historical criticism of the sources of a narrative, than the mathematical and physical criticism of an hypothesis in natural science ; but essentially it must, like all criticism, work with every implement of the whole of logic, now inductive, now deductive, and must give to experience what belongs to experience, and to ideas what belongs to ideas.

And the error of the disciples of common sense by no means lies in a one-sided departure from experience. It would be nearer the truth if we were to understand the German phrase, ' Gesunder Menschenverstand ' (sound common sense), rather on the analogy of ' cotton-stocking manufacturer,' and similar elegant formations. For it means, in fact, if not etymologically, the average understanding of a sound man, *i.e.*, of a man who, along with a crude logic, applies still sound senses, who in his judgments besides understanding allows play to feeling, intuition, experience, knowledge of facts, in an irregular way, so that in matters of daily life within the limits of common interests the result is a good and never eccentric judgment.

The logic of daily life is therefore successful, although it swallows camels and never strains out gnats. The influence of universal prejudice upon its results the great public does not detect, because it is all involved in the same errors. And thus sound common sense celebrates most of its triumphs in such achievements as the contempt of all efforts at reform, the defence of police guardianship, of a cruel criminal law, of the keeping under of the 'common people,' of the necessity of mechanical institutions, and the advantages of Gotham over all other towns of Europe. We learn to know it from a better side, however, where prejudice loses its influence, but where judgment, according to the subject-matter, must co-operate with reality and experience. Even the successes of Bentley in the criticism of Horace, of Niebuhr in the reform of Roman history, of Winckelmann in the spreading of a deeper comprehension of antiquity, of Humboldt in the sure casting of the world-reaching nets of general investigation, rest in great part upon a combination of the radical scientific understanding with a greater knowledge of men and of the world, or with a more vigorous reality, than commonly belong to the arm-chair student; and even in philosophical criticism this element becomes only relatively less important, without ever entirely losing its significance. It contributes to the achievement of the best work, so far as it serves and completes conscientious workmanship, while it fosters and develops every kind of vanity in the opposition against scientific thought. Kant felt this keenly in comparing so superior a mind as Hume with the representatives of common sense; but he confused greater power and keenness of thought with speculative method. It was nothing but force of logic by which Hume woke him from his dogmatic slumber; if Kant had merely reacted against the attack of Hume by the discovery of the Categories his reaction would not have been justified; but behind this luxuriant foliage of speculation lurks the profounder idea that might make him the Reformer of philosophy. It is the view that man's experience is a product of certain fundamental ideas, the whole import of which lies in this fact, that they do determine experience. The controversy as to the idea of cause is understood generally. Hume is right in annihilating the supernatural, as it were revealed, origin of these ideas; he is wrong in that he deduces them from experience, since we are quite incapable of experience at all without being from the first so organised as to combine subject and predicate, cause and effect.

Strictly speaking, it is of course not the ideas themselves that exist prior to experience, but only those dispositions by which the impressions of the outward world are combined and arranged in accordance with these ideas. We might say, the body is *a priori*, if only the body itself in its turn were not merely an *a priori* given mode of conceiving purely intellectual phenomena. (Comp. note 25.) Perhaps some day the basis of the idea of cause may be found in the mechanism of reflex action and sympathetic excitation; we should then have translated Kant's pure reason into physiology, and so made it more easily conceivable. But the question essentially continues the same; for when once simple faith in the reality of the phenomenal world is expelled, the step from the physical to the intellectual is no longer a great one; only that, of course, the purely intellectual element will always remain unknown, just because we can only conceive it in sensuous images.

As the judgment of the idea of causality has become so far-reaching in its importance, we will not neglect to give here, in four short propositions, a summary view of the different doctrines as to this idea, including our own.

I. The old Metaphysic: The idea of cause springs, not from experience, but from the pure reason, and is, thanks to this higher origin, valid and applicable even beyond the limits of human experience.

II. Hume: The idea of cause cannot be derived from the pure reason, but rather springs from experience. The limits of its application are doubtful, but at all events it cannot be applied to anything that transcends our experience.

III. Kant: The idea of cause is a primary idea of the pure reason, and as such underlies our whole experience. For this reason, therefore, it has unlimited validity in the sphere of experience, but beyond it has no meaning.

IV. The writer: The idea of cause is rooted in our organisation, and is, in point of the disposition to it, before all experience. For this very reason it has unlimited validity in the sphere of experience, but beyond it absolutely no meaning.

To the sphere of experience belongs also all that is inferred from immediate experience, and in general whatever is conceived on the analogy of experience ; thus, *e.g.*, the doctrine of Atoms.[31] Epikuros, however, without any reason, assumed for his atoms a deviation from the straight line, a view that Kant, usually so moderate, at once disposes of as 'monstrous.'[32] He would surely never have allowed himself to dream that, after more than half a century, a countryman and intellectual relative of the great Hume would write down the following sentence :—

"I am convinced that any one accustomed to abstraction and analysis, who will fairly exert his faculties for the purpose, will, when his imagination has once learnt to entertain the notion, find no difficulty in conceiving that

[31] As appears from the context the 'sphere of experience' is only spoken of in that sense in which alone an entire disjunction exists between the transcendental and the empirical, between the spheres of 'phenomena' and 'noümena.' That this quite agrees with Kant's use must be at once obvious to every one who knows Kant's writings. Nevertheless, I have been obliged in my 'Neue Beitr. zur Gesch. d. Mat.' (Winterthür, 1867), S. 31-36, to produce an elaborate proof of this, and I will not deny that the bitterness with which I have replied to the pedantries of the since deceased Professor Schilling was provoked by nothing so much as his conspicuous ignorance of Kant in this point. If I had already witnessed the controversy between Kuno Fischer and Trendelenburg, I should assuredly have judged Schilling more gently.

[32] In the preface to the 'Allgem. Naturgesch. u. Theorie des Himmels' (1755): "Epikur war gar so unverschämt, dass er verlangte, die Atomen wichen von ihrer Bewegung ohne alle Ursache ab, um einander begegnen zu können" (Hartenst., i. 217).

in some one, for instance, of the many firmaments into which sidereal astronomy now divides the universe, events may succeed one another at random, without any fixed law; nor can anything in our experience or in our mental nature constitute a sufficient, or indeed any, reason for believing that this is nowhere the case." [33]

Mill regards belief in causality as a mere consequence of involuntary induction. From this it necessarily follows that upon our earth, just as well as in the remotest firmaments, something might happen without any cause; and Epikuros, who was only untrue to the law of cause in that one instance, might with all reason answer Mill in his favourite formula: " Then anything might come from anything ! " ' Quite true, indeed,' Mill will answer, ' only it is not at all *probable;* we'll talk about it again, so soon as such a case occurs.' And if then a case occurs that seems to contradict all the previous notions of science, Mill will just like us, who hold the idea of cause as given *a priori,* suspend his judgment on this case until science has studied it more exactly. He will always be able to maintain that he has so much regard for induction, that he cannot yet surrender the hope of ranging this case under the universal law of cause. The proof of the contrary will be a suit *in infinitum;* the matter threatens to run into an empty logomachy, if it is not conceded that the adherents to the *a priority* of the causal law are right *a priori* and before experience. Mill would perhaps not have erred so far, if he had distinguished between the law of cause in general and the conception of it in our modern physical science. This latter conception, according to which all causes and effects stand in the strictest connexion of natural laws, and outside these no thing or idea is allowed any causal significance,—this particular scientific conception of the law of cause is indeed new, and has been acquired by induction within historical times. The necessity proceeding immediately from the nature of the human mind to

[33] Mill, Logic, 6th ed., ii. 98.

assume a cause for everything, is, in fact, often very unscientific.   It is due to the idea of cause that the monkey
—in this respect, as it seems, humanly organised—gropes
with its paw behind the mirror, or turns the mocking thing
round, in order to seek the cause of the phenomenon.   It
is due to the law of cause that the savage attributes the
thunder to the car of a god, or at an eclipse imagines that
a dragon is trying to swallow up the light-giver.   The law
of cause makes the babe associate the appearance of its
mother with its own cry, and so gives rise to experience.
The privileged noodle, however, who attributes everything
to chance, thinks of chance—if he thinks at all—as a demonic thing whose malice contains a sufficient explanation
of all his failures.[34]

Our modern Materialists will as to this question, perhaps, be a little inconsistent with themselves.   Inclined, on
the one hand, to draw everything from experience, they
will not like to make an exception in the case of the
law of cause.   On the other hand, the unconditional
and unlimited validity of the natural laws is rightly one
of their favourite principles.   Czolbe, indeed, seems to
range himself quite decidedly * on Mill's side; but by
innate laws of thought he understands such as from our
birth lie as logical principles in our consciousness.   In

[34] It is, of course, quite another question whether the law of cause must not ultimately be brought into so purified a shape, that the anthropomorphic ideas that we associate with the notion of Cause, as with that of Necessity, of Power, and so on, may entirely vanish, or at all events be reduced to a harmless minimum.   In this sense, indeed, even the category of causality can lay claim to no sanctity, and if, *e.g.*, Comte entirely dismisses the notion of cause, and replaces it by the notion of invariable sequence, this procedure can by no means be impugned on the ground of the *a priority* of the notion of cause.

Even in this an indispensable factor may be separated from the ingredients furnished by imagination, and the more intellectual culture advances, the more such will a purification (as, *e.g.*, even in the notion of *power*) be felt to be needed.   As to causality it is in truth, as will later appear, of the utmost importance, once for all, to displace at least one of the anthropomorphic ideas mixed up with it; that which attributes to the cause (the *Ur-sache*), as though it were the active, generative element, higher consequence and importance than to the effect.

* *Sensualismus*, S. 64.

which way he would have decided after this misunderstanding has been removed cannot be quite clearly determined from his statement. At all events, in his postulate that our ideas must be such as are clearly conceivable, Czolbe has set up a metaphysical principle which it is quite impossible to harmonise with Mill's system, and which carries us even beyond Kant in the other direction. With Büchner we find the necessity and invariableness of natural laws most strongly emphasised, and yet the belief in these laws is derived from experience. At the same time, even Oersted's metaphysical principle of the unity of the laws of thought and the laws of nature is occasionally treated as true.

Perhaps many of our modern Materialists would be inclined to elevate this uncertainty of which we are speaking into a principle, and to declare the whole distinction between the empirical and the rational conception of the notion of cause to be useless refinement. This is, of course, to give up the ground, for it is obvious that for the practical application of the notion of cause it is sufficient to draw it from experience. More exact investigation can have no object except in a purely theoretical interest; where we have to do with ideas keenness of logic is as indispensable as exact analysis in chemistry.

The most favourable position for our modern Materialists would be for them, on the whole, to go with Hume and Mill, and to avoid the fatal consequences of a possible exception to the law of causality by insisting upon the infinitely slender probability of such an exception. This is, at all events, sufficient to dispose of the lovers of miracle, for we may always require, as though it were demanded by the *morality of thought*, that our assumptions should rest, not upon vague possibility, but upon probability. This does not, however, dispose of the real question; for the true difficulty lies in this, that from the outset two sensations could never be combined into an experience of their connexion, unless the ground of their interdependence as cause and effect were determined by the disposition of our mind.

From this point, indeed, there falls quite a new light upon the relation of the phenomena to the ' thing-in-itself.' If the idea of causality is a category in Kant's sense, then, like all the categories, it has validity merely in the sphere of experience. Only in combination with the intuitions that sense supplies can these ideas be referred to an object. Sensibility realises the understanding. But how, then, is it possible, if this is so, to conclude to a 'thing-in-itself' that stands behind the phenomena ? Does not the idea of cause then become transcendental ? Is it not applied to a supposed hypothetical object that lies beyond any possible experience ?

This objection has, from the first replies to the ' Critick' down to the present, always been supposed a fatal blow to Kant ; and even we ourselves, in the first edition of this work, assumed that the 'armour of the system' is thereby crushed in. A more careful inquiry, however, shows that this blow does not find Kant unprepared. What we announced as a correction of the system is, in fact, exactly Kant's own view; the 'thing-in-itself' is a mere idea of limit. 'The fish in the pond,' we remarked, 'can swim only in the water, not in the earth ; but yet it may strike its head against the ground and sides.' So, too, we might with the notion of cause survey the whole realm of experience and find that beyond it lies a sphere which to our knowledge is absolutely inaccessible.[35]

[35] The change in my views on this point had already been prepared by my new studies, when the important work of Dr. Cohen on Kant's ' Theorie der Erfahrung ' appeared, which led me to another entire revision of my views on Kant's system. The result was that I was obliged on most points to adhere to Dr. Cohen's interpretation, so far as the objective exposition of Kant's views was concerned, always with the reservation that Kant still seems to me far from being so free from inconsistencies and hesitations, as appears from Dr. Cohen. We have now the beginnings of a 'Philology of Kant' that will probably soon find imitation, and it is quite natural that this, like the Aristotle-philology of the school of Trendelenburg, has its principal motive in trying to conceive the object of its studies as a consistent whole. The points in which this is impossible will

We do not, then, really know whether a thing-in-itself exists. We know only that the logical application of our laws of thought leads us to the notion of an entirely problematical something which we assume as the cause of the phenomenon so soon as we have recognised that our world can only be a world of representation. If it is asked, But where, then, are things? the answer runs, In the phenomena. The more the 'thing-in-itself' refines itself away to a mere representation, the more the word phenomena gains in reality. It embraces everything that we can call 'real.' The phenomena are what the ordinary understanding calls things; the philosopher calls the things phenomena, in order to denote that they are not something existing entirely outside myself, but a product of the laws of my understanding and my sensibility. The same laws lead me, then, on the analogy of the relations of cause and effect, as I daily observe them in the individual facts of experience, to suppose a cause for this great whole of the world that appears to me. Empirical investigation in the hand of the notion of causality showed us that the world of the ear does not correspond to the world of the eye, that the world of logical inferences is other than that of immediate intuition. It shows us that the whole of our world of appearances depends upon our organs, and Kant has the lasting credit of having shown that here our categories play the same part as our senses. If now the comprehensive view of the world of appearances leads us to the idea that this, too, in its collective relations is conditioned by our organisation, we must, driven by analogy, suppose that even where we can acquire no new organ to supplement and improve the others, still a whole infinity of different interpretations is possible; nay, that in fine all these different views of differently organised beings have a common unknown source as their origin, the thing-in-

thus be most certainly revealed. The important passages for the interpretation of the thing-in-itself here laid down are especially in the sections on Phänomena u. Noümena, and on the Amphibolie der Reflexionsbegriffe.— Cp. besides, Cohen, K. Th. d. E., S. 252 f.

itself as opposed to the things of appearance; then we quietly yield to this view, so far as it is a necessary consequence of the use of our understanding, even though the same understanding, upon further investigation, must confess that it has itself created this antithesis. We find everywhere nothing but the usual empirical opposition between appearances and existence, which, of course, exhibits endless degrees to the reason. What at this stage of consideration is existence, appears again at another, in relation to a deeper concealed existence, as appearance. The true essence of things, the last cause of all phenomena, is, however, not only unknown to us, but even the idea of it is nothing more and nothing less than the last outcome of an antithesis determined by our organisation, and of which we do not know whether, beyond our experience, it has any meaning at all.

Kant denies that the question as to the nature of things in themselves has any interest: so entirely is he in harmony here with the empiricist who, to use an expression of Czolbe's, contents himself with the given world. "What things may be in themselves," he says in the section on the *Amphibolie der Reflexionsbegriffe*, "I know not, and do not need to know, because a thing is never presented to me otherwise than as a phenomenon;" and, further, he declares the "internal in matter," or the thing-in-itself which appears as matter, to be "a mere chimera." The complaints that we do not see into the interior of things—with a clear allusion to that saying of Haller's that was so distasteful to Goethe—are "silly and unreasonable;" for such people desire that we should be able to know things and even to perceive them without senses. But "into the interior of nature," that is the orderly relations of phenomena, "penetrate observation and analysis of phenomena, and no one can say what progress this knowledge may make in time." [36]

[36] The well-known verses:
"In's Inn're der Natur
    Dringt kein erschaffner Geist;
        Glückselig! wem sie nur
            Die äuss're Schale weist!"
over which Goethe (Gedichte, Abth.

As it is with the notion of causality, so it is also with
the rest of the Categories; they underlie our whole experience, but are entirely useless for the purpose of overstep-
ping the province of possible experience, and of being
applied to those transcendental objects, to secure a knowledge of which was the aim of the old metaphysic. That
Kant created a new metaphysic, in thinking that he could
with certainty deduce all the *a priori* elements of our
thought from a single principle, is the weak side of his
theoretical philosophy. Though it was nevertheless precisely this supposed discovery that led him to appear as
the reformer of philosophy, we must not forget that hardly
any one resists the fascination of such brilliant conjectures,
and, what is more important, that even here there is an
underlying core of truth.

Kant believed, that is to say, that he could deduce the
primitive conceptions of the understanding from the different forms of the judgment, as they are or should be taught
in logic. If, then, we were sure that we knew the real
and permanent primary forms of judgment, it would not
be illogical to conclude from these to the true fundamental
conceptions, as it must be supposed that the same qualities
of our organism which determine our whole experience
give their stamp also to the various tendencies of the
activity of our understanding.[37] But whence are we to

Gott u. Welt: 'Allerdings. Dem
Physiker') for sixty years 'cursed in
secret,' are to be understood in the
sense of Leibniz's philosophy, according to which all sensuous intuition,
and therefore also our whole view of
nature, is only the confused representation of a divine pure thought (or
intellectual, not sensuous, intuition).
According to Kant, the interior of
nature in the sense of the transcendental basis of phenomena is indeed
inaccessible to us, but we are also not
at all concerned to inquire into it,
while the interior of nature in the

sense of natural science is open to an
unlimited progress of knowledge.

[37] Cp. *supra* note 25.   With
reference to Cohen, Kant's The. der
Erfahr., S. 207, let me here add
further that it is not enough to defend Kant by saying that his *system*
continues to exist, though individual
categories must fall away or be otherwise deduced. It is quite true that
the system rests upon the transcendental deduction of the categories,
and not upon the metaphysical—that
is, that the true proof of Kant lies in
this, that these ideas are demonstrated

learn the simple and necessary elements of all judgment, for only these are able to supply us with true categories?

The "deduction from a principle," altogether a most seductive procedure, consisted, however, at bottom only in this, that five perpendicular and four transverse lines were made, and the twelve compartments thus formed were filled up; though it is quite obvious, *e.g.*, that of the judgments of Possibility and Necessity, at most only one can be an original form, from which the other is produced by the use of negation. In this respect the purely empirical procedure of Aristotle was essentially better, because at least it did not lead to such dangerous self-delusions. The error which Kant fell into was indeed for a disciple of the German scholastic philosophy, which only slowly with immense effort of mind had torn itself from tradition, very natural. Kant over-estimated the value of the work he supposed formal logic to have accomplished by way of preparation, just as he also over-estimated the table-work of empirical psychology—at least as to its applicability

a priori as conditions of the possibility of synthetic knowledge. We might then suppose that it is indifferent whether such a fundamental idea is set aside by a more exact analysis, so long as that *persistent factor* in it (cp. also note 34) is retained, which underlies the synthesis *a priori*. But here we must observe that this analysis, going beyond Kant, will very probably lead at the same time to a reduction (perhaps to a completion) of the table of Categories, and that thus of course a pretension of Kant's, which is very important for the developing of his system (viz., absolute completeness of his table of Categories), would be destroyed. If we push too far the emphasis on the *merely transcendental* standpoint, we come, as already hinted, to the tautology, that experience is to be explained out of the conditions of possible experience in general. If transcendental deduction is to afford a synthetic result instead of this tau-tology, the categories must necessarily be something more besides being conditions of experience. This with Kant is to be sought in their designation as "primitive conceptions of the pure reason," while we have here substituted 'Organisation' instead. For this very reason, however, Kant's aim must be to discover the ultimate and permanent "primitive conceptions," and not any casual network of anthropomorphically tinctured conceptions, of which it cannot even be said whether one or several of them correspond to the ultimate, logically indispensable, primitive conceptions. Let me observe still further on this occasion that we cannot only, as Comte has shown, dispense with the conception of 'cause,' but that the conception of 'possibility' and 'necessity' in particular, as we hope to show later, may be entirely dismissed from philosophical employment.

for a complete classification of the mental activities. He did not reflect that in the traditional logic, owing to its natural connexion with grammar and language, there still linger psychological elements, which in their anthropomorphic constitution are very different from the strictly logical element in logic, which indeed is even yet awaiting a rigid purification from these admixtures. At the same time, however, in taking the division of judgments not unaltered from the scholastic logic, but filling up his dozen by many reflections of very various value, he followed unmistakably that architectonic instinct of the metaphysician, which has its place in the creations of speculation, but not in a critical investigation of the foundations of the understanding. The further, therefore, he ventured in applying his four main heads of quantity, quality, relation, and modality with the trichotomy of their subdivisions, the more he lost the safe ground of criticism from beneath his feet,[38] and reached that dangerous province of creation out of nothing into which his successors soon strike out with full sails, as though they were about to conquer a world, while really they were only going to wander fruitlessly on what Kant has so rightly called that " wide and stormy ocean, the true home of mirage."

It would lead us too far to enter here upon a special criticism of the table of Categories. It is more important for the subject of Materialism, instead of dealing with the other Categories, to look further into the origin of those *ideas* which constitute the core of the whole controversy. If we will believe Schleiden, Kant has for ever impregnably established the ideas of God, Freedom, and Immortality. Instead of this we find in the sphere of theoretical philo-

[38] It must here be expressly observed that this applies, not only to the often untenable constructions in the 'Critick of Practical Reason,' but that the evil appears very plainly even in the 'Systematische Vorstellung aller Grundsätze' (to say nothing of the 'Metaphysische Anfangsgründe '), so that if any one wished to support the twelve Categories *from this point*, a serious criticism would assuredly not result in favour of the 'deduction from a principle.'

sophy especially only a deduction that is, if possible, even more doubtful than that of the Categories. While Kant deduced these from the forms of judgment of the usual logic, he found himself obliged—it is hard to say why—to deduce these ideas as pure conceptions of the reason from the forms of syllogisms. Here again he believed that he had thus found a guarantee for the complete securing of the ideas of pure reason, and very ingeniously developed out of the categorical syllogism the idea of the Soul, out of the hypothetical the idea of the World, and out of the disjunctive the idea of God.

The Categories, according to Kant, serve only for the use of the understanding in experience. What purpose, then, do the ideas serve? Considering the important part that these ideas play in the materialistic controversy of our days, it will not be uninteresting to hear a few words more from Kant on this very point. However little value we may attribute to the deduction of these ideas of the reason, all the more must we admire, in criticising the part they play in our knowledge, the admirable clearness of a great intellectual leader.

Kant observes in the *Prolegomena* (§ 44), "That the idea of reason is not, like the Categories, of any service to the use of our understanding in experience, but with respect to that use is quite dispensable, and even an impediment to the maxims of the rational cognition of nature, though necessary in another respect still to be determined.

"Whether the soul is or is not a simple substance is of no consequence to us in the explanation of its phenomena; for we cannot render the notion of a simple being intelligible by any possible experience, sensuously or *in concreto.* The notion is, therefore, quite void as regards all hoped-for insight into the cause of phenomena, and cannot at all serve as a principle of the explanation of that which internal or external experience supplies. So the cosmological ideas of the beginning of the world or of its eternity cannot be of any greater service to us for the explanation of any event in the world itself. And, finally, we must, according to a right maxim of the philosophy of nature, refrain from all explanations of the design of nature drawn from the will of a Supreme Being, because this is no longer natural philosophy, but an acknowledgment that we have reached its limits." *

More cannot be demanded by those of our modern 'Materialists' who have no wish at all to be metaphysicians, and whose only object is to clear the way everywhere for exact investigation, while it remains quite indifferent to them what may be supposed beyond this investigation on whatever grounds. The *dogmatic* Materialist, however, will ask, What then can these ideas do if they can exercise no influence whatever on the course of the positive sciences? He will not only suspect that they will after all sneak again by some back way into the sphere of inquiry, and oppose themselves to the progress of the sciences, but he will no longer recognise anything outside sensuous experience, since he maintains as a metaphysical dogma that the world is as it appears to us through our senses. This suspicion, let us observe, is only too well grounded; where, that is, we have to do with certain Kantians, and not with Kant himself. Has not the combination of bureaucratic fanaticism with philosophical impotence brought it about that Kant's doctrine of freedom was abused even in judicial psychology—a science that becomes the death-instrument of juristic pedantry so soon as it leaves the ground of the strictest empiricism? [39] As to the metaphysical dogma of the absolute objectivity of the sense-world, on the other hand, the ideas will be very easily able to maintain their own peculiar position.

Reason, the mother of these ideas, is in Kant's view directed to the sum of all possible experience, while the

* Mahaffy, iii. 120.

[39] Cp. my essay 'On the Principles of Legal Psychology, with special reference to Ideler's Lehrbuch der jur. Psych.' in the Deutsche Zeitschr. für Staatsarzneikunde, Neue Folg., Bd. xi., Heft 1 and 2: Erlangen, 1858.

understanding occupies itself with the particular. Reason finds satisfaction in no amount of knowledge, so long as it has not embraced the whole. Thus the reason is systematic, just as the understanding is empirical. The ideas Soul, World, God are only the expression of those efforts after unity that lie in our rational organisation. If we attribute to them an objective existence outside ourselves, we fall at once into the shoreless sea of metaphysical errors. So long, however, as we hold them in honour as *our* ideas, we only satisfy an irresistible demand of our reason. These ideas do not serve to extend our knowledge, but they do serve to refute the assertions of Materialism, and thereby to make way for the moral philosophy which Kant holds to be the most important branch of philosophy.

What justifies the ideas as opposed to Materialism is then not their claim to a higher truth, whether it be demonstrated or whether it be revealed and indemonstrable, but precisely the opposite of this; the complete and absolute renunciation of any theoretical validity in the sphere of the knowledge that has for its object the external world. From figments of the brain the ideas are chiefly distinguished by the fact, that they do not crop up occasionally in an individual man, but that they are based in man's natural disposition,[40] and that they have a utility which does not belong to ordinary figments of the brain. Thus criticism is powerless against the ideas, while it sets aside all dogmatic metaphysic, and therefore dogmatic Materialism too. If the proof were conclusive that the ideas in the number and shape in which Kant deduces them were an absolutely necessary result of our natural

[40] 'Natural disposition of man' is more correct; 'natural disposition of the human mind,' as I wrote in the first edition, is more popular. It is not without interest to see how Kant, *e.g.*, in the introduction to the second edition, pt. vi., avoids the expression 'natural disposition of the mind,' or even 'of the soul,' precisely in order to prevent its appearing as though this 'disposition' is something different from the physical organisation. On the other hand, he talks quite unconcernedly of the nature or the impulses of the 'reason,' by which is understood only a function of man, without deciding as to the relation of body and soul. Comp. note 25.

disposition, they would thus have an inexpugnable right upon their side. If, furthermore, this natural disposition of ours be discovered by pure reason, without any experience, there would assuredly be in it an essential branch of knowledge. Let us imagine, to make this clear, a man who takes a kaleidoscope for a telescope. He supposes that he perceives extremely remarkable objects, and observes them very diligently. He must now be shut up in a narrow room. On one side it has a window, affording him a narrowed and disturbed view outwards ; on another side the tube, with which he supposes that he sees afar, is fastened in the wall. This outlook he is specially fond of. It charms him more than the window; assiduously he seeks in this way to perfect his knowledge of the wonders in the distance. This is the metaphysician who despises the narrow window of experience, and lets himself be deceived by the kaleidoscope of his ideal world. But if now he observes this deception, if he proves the nature of the kaleidoscope, it may still even be for him, despite the cruel disenchantment, an object of interest and knowledge. He asks no longer, What is the meaning of the wonderful pictures that I see there in the distance ? but, What is the constitution of the tube that gives rise to them ? So there might lie in this a source of knowledge that might be just as important as the outlook from the window.

Our readers will already observe that here there remains the same doubt that we asserted against the categories. It must be admitted that such a disposition may exist in our reason, as necessarily presents to us ideas which have nothing to do with experience. It must be admitted that such ideas, if we have freed ourselves from the deceptive appearance of an external knowledge, may still be, even in a theoretical sense, an extremely valuable intellectual possession ; but we have no means of deducing them with certainty from a principle. We find ourselves here simply on the ground of *psychology*—so far that is as such a science may be spoken of as already existing—and only the universal method of special scientific inquiries can lead us to a knowledge of such natural dispositions, if such knowledge be possible at all.[41]

But now as to the *necessity* of the ideas, it must, in the extent in which Kant maintains it, be decidedly controverted. Only for the idea of the soul, as a unitary subject for the multeity of sensations, may it be said to be probable. As to the idea of God, so far as a rational Creator is opposed to the world, there is no such natural disposition. This is proved not only by the Materialists through their mere existence ; it is proved also by many of the greatest thinkers of ancient and modern times, Demokritos, Heraklitos, Empedokles, Spinoza, Fichte, Hegel. Far as these last two on the main question — like the astronomer Tycho—have fallen behind Kant, yet they serve here as examples of vigorous thinkers, with a leaning to the abstract, who by no means confirm the ideal of the pure reason of a rational originator of the universe in Kant's sense.

While treating the idea of the world as a totality of all phenomena in their causal connexion, Kant tries to solve also the problem of the will. But this very problem plays a great part in the materialistic controversy of our day ; and while the Materialists usually confine themselves to a simple denial of free will, unskilful opponents appeal often enough to Kant, as though he had proved incontrovertibly the existence of free will. From either point of view, then, it must throw light upon the matter, if we succeed in sketching Kant's real view, with a few firm and comprehensive traits.

In the phenomenal world, everything hangs together as

[41] That psychology, in the sense in which alone it can in future be called a science, must start not from a notion of a soul, but from the psychical functions, we shall show further on. The relation of 'body and soul' in the sense of the old metaphysic, need, therefore, by no means be decided in the materialistic sense. It is simply beyond discussion, as something to which actual investigation within the limits of possible experience never leads. See previous note.

cause and effect. To this the human will is no exception. It is entirely subject to the law of nature. But this law of nature itself, with the whole succession of events, is only phenomenon, and the natural disposition of our reason necessarily leads us to assume besides the world that we perceive with our senses another imaginary world. This imaginary world, so far as we form any definite idea of it, is a world of illusion, a figment of the brain. So far, however, as we regard it merely as the general notion of the nature of things that lies beyond our experience, it is something more; for precisely because we recognise the phenomenal world as a product of our organisation, we must also be able to assume a world independent of our forms of knowledge—the 'intelligible' world. This assumption is not a transcendental knowledge, but merely the ultimate consequence of the use of the understanding in judging of what is given us.

Into this intellectual world Kant removes the freedom of the will, that is, he abolishes it altogether from the world that we usually call the real world—from our phenomenal world. In this latter everything is related as cause and effect. These alone can, leaving the criticism of the reason and metaphysic out of view, be the object of scientific inquiry; they alone can form the basis of a judgment on human actions in daily life, in medical or judicial investigations, and so on.

We must judge quite otherwise in the sphere of practice, in the struggle with our own passions, in education, or wherever we are concerned not to judge as to the will, but to exercise a moral effect. There we must start from the fact, that we find within ourselves a law that unconditionally prescribes to us how we ought to act. This law, however, must be associated with the conception that it can also be carried into effect. 'Thou canst, for thou oughtst,' says the inner voice; not, 'Thou oughtst, because thou canst;' because the sense of duty is present quite independently of our power. Whether Kant was justified

in basing his whole practical philosophy on the idea of
duty we leave for the present undetermined. We simply
insist upon the fact. Considering the enormous influence
which Kant, understood or misunderstood, has exercised
upon the treatment of these questions, we spare ourselves
and our readers endless discussions as to modern controversies, if we only succeed in clearly and fully exhibiting
the essential course of Kant's ideas, without losing ourselves in the labyrinth of these endless definitions of his,
which remind us of Gothic ornamentation.

Quite independently of all experience Kant believes
that he can find in the human consciousness the moral
law, which as an inner voice commands absolutely, but is,
of course, not absolutely obeyed. But just because man conceives the unconditional fulfilling of the moral law as possible, a conditional influence also is exercised upon its real,
and not its merely imaginary, accomplishment. The conception of the moral law we can only regard as an element
of the mental process as matter of experience, which has to
struggle with all other elements, with impulses, inclinations, habits, momentary influences, and so on. And this
struggle, together with its result—the moral or immoral
act—follows in its whole course the universal natural
laws to which man in this respect forms no exception.
The conception of the unconditional has, therefore, in experience only conditional force ; but yet this conditional force
is all the stronger, the more purely, clearly, and strongly
the man can hear within himself that unconditionally
commanding voice. But the conception of duty which
calls to us, 'Thou shalt,' cannot possibly continue clear and
strong, if it is not combined with the conception of the
possibility of carrying out this command. For this reason,
therefore, we must, with regard to the morality of our
conduct, transfer ourselves entirely into the intellectual
world in which alone freedom is conceivable.[42]

[42] In the First Ed. we were content to set out this side of the Kantian
doctrine of freedom, thinking that it
contains, at least from a theoretical

So far Kant's doctrine of freedom is perfectly clear and —apart from the question of the *a priority* of the moral law—invulnerable. He still wants, however, a bond which shall give greater certainty to the doctrine of freedom, while at the same time it binds together the practical and the theoretical philosophy. In establishing this bond, Kant gives to his doctrine of freedom a mystic background, which seems desirable for the moral impulse of the soul, but which at the same time seriously confuses that clear and definite doctrine of the relation of the world of phenomena to the world of things-in-themselves, which we have set out above, and lands the whole system in uncertainty.

This bond is the idea that, in order to be able to support *practically* the doctrine of freedom, we must *theoretically* assume it as at least possible, although we cannot know in what way it is possible.

This postulated possibility is built upon the notion of things in themselves as opposed to phenomena. If the phenomena were the things in themselves, as Materialism maintains, freedom could not be saved. The bare idea of freedom is not enough for him, unless it is related to the phenomena exactly as is an idea to reality, or poetry to history. Nay indeed, Kant goes so far as to say, "Man

standpoint, the kernel of the question, and that passages like those from the *Kritik d. pr. V.* (Hart., v. S. 105), which are discussed further on, might be regarded as deviations from the essential principle, while the whole doctrine of the "objective reality" of the idea of freedom only serves to darken the real question. The present fuller exposition is connected with my renouncing the attempt to be so very popular and easy, but will, I hope, be intelligible to that class of readers who are most interested in a scientific history of Materialism. An important point is, that even this mystical character which the doctrine of freedom acquires in passing over into the sphere of practice does not exclude the strict rule of the laws of nature in empirical psychology, and that therefore even in this sphere Kant's "transcendental freedom" is very different from that theory of freedom which Schleiden, Ideler, and other 'Kantians' have read into him. The proofs of our several propositions which attempt to give shortly, for the most part, the sense and spirit, and not the words, of the Kantian theory, must be here dispensed with, as the notes would otherwise, with any pretensions to thoroughness, have extended themselves into a book.

would be a marionette or a Vaucanson's automaton put together and set agoing by the supreme master of mechanism," and the consciousness of freedom would be mere delusion, unless the actions of man were "mere determinations of man as phenomenon."

It must be observed that Kant, even after this hazardous step, still remains at peace with the scientific study of man. The world of phenomena, to which man belongs as a portion of them, is thoroughly governed by the law of cause; and there is no action of man, not even the supreme heroism of duty, which is not, physiologically and psychologically considered, determined by the antecedent development of the individual, or by the shaping of the situation in which he finds himself placed. On the other hand, Kant holds the idea to be indispensable, that the very same series of events which in the world of phenomena presents itself as a causal series, is in the intelligible world based upon freedom. This idea appears theoretically as possible only, but the practical reason treats it as actual, nay, it converts it, through the irresistible force of the moral consciousness, into an assertory principle. We know that we are free, although we do not see how it can be so. We are free as rational beings. The subject exalts itself in the certainty of the moral law above the sphere of phenomena. We think of ourselves in moral action as a thing in itself, and we have a right to do so, although the theoretical reason cannot follow us here. There is nothing left her, as it were, but in the moment of action to marvel at the wonder, which she at the same time, in the moment of examination, must again find too easy, and cannot take up into the sure possession of knowledge.

This whole train of thought is wrong from the very outset. Kant wished to avoid the obvious contradiction between the Ideal and Life; but this is impossible. It is impossible because the subject, even in the moral struggle, is not noümenon but phenomenon. The corner-stone of the critical philosophy—that we do not know even ourselves as we are in ourselves, but only as we appear to ourselves—can no more be overturned by the *moral* will than by the will in general, after the fashion of Schopenhauer. But even if we would suppose with Schopenhauer that the will is the thing in itself, or with Kant that in moral willing the subject is a rational thing, even this could not protect us from that contradiction ; for we have to do in every moral struggle, not with the will in itself, but with our *conception* of ourselves and of our will, and this conception remains unavoidably phenomenon.

Kant, who in the Prolegomena explains his own view to be that truth lies only in experience, has by a stroke of the pen turned all experience into a game of marionettes; while, at the same time, the whole difference between an automaton and a morally acting man is undoubtedly *a difference between two phenomena.* In the phenomenal world those notions of value have their root, by which we find here mere mechanicalness and there exalted earnestness. We conceive the one and the other with our senses and ideas, and establish a distinction which is not in the least impaired by the circumstance that we find in both the common feature of necessity. But even if it were so impaired, yet here again the translation into the 'thing-in-itself' would not help us. To compare them, everything, and not only the moral will, must be transferred into the world of noümena, and what then becomes of the marionette? What of the mechanism of nature in general? There the difference in our estimation will perhaps disappear, which in the world of phenomena has its roots sure and independent of any psychological views as to the will.

All these objections, however, touch only the equivocal position into which by that fatal turning the thing in itself is brought, and the construction of a knowledge that is yet no knowledge, of a science which, according to our own presuppositions, cannot be called science. Kant would not understand, what Plato before him would not understand, that the 'intelligible world' is a world of poesy, and that precisely upon this fact rests its worth and nobleness. For poesy, in the high and comprehensive sense in which it must be taken, cannot be regarded as a capricious playing of talent and fancy with empty imginations for amusement, but it is a necessary offspring of the soul, arising from the deepest life-roots of the race, and a complete counterbalance to the pessimism which springs from an exclusive acquaintance with reality.

It was not that Kant had no sense for this view of the intelligible world, but his whole development, and the age in which his intellectual life had its roots, prevented him from breaking fully out into the light in this point. As it was denied him to find for the powerful structure of his ideas a noble form, free from mediæval fancifulness, so his positive philosophy never attained a full and free development. His philosophy, however, stands with Janus-countenance on the border of two ages, and his relations to the great epoch of German poetry go far beyond the character of a casual and isolated stimulus. And therefore the false subtleties in his deduction of freedom may speedily be forgotten; the loftiness with which he conceived the idea of duty kindled a flame in youthful minds; and many a passage of his writings, in all the simplicity of their awkward expression, exercised an entrancing influence, as of a heroic song, upon those spirits that were seized by the ideal character of the age. "There is also a teacher of the ideal," said Kant towards the end of the *Critick*, and him alone must we call the philosopher. He himself, despite all errors in his deductions, has become such a "teacher of the ideal." Especially has Schiller, with a spiritual divination, seized the core of his doctrines and purified them from scholastic dross.

We shall hardly find a more eloquent testimony for the importance which we have here attributed to poesy than the fact that Schiller in his prose writings repeatedly shares, nay even surpasses, the faults of the Master, while in his poetry he is thoroughly consistent. Kant believes that we can only 'think,' and not 'intuite,' the intelligible world, but that what we think about it must possess 'objective reality.' Schiller has, rightly enough, made the intelligible world visible to sense in treating it as a poet; and in so doing he has trodden in the steps of Plato, who, in contradiction to his own dialectic, produced his noblest creations when he made in the mythos the supersensuous become sensuous.

Schiller, the 'poet of freedom,' might venture openly to transpose freedom into the 'Realm of Dreams' and the 'Realm of Shadows,' for beneath his hand dreams and shadows were raised to the ideal. The wavering became a fixed pole, the fleeting a godlike form, the play of caprice an everlasting law, as over against life he set the ideal. Whatever of good religion and morality contain cannot be more purely and forcibly expressed than in that immortal Hymn which closes with the passage through the sky of the tortured Son of God. Here is embodied the flight from the limits of the senses into the intelligible world. We follow the God who, 'flaming, parts Himself from man,' and now dream and truth change their parts— the heavy dream-picture of life sinks, and sinks, and sinks.

.   .   .   .   .   .

Later we shall come upon these thoughts again. Here let us only add, that the historical importance that Kant's ethic attained must seem to us, not only intelligible, but even justifiable, as soon as we regard it in the proper light. The lasting achievements of Kant's philosophy lie in the criticism of the pure reason, and even here only in a few fundamental principles; but a philosophy is not important only through those elements of it that stand the test of the understanding, and are numbered among the assured treasures of human knowledge. Creations of a bold and, as it were, unconsciously poetic combination, which a strict criticism must again destroy, may through their spirit and content exercise a deeper and nobler influence than the most luminous doctrines; and human culture can no more spare the stimulating glow of these revelations, perishable though they be in form, than the illuminating light of criticism. No thought is so calculated to reconcile poesy and science as the thought that all our 'reality'—without any prejudice to its strict connexion, undisturbed by any caprice—is only *appearance*. Yet this truth still remains for science, that the 'thing-in-itself' is a mere limitative idea. Every attempt to turn its negative meaning into a positive one leads us undeniably into the sphere of poesy, and only what endures when measured by the standard of poetic purity and nobleness can claim to serve a generation as instruction in the ideal.

CHAPTER II.

ENGLAND, France, and the Netherlands, the true homes of modern philosophy, retired towards the end of the last century from the theatre of metaphysical war. Since Hume England has produced no great philosopher, unless we concede this rank to the acute and energetic Mill. A similar interval lies in France between Diderot and Comte. In both countries we find meanwhile in other spheres progress and revolutions on the most splendid scale. Here the most unexampled movement of industry and commerce with general consolidation; there the Revolution that shook Europe, and the development of a tremendous military power. These were two very different, indeed quite opposite, turns of national development, that nevertheless agreed in this, that the 'Western Powers' devoted themselves entirely to the tasks of real life. Meanwhile metaphysics were left to us in Germany.

And yet it were the greatest ingratitude, if we were to look back upon those great epochs of purely intellectual effort with depreciation or even with lack of sympathy. It is true that we, like Schiller's Poet, came off empty at the partition of the world. It is true that the intoxication of Idealism with us—perhaps we may say, and its after-pangs also—is now over, and that we are no longer content with a spiritual sojourn in the heaven of Zeus. We are reaching manhood later than other nations, but we have also experienced a more beautiful, richer, if almost too enthusiastic a youth; and it must be proved whether our people has been enervated by these intellectual delights, or whether in its ideal past it possesses an inexhaustible spring of force and freshness, that needs only to be diverted into the channels of a new productiveness to achieve great results. The *one* practical fact that falls in this period of Idealism, the rising of the people in the liberation wars, bears indeed the character of a dreamy half-heartedness, but it betrays at the same time a mighty force that is as yet only dimly conscious of its aim.

It is remarkable how our national development, more regular than that of ancient Hellas, started from the most ideal and approximated more and more to the real. At first came Poetry, whose classic age had reached its zenith in the common activity of Goethe and Schiller, when Philosophy, set going by Kant, began its stormy course. After the extinction of the Titanic efforts of Schelling and Hegel, the serious study of the positive sciences came to the front. To the old fame of Germany in philosophical criticism now succeed brilliant conquests in every branch of knowledge. Niebuhr, Ritter, and the two Humboldts may here be especially named as pioneers. Only in the exact sciences, which most concern us in connexion with Materialism, is Germany supposed to be behind England and France; and our men of science are glad to shift the blame of this upon philosophy, that has overgrown everything with its structures of fancy, and has smothered the spirit of sound inquiry. How this is we shall soon see. Here it is enough to observe that at all events the exact sciences stand nearest to the tasks of practical life that at present lie before us, and that their late unfolding in Germany entirely corresponds to the course of development here indicated.

We have seen in the First Book how early Materialism planted itself in Germany; how it was by no means first introduced from France, but, coming here direct from England, had struck out peculiar roots. We have seen how, in fact, in Germany the materialistic controversy of the last century was carried on with special vigour, and how the dominant philosophy, despite its apparently so easy triumph, in this contest only exhibited its own weakness.

Materialism, without doubt, increased in the general modes of thought, while Klopstock had long ago laid the germ of that luxuriant Idealism in the ground of poetry. That Materialism could not openly show itself is, considering the state of things then in Germany, easily intelligible. We detect its presence more by the persistent polemics against it than by positive creations. And yet we may regard Kant's whole system as a splendid attempt to abolish Materialism for ever, without therefore falling a prey to scepticism.

If we look to the external success of this attempt, it may seem significant enough that from Kant's appearance until the immediate past Materialism in Germany seemed almost blown away. The isolated attempts to explain naturally the origin of man through the development of an animal form, amongst which that of Oken (1819) made most sensation, belong by no means to the succession of strictly Materialistic views. Pantheism, on the contrary, thanks to Schelling and Hegel, became the prevailing mode of thought in the philosophy of nature, a view of things that, with a certain mystical depth, at the same time all but necessarily contains within itself the danger of fantastical extravagances. Instead of strictly separating experience and the sense-world from the ideal, and then seeking in the nature of man for the reconciliation of these spheres, the Pantheist effects the reconciliation of Spirit and Nature by a dictum of the imaginative reason without any critical mediation. Hence the pretensions to the knowledge of the Absolute which Kant thought his Criticism had banished for ever. Kant, of course, knew well enough, and foretold unequivocally, that his philosophy could not possibly expect an immediate victory, since centuries had passed before Copernicus's theory had prevailed over the

prejudices that opposed it. But could the sober and
yet vigorous thinker have allowed himself to fancy that,
scarcely twenty-five years after the first propagation of
his Criticism, a work like Hegel's *Phänomenologie des
Geistes* would be possible in Germany? And yet it was
his own appearance that called forth our metaphysical
Sturm-und-Drang period. The man whom Schiller compared to a constructing king not only afforded nourishment to the 'dustmen' of interpretation, but he begat also
a spiritual dynasty of ambitious imitators, who, like the
Pharaohs, piled one pyramid upon another into the sky,
and only forgot to base them upon *terra firma*.

We are here not concerned to develop how it came
about that Fichte seized upon one of the darkest points
of Kant's philosophy—the doctrine of the original synthetic unity of apperception,—in order to deduce from it
his creative Ego, as Schelling from the A = A, as it were
from a hollow nut, conjured forth the universe; how
Hegel could declare *Sein* and *Nichtsein* to be identical,
amid the joyful acclamations of the inquisitive youth of
our universities. The time is over when one heard men
talking of Ego and Non-ego, of the Absolute and the Idea,
at every street-corner in the homes of the Muses, and
Materialism does not require us to describe it to our
readers. That whole epoch of philosophical romanticism
has not down to our own day produced one single point
of permanent value for the criticism of the materialistic
question. Every criticism of Materialism, from the standpoint of imaginative metaphysic, can only serve the purpose of an explanation between two co-ordinate standpoints. Where we cannot, as with Kant, reach a higher
point of view, we must decline such excursions.

That we cannot look down with the depreciation that
has now become fashionable upon the services of Schelling
and Hegel, but especially of the latter, is quite a different
matter. A man who gives to the enthusiastic tendency of
several decades a dominant and overwhelming expression

can never be altogether unimportant. But if we consider only the influence of Hegel on the writing of history, especially with reference to the treatment of the history of civilisation, it must be admitted that in his own way he has mightily contributed to the advancement of science.[43] The poesy of ideas has a high value for science, if it proceeds from a rich and many-sided scientific culture. The ideas which the philosopher of this stamp produces are more than dead rubrics for the results of inquiry; they have a wealth of relations to the essence of our knowledge, and therefore to the essence of that experience which is alone possible to us. If inquiry uses them rightly, it can never be hindered by them; but if it submits to be manacled by a philosophic dictum, then it loses its own proper life. Our doctrine of the invalidity of all metaphysic as opposed to strict empiricism, whenever it is a question of a definite piece of knowledge, lies unconsciously in human nature. Every one believes in the experiment he has clearly seen, and still more in that which he has made himself. Inquiry was able in its first childish

[43] If sometimes Hegel's influence upon the writing of history is singled out as mischievous, the charge rests especially upon that inclination to bend the facts to suit a philosophical theory, of which we have found so striking an example in the History of Materialism (comp. p. 49, foll.). It is too easy, however, to forget in what a poor condition was the writing of history in Germany before Hegel. Not unjustly, says Zeller (Gesch. d. deutschen Phil., S. 824), "If our own historical writing no longer contents itself with the learned discovery and critical sifting of traditions, with the ordering and pragmatic exposition of facts, but, above all, seeks to understand the deep-lying connexion of events, and to take a large view of the historical development and the intellectual forces that govern it, this progress is not last to be referred to the influence which Hegel's Philosophy of History has exercised even upon those who have never belonged to his school." The true point of view is somewhat missed in opposing to the 'idealistic' tendency in history which began with Kant and Schiller the present tendency as absolutely realistic. When Alex. v. Humboldt (cp. Tomaschek, Schiller in s. Verh. zur Wissensch, S 130) compares the idealistic tendency with the assumption of "vital force" in physiology, we might perhaps more correctly represent the relation of idea and fact in the influence of Darwin's theory upon the study of natural history. We may here, too, dismiss the inclination to construction from a tendency rigidly starting from the facts, without overlooking the importance of so great a point of view for the apprehension and appreciation of the individual.

beginnings to burst the bands of the Aristotelian metaphysic that had been hardening for thousands of years, and
shall a Hegel have brought it in its manhood out of Germany as if by mere sleight of hand ?   In the next section
we shall see better what is the true state of the case!

If we now ask ourselves how Materialism emerged again
after Kant, we must remember above all that the flood of
Idealism which burst over Germany had swept away with
it not only Materialism, but at bottom even the properly
critical element in the criticism of reason, so that in this
respect Kant has had almost more influence upon our own
day than upon his contemporaries.   The elements of the
Kantian philosophy, which *permanently* destroy Materialism, very slightly asserted themselves, and those that
momentarily supplanted it might themselves naturally be
supplanted upon a fresh change in the character of the
time.

Most of our modern Materialists are, of course, inclined
a priori, and before any examination, to deny roundly the
connexion of their views with De la Mettrie, or even with
Demokritos.   The favourite view is that modern Materialism is a simple result of modern science, and for this
very reason not at all to be compared with similar views of
ancient times, because our modern sciences did not exist
in these earlier times.   In that case this book need not
have been written.   But if it were allowed us to develop
successively the decisive principles in the simpler views
of earlier times, we must at least have placed the next
chapter before the present one.

Let us guard against a very possible misunderstanding.
When we maintain the historical connexion we do not, of
course, mean by it to explain Büchner's ' Kraft und Stoff'
as an unacknowledged use of ' L'Homme Machine.'   Not
even a stimulus from the reading of such works, nay, not
even the slightest knowledge of them, is required to justify
us in supposing an historical connexion.   As the heat-
rays of the glowing coal scatter themselves in every

direction from one point, in order, when thrown back from the elliptic mirror, to ignite the glowing tinder, so the influence of an author—and especially of the philosopher—loses itself in the consciousness of the crowd, and from out this consciousness the scattered principles and views act upon the later-ripening individuals, whose receptivity and position determine their suitability to collect such rays. That our comparison halts is matter of course, but still it explains one side of the truth; now for the other!

If Moleschott could say that the man is the sum of parents and nurse, of place and time, of air and weather, of sound and light, of food and dress, we may venture to lay down a similar canon for intellectual influences. 'The philosopher is the sum of tradition and experience, of brain-structure and environment, of opportunity and study, of health and society.' Somewhat thus might run the canon, which should at all events show, obviously enough, that even the materialistic philosopher cannot attribute his system to his studies only. In the historical connexion of things one step strikes upon a thousand threads, and we can follow only one at once. Indeed we cannot always do even this, because the coarser and visible thread branches into innumerable smaller threads, that partially escape our view. That the influence of the modern sciences upon the special development of Materialism, and particularly upon its spread and wider propagation, is very great, need not be said. Our exposition, however, will sufficiently show that most of the questions we have now to do with are just the old ones, and that only the material is changed, but not the aim or the method of demonstration.

It must, of course, be at once admitted that the influence of the physical sciences was always calculated, even during our idealistic period, to maintain and advance materialistic principles. With the awakening, therefore, of a keener and universal feeling for the natural sciences, such views naturally at once found themselves at home, even though they may not at once have assumed a dogmatic attitude. And we must not forget that the study of the positive sciences remained cosmopolitan, while philosophy in Germany struck out an isolated path corresponding to the general feeling of the nation. The German man of science, however, must have necessarily shared not only in the sympathy with the inquiries of foreigners, but also the spirit in which these inquiries were instituted and the ideas that linked the details together. In the most influential nations it was the views of the seventeenth and eighteenth centuries that on the whole prevailed, even though, as a rule, any attempt to push things to their consequences was avoided. In France especially a materialistic basis was given to physiology by Cabanis, just at the very moment when in Germany Idealism was being carried to the highest pitch by Schiller and Fichte (1795 and onwards). As a philosopher, indeed, Cabanis was anything but a Materialist.[44] He leaned to a pantheism bordering on the Stoic doctrine, and regarded the knowledge of ' first causes ' (we might say, in Kant's language, of the ' thing-in-itself ')

[44] Cf. Cabanis, Rapports du Physique et du Moral de l'Homme et Lettre sur les Causes Premières, 8e ed. augm. de Notes, &c., par L. Peisse: Paris, 1844. The first half of the work was read towards the end of 1795 in the Academy, and printed in its Proceedings, 1798–99 ; the second half appeared with the collected works in 1802. The 'Letter on First Causes,' one of his last productions, was only published long after the author's death—in 1824. There has been much controversy whether the pantheistic philosophy of the Letter, and especially the clearly expressed *Vitalism* (assumption of a *substantial* vital force over and above the organic forces), are consistent or not with the materialistic spirit of the principal work. The editor, Peisse, has shown in the prefixed essay on the life and doctrines of Cabanis, and in several of his notes, that we must not look in Cabanis for any strict philosophical consistency; that his writings may contain many small vacillations and even contradictions, but that there is no occasion to suppose a change of view, or a conscious retractation between the chief work and the metaphysical Letter. Thus, *e.g.*, it is shown from a passage in an earlier work that Cabanis, even before writing the ' Rapports,' was a decided adherent of Stahl's ' Vitalism.' His leaning to pantheism can be easily gathered from the historical section of the ' Rapports,' especially from his views of the natural philosophy of the Stoics. It is by no means incompatible with this that we find in Cabanis nearly all the watchwords of our modern Materialists, as, *e.g.*, the idea that *thoughts are a secretion of the brain* (*loc. cit.*, S. p. 138).

as impossible.[45] He often controverts the doctrine of Epikuros. But in the scientific study of man he is the pioneer of the *somatic method*. In the sphere of phenomena, or, as it is expressed in his phrase, when we deal with the 'secondary causes,' which alone are accessible to man, we find intellectual functions everywhere dependent upon organisation, and sensation is the basis of thought and action. To the demonstration of this connexion his work is devoted, and his readers and disciples naturally keep to the heart of his theme, to the aim and matter of his work, without troubling themselves much with any introductory or casual expressions of a philosophic character. Since Cabanis, therefore, the resolution of mental functions into the activity of the nervous system has kept its ground in physiology, whatever individual physiologists may have thought as to the ultimate grounds of all things. It belongs to the nature of the special sciences that subject-matter and method go from step to step, while the philosophical background is constantly changing, if indeed it exists at all. The mass of men hold fast to the comparatively constant factor, and regard as justified only what is obvious, useful, and practical. In this way there must necessarily be developed from the study of the special sciences—so long as philosophy is not in a position to assert its counter-influence amongst all educated men—an ever new Materialism, which is perhaps only the more obstinate the less it is consciously regarded by its disciples as a philosophical theory of things. But for the same reasons this Materialism does not far overstep the limits of special studies. It must be deeper reasons that suddenly excite the scientific student to examine the principles that underlie his notion of the world, and this process is inseparable from that reflection and collection of ideas under one single point of view, the philosophical character of which is unmistakable.

That such a turn took place just in Germany while in

45 Cf. II. Mémoire, § 8, pp. 141, 142.

England and France Materialism ceased to appear con-
spicuously in the arena, depends no doubt upon the circumstance that here men had become more accustomed than in
any other country to philosophical controversies. We may
say that Idealism itself lent assistance to Materialism in
awaking the sense for the systematic working out of leading ideas, and in provoking by its very opposition the
young and aspiring natural sciences. To this was added
that in no country had such general freedom been attained
from religious prejudices and ecclesiastical pretensions,
and one's own ideas, as it were, so much claimed as a
necessity for all educated persons. Here, too, it was
Idealism that had prepared the way in which Materialism
might later move along, almost without any hindrance
worth naming; and if this circumstance is often entirely
overlooked by Materialists, or even entirely misrepresented,
this is only one of the many signs of the unhistorical sense
that is so often found combined with Materialism.

At the same time, we must not forget that there has never
been wanting in Germany a sense for the scientific consideration of things, though this tendency in the flowering
time of our national literature was thrown into the shade
by ethical elevation and speculative enthusiasm. Kant
himself was quite the man to combine the two tendencies
in his thinking, and especially in his pre-critical period he
not unfrequently comes very near to Materialism. His
pupil and opponent, Herder,[46] was thoroughly imbued with
scientific modes of thought, and might perhaps have been
able to do much more for the development of the scientific
sense in Germany, if he had been content to work for his
ideas in positive fashion, instead of engaging with Kant
in a controversy over principles, bitter and full of misunderstandings. How far Goethe was carried by genuine

---

[46] We can here refer to the clever
and instructive 'Geschichte der Ent-
wickelung der Naturwissenschaftl.
Weltanschauung in Deutschland' by
Dr. H. Böhmer. The author indeed
exalts Herder at the expense of Kant,
and favours a 'Realism' the defects
of which we hope to show farther on.

scientific feeling is every day becoming more generally recognised. In many of his expressions we observe a calm and gentle tolerance towards the one-sidedness of the idealistic tendency, the kernel of truth in which he knew how to value, while at the same time his mind felt itself gradually drawn more and more decidedly to the objective view of nature. His relation to the philosophy of nature school must therefore not be misinterpreted. He, the poet, was at least freer from fantastic extravagance than many a professed man of science. But even the philosophers of nature show us in truth only an odd fusion of the universally ruling Romanticism with genuine receptiveness for the observation of phenomena and the tracing of their connexions. With such preparations the general transition of the nation from the period of Idealism to a sober and objective mode of thinking must in time necessarily bring Materialism also again to the front.

If we wish to fix a definite point to describe as the end of the idealistic period in Germany, no such distinctive event offers itself as the French Revolution of July 1830.

The idealistic patriotism of the times of the liberation had become soured in prison air, languishing abroad, and evaporating beneath the indifference of the masses. Philosophy had lost its charm since it had entered into the service of Absolutism. The magnificent abstraction which had created the formula that the *actual* is at the same time the *rational* had in the North of Germany performed the meanest beadle-offices long enough to excite a universal distrust of philosophy. In poetic literature men had become sated with Romanticism, and Heine's *Reisebilder* had struck a note of frivolity that one would hardly have looked for in the country of Schiller. The author of this characteristic product of the time took up his abode in Paris in 1830, and it became the fashion to despair of Germany's future, and to regard the more realistic France as the model of the new epoch. About the same time the spirit of enterprise in commerce and industry began to bestir itself. Material interests developed, and, as in England, they soon combined with the natural sciences against everything that seemed to turn man aside from his immediate purposes. Yet literature for some decades still dominated the national point of view; but into the place of Classicism as well as Romanticism Young Germany forced its way. The rays of materialistic modes of thought gathered themselves together. Men like Gutzkow, Th. Mundt, and Laube by their writings contributed much of the leaven of Epikurean views. The last especially tugged hard at the mantle of honour with which our philosophy had concealed the deficiencies of its logic.

Yet it is just Epigoni of the great philosophical epoch to whom the revival of Materialism is commonly referred. Czolbe regards D. F. Strauss as the father of our modern Materialism; others, with more justice, name Feuerbach.[47] It is certain that in the use of this name too exclusive reference has been had to religious controversies; and yet Feuerbach stands so near to Materialism that he demands special consideration.

Ludwig Feuerbach, the son of the famous criminal lawyer, early displayed an earnest, laborious nature, and more character than spirit and vivacity. Drawn into the vortex of Hegelian enthusiasm, in his twentieth year he started as a student of theology upon his pilgrimage to Berlin, where Hegel was then (1824) already clothed in the full dignity of the state philosopher. Philosophemes in which being was not replaced by not-being, and the positive obtained from the negative, were in official edicts characterised as "shallow and superficial."[48] Feuerbach's

---

[47] There can here be no question, of course, of Strauss's latest appearance.

[48] In a circular rescript from the Ministry of Education and Medicine, of 21st August 1824: "The Royal Science Examinations Commission is invited at the same time to have strict regard to the thoroughness and inward content of philosophy and its study, in order that the *shallow and superficial philosophemes* which have recently but too often formed the whole study of philosophy may at length yield to a thorough training in philosophy, and that the true philosophical study may again receive its honoured and valuable position, and

thorough nature worked its way from the Hegelian abysses into a certain "superficiality," without, however, ever losing the traces of the Hegelian profundity. To a clear logic Feuerbach never attained. The nerve of his philosophising remained, as everywhere in the idealistic epoch, divination. A "consequently" in Feuerbach does not, as with Kant and Herbart, carry the force of a real, or at least intended, inference of the understanding, but it means, as with Schelling and Hegel, a leap to be taken in thought ; and therefore his system, too, floats in a mystic gloom which is by no means adequately illuminated by the emphasis put upon sensibility and picturableness.

"God was my first thought, Reason my second, Man my third and last thought." By this expression Feuerbach denotes not so much different phases of his philosophy as rather merely the stadia of his youthful development; for soon after his habilitation (1828) he openly set forth the principles of his humanity-philosophy, to which he afterwards held unshakably fast. The new philosophy is to hold the same relation to Hegel's philosophy of reason as this holds to theology. A new epoch is now therefore to begin, in which not only theology but also metaphysic appears as an obsolete standpoint.

It is remarkable how nearly this view coincides with the doctrines which about the same time the noble Comte, a lonely thinker and friend of man, struggling with poverty and depression, was trying to assert in Paris. Comte, too, speaks of three epochs of humanity. The first is the theological, the second the metaphysical, the third and last is the *positive, i.e.,* that in which man applies himself, with

the academic youth, instead of being confused and darkened by that sham-philosophy, may be led by a thorough training in the genuine philosophic spirit to the clear, right, and thorough application of their mental powers." Rönne, Unterrichtswesen des Preuss. Staates, ii. S. 42. "That sham-philosophy" is probably Bencke's ; cf. Ueberweg, Grundr. d. Phil., iii. 3 Aufl. 319. The tendency and effect of the edict must, under the then circumstances, necessarily have been directed to a monopoly for the philosophy of Hegel.

all his might and main, to reality, and finds his satisfaction in the resolution of actual problems.[49]

In common with Hobbes, Comte places the aim of all science in the knowledge of the laws that regulate phenomena. "To see, in order to foresee; to inquire what is, in order to conclude what will be," is for him the task of philosophy. Feuerbach, on the other hand, declares, "The new philosophy makes man, including nature as the basis of man, the one universal and highest object of philosophy,"—makes anthropology, therefore, including physiology, the universal science.[50]

In this undue prominence given to man lies a trait which is due to the Hegelian philosophy, and which separates Feuerbach from strict Materialists. That is to say, it is only the philosophy of spirit over again that meets us here in the shape of a philosophy of sensibility. The genuine Materialist will always incline to turn his gaze upon the great whole of external nature, and to regard man as a wave in the ocean of the eternal movement of matter. The nature of man is to the Materialist only a special case of universal physiology, as thought is only a special case in the chain of the physical processes of life. He likes best to range the whole of physiology in the general phenomena of physics and chemistry, and chooses

---

[49] On Comte and his system, cf. 'Auguste Comte and Positivism,' by John Stuart Mill: London, 1865. A brief view of the idea and aim of Positivism is given in the 'Discours sur l'Esprit Positif,' par M. Auguste Comte : Paris, 1844 (pp. 108, 80). Comte's chief work is the six-volumed 'Cours de Philosophie Positive,' 1830–42; second edition, with Preface by Littré, 1864. Comte has only recently received any attention in Germany. In Ueberweg's Hist. of Philos., (Grundr, iii. 361 ff. E. T. ii. 344), there is a short account of him by Paul Janet, which, however, is so far unjust to Comte that it makes his doctrine of the three stages, theological, metaphysical, and positive, merely the *negative* part of his philosophy, so that as positive part we have only two notions, "a certain historical hypothesis," and "a certain co-ordination of the sciences." In fact, his positive achievement lies chiefly in the attainment and consistent carrying out of the idea of the 'positive,' which is peculiar to Comte. More exact information is given by Dühring, Krit. Gesch. d. Phil., 2 Aufl.: Berlin, 1873, S. 494–510.

[50] Grundsätze der Philos. d. Zukunft : Leipzig, 1849, S. 81, § 55.

to give man too insignificant rather than too important a place in the series of existences. In practical philosophy, indeed, he will occasionally go back to the nature of man, but there, too, he will have little inclination to ascribe divine attributes to his nature, as Feuerbach does.

The great relapse of Hegel compared with Kant consists in his entirely losing the idea of a more universal mode of knowing things as opposed to the human mode of knowing them. His whole system moves within the circle of our thoughts and fancies as to things, to which high-sounding names are given, without our ever getting to understand what validity can be attached to phenomena and to the notions collected from them. The antithesis between "essence" and "appearance" is in Hegel nothing more than an antithesis of two human modes of conception, which are soon again confounded. The phenomenon is defined as the appearance filled with the essence, and reality is thus where the phenomenon is the entire and adequate manifestation of the essence. The delusion that there can be any such thing as "entire and adequate manifestation of the essence" in the phenomenon has extended to Feuerbach also, and yet he explains reality as being simply sensibility, and this it is that brings him near to the Materialists.

"Truth, reality, sensibility are identical. Only a sensible being is a true, a real being; only sensibility is truth and reality." "Only through the senses is an object in the true sense given — not through thought in itself." "Where there is no sense there is no being, no real object." "While the old philosophy had started from the principle: I am an abstract, merely thinking being; the body is no part of my being; the new philosophy, on the other hand, begins with the principle: I am a real, a sensible being; the body is part of my being; nay, the body is its totality, is my ego, is itself my essence." "True and divine is only what needs no demonstration, what is immediately certain of itself, speaks for and asserts itself immediately, carries immediately with it the affirmation that it is—the absolutely certain, the absolutely indubitable, the sun-clear. But clear as the sun is only the sensible; only where sensibility begins does all doubt and controversy cease. The secret of immediate knowledge is sensibility." [51]

These propositions, which stand in Feuerbach's 'Grundsätze der Philosophie der Zukunft' (1849), almost as aphoristically as we here put them together, sound materialistic enough. And yet we must observe that sensibility and materiality are not identical notions. Form is not less an object of the senses than matter; indeed, true sensibility gives us always the unity of form and matter. We attain these ideas only by abstraction, by thought. By further reflection we then attain to a comprehension of their relation in any particular mode. As Aristotle everywhere gives the precedence to form, so all Materialism gives it to matter. It is one of the absolute criteria of Materialism that force and matter are not only conceived as inseparable, but that force is, in fact, conceived as a property of matter, and, moreover, that from the interaction of matter and its forces all the forms of things are deduced. We may make sensibility a principle, and still, in the essential foundation of the system, be Aristotelian, Spinozist, and even Kantian. Let us only assume, for example, that what Kant expresses as conjecture is fact, viz., that sensibility and understanding have a common root in our nature. Let us then go a step farther, and deduce the categories of the understanding from the structure of our organs of sense; the principle may still remain that sensibility itself, which thus underlies the whole phenomenal world, is only the mode in which an existence, whose real properties we do not know, is affected by other existences. There is then no logical reason to prevent our so defining reality that it coincides with sensibility, while we must, of course, maintain that behind what is thus for man

[51] These principles are in sects. 32, 33, 37, and 39 of the 'Grundsätze der Phil. d. Zukunft.'

reality a more universal existence is concealed, which, if conceived by different organs, appears also different. We might, in fact, retain the ideas of the reason together with the basing of the practical philosophy upon the consciousness of the moral agent that is peculiar to Kant; only, of course, the intelligible world must be conceived under the figure of a sensible world. Instead of Kant's sober morality, there would then result a many-coloured and glowing religion, whose sensibility, being the result of thought, could not indeed lay claim to the reality and objectivity of immediate sensibility, but might well pass, like Kant's ideas, for a representation of the higher and more universal reality of the intelligible world.

In this slight digression into the realm of possible systems, we have, indeed, got pretty far from Feuerbach; but hardly much farther than Feuerbach himself is removed from strict Materialism. Let us, then, look also at the idealistic side of this philosophy of sensibility !

" Existence is a secret of intuition, of sensation, of love. Only in sensation, only in love has This—this person, this thing—that is, the individual—absolute worth, is the finite, the infinite; herein, and only herein, consist the infinite depth, divinity, and truth of love. In love alone is the God who numbers the hairs upon our heads, truth and reality." " Human sensations have no empirical, anthropological meaning in the sense of the old transcendental philosophy; they have an ontological, metaphysical meaning; in sensations, yes, in everyday sensations, are concealed the deepest and highest truths. Thus is love the true ontological proof of the existence of an object outside our brain; and there is no other proof of existence than love and sensation generally. That only exists whose existence brings thee joy, whose non-existence brings thee pain." [52]

Feuerbach had at least so much after-thought that he did not, *e.g.*, regard the existence of living and thinking

[52] *Loc. cit.*, § 34.

beings in Jupiter or in a distant solar system as exactly impossible. And yet, if all philosophy is treated as if man were the only, indeed the only conceivable being of cultivated intellectual sensibility, this is, of course, a deliberate self-limitation. Feuerbach is in this respect Hegelian, and at bottom favours with Hegel the principle of Protagoras, that man is the measure of things. True with him means what is true for man; that is, what is apprehended with human senses. Hence he declares that sensations have not merely anthropological but metaphysical meaning; that is, that they are to be regarded not merely as facts in the individual man, but as proofs of the truth and reality of things. Hence also an advance in the subjective value of the sensible. If sensations are the basis of the metaphysical element, they must also, psychologically speaking, be the proper substance of everything intellectual.

"The old absolute philosophy rejected the senses merely into the sphere of phenomena, of finite things, and yet in contradiction to this make the absolute, the divine, the subject-matter of art. But the subject-matter of art is the subject-matter of sight, of hearing, of feeling. And therefore not only the finite, the phenomenal, but also the true, divine essence is an object of the senses—the senses the organs of the absolute.

"We feel not only stones and wood, not only flesh and bone, we feel also feelings when we press the hands or lips of a feeling creature; we catch by the ears not only the rushing of the water and the rustling of the leaves, but also the earnest voice of love and wisdom; we see not only mirror-surfaces and coloured figures, but we look into the glance of man. Not the external, then, but also the internal, not only flesh but spirit, not only the thing but the Ego is an object of the senses. Everything, therefore, is sensibly apprehensible; if not immediately, at least mediately; if not with the vulgar, untrained senses, at least with the cultivated senses; if not with the eye of the anatomist or chemist, at least with the eye of the philosopher." [53]

But are not the 'cultivated senses' and the 'eye of the philosopher' in truth a co-operation of the senses with the influence of acquired conceptions? We must concede to Feuerbach that this co-operation cannot be conceived so merely mechanically as the sum of two functions, a sensible and an intellectual. Together with the intellectual development the senses also are really trained to the knowledge of the perception of the intellectual, and it is very probable that even when we are thinking of the sublimest and apparently the most 'supersensible' objects, the sense-centres of the brain very essentially co-operate. If, however, we wish to separate the sensible element in contemplation from the intellectual, this may be done just as well in art as in any other sphere. The ideal in the head of Juno lies not in the marble, but in its *form*. Sense, as such, sees primarily the white gleaming marble; to the perception of the form some degree of cultivation is necessary, and in order to appreciate the form itself completely, thought must come out to meet the thought of the artist. Now it may well be—and this goes farther even than Feuerbach's standpoint—that even the abstractest thought builds itself up in the material of sensations, just as the most delicate drawing necessarily requires chalk or pencil; we shall then be still able to distinguish the *form* of the succession of sensations from the material element of the sensations, just as much as we distinguish the form of Cologne Cathedral from the trachyte blocks of which it is constructed. The form of the cathedral, however, may be represented in a drawing; is the notion very remote that that form of the succession of sensations, which is the spiritually significant element in the intuition of a work of art, is essentially independent of the correct material of human sensation, to which it is, of course, for us more

[53] *Loc. cit.*, §§ 40, 42.

immutably annexed ? The idea is indeed transcendental, but it contains no contradiction.

The worst point is at bottom this, that Feuerbach, besides sensation, still recognises, quite in the spirit of Hegel, an absolutely sensationless thought, and thereby introduces an irremediable discord into the nature of man. The prejudice that there must exist a sensationless, quite pure abstract thought, Feuerbach shares with the masses; unfortunately also with the great mass of physiologists and philosophers. But it fits his system less than any other. Our most significant ideas work themselves out in the finest material of sensation, so fine as to be indiscernible by careless self-observation, while the strongest sensations often have but a subordinate value in relation to our personality, and still less logical content. But there can hardly be a sensation in which there is not also felt a relation to other sensations of the same class. When I hear the sound of a bell, my sensation is conditioned in its very first immediateness by my knowledge of the bell. It is just because of this that an entirely strange sound is so unusually exciting. The universal is in the particular, the logical in the physiological, as matter is in form. What Feuerbach tears asunder metaphysically is only logically separable. There is no pure thought, containing only the universal. There is also no sensation having nothing of the universal. The individual sensible thing, as Feuerbach conceives it, does not, in fact, occur, and therefore also it cannot be the only reality.

It has always seemed remarkable to us that intelligent opponents have often urged it against Feuerbach that his system must morally lead necessarily to pure Egoism. The very contrary of this might rather be objected, namely, that Feuerbach expressly recognised the morality of theoretical Egoism, while the consequences of his whole system must necessarily lead to the very opposite. He who derives the notion of existence even from love cannot possibly retain the morality of the " Système de la Nature."

Feuerbach's peculiar moral principle, which, it is true, he sometimes flatly contradicted, must rather be denoted by the pronoun of the second person; he invented Tuism! Let us hear the basis!

"All our ideas spring from the senses; so far Empiricism is perfectly true, only it forgets that the most important and essential object of the senses to man is man himself—that the light of consciousness and understanding is kindled only in the glance of man at man. Idealism is therefore right in seeking in man the origin of ideas, but wrong in trying to derive them from isolated man as a being existing for himself and fixed as a soul—in a word, from the Ego without the sensuously given Thou. Ideas arise only through communication, only out of the converse of man with man. Not alone, but only in virtue of a duality, we attain to ideas and to reason. Two human beings appertain to the production of man, as well of spiritual as physical man; the community of man with man is the first principle and criterion of the true and the universal.

"The individual man by himself does not contain the nature of man in himself, either in himself as a moral or as a thinking being. The nature of man is contained only in the community, in the unity of man with man—a unity, however, which rests only upon the reality of the distinction of I and Thou.

"Isolation is finiteness and limitation, community is freedom and infinity. Man by himself is but man; man with man, the unity of I and Thou, is God."[54]

---

[54] *Loc. cit.*, §§ 42, 61, 62. These very important passages have been quite overlooked by, *e.g.*, Schaller in his 'Darstell. u. Kritik der Phil. Feuerbachs,' Leipzig, 1847, and it is therefore not to be wondered at that he identifies Feuerbach's ethic with Stirner's, and so concludes that Egoism and sophistic, 'die principielle Entsittlichung des Geistes,' as inevitable consequences of Feuerbach's principles. Here let us only add farther, that it was tempting enough to parallel Feuerbach's 'Tuism' with Comte's 'Altruism;' but still, without long explanations, it would have been impossible to exhibit their common features without allowing the similarity to appear greater than it really is. Feuerbach always starts

A little consecutiveness must have led Feuerbach to deduce from these principles that all human morality and the higher spiritual life rest upon the recognition of another. Instead of this, he relapsed into theoretical Egoism. The blame of this must be sought partly in the want of connexion in his speculation, partly in his struggle against religion. Opposition to the doctrines of religion carried him away into recognising the morality of Holbach, which is opposed to his system. The man who in German literature has most preached Egoism recklessly and logically—Max Stirner—finds himself in distinct opposition to Feuerbach.

Stirner went so far in his notorious work, ' Der Einzige und Sein Eigenthum' (1845), as to reject all moral ideas. Everything that in any way, whether it be external force, belief, or mere idea, places itself above the individual and his caprice, Stirner rejects as a hateful limitation of himself. What a pity that to this book—the extremest that we know anywhere—a second positive part was not added. It would have been easier than in the case of Schelling's philosophy; for out of the unlimited Ego I can again beget every kind of Idealism as *my* will and *my* idea. Stirner lays so much stress upon the will, in fact, that it appears as the root force of human nature. It may remind us of Schopenhauer. Thus are there two sides to everything!

Stirner does not stand in so clear a relation to Materialism, nor has his book had so much influence, that we need linger with him. It is rather time for us to turn to the present.

The breaking up of German Idealism, which we date from the year 1830, passed gradually into a struggle against the existing powers in State and Church, in

from the individual who seeks his completion in another, and only comes to act for the whole by personal affection. In Comte society and man's social impulse is the starting-point; and his moral law, 'vivre pour autrui' does not flow freely, like a passion from the heart, but must be supported by the notion of duty towards society.

which philosophical Materialism played directly only a subordinate part, although indeed the whole character of the time began to incline towards Materialism. We might close the record of German poetry with the year 1830, and we should lose little of real importance. Not only was the Classical period over, but the Romanticists also had sung themselves out; the Schwabian school was past its bloom, and even of Heine, who exercised so large an influence upon the new period, almost everything that is animated by the breath of Idealism lies before that point. The famous poets were dead or dumb, or had taken to prose; what was still being produced bore an artificial stamp. It is impossible to demand a more speaking proof of the inner connexion between speculation and poetry than the way in which this transition is mirrored in philosophy. Schelling, once the most conscious representative of the ideas of the time, an exuberant apostle of production, produced nothing more. The age of genius, with its quickly ripened fruits, was gone by, like a flood-tide that has given way to the ebb. Hegel, who seemed to dominate the age, tried to confine the idea into ossified formulas. In his system, indeed, the influence of the great idealistic period upon the younger generation still continued most decidedly—but with what transformations! Most of all, the understanding of Schiller disappeared, as was shown by the approval that the public gave to Börne's worthless criticism.

Gervinus, who gave distinct expression to the idea that our period of poetry had for a time come to an end, ventured the opinion that a period of *political* activity must now follow, in which Germany, under the guidance of a political Luther, should raise itself to a higher form of existence. But he forgot that to such a regeneration of form a new idealistic impulse would have been necessary, and that to the realistic period then beginning material welfare and the development of industrial activity ranked first in importance. It was towards France—" realistic "

France—that men loved to look even from a political point
of view.   But what so specially endeared the July mo-
narchy and French Constitutionalism to the men who now
gave the tone in Germany was their relation to the material interests of the monied classes.   Now for the first
time was it possible in Germany for a merchant and a
promoter of limited companies like Hansemann to become
the leader of public opinion.   Chambers of commerce and
similar societies shot up at the beginning of the 'thirties'
like mushrooms from the ground.   In education, poly-
technic institutes, institutions for technical teaching, and
commercial schools were established by the citizens of
flourishing towns, while the undeniable failings of the
grammar-schools and universities were regarded through
the magnifying-glass of failing sympathy.   Governments
tried here to check, there to anticipate, but on the whole
showed themselves seized by the same spirit.   A small
but characteristic feature was that gymnastic training,
which had been abolished because of its idealistic tendencies, was now readmitted on sanitary grounds.   The chief
activity of Governments was directed to the means of
transport, and the most important political result of the
whole decade was the German Customs Union.   Still more
important, of course, subsequently were the railways, in the
construction of which the principal towns eagerly rivalled
one another.   Exactly at the same time the interest for
natural science at last established itself in Germany also,
and the most important part in the movement was taken
by a science most closely connected with practical interests—that of chemistry.   After Liebig at Giessen had
secured the first laboratory at a German university, the
barriers of prejudice were broken down, and as one able
chemist after the other issued from Giessen, the other
universities saw themselves obliged in time to follow the
example that had been set.   One of the most important
homes, moreover, of the natural sciences was found in
Berlin, where Alexander von Humboldt, already a Euro-

pean celebrity, had taken up his abode in 1827. Ehren-
berg, Dove, and the two Roses, the chemist and the mine-
ralogist, were already at work here in the 'thirties.' To
them joined himself Johannes Müller, who had indeed in
his youth passed through the school of the philosophers
of nature, but without losing the sober energy of the scientific student. Through his 'Handbuch der Physiologie'
(1833), as well as through his indefatigable activity as a
teacher, he became the most influential pioneer of the rigidly
scientific tendency in physiology; powerfully supported,
indeed, by the still deeper and more accurate investigations
of Ernst Heinrich Weber, who worked at Leipzig. There
was, besides, the French influence, which had again become
very great in Germany, and which worked also in this direction. The inquiries of Flourens, Magendie, Leuret, Longet in
the field of physiology, and especially, too, in the physiology
of the brain and the nervous system, created an immense
sensation among the specialists of Germany, and prepared
the ground for the subsequent appearance of Vogt and
Moleschott. Even then in Germany it was common—if
not with the publicity that came later—to draw from
these inquiries conclusions as to the nature of the soul.
Even in the treatment of mind-diseases, the most powerful
impulse to reform came from France. For nothing was
so well adapted to put an end for ever to the transcendental dreams of the theologising Heinroth and his disciples as the study of Esquirol's valuable work, which was
translated into German in 1838. In the same year also
appeared a translation of Quetelet's work on Man, in
which the celebrated Belgian astronomer and statistician
endeavoured to supply a natural theory of human actions
based upon figures.

The most important effect was produced by the retiring
of the idealistic flood-tide in the sphere of religion. The
enthusiasm for pious Romanticism and poetical Ecclesias-
ticism disappeared, and left as a sediment the Materialism
of a new belief in the letter, and a soulless principle of

authority. While Hengstenberg gave the tone in this
direction from Berlin, in the South of Germany the Tübingen School, on the contrary, proceeded with an unwonted
keenness to examine the ecclesiastical traditions with the
weapons of exact science. While there was even in these
efforts—which were at first still combined with an admiration of Hegel—decidedly more genuine Idealism than in
the activity of Hengstenberg and his favourers and disciples, yet the application of a cool and strictly rational
criticism to the Bible and to ecclesiastical history belonged
to the signs of the new age, in which the practical and
rational were everywhere asserting themselves.

It cannot, however, be denied that, besides this general
tendency of the age to the practical and material, a lively
fermentation of mind was kept up by the demand for a
better political condition, and by the hatred of the cultivated classes against the reactionary attitude of the Governments. Great as was the sense of weakness in politics,
just as great was the feeling of strength in literature, as
well imaginative as scientific. The productions of 'Young
Germany' received, through the spirit of opposition which
expressed itself through them, an importance far greater
than their intrinsic merits deserved. In the year 1835—
the same year in which the first railway was opened in
Germany—appeared Mundt's 'Madonna' and Gutzkow's
'Wally,' a book that sent its author to prison for his
attack upon Christianity. And yet another book that
appeared in the same year was to strike still deeper at
the roots of the Government-Christianity, that was then
treated as the shield of all authority—Strauss's 'Life of
Jesus. With this book Germany took up the part of
leader in that struggle, which had been begun in England
and continued in France, for the application of free criticism to religious traditions. Historical and philological
criticism had already become the central feature of German science. Here reasons and counter-reasons were
easier to grasp than in the field of speculation, and the

book became, as it were, a direct challenge to every one who believed himself to possess the knowledge necessary to examine it. All those transitional standpoints, still coloured by the ideal but undecided, that survived from the age of Romanticism and the older Rationalism, were broken on the critical questions that henceforth predominated. There was a sharper division between men's minds than before.

In the 'forties' the impetus towards a new state of things became aggressive. Men were no longer content to venture a free word or express a bold idea, but they described the existing state of things as absolutely intolerable. When Ruge gave the signal with the 'Hallische Jahrbücher,' the struggle for political liberty combined with scientific and social efforts of many kinds into a united storm of opposition. The ecclesiastical state of things especially became the object of attack, and hence materialistic ideas on the whole became welcome allies, while at the same time Hegelianism and rationalistic criticism occupied the foremost place. In religion those chains were especially galling which an ever-increasing attempt at rehabilitation threatened to impose upon science: in politics the attempts of a vague Romanticism to conjure up the ideas of bygone ages were most irritating. It might almost seem as though a scientific impulse struggling against the barriers of political force was the secret of the tension that soon began to discharge itself. The movement, as ever, became in its progress more idealistic. Religion and poetry were summoned to the fight. Political party reached its height. German Catholicism made the first vent; then a series of storms traversed all Europe, and the year 1848 gave sudden vent to the long-suppressed discontent.

While Materialism had taken its share in the beginnings of this movement, at the moment of the decisive contests, on the other hand, it fell completely behind the idealistic impulses. It was the rebound from the *reaction* that dis-

posed men's minds again eagerly to take up the question
of Materialism, and to set forth the *pro* and *con* from many
standpoints, if not quite with thoroughness.

A peculiar change in the direction of the general movement of progress may often be observed in Germany.
After a period in which certain ruling ideas gather all
their forces together into a common impulse, there follows
another in which each worker busies himself in his own
pursuit. Thus there now arose congresses, excursions, general
festivals, central organisations for all possible branches
and movements in ever-increasing numbers; and in this
very system of co-operative action a new social power
quietly and practically developed. But material interests
raised themselves with special energy after the political
flood of 1848 with the first signs of decided ebb. Austria,
which had been shaken to its foundations, tried to achieve
a thorough regeneration on the basis of industrial progress.
In feverish haste Von Bruck created street after street;
commercial treaties, speculations, and financial measures
rapidly succeeded each other. Private activity followed
suit. In Bohemia were started collieries, furnaces, railways. In South Germany the cotton industry made a
great start forward. In Saxony nearly every branch of
metal and textile industry was developed more than
ever before. Prussia plunged desperately into mining
and smelting. Coal and iron became the watchword of
the age. Silesia, and still more the Lower Rhine and
Westphalia, tried to rival England. In a period of
scarcely ten years the coal production of Saxony doubled;
on the Rhine and in Westphalia it trebled; Silesia came
between. The value of the iron ore produced in Silesia
doubled itself; in the western half of the kingdom of
Prussia it multiplied fivefold. The value of the collective
mining and smelting production more than trebled. The
railways were made available for goods transport on an
immense scale, and gained an amount of traffic that no
one would have anticipated. Shipping increased, and

exports reached in some cases an extravagant extent. An attempt was made to further German unity after the loss of the Parliament by a system of weights and coinage. Thus, characteristically enough, almost all that was saved out of the great movement for unity was the code of regulations for bills of exchange.

With material progress there went hand-in-hand again a new impulse in the natural sciences, and chemistry especially came into even closer relations with life. People might now have contented themselves with positive facts, and especially with the usable results of these sciences, and, for the rest, favoured, as was done in England, a convenient and unthinking orthodoxy. This would have been practical Materialism completely realised; for nothing more surely economises our forces for production, nothing so ensures careless enjoyment, nothing so steels the heart against the hateful shocks of sympathy and of doubts of our own perfection, as that entire spiritual passiveness which rejects as useless all reflection upon the connexion of phenomena and upon the contradictions between experience and tradition.

Germany can never entirely surrender itself to this Materialism. The old creative impulse will not rest; the efforts for the unity of the Fatherland might for a season be forgotten, but not those for the unity of the reason. This architectonic lies closer to our hearts than the architecture of our medieval cathedrals. And if the specially privileged architectress sleeps, meanwhile other trades assert the freedom of commerce, and chemists and physiologists seize the trowel of metaphysic. Germany is the only country in the world where the apothecary cannot make up a prescription without being conscious of the relation of his activity to the constitution of the universe. It is an ideal trait, that gave us, during the profoundest stagnation of philosophy, at least the *Materialistic controversy*, as a reminder to the easily contented masses of the "educated" that, outside the daily habit of labour and experiment, there lies still an infinite realm, to wander through which refreshes the mind and ennobles the soul.

One merit must ever be exalted in the German science of those days—that as well as it could it took up the gauntlet that was flung down by the arrogant blasphemers of science. There is no surer sign of the impotence and degradation of philosophy than that she was silent while the miserable protégés of miserable princes tried to put a curb upon thought.

It is true, indeed, that men of science were irritated too by men from their own ranks, who, without the least scientific justification, found themselves moved to oppose the spirit that ruled in scientific research. The 'Allgemeine Zeitung,' which had gone over and dedicated the columns of its once more respectable supplements to the less scientific amongst the academic professors, may claim its share in the kindling of the controversy. The year 1852, with its very outset, produced Rudolf Wagner's 'Letters on Physiology.' In April Moleschott subscribed the preface to the 'Circle of Life,' and in September Vogt announced in his 'Pictures of Animal Life' that it was time to make a stand against the increasing plague of authority.

Of the two champions of the Materialistic tendency, the one was an Epigonus of the Philosophy of Nature; the other had been an imperial administrator, and was consequently a desperate Idealist. Both men, though not without the stimulus of original research, shine chiefly in their talent for exposition. If Vogt is clearer and sharper in detail, yet Moleschott had given more thought to the rounding of the whole. Vogt more frequently contradicts himself; Moleschott is richer in propositions to which it is impossible to attach any definite meaning. Vogt's chief work in this controversy—'Köhlerglaube und Wissenschaft'—first appeared after that meeting of men of science at Göttingen in 1854 which almost repeated for us the drama of the great religious controversies of the Reformation age. To the period of warmest controversy (1855) belongs also Büchner's 'Kraft und Stoff,' a work that perhaps created a greater sensation, and was at all events more bitterly condemned, than any other book of the kind. We must distinctly repel the reproaches of immorality that were sought to be made against Büchner, chiefly with reference to his first edition. On the other hand, we can as little recognise the claim to an independent philosophical importance which Büchner sets up. Let us, therefore, first of all examine his pretensions to philosophy !

In the preface to his work, after showing reasons for rejecting the technical language of philosophy, Büchner writes:—

"It lies in the nature of philosophy that it should be common property. Expositions *which are not intelligible to an educated man* are scarcely worth the ink they are printed with. Whatever is clearly conceived can be clearly expressed." *

In these words Büchner sets up an entirely new idea of philosophy, without, however, precisely defining it. What had hitherto been called philosophy was never the common property of all, and could not be understood by "every educated man," at least not without deep and thoroughgoing preparation. The systems of Herakleitos, Aristotle, Spinoza, Kant, Hegel, demand the most strenuous exertions, and if, even then, not everything in them is intelligible, this may be the fault of these philosophers. That their works were worth more to our forefathers than the ink they are printed with is clear, because otherwise they would not have been printed, sold, paid for, praised, and in many cases even read. It is obvious, however, that Büchner directs his words only at the living, in the most perverse sense of the word. What those systems may have been worth in the past he omits to inquire. Nor does he linger over the question what influence the

* Force and Matter, edited by J. F. Collingwood, 2d ed. 1870, p. xix.

past has exercised upon the present, and whether, it may be, a necessary process of development connects our present speculation with the exertions of those philosophers. We must also assume that Büchner admits the importance of the history of philosophy, for, like many objects of nature, it will probably also be the case that human thought deserves a study that must not be limited to the most superficial products of speculative activity. Büchner has himself written an essay upon Schopenhauer, in which, indeed, he only endeavours to give the general public some idea of the peculiar speculations of this philosopher, but yet also recognises that Schopenhauer must still exert "an important influence upon the course of our present philosophical development." And yet Schopenhauer represents an Idealism which, by the side of Kant, must be described as reactionary, and which is, moreover, by no means easy to understand.

Büchner again by no means demands merely a better and more intelligible exposition of philosophy; for in what hitherto had been called philosophy there occurred questions which could not be made much more intelligible by the most popular exposition, just because the difficulty lies only in the matter. So far, indeed, we should entirely agree with Büchner that it is quite time to at length eradicate to the last relic the so-called esoteric form of teaching. It is true that most philosophers would be very conveniently disposed of if the radicalism of their peculiar principles were as intelligible as the tractableness of the practical applications that are often brought about by the most singular evasions; but that would have been no great misfortune for the progress of humanity. Kant, who was a straightforward thinker, and who might, moreover, rely upon the great King and the liberal-minded Minister Von Zedlitz, had yet retained so much of the old esoteric principles, that, for instance, he regarded Materialism, because of its intelligibleness, as more dangerous than Scepticism, which presupposes more.

Kant's own deep radicalism is, partly by the difficulty of his standpoint, but partly too by his language, so much hidden, that it only completely reveals itself to the most penetrating and most unprejudiced examination; so much so, that Büchner would perhaps find here more that might be of use in modern speculation than in Schopenhauer, if he would only work his way into the system. While, then, we must agree with Büchner that the intentional difficulties put in the way of the uninitiated must for ever be put an end to, we cannot, on the other hand, hope or wish that the difficulties lying in the subject-matter itself should be banished from the sphere of philosophy. On the one side stands the inevitable consequence of the great democratic era, which no longer admits any secrets of illumination and free thought, and which is anxious to make accessible to the masses the fruits of all that has been achieved by the combined efforts of humanity. But on the other side stands the wish, despite this considera-tion for the needs of the masses, not to allow science to be impoverished, and, if possible, to prevent the overthrow of modern culture by maintaining all our treasure of philoso-phical insight. This openness also with regard to the consequences of philosophical doctrine is not desirable so much as a concession to the large mass of the educated, but as an aid to the emancipation of that *largest* mass of all—the lower classes, who are attaining the conscious-ness of their own higher destiny. Our 'educated' classes, on the contrary, are already so blasé in their polished superficiality, that there is certainly no object in pretend-ing to them longer that there is nothing in philosophy to which they need do more than stretch out their hands in order to know as much as the most famous philosophers. If we wish to give the name of philosophy to that popular intelligence which draws just enough from the results of science to dispel the absurdest superstition, then we must discover a new name for that philosophy which contains the combined theory of all the sciences. Or will it be denied that, even in the present condition of science, any philosophy in this sense is yet possible?

At all events, the principle that whatever is clearly conceived can be clearly expressed, true as it may be in itself, is capable of great abuse. The great Laplace, in his analytical theory of the calculus of probabilities, has assuredly given a perfect model of clear development, and yet there will not be many amongst those who have only studied a little mathematics for the purposes of a general education who will be able, even with some exertion, to understand this work. In mathematics generally, even the clearest calculation will be as unintelligible as a foreign tongue to any one who is not familiar with the ideas that are employed. But just the same thing may happen in philosophy. Passing over other proofs, we can only point out here that there is no single branch of mathematics which is not also capable of philosophical treatment. Laplace himself subjected the first principles of the calculus of probabilities to a philosophical treatment, and this work is not so much easier to understand than the analytical theory because it is *philosophical*, but rather because it treats only of *principles*. Nevertheless, even this ' philosophical essay on probabilities' would still present serious difficulties to many ' educated' persons.

Here, of course, it is in favour of Büchner's view that philosophy has come forward not merely as the quintessence of the sciences, as the final result of the comparison of their results, but no less as an introduction and preparation. This latter was the sense in which Scholasticism conceived philosophy, and down to the most recent times it continued to be the usual practice in our universities to precede special studies by philosophical lectures. But in England and France the philosophical treatment of things has often actually been confounded with the popular treatment of them. And hence it comes about that Büchner is esteemed in Germany more as a popular polemical writer, while his numerous supporters in England and

France are much more ready to concede him pretensions to philosophical importance.

One of the most remarkable proofs of the relativity of our ideas, moreover, may be found in this very fact, that those qualities that make Büchner seem *clearer* to the general public are the very opposite of what stricter science calls clear. If Büchner had taken, for instance, the idea of hypothesis in a scientific sense, he would probably have remained unintelligible to many of his readers, since it requires no inconsiderable logical training, as well as some idea of the history of the sciences, to grasp this idea in such a shape as to be clear to an accurate thinker. But in Büchner 'hypothesis' means any kind of unjustified assumption, as, *e.g.*, the deduced principles of philosophical speculation.[55] The expression 'Materialism' stands now in its historically proper sense, now is equivalent to 'Realism,' and again to 'Empiricism.' There are, in fact, passages where this most positive of all philosophical ideas is used in a purely negative sense, and almost coincides with Scepticism. There are still greater variations in the meaning of 'Idealism,' which often seems to be almost synonymous with 'orthodoxy.' Just because of this vague use, however, such ideas seem clear to those who do not know the exact force of the terms, and yet feel the necessity of using them. It is much like using one pair of spectacles for different distances and eyes. The man who sees farther in these matters with the naked eye finds everything uncertain through Büchner's spectacles. The man, on the other hand, who is extremely short-sighted thinks that he sees very clearly through this medium, and does in fact really see more clearly than without this assistance. Only it is a pity that the spectacles are at the same time strongly coloured! In particular, it is con-

---

[55] Most extravagant is the use of the word 'hypothesis' in the 'Concluding Observations' to 'Force and Matter,' S. 259 ff., 1st edition, E.T., 251 *sqq.* Here even religious dogmas are called hypotheses. On the other hand, the correct use is found, *e.g.*, in 'Natur u. Geist,' S. 83, where Atomism is called a 'scientific hypothesis.'

stantly happening to Büchner that he regards the real
doctrines of philosophers as too simple, because he observes
that in life they are often combined in a conservative way
with absurd ideas of daily life. Thus the chapter on
' Innate Ideas ' especially can only awake in us dim recollections of the phrases of some unlearned preacher, or the
doubtful terms of a reading-book for industrious boys,
while we should search modern philosophy in vain for a
principle that really sets up the doctrines that Büchner
attacks. Here, then, we see also that it is a just punishment for the awkward speech of our gentle philosophers
that they must have their ears boxed, as it were, in the
open street, without the public feeling the slightest sympathy with them.

As Büchner is hesitating and capricious in the use of
individual ideas, so, of course, he cannot be regarded as
the representative of a sharply expressed and decided
positive principle. Keen, relentless, and consistent is he
only in negation; but this keen negation is by no means
the result of a dry, purely critical understanding; it
springs rather from a wild enthusiasm for the progress
of humanity, for the victory of the true and beautiful.
Whatever stands in the way of this he has studied sufficiently to follow it up relentlessly. Much, too, that is
harmless seems to him suspicious; but whatever is un-
suspected, when he does not suppose that there is any
trickery, any malicious delaying of scientific and moral
progress, all this he can use. Büchner is essentially an
idealistic nature. He comes of a family of rich poetic
gifts. One of his brothers died early as a poet full of
promise; another has made a name as a poet and an historian of poetry; his sister, Luise Büchner, is known far
and wide as a talented authoress, and as the collector of the
poetry of German women. He himself was distinguished
as a student—in this resembling De la Mettrie—chiefly
by literary, philosophical, and poetical studies, and by his
successes in style. In his case, too, it was his father's

wish that made him take to medicine; and here again he may be compared with his French predecessor in the fact that he at once took sides in his new pursuit, and joined the Rational School. More serious and solid than the Frenchman, he applied his rich and many-sided abilities partly to scientific inquiries, but partly to the popular exposition and the appreciation from a social and political standpoint of the results of our recent researches in physical science. Amid all this activity he never lost sight of the mighty task of advancing humanity.

Although Büchner, stimulated by Moleschott, and in a similar rhetorical way in many of his utterances, gave in his adherence to the most decided Materialism, yet his peculiar tendency—which is indeed only with difficulty to be ascertained from contradictory passages—is rather relativistic.[56] The ultimate riddles of life and of existence are, he often says, not to be solved.[57] But empirical inves-

[56] We must regard as relativistic (if not rather idealistic) the principle, borrowed from Moleschott, that things in general exist only for each other (cf. note 58). Here, too, belongs his doctrine of the infinity of smallness and the necessarily involved relativity of the idea of an atom (cf. Kraft u. Stoff, 1 Aufl., S. 22 ff.; Natur u. Geist, S. 82 ff.). That, notwithstanding, the atoms are treated as facts, discoveries, and so on, must not surprise us in Büchner.—In the Sechs Vorl. über d. Darwin'sche Theorie: Leipzig, 1868, S. 383 ff., Büchner expressly rejects *systematic* Materialism, and would call his philosophy 'Realism.'

[57] The passages in point are, of course, principally in 'Natur und Geist' (Frankf., 1857), an entirely unsuccessful attempt of an otherwise skilful writer to introduce his philosophy to the general public in a calm and impartial exposition. Comp. S. 83: "Da unsre Erkenntniss nicht in das Innerste der Natur reicht und das eigentliche tiefste Wesen der Materie

wahrscheinlich immer ein unlösbares Problem für uns bleiben wird;"—S. 173: "Dass ich es vorziehe, Dir unsre Unwissenheit über Zeit und Ewigkeit, über Raum und Unendlichkeit einzugestehen." It is highly characteristic of Büchner's mode of thought when, at S. 176 ff., with reference to the question of the infinity of space and time, he makes the representative of his own standpoint ('August') content himself with saying that the limits which space, time, and causality seem to set to our ideas "are so remote that they scarcely touch my philosophical view of the world and matter." Very noteworthy, too, is the following passage from the first edition of 'Kraft und Stoff' (which was later almost entirely omitted), S. 261: "Hinter dem, was unserer sinnlichen Erkenntniss verschlossen ist, können ja alle denkbaren Dinge existiren, aber Alles dieses kann sie" (die 'Hypothese') "nur willkürlich, nur ideell, nur metaphysich. Wer die Empirie verwirft, verwirft alles

tigation, which only can conduct us to truth, forbids the assumption of anything supersensuous. If we overstep in our speculation the limits of experience, we land ourselves in error from which there is no deliverance. Faith, which then, however, has no longer anything to do with facts, may extravagate into those realms, but reason cannot, may not, follow. Philosophy must proceed from the natural sciences; we must hold fast to what they teach us until by the same method we attain a deeper insight. It is observable that Büchner does not allow any poetical or symbolical value to philosophical or religious principles. He has with his own poetical nature once broken with these questions, and now everything with him is true or false. But this is really to deny not only speculation and religious faith, but even all poetry that gives to ideas figurative expression.

Both Moleschott and Büchner frequently exhibit in the treatment of single questions a genuine philosophical acuteness, which gives place again, however, to scarcely intelligible trivialities. Thus, for instance, in Büchner's 'Force and Matter,' the greatest part of the chapter on 'Thought' is a pattern of cautious dialectic; it is true it is only a fragment, for the admirable criticism of Vogt's famous utterance as to the relation of thought to the brain closes with a complete dualism of force and matter, which is then not reconciled, but only obscured by the rapid flow of words.

" Thought, spirit, soul are not material, not a substance, but the effect of the conjoint action of many materials endowed with forces or qualities." He compares this effect with that of a steam-engine, the force of which we cannot see, smell, or touch, while the steam expelled by it is a mere bye-thing, and has nothing to do with " the object of the engine." Every force can only be " inferred " from its

menschliche Begreifen überhaupt und hat noch nicht einmal gesehen, dass menschliches Wissen und Denken ohne reale Objekte ein non ens ist." That is pretty much what Kant says, only in somewhat different words.

manifestations, or, as it stood in the first edition—much more logically and more in harmony with the context— "ideally constructed." Force and matter are inseparable, but are nevertheless *in thought* very far removed from each other, "nay, in a certain sense, absolutely negative each other." "At least we do not know how spirit, force, could be defined as anything else than as something immaterial, something in itself excluding matter or opposed to it."

The most credulous spiritualist does not need more in order to base his whole edifice; and here again we can see clearly how little room there is to hope that the mere propagation of the materialistic view of nature, with all the knowledge that supports it, will ever be enough to eradicate religious or superstitious opinions to which mankind inclines for reasons that have their roots deeper than in his theoretical views of natural things. That force and matter are inseparably united is, with regard to the visible and apprehensible world, sufficiently proved. But if force is something essentially supersensuous, why shall it not exist in a world that our senses cannot apprehend, either of itself or in conjunction with immaterial substances?

Very much truer and more consistent than that of Büchner is the conception of the older Materialists, who resolve all force into motion, pressure, and collision of matter, and, as was admirably done by Toland in particular, conceive matter as moved in itself, and in fact rest itself as a mere special form of motion.

But independently of the difficulties in the way of carrying out this conception that result from modern physics, with its absolutely incomprehensible action at a distance, there is another point that is equally difficult for every kind of Materialism, only that the difficulty is more concealed in the vague conception of Büchner, which confusedly mixes up mechanical force and spirit. I mean that Büchner formed his whole philosophy, and wrote his principal work, without knowing the law of the persistence of force. When he afterwards came to know it, he devoted

a special chapter to it, and simply ranged it among the
new supports of his materialistic philosophy, without ever
thoroughly illuminating every corner of his structure with
the light of this most important doctrine.   Otherwise it
must easily have occurred to him that even the processes
in the brain must be strictly subject to the law of the
persistence of force, and thus, as we shall see better
farther on, all forces inevitably become *mechanical*, become movements and elastic forces.   We may this way
construe mechanically the whole man, including all his
intellectually significant acts, but everything that goes
on in the brain will be pressure and motion, and from
this to ' spirit,' or even to conscious sensation only, the
way is exactly as far as from matter to spirit.

How little clearness Büchner attained on this point is
shown by a very curious addition which he introduced
into his later editions, while retaining the whole confusion
of spirit and force.   He finds here that the brain, which
produces so peculiar an effect as spirit, of all the organs alone
becomes *weary* and needs sleep, " a circumstance which
establishes not merely an essential distinction between
these organs, but also between psychical and mechanical
activity in general."   Later on the muscles occur to him,
and with a superficiality scarcely pardonable in a physiologist he adds, " The same may be said of those muscles
which are set in motion from the brain through the nervous system—the voluntary muscles."   Büchner has, of
course, not bethought himself that the muscles also become
weary if the elastic energy collected in them is used up,
while the brain would still long be able to transmit to
them fresh efferent stimuli.

The reason why men so able and honest as Moleschott
and Büchner have not a more thorough grasp of their subject must not therefore be sought merely in the fact that
from the first they put popular exposition in the place of
philosophy, for even within these limits a much higher
standard may be demanded, and popular exposition may

really have philosophical value without quite exhausting the business of philosophy. But then the exposition must be based at least upon a definite theory carried out with clearness and consistency, and with the majority of our Materialists this is not the case. The reason of this may be looked for in the influence of the philosophy of Schelling and Hegel.

We called Moleschott above an Epigonus of the philosophy of nature, and deliberately so. And he is so, not because in his younger days he industriously studied Hegel and later favoured Feuerbach, but because this intellectual tendency is still everywhere observable in his nominally so consistent Materialism; and that just in what are metaphysically the decisive points. Much the same thing is noticeable in Büchner, who not only frequently sets up as an authority Feuerbach, a powerfully *stimulating* but thoroughly unclear thinker, but even in his own utterances often enough wanders into a vague pantheism.

The point here especially in question may be quite clearly indicated. It is, as it were, the apple in the logical fall of German philosophy since Kant—the relation between subject and object in knowledge.

According to Kant, our knowledge arises from the reciprocal action of the two things—an infinitely simple principle, yet one which is constantly being lost again. It follows from this view that our phenomenal world is not merely a product of our conception (Leibniz, Berkeley); that again it is not an adequate picture of actual things, but is a result of objective influences and of the subjective shaping of them. Not, then, what an individual man, through accidental temperament or defective organisation, knows thus or thus, but what mankind in general, through their sensibility and understanding, *must know*, this Kant called in a certain sense objective. He called it objective so far as we speak only of our experience; transcendental, on the other hand, or, in other words, false, if we apply such knowledge to things in themselves, that is, things existing absolutely quite independently of our knowledge.

His successors, however, thirsted again after absolute knowledge, and entirely abandoning the path of sober explanation, found themselves another by the dogmatic aid of their philosophemes. Then arose the grand axiom of the unity of the Subjective and Objective, the fabulous *petitio principii* of the unity of Thought and of Existence, in which even Büchner is still involved.

According to Kant, there is such a unity only in experience; but this unity is a fusion; it is neither pure thought nor does it give us pure existence. But now, according to Hegel, the contrary should be the case; this absolute thought must coincide with absolute existence. This notion gained ground because of its magnificent absurdity, which corresponded with the need of the age. It is the basis of the notorious Philosophy of Nature. In the troubled fermentation of the Hegelian School it was often found impossible to decide what this notion actually meant. It might, to begin with, be regarded as an actual metaphysical principle, or as a colossal categorical imperative intended to limit metaphysic. In the latter case we approach to Protagoras. Shall we so define the notion of the true, the good, the real, and so on, that we *name* true, good, real, and so on, only that which is so for man; or shall we imagine that what man recognises as such is equally valid also for all thinking beings that do or can exist?

The latter view, which only is peculiar to the true original Hegelianism, leads necessarily to Pantheism; for it already presupposes as an axiom the unity of the human spirit with the spirit of the universe and with all spirits. Part of the Epigoni, nevertheless, held with Feuerbach to the categorical imperative; real means what is real *for man;* that is, because we *can* know nothing of things in themselves we *will* know nothing of them—and there an end!

The old metaphysic would have a knowledge of things

in themselves; the philosophy of nature relapsed into this error. Kant stands alone at the sharp and perfectly clear standpoint that of things in themselves we know only one thing, precisely that one thing which Feuerbach has neglected, namely, that we *must presuppose* them as a necessary consequence of our own understanding; that is, that human knowledge shows itself as a small island in the vast ocean of all possible knowledge.

Feuerbach and his followers, just because they do not observe this, are constantly falling back into transcendental Hegelianism. In the case of Feuerbach's 'sensibility,' it is often very difficult to think of ear and eye, to say nothing of the use of these organs in the exact sciences. His sensibility is a new form of absolute thought, which is wholly independent of the facts of experience. That he notwithstanding gained so great an influence over certain men of science is to be explained not from the nature of the empirical sciences, but from the effects of the philosophy of nature upon 'Young Germany.'

Let us look for a moment at the after-pains attending the birth of the absolute spirit in Moleschott!

In the 'Kreislauf des Lebens,' this skilful writer discusses also the sources of knowledge in man. After a very striking eulogy of Aristotle and a passage upon 'Kant,' in which Moleschott attacks a phantom of this name with principles which the real Kant might concede without affecting his system, there follows the passage that is in our mind. It begins with admirable clearness only to pass gradually over into a metaphysical haze, which even in our mist-haunted Fatherland it would be difficult to match. In accordance with our purpose we will here exhibit the darkest mists in italics:

" All facts, every observation of a flower, or an insect, the discovery of a world, or the detection of the characteristics of man, what else are they but relations of objects to our senses? If a rotifer has but one eye consisting of a cornea only, will it not receive other pictures of objects than the spider, which exhibits in addition lenses and vitreous bodies? And accordingly the knowledge of the insect, the knowledge of the effects of the outer world is different in the case of the insect and in the case of man. Above the knowledge of these relations to the instruments of his apprehension neither man nor God can raise himself.

"Thus then we know everything in relation to ourselves; we know what the sun looks like to us, how the flower smells to man, how the vibrations of the air affect a human ear. This has been called a limited knowledge, a human knowledge conditioned by the senses, a knowledge that merely observes the tree as it is to us. That is very little, it has been said; we must know how the tree is in itself, that we may not longer delude ourselves that it is as it appears to us.

" But where then is this tree in itself that we are looking for? Does not all knowledge presuppose some one that knows, and consequently a relation between the object and the observer? The observer may be an insect, a man, or, if there are such things, an angel. If the two things exist, the tree and the man, *it is just as necessary for the tree as for the man that it stands to him in a relation that manifests itself by the impression upon his eye. Without relation to the eye into which it sends its rays there is no tree. It is simply by this relation that the tree is in itself.*

" All existence is an existence by means of qualities. *But there is no quality that does not exist simply through a relation.*

" Steel is hard as opposed to soft butter, ice is only cold to the warm hand, trees only green to a healthy eye.

" Or is green anything but a relation of light to our eye. And if it is nothing else, *then is not the green leaf so in itself, just because it is green for our eye.*

" *But then the wall of separation is broken down between*

the thing as it is to us and the thing in itself. Because an object is only through its relation to other objects, for instance, through its relation to the observer, because the knowledge of the object resolves itself into the knowledge of their relations, all my knowledge is an objective knowledge."

It is true enough indeed that all our knowledge is objective knowledge, for it relates to objects. Nay, even more; we must suppose that the relations of the object to our senses are regulated by rigid laws. Through sensible empirical knowledge we stand in as complete a relation to the objects as our nature allows. What more do we need to call this knowledge objective? But whether we perceive the objects as they are *in themselves* is quite another question.

Let us only look now at the italicised passages, and ask in what part of the primeval philosophic forest we are? Are we among the extremest idealists, who do not suppose at all that there is anything without us corresponding to our conceptions of things. Is the tree really out of the world when I shut my eyes? Is there no world at all outside me? Or are we amongst the pantheistic dreamers, who imagined that the human mind can conceive the absolute? Is the green leaf green in and for itself, because it produces this impression upon the human eye; while the eyes of spiders, chafers, or angels are of less importance? There are, in fact, few philosophic systems which cannot be discovered in these principles more easily than Materialism. And how is it then with the basis of this oracle?

As it is merely the contrast to our blood-heat that makes us call ice cold, is there consequently no absolute constitution in the ice independently of any feeling, in accordance with which it enters into a certain interchange of heat-rays with its environment—whether this environment feels or not does not matter? And if this interchange essentially depends upon the temperature and other properties of the environing bodies, does it not at the same time

depend also upon the ice? Is not this constitution by
which the ice undergoes in this case one interchange, and
in another a different interchange of heat-rays, simply a
property belonging to the ice in itself? To our feeling
the property regularly produces the impression of cold.
We denote it, then, according to the impression that it
makes upon us—we call it cold; but we can easily distinguish between the physiological process in *our nerves* and
the physical process in *the body itself.* This latter is *in
relation* to the former the thing in itself. Whether we
may not still further leave out of account not only our
nerves of sensation but also our rational apprehension,
and seek behind the ice a thing-in-itself, neither existing
in space nor time, is a question we do not at all discuss
here. We need but a single step in order to show that the
qualities of things are distinguishable from our conceptions, and that a thing may have qualities, that it may
exist, without our perceiving it.

When worm, chafer, man, and angel perceive a tree, are
there then *five trees?* There are four conceptions of a
tree, presumably very different from each other; but they
refer to one and the same object, as to which no individual
can know how it is constituted in itself, because it only
knows its own conception of it. Man has only this one
advantage, that by the comparison of his organs with those
of the animal world and by physiological investigations,
he succeeds in regarding his own conception as being just
as imperfect and one-sided as those of the different kinds
of animals.

How is it, then, that the dividing wall between the thing
as it is to us and the thing in itself is broken down? If
the thing exists only in its relation to other objects, this
metaphysical principle of Moleschott's can only reasonably
be taken to mean that the thing in itself exists through
the sum of all its relations to other objects, but not through
a limited portion of them. If I close my eyes, the rays of
light which proceeded from the different parts of the tree

to the retina fall now upon the outer surface of my eyelids. That is the only change that has taken place. Whether an object can still exist that cannot interchange light, heat, and sound rays, or electric currents, chemical changes, and mechanical movements with *any* other object, that is, of course, a question. It would be an admirable field for the subtleties of the philosophers of nature. But even if we solve the problem by agreeing with Moleschott, there still always remains between the thing in itself and the thing as it is to me a difference that is nearly as great as the difference between a product of an infinite number of factors and one particular factor of this product.[58]

[58] This entirely applies also to Büchner, who in note 82 to his book, 'Die Stellung des Menschen in der Natur,' Leipzig, 1870, by way of gratitude for our recognition of his poetical nature has devoted a song of praise to the 'thing in itself,' and has prefixed to it a prolix, but not particularly clear, polemic. The total misunderstanding of the Kantian principle that our ideas do not order themselves in accordance with things, but things in accordance with our ideas, we may here leave untouched. Any one who cannot see how this is to be understood from our section on Kant will not learn it from a new discussion in this note. Büchner tries first to resolve the distinction between the thing in itself and the phenomenon into the old distinction of *primary* and *secondary* qualities, but still does not venture to draw the only true consequence of Materialism, that the atoms in movement are the 'thing in itself.' The importance of the physiology of the sense organs for this question is as superficially disposed of by Büchner without going at all into the scientific side of the question, as Materialism often is disposed of by saying that in the main we knew all this long ago. What the present position of science can do to give new and deeper foundations to the general idea that had appeared long ago is most sharply emphasised by Büchner when it suits him, and entirely ignored when it presents difficulties to his standpoint. That, moreover, the Kantian 'thing in itself' is a "new thought-thing," is "unrepresentable," "unknowable," and so on, we do not need to learn from Büchner. "Unthinkable," however, is a very different thing, although Büchner adds it in the same breath with the other predicates. He asserts, however, the thing in itself to be unthinkable "because all things exist only for each other, and without reciprocal relations have no significance." But if these "*relations*" of a thing to man are its *qualities* as perceived *by us*—for what else can they be?—does not this very statement assert the 'thing in itself'? It may be that the thing *without any relations* means nothing, as Büchner supposes, in common with dogmatic Idealism; yet even then it is conceived as the origin of all its real relations to various other things, something more than the mere *relation to ourselves*, which comes to consciousness within us. But the *latter* only is what popular language calls 'the thing,' and which the critical philosophy, on the contrary, calls '*the phenomenon.*' Further on Büchner shows by the way

No ! The thing in itself is not the thing as it is to me; but I may perhaps deliberately substitute this for it; as, for example, I substitute my notion of cold and heat for the actual temperature of bodies. The old Materialism naïvely regarded both as identical. But two things have made this for ever impossible—the victory of the undulation theory and the philosophy of Kant. We may, indeed, push on past their influence, but that is not the way to make an epoch. We should have to settle with Kant. This the philosophy of nature did in the shape of a delirium of revelation which elevated absolute thought to a divinity. A serious settlement must take a very different form. We must either admit the distinction between the thing in itself and the phenomenal world, and content ourselves with improving Kant's development of it, or we must throw ourselves into the arms of the categorical imperative, and thus to a certain extent try to combat Kant with his own weapons.

Here, indeed, there is still a side-door open to us. Kant made use of the infinite void space beyond human experience in order to make room to construct his intelligible world. He did this by means of the categorical imperative, 'Thou canst because thou must.' And therefore there must be freedom. In the actual world of our understanding there is none. Therefore it must exist in the intelligible world. We cannot, indeed, conceive for a moment the possibility of freewill; but we can vaguely think it possible that there are causes in the thing in itself which exhibit themselves in the organ of our rational consciousness as freedom, although, regarded with the organ of the analytic understanding, they present only the picture of a chain of cause and effect.

What, then, if we now start with another categorical

in which he refers the subjectivity of sense-perceptions to particular illusions of the senses, that in this sphere he has not yet sufficiently acquainted himself with the results of experience. He promises to return to the subject in a more suitable place. If this is done with the necessary knowledge, there should be no great difficulties in the way of understanding it.

imperative ? What if we put at the head of all positive
philosophy the principle, ' *Content thyself with the world
that is given thee !* ' Is not, then, the Fata Morgana of the
intelligible world annihilated as by a magic wand ?

Kant would first maintain that *his* categorical imperative, which from within bids us do the right, is a *fact* of
the internal consciousness, of the same necessity and
universality as the natural law in external nature; but
that this new imperative, which we will call by the name
of Feuerbach, is not necessarily found in man, but rather
rests upon subjective caprice. Here, then, the opposite
party has a not unfavourable game. It is easy to show
that the moral law, as a matter of history, only slowly
develops itself, and that it can only have a necessary and
unconditionally valid character in those cases where it
exists in consciousness at all. But if a further historical
development brings into play the principle of contentment
with this world as the basis of the moral consciousness, no
one can make any answer to this. It must show itself.

But, of course, it must *show itself;* and here comes the
more serious difficulty. Kant has this on his side, that in
every educated individual the moral law attains to consciousness. Its content may in many respects be very
various, but the form is there. The fact of the inner
voice is certain. We may criticise its universality; we
may, on the contrary, extend it to the higher animals: but
this does not at all change the main fact. But as to
Feuerbach's imperative, the fact has still to be proved that
we *can* really content ourselves with the phenomenal
world, and with its sensible apprehension. If the fact is
proved, then we will readily believe also that an ethical
system may be constructed upon it; for what limit is
there to construction ?

As Kant's system might have been at variance with the
knowledge of the understanding if this variance had not
been provided for from the first, so the system of contentment stands apparently at variance with the efforts of the

reason towards unity; with art, poetry, and religion, in which lies the impulse to exalt ourselves above the limits of experience. There yet remains the attempt to get rid of these contradictions.

Accordingly, naïve Materialism would hardly have come up again in our own time in systematic shape, as indeed it can hardly do again after Kant. The unconditional belief in atoms has disappeared, like other dogmas. It is no longer supposed that the world is absolutely so constituted as we perceive it with ear and eye; but it is maintained that with the world in itself we have nothing to do.

One only of the modern Materialists has attempted a really systematic solution of the difficulties that present themselves against this standpoint. The same thinker, however, has gone still further. He has, in fact, made an attempt to demonstrate, or at least to render probable, the agreement of the actual world with the world of our senses. This Czolbe undertook in his 'New Exposition of Sensationalism.'

Heinrich Czolbe, the son of a landowner in the neighbourhood of Danzig, devoted himself in early youth to theological and philosophical questions, although he took up medicine as his special pursuit. Here, too, we find the starting-point for his later course in that philosophy of nature which our modern Materialists are so fond of representing as the opposite extreme to their own efforts, and yet by which Carl Vogt alone among their leaders has remained quite unaffected. In Czolbe's case Hölderlin's 'Hyperion' especially was of decisive importance, a work which embodied, in wild and magnificent poetry, the Pantheism due to Schelling and Hegel, and glorified the Hellenic unity of spirit and nature, as compared with German civilisation. Strauss, Bruno Bauer, and Feuerbach, moreover, helped to determine the young doctor's tendency. But it is remarkable that it was a philosopher—and in fact a professor of philosophy, unless that is, as Feuerbach says, a contradiction—who at length gave him the final impulse to the elaboration of his peculiar materialistic system.

It is Lotze—the man whom Carl Vogt occasionally decorates as joint-manufacturer of the genuine Göttingen soul-substance with the title of a speculating Struwelpeter —Lotze, one of the acutest, and in scientific criticism one of the surest, philosophers of our day—who did this involuntary service to Materialism. The article 'Vital Force' in Wagner's 'Handwörterbuch' and his 'General Pathology and Therapeutic as Mechanical Sciences,' annihilated the phantom of a vital force, and introduced some degree of order into the lumber-room of superstition and confusion of ideas that medical men called Pathology. Lotze had trodden the right path; for, in fact, it is amongst the tasks of philosophy, while making a critical use of the facts supplied by the positive sciences, to react upon them, and to exchange for the gold of special research the results of a wider survey and a more rigid logic. He would no doubt have met more recognition in this course if Virchow had not simultaneously appeared as practical reformer of Pathology, and if Lotze himself had not adopted a peculiar metaphysic of his own, of which it is difficult to understand how it could maintain itself by the side of his own critical acumen.

Czolbe was stimulated by the rejection of the 'supersensuous idea' of vital force to attempt to make the rejection of the supersensuous the principle of philosophy. As early as 1844, his inaugural dissertation on the Principles of Physiology shows these efforts; but it was only eleven years later, when the Materialistic controversy was in full swing, that Czolbe came forward with his 'New Exposition of Sensationalism.'

As we have, generally speaking, taken the idea of philosophical Materialism in a tolerably narrow sense, we must first explain why we here devote special attention to a system calling itself 'Sensationalism.' Czolbe himself must have chosen this term because the idea of sensible presentation throughout determines his course of thought. This sensible presentation, however, consists in this, that everything is resolved into *matter and its motion.* Accordingly sensible presentation is only a regulative principle, and the metaphysical element is matter.

If we wish to distinguish strictly between Sensationalism and Materialism, we must give the former name only to those systems which hold to the origin of our knowledge from the senses, and attach no importance to the power of constructing the universe from atoms, molecules, or other modifications of matter. The Sensationalist may assume that matter is mere representation, because what we have immediately in perception is only sensation and not 'matter.' But he may also, like Locke, be inclined to refer spirit to matter. So soon, however, as this becomes the essential basis of the whole system, we have before us genuine Materialism.

And yet in Czolbe, too, we no longer find the old naïf Materialism of earlier ages. It is not merely the uniform personal modesty of the author that makes him almost universally throw his views into hypothetical form. He has brought with him enough of Kant to know the doubtfulness of metaphysical dogmas. In general his system stands to Kant, whom he chiefly combats, in a changeful relation, which offers at least as many analogies as oppositions. And therefore a consideration of Czolbe must make much clearer the results that we attained in the last chapter.

Czolbe is of opinion that, despite the passionate strife for and against Materialism, nothing has yet been done to bring this view of things into a satisfactory system. "What in recent times Feuerbach, Vogt, Moleschott, and others have accomplished forms but suggestive and fragmentary assertions, which upon a deeper examination of the matter leave us unsatisfied. As they have only generally maintained the possibility of explaining everything in a purely natural way, but have never attempted a more particular proof of this, they are still at bottom entirely on the ground of the religion and speculative philosophy which they attack."[59] We shall see sufficiently that even Czolbe never leaves this ground.

Czolbe admits that the principle of his Sensationalism, the exclusion of the supersensuous, may be called a prejudice or a preconceived opinion. "But without such a *prejudice* the forming of a view as to the connection of phenomena is altogether impossible." Besides internal and external experience, he regards *hypotheses* as a necessary element in the forming of a philosophy of things.

Well, prejudice or oracle, hypothesis or poesy, is a question that has yet to be decided. But if the hypothesis is not only to appear in the course of the philosophy, but in the humble guise of a 'prejudice' receives us on the very threshold, we must surely ask, What, then, determines the choice of this or the other original hypothesis? To this question Czolbe has two very different answers. According to one he reached it by induction; according to the other, morality, as in Kant, forms the foundation of the whole positive philosophy, since by the strict use of the understanding nothing of the kind, as a metaphysical principle, can be attained. Both answers may in their way be right. Czolbe sees how Bacon brings about an advance in philosophy by the exclusion of the supersensuous; why should not a new advance be attained by continuing this method? Lotze has banished vital force; why should we not be able to banish all transcendental forces and existences?

As, however, the "Exposition of Sensationalism" proceeds not inductively, but deductively, this induction cannot well form the strict basis of the system: it was only the occasion. The basis lies in the ethic, or rather in the categorical imperative so often mentioned: Content thyself with the world that is given thee.

It is peculiar to Materialism that it is able to establish

[59] N. Darstellung des Sensualismus: Leipzig, 1855. Vorwort, S. vi.

its moral theory without any such imperative, while the philosophy of nature rests upon a practical principle. Thus Epikuros had a moral doctrine which supported itself upon the impulse of nature, while he reduced into the form of a moral law the purification of the soul from superstition by the knowledge of nature.

Czolbe derives morality from the *goodwill* which necessarily develops itself in the intercourse of man with man. The principle of the exclusion of the supersensuous, however, has a definite *moral* aim.

Here our philosopher's theory is very deeply rooted, although he generally puts it forth only in modest and even inadequate terms, or even falls back upon authority. Through our whole epoch runs, as a grand characteristic, the expectation of a great and fundamental, though it may be a quietly and peacefully accomplished, reform of all our views and circumstances. There is a feeling that the era of the Middle Ages is only now drawing to its conclusion, and that the Reformation and even the French Revolution are perhaps only the first dawnings of a new light. In Germany the influence of our great poets combined with the political, ecclesiastical, and social efforts of the time to promote views and inclinations of this kind. But the watchword was given in this, as in so many other respects, by the philosophy of Hegel, through its demand for the unity of nature and spirit, which stood through the long period of the Middle Ages in such sharp antithesis. Fichte already had ventured to apply the outpouring of the Holy Spirit which is spoken of in the New Testament to the light of his own day with the same boldness with which Christ and the Apostles had interpreted the prophets of the Old Testament. Natural insight is only attaining its full development in our own epoch, and is thus manifested as the real Holy Spirit that is to lead us into all truth. Hegel gave to these ideas a more definite direction. His view of the world's history makes the dualism of spirit and nature a great transitional stage between a lower stage and a higher and purer stage of unity—an idea which, on the one hand, retains points of connection with the innermost motives of ecclesiastical doctrine, and, on the other, has given rise to those exertions which have for their object the entire setting aside of all religion. As these views made way, it was inevitable that Germany should turn its gaze back to classical antiquity, and especially to Greece, where that unity of spirit and nature, towards which we must again approximate, had as yet been most fully manifested. It is in particular in a passage of Strauss that Czolbe finds the results of these speculations happily condensed.

"What Julian endeavoured to maintain from the past," says Strauss in his essay on Julian, "is materially related with what the future ought to bring to us. The free harmonious humanity of Hellenism, the self-supporting manliness of Roman antiquity, is the goal towards which we are about to struggle from out of the long Christian interval, enriched 'with the spiritual and moral gains we have derived from it.' If we ask what will be the philosophy of the future, Sensationalism may so far answer to this view of Strauss, as clearness of conception seems to determine a unity in the harmony of our whole conscious life, and resignation to what knowledge shows us to be impossible or non-existent, a certain manliness of soul or feeling."

Thus Czolbe, and the circumstance that in his later treatise on the origin of self-consciousness he comes back upon this passage, still more clearly exhibits its fundamental importance for his Sensationalism.

"To what has already been said upon the æsthetic significance of Materialism must here be added, that as the true mean or moderation was an essential note of Greek artistic work, so our efforts in this respect also satisfy æsthetic demands. The historical ideal of every effort of this kind, however, was first pointed out with

joyful confidence by the true author of modern Materialism, David Strauss." [60]

Here, again, we see that Strauss has the honour of being
designated the father of contemporary Materialism; for
Czolbe in fact regards all Materialism as having sprung
from this moral and æsthetic germ. Czolbe's whole nature
is essentially devoted to the ideal, and his intellectual
development is ever more decidedly leading him in this
direction. But this by no means deprives his exposition
of Sensationalism of the interest that it possesses for us
through the peculiar way in which it is carried out. Let
us listen, therefore, to another passage!

" The so-called moral needs arising from dissatisfaction
with our earthly life might just as properly be called
immoral. It is indeed no proof of humility, but rather of
arrogance and vanity, to improve upon the world we know
by imagining a supersensuous world, and to wish to exalt
man into a creature above nature by the addition of a
supersensuous part. Yes, certainly, dissatisfaction with
the world of phenomena—the deepest root of supersensuous ideas—is not a moral reason at all, but rather a moral
weakness! Since, just as the moving of a machine requires
the smallest exertion of strength, if we only know exactly
where to apply it, so the systematic development of true
principles often demands much less acumen than the
development of false ones;—*thus Sensationalism does not
require greater acuteness, but does require deeper and truer
morality.*" [61]

Czolbe's 'System' had many incurable weaknesses, but
his life was marked by a deep and genuine morality. He
laboured ceaselessly at the perfection of his philosophy;
and if in doing so he soon left stricter Materialism behind
him, yet he remained unchangeably true to his principle

---

[60] Entsteh. d. Selbstbewusstseins, Leipzig, 1856, S. 52 ff.; N. D. d. Sensualism., S. 5. Comp. also Czolbe, Die Grenzen u. d. Urspr. der Men- schl. Erkenntniss, Jena u. Leipzig, 1865, S. 280 ff.

[61] N. D. d. Sensualism., S. 187 ff.

of contentment with the world that is given us, and the exclusion of everything supersensuous. The opinion that the world in its present condition is eternal, and subject only to trifling variations, and the theory that light and sound waves, which he conceives as having light and sound in themselves, propagate themselves mechanically through the nerves of sight and hearing into the brain, formed two pillars of his system, which accordingly was from no side subjected to more passionate assaults than from that of exact science. Here he showed himself obstinate, and regarded all the counter-proofs of science as mere illusions, which on further investigation would disappear.[62] There can be no doubt, therefore, that while he believed himself to be carrying the mechanical theory of nature to its extreme consequences, he was really lacking in the strict appreciation of the mechanical element.

On the other hand, he early recognised that *mechanism* in the atoms and *sensation* are two different principles, and consequently he did not hesitate to adopt into his philosophy the consequences of this recognition, since they were not at variance with his ethical principle. In a book published in 1865 on the ' Limits and Origin of Human Knowledge,' he accordingly supposes a sort of ' world-soul,' which consists of sensations that are immutably bound up with the vibrations of atoms, and that only condense themselves in the human organism, and are aggregated into the sum of the life of the soul. To these two principles he adds yet another: the organic base-forms, made · up from all eternity of atomic groups, from the co-operation of which, in the mechanism of events, organisms are to be explained. We can understand that with such principles

---

[62] In the treatise, ' Ueber die Grenzen u. d. Ursprung der menschl. Erkenntniss,' 1865, Czolbe expresses himself as to the processes in the nerves of sensations more in accord with rational physiology (S. 210 ff.); on the other hand, the view of the immutability of the world-order, the eternal existence of our solar system, &c., still occurs (S. 129 ff.), and is attacked with a striking depreciation of the undeniable consequences of mechanics.

Czolbe could make no use of Darwin's theory. He admitted that by Darwin's principle certain modifications in the constitution of organisms are ingeniously and happily explained, but he was unable to make use of the theory of descent.

These difficulties in his standpoint, and his excessive inclination to build hypothesis upon hypothesis,[63] lessen the importance of a philosophical attempt which must excite great interest from its ethical starting-point, and the relation of his theory to its ethical foundation. Even in the 'Origin of Self-Consciousness' Czolbe says, with the frankness peculiar to him: "I can well conceive what people . . . will say; nay, it seems even to myself that I am carried, by the consequences which my principle has forced upon me, into a fairy (märchenhafte) world of ideas." With this recognition of the weaknesses of his own standpoint was combined the utmost toleration for other views. "Never," he says in the book he published in 1865, "have I shared the opinion of the best-known representatives of Materialism, that it is the force of scientific facts which compels us to the principle of the exclusion of the supersensuous. I have always been convinced that the facts of external and internal experience are very equivocal, and can be interpreted even on the supposition of another world theologically or spiritualistically, with full right, or even without any logical flaw." And again: "As Rudolf Wagner once declared that it was

---

[63] The doubtful character of the method inaugurated by Czolbe is easy to perceive. Good and great hypotheses contain for the most part a single assumption, which may in many cases be verified: here, on the other hand, we have a long series of hypotheses which can hardly be tested at all by experience. They do not stand alone, moreover, nor serve to explain particular cases, as often happens in natural science, but each is a necessary support of the other and for the whole system. If only one is false, then the whole system is false. If we put the probability of the truth of each single hypothesis as equal to the probability of the contrary, and therefore $= \frac{1}{2}$, then the probability of the truth of the whole system will be $\frac{1}{2n}$, where n denotes the number of hypotheses. Upon this simple mathematical law rests the weakness of all constructions with the aid of necessary hypotheses, —though we feel this, indeed, without mathematical proof.

not physiology that drove him to assume an immaterial soul, but the idea of a moral order which was immanent in and inseparable from himself; as he assumed in the brain of those who think theologically, as a necessary condition of this idea, an organ of faith, so I openly declare that in my case too it is neither physiology nor the rational principle of the exclusion of the supernatural, but primarily the moral feeling of duty towards the natural world-order and contentment with it, that compels me to the denial of a supernatural soul." "A certain chemical and physical constitution of the brain-substance" may be more suited to the religious need, another to the atheistic. Materialism, like its opposite, springs not from knowledge and reason, but from faith and feeling.[64]

We shall abundantly see how much truth is contained in this extreme view; but here we must above all remember that it, obviously in connection with the yielding and unthorough conception of natural science which we found in Czolbe, uselessly gives up the strong side of Materialism. It deviates from the right attitude at least as much in the opposite direction as Büchner does to the side of excessive confidence and naïf confusion of what is probable and what is proved. The understanding is not so neutral in these questions as Czolbe thinks, but it leads, in fact, inductively to the highest probability of a strictly mechanical cosmology, by the side of which transcendental identity can be maintained only in a 'second world.' But, on the other hand, the assumption of an intelligible world is far from justifying every 'theological' or 'spiritualistic' interpretation of experience. Here Czolbe was only consistent in inconsistency. His aversion to Kant, whose 'intelligible world' is, in fact, quite reconcilable with all the results of natural inquiry, misled him into frequently abusing Kant, while he admitted the extremest doctrines of ecclesiastical orthodoxy as relatively justified—although these doctrines by no means content

[64] Die Grenzen u. Ursprung der Menschl. Erkentniss, S. 50, 51.

themselves with a 'second world' behind the world of phenomena, but by their dogmas often come into conflict with the most irrefutable consequences of the facts of experience.

Czolbe indirectly gained an additional interest for the history of Materialism through his lively intercourse with Ueberweg at the time when the latter was developing his Materialistic philosophy, of which we shall hereafter speak. A posthumous work of Czolbe's, which, amongst other things, is said to contain an account of Ueberweg's philosophy, is still to be expected. Czolbe died in February 1873, highly esteemed by all who knew him, and prized because of his noble efforts by men of the most opposite opinions.[65]

[65] More precise information as to Czolbe and his views is afforded in a good biographical sketch by Dr. Ed. Johnson, in the 'Altpreuss. Monatsschrift,' Bd. x., Heft 4, S. 338–352 (also reprinted, Königsberg, 1873).

SECOND SECTION.

THE NATURAL SCIENCES.

THE NATURAL SCIENCES.

——◆——

CHAPTER I.

MATERIALISM AND SCIENTIFIC RESEARCH.

MATERIALISM always rests upon the contemplation of nature; but in our own days it cannot content itself with a possible explanation of natural events by means of its theory: it must take its stand upon scientific research, and it gladly accepts this forum, because it is convinced that here it must win its cause. Many of our Materialists go so far as to represent the philosophy to which they attach themselves as a necessary consequence of the scientific spirit—as a natural result of the enormous development and advance which the natural sciences have attained since the speculative method has been abandoned, and the exact and systematic investigation of facts has taken its place. We must not, therefore, be surprised if the opponents of Materialism eagerly seize upon any utterance of a great man of science which repudiates this supposed consequence, or even represents Materialism as a mere misinterpretation of the facts, as a fallacy of superficial inquirers, not to call them absolute triflers.

It was an utterance of this kind when Liebig, in his 'Chemical Letters,' spoke of the Materialists as 'dilettanti.' But although it may be true enough in general that the profoundest inquirers, the discoverers and inventors, the chief masters in any special department, do not usually concern themselves with the promulgation of Materialism; and though men like Büchner, Vogt, or even Czolbe, have exhibited many deficiencies before the judgment-seat of strict method, yet we cannot give an immediate adhesion to Liebig's view.

In the first place, it is quite natural that, in our present subdivision of labour amongst specialists, the man who has directed his whole intellectual energy to the prosecution of a particular branch of science has not the inclination, and often not the capacity, to traverse the whole sphere of the physical sciences, in order to collect from every side the best-established facts of other inquirers, and to weave them into a collective whole. For him it is a thankless labour. His eminence rests upon his discoveries, and these he can only hope to make in his own special department. However much justice, therefore, there is in the demand that every scientific inquirer must possess a certain degree of general scientific training, and especially that he should know as accurately as may be the departments nearest to his own, this is only to correct some of the results of the division of labour, and not to remove the principle altogether. It may very well be, indeed, that a specialist, through his efforts to secure a general scientific culture, may attain to a definite view as to the nature of the universe, and the forces that are at work in it, without feeling the least desire to press his own view upon others, or to set it up as the only possible view. Such a reserve may be due to the best motives, for the specialist will always be conscious of a great difference between the foundations upon which his special knowledge rests and the subjective basis of whatever he may have appropriated from the results of the investigations of others.

Special studies, then, produce caution; but they also produce sometimes narrowness and arrogance. This is especially striking when such an inquirer declares his own attitude towards the neighbour sciences as the only admissible one, when he forbids others to pronounce a judgment on the subjects of his own department, when, therefore, he absolutely rejects the necessary procedure of those who make a collective view of nature the object of their exertions. If, for example, the chemist will forbid the physiologists to say anything of chemistry, or if the physicist spurns the chemist as a 'dilettante' if he ventures a word as to the mechanism of atoms, he ought to consider whether he has really any positive justification for this arbitrary course. If he has not, if a sort of guild coins, as it were, a set of police regulations against 'dabblers' without examining their labours, such pretensions cannot be too severely condemned. But such arrogance is most pernicious when it is not a question of propounding new views, but of bringing into a new connection merely the admitted facts that have been taught us by the specialists themselves, of combining them with facts from another department into far-reaching conclusions, or of giving them a new interpretation in reference to the deriving of the phenomenon from the ultimate grounds of things. If the results of science were such that no one could interpret them but he who has discovered them—and this would be the logical result of such a pretension—it would be a sad outlook for the co-ordination of knowledge and for our whole higher culture. A shoe is in certain respects best judged by the shoemaker, in others by the wearer, and in others again by the anatomist, or by the painter and sculptor. An industrial product is judged not only by the manufacturer but also by the consumer. The man who buys a tool can often make a better use of it than the man who made it. These examples are trivial enough, but they have their application here. He who has diligently traversed the whole realm of the natural sciences in order to obtain a picture of the whole, will often see the meaning of a particular fact better than its discoverer.

We easily see, moreover, that the task of the man who seeks to gain such a collective picture of nature is essentially *philosophical*, and we may ask, therefore, whether the Materialist may not far more justly be charged with philosophical dilettanteism. This has often enough been done, but this does not help us to an unprejudiced critical appreciation of Materialism. Correctly speaking, by a dilettante we should mean one who has not gone through any thorough schooling; but what school is there for the philosopher which, on the ground of its achievements, might draw such a line between what is warranted and what is unwarranted? In the positive sciences, as in the arts, we can nowadays say what is schooling; but not in philosophy. Leaving out of account for the present the special meaning of the term when it refers to the carrying on by others of the practice of a great master, we still know well enough always what is meant by a trained historian, philologist, chemist, or statistician; but amongst 'philosophers' the term is for the most part only misapplied. Nay, the misuse of the idea itself, thoughtlessly continued, has done the utmost injury to the dignity and importance of philosophy. If we wished, independently of discipleship to a particular system, to give a general idea of philosophical training, what could it include? Above all things, a strict logical education in serious and close attention to the rules of formal logic and the bases of all modern sciences, in the doctrine of probabilities, and the theory of induction. But where in our days is such an education to be found? Hardly one university professor in ten possesses it, and least of all is it to be found amongst the "——ians," whether they call themselves after Hegel, Herbart, Trendelenburg, or any other head of a school. The second requisite would be a serious study of the positive sciences, if not to the extent of a mastery of them all in detail—which is impossible and unnecessary—yet at least in order to appreciate their present course and condition from their historical development to the extent of thoroughly understanding their interconnection, and of understanding their methods as deduced from the principles of methodology generally. And we ask again, Where are those who have been so trained? Again, surely, amongst the "——ians" least of all. Hegel, for instance, who very lightly dispensed with the first requisite, at least endeavoured by serious intellectual exertion to satisfy the second requisite. But his 'disciples' do not study what Hegel studied; they study Hegel. And the result of this we have sufficiently seen: a hollow edifice of phrases, a philosophy of shadows, whose arrogance must disgust every one who has been trained in serious subjects. Only in the third or fourth place would come in a true philosophic training the thorough study of the history of philosophy. If, as now generally happens, this is made the first and only condition besides the adoption of some definite system, the inevitable result must be that the history of philosophy too becomes a mere playing with shadows; the formulas under which earlier thinkers tried to comprehend the world are disconnected from the scientific soil from which they grew, and so lose all their real import.

Let us leave aside, then, the charge of dilettanteism, because there is properly nothing to be opposed to it, and because precisely in the sphere of philosophy the advantage of a fresh originality often outweighs all the traditions of the schools. With regard to the exact sciences, the Materialists are justified by the philosophical tendency of their work, though, of course, only so far as they rightly appreciate facts, and confine themselves to inferences from these facts. If they venture, however much they may be driven by the connection of their system, upon conjectures which do violence to the observed facts in the empirical sciences, or if they wholly leave out of account important results of investigation, they are justly liable, as is every philosopher in like case, to the blame of specialists; but these specialists do not thereby acquire a right to treat contemptuously all the efforts of such writers. With regard to philosophy, however, the Materialists are by no means fully justified, even though we must maintain that the reproach of dilettanteism can have no definite meaning here.

From the first, the very undertaking to construct a philosophical theory of things exclusively upon the physical sciences must in these days be described as a philosophical one-sidedness of the worst kind. By the same right by which the empirical philosopher like Büchner opposes himself to the one-sided specialist, may every thoroughly-trained philosopher in his turn oppose himself to Büchner, and reproach him with the prejudices that necessarily result from the limitation of his field of view.

Two objections, however, present themselves to this claim on the part of philosophy: the first is specifically Materialistic, the second is supported by very many representatives of the exact sciences who can by no means be numbered with the Materialists.

There is nothing outside nature is the first objection to the demand of philosophy that we should seek a wider basis. Your Metaphysic is a science falsely so called, without any sure basis; your Psychology is nothing without the physiology of the brain and nervous system; and as to Logic, our successes are the best proof that we are better placed as to the laws of thought than you with your impotent scholastic formulas. But Ethic and Æsthetic have nothing to do with the theoretical basis of philosophy, and may be constructed upon a Materialistic foundation just as well as on any other. What, under these circumstances, can the History of Philosophy do for us? It can be, from first to last, nothing but a history of human errors.

We see ourselves brought here to the question, recently become so famous, of the *limits of the knowledge of nature,* to which we must presently devote a thorough consideration. But first a few remarks on the second objection.

The philosophers, it is often said in the scientific camp,

have an *entirely different way of thinking* from ours. Any contact with philosophy, therefore, can only be hurtful to scientific research. They are simply disparate provinces, and they must remain disparate.

We pass by the question how often this view means exactly what it says, and how often, on the contrary, it is a euphemistic way of expressing the opinion that philosophy is simple nonsense. The fact remains that the doctrine of the complete difference in the way of thinking is very widely spread amongst scientific men. A very lively expression was given to it by the eminent botanist Hugo von Mohl in an address to celebrate the establishing of a scientific faculty in the University of Tübingen.[1] But the Materialists naturally do not consider themselves included in this idea of 'philosophy.' They profess to gain their ideas of the world by means of scientific thinking, and at most admit that they make a larger use of hypothesis than is admissible in special researches.

This whole way of looking at the matter rests upon a one-sided reference to our post-Kantian philosophy, with a complete misunderstanding of the character of modern philosophy from Descartes to Kant. The activity of the followers of Schelling and Hegel, of the Neo-Aristotelians, and of other recent schools, is only too well calculated to justify the repugnance with which scientific men usually turn away from philosophy; but, on the other hand, the whole principle of modern philosophy—if we do not include in that term the corruptions of German philosophical Romanticism—is entirely different. We have here, with a few exceptions not worth mentioning, a strictly scientific mode of thought with regard to everything that is given us by means of the senses; but almost as universally also an attempt to overcome by speculation the one-sidedness of the notion of the world that is thus given us.

[1] We subjoin a passage from the first edition with reference to the fact of the formation of a special scientific faculty, which has had to give up its place in the text in order to preserve a stricter consecution of ideas and to admit new material. [See Note A. at end of chapter.—Tr.]

Descartes is not so much a man of science as a mathematician. He has some serious defects, but he has in other points really advanced science, and no one will assert that he was lacking in a true scientific mode of thought. Yet he assumed, besides the corporeal world, a world also of the soul, in which everything that exists externally is only *represented;* and thus, great as are the defects inherent in his system, he touched the very point at which all Materialism must make a halt, and to which the most exact scientific inquiry at last finds itself brought.

Spinoza, the great champion of the absolute necessity of all existence and of the unity of all natural phenomena, has so often been reckoned with the Materialists, that it is almost more necessary to point out his difference than his agreement with the Materialistic view. It is, however, the same point again in which this difference appears: the whole picture of the world, to which the mechanical theory of the universe leads us, is only *one side* of the nature of things, which, of course, stands in entire harmony with the other, the intellectual side. The English philosophers ever since Bacon employ, almost without exception, a method which harmonises very well with the scientific mode of thought; and in England that conflict between philosophy and science, of which so much is heard here, has never been known. The phenomenal world is conceived by the leading English philosophers on the same principles as it is conceived by our Materialists, even though but few of them remain, like Hobbes, absolutely Materialist. But Locke, who in natural science, like Newton, assumed the doctrine of atoms, based his philosophy not upon matter, but upon subjectivity, even though in a sensationalistic sense; and he doubts whether our understanding is competent to the solution of all the problems that present themselves—a beginning of the Kantian Criticism, which receives a notable advance in the hands of Hume. There is not one of these men who did not regard it as obvious that everything in nature proceeds naturally, and the occasional concessions to ecclesiastical views are transparent enough. They are, however, with the exception of Hobbes, far from identifying the picture of the world as it is presented to our understanding and senses with the absolute nature of things, and in all the curious modifications of the systems there everywhere appears the point which distinguishes the modern philosophy from the ancient—regard to the fact that our idea of the world is essentially *representation.*

With Leibniz the idea of the world as representation is carried to an extreme in his attributing representation to the monads ; and yet at the same time Leibniz, in his conception of the phenomenal world, favours the strictest mechanism, and the way in which he handles a problem of physics does not differ from the procedure of other physicists. The relation of philosophy to Materialism at length attains the utmost clearness in Kant. The man who first developed the doctrine of the origin of the heavenly bodies from the mere attraction of scattered matter, who had already recognised the main features of Darwinism, and who did not hesitate to speak in his popular lectures of the development of man from an earlier animal condition as something obvious, who rejected the question of the ' seat of the soul ' as irrational, and often enough let it appear that to him body and soul are the same thing, only perceived by different organs, could not possibly have had much to learn of Materialism ; for the whole philosophy of Materialism is, as it were, incorporated in the Kantian system, without changing its more idealistic character. That Kant dealt with all the objects of natural science in a scientific way there is no doubt ; for the ' metaphysical principles of natural science ' contain only an attempt to discover the axiomatic foundations *a priori,* and do not fall, therefore, within the sphere of empirical inquiry, which everywhere rests upon experience, and regards the axioms as given. Thus Kant leaves the whole compass of scientific thought in its place and in its dignity, as the great and only means of extending our experience of the world given to us through our senses, of systematising it, and thus making this world intelligible to us in the causal connection of all phenomena. Were it well done then, if such a man at the same time did not rest in the scientific and mechanical theory of the world, if he asserted that this is not the end of everything, that we have reason to take the world of our ideas also into account, and that neither the phenomenal world nor the ideal world can be regarded as the absolute nature of things—were it well done to pass unsuspectingly by or to ignore the whole assertion, just because we do not feel the need for wider and deeper examination ?

If it may be the specialist is afraid of being drawn away too far from his subject by the prosecution of such ideas, and if he prefers, therefore, to content himself with a few vague ideas on this head, or even to decline philosophy altogether as a foreign subject, there will not be much to say against it. But whoever, like our Materialists, comes forward as a ' philosopher,' or even thinks himself called to be an epoch-making reformer of philosophy, cannot evade these questions. To come to a thorough explanation with them is the only way in which the Materialist can claim a permanent place in the history of philosophy. Without this effort of the mind, Materialism—which, indeed, otherwise can only clothe old ideas in new material—remains for the most part nothing but a battering-ram directed against the crudest conceptions of religious tradition, and a significant symptom of a profound intellectual ferment.[2]

[2] Büchner has written a ' Criticism of Himself' on the occasion of the twelfth edition of ' Force and Matter' (in the third edition of ' Natur u. Wissenschaft,' Leipz., 1874), in which he regards it as a chief merit of his to have helped *philosophy* to vindicate her claims in the sphere of the natural sciences. He admits that other circumstances have contributed to this, but "it was ' Force and Matter' that paved the way and opened the contest in such a manner that it secured the universal sympathy of learned and unlearned, and could not be laid again to rest without a definite result. In this sense, then, ' Force and Matter' may, and indeed must,

It is, however, remarkable that the very point which the systematisers and apostles of the mechanical cosmology so carelessly pass by—the question as to the *limits of natural knowledge* has found full appreciation amongst deep-thinking men engaged in special researches. Thus it is shown that genuine and thorough special studies, in combination with solid general culture, easily lead to a deeper. insight into the essence of nature than a mere encyclopædic excursion through the whole realm of physical research. The man who is securely master of a single field, and here sees into the heart of every problem, has won a sharpened eye for all related fields of inquiry. He will everywhere easily find his way, and so, too, will quickly attain to a general view, which may be described as genuinely philosophical, while studies which are wider in their reach may easily retain that lack of thoroughness which marks every philosophical system that evades the questions belonging to the theory of knowledge. And therefore it deserves also to be specially observed, that the most eminent of our scientific men who have ventured to

be called 'epoch-making,' and the book must be always regarded in the history of science so long as such a history exists." But Büchner might much more claim a permanent mention of his name in the general history of intellectual development, on the ground that he was the man who trumpeted abroad with striking success at the right moment what many were thinking, a thing which assuredly many, as well from the scientific as the philosophical side, could have done better. Whether more successfully, too, is another question, since his very lack of scientific precision and his dallying with the superficial aspect of phenomena were very essential to Büchner's success. When Büchner attributes scientific importance to his 'theory,' he certainly deceives himself, since neither in general nor in detail does he contribute anything essentially new, but, in fact, often falls considerably short of the requirements of his task, viz., to present a general view of the mechanical theory of the world. Thus, for instance, Büchner, in his 'Criticism of Himself,' represents the doctrine of the persistence of force as a subsequent and confirmatory complement of his standpoint, since he dates it very naïvely from the fifth edition of his book, although every thorough man of science and philosophy *must* have been acquainted with this important doctrine as early as 1855, when the first edition of 'Force and Matter' appeared. Why, Mayer had announced the law in 1842; in 1847 came Helmholtz's 'Abhandlung von der Erhaltung der Kraft;' and in 1854 the same physicist's *popular* essay, 'Ueber die Wechselwirkung der Naturkräfte,' was in a *second* edition!

enter the domain of philosophy, nearly all, from whatever
starting-point, have come upon the problems of the theory
of knowledge.

Let us first consider the much-discussed lecture, ' On
the Limits of the Knowledge of Nature,' which Du Bois-
Reymond delivered at the meeting of the German Scientific and Medical Association at Leipzig in 1872. The
lecture itself, as well as sundry answers to it, will give us
abundant opportunity to exhibit in the clearest light the
salient point in the whole criticism of Materialism.

All knowledge of nature has its ultimate aim in the
mechanism of atoms. Accordingly, Du Bois-Reymond
sets up as an extreme, to the human mind unattainable, but still intelligible, goal, a complete knowledge of
this mechanism. Starting from an expression of Laplace's
he teaches that " a mind which should know for a given
very small period of time the position and movement of
all the atoms in the universe, would also necessarily be in
a position to derive from these, in accordance with the
laws of mechanics, the whole past and future. It could,
by an appropriate treatment of its world-formula, tell us
who was the Iron Mask, or how the ' President' came to
grief. As the astronomer predicts the day on which, after
many years, a comet again appears in the vault of heaven
from the depths of space, so this ' mind' would read in its
equations the day when the Greek cross will glitter from
the mosque of Sophia, or when England will burn its
last lump of coal. If put down in the world-formula
$t = - \infty$, the riddle of the original condition of things would
solve itself to it. It would see in endless space matter
either already moved or unequally distributed, since, if it
were equally distributed, the equilibrium would never have
been disturbed. If it let t increase indefinitely in the positive sense, it would learn whether it is after an infinite or
finite period that Carnot's principle threatens the universe
with icy cessation." All qualities arise first through
the senses. " The Mosaic ' there was light' is physiolo-

gically false. Light first was when the first red eye-point of an infusorium for the first time distinguished between light and dark." " Dumb and dark in itself, that is, without qualities, as it appears from a subjective analysis, is the world also for the mechanical theory resulting from objective inquiry, which, instead of light and sound, knows only vibrations of a primitive substance devoid of qualities, which has become matter that may here be weighed, and there not."

There are now two places where even the mind imagined by Laplace would have to halt. We are not in a position to conceive the atoms, and we are unable, from the atoms and their motion, to explain the slightest phenomenon of consciousness.

We may turn and twist the notion of matter as we like, we always come upon an ultimate something that is incomprehensible, if not absolutely contradictory, as in the hypothesis of forces that act at a distance through empty space. There is no hope of ever solving this problem ; the hindrance is transcendental. It rests upon the fact that we can in fine conceive of nothing without any sense qualities, while, at the same time, our whole knowledge is directed towards resolving the qualities into mathematical relations. Not without justice, therefore, Du Bois-Reymond goes on to mention that all our knowledge of nature is, in truth, no knowledge at all, that it affords us merely the substitute for an explanation. We shall never forget that our whole culture rests upon this ' substitute,' which in many important respects perfectly replaces the hypothetical absolute knowledge; but it remains strictly true that the knowledge of nature, if we follow it to this point, and try to press farther on with the same principle that has brought us so far, reveals to us its own inadequacy, and sets a limit to itself.

Du Bois-Reymond finds no serious difficulty for the knowledge of nature in the origin of organisms. Where and in what shape life first appeared we do not know, but the mind that Laplace imagined in possession of the world-formula could tell us. Crystal and organism differ from each other as a mere building differs from a factory with its engines and machinery, into which raw material pours, and from which manufactures, waste materials, and refuse pour out again. We have here nothing more than an "extremely difficult mechanical problem." The richest nature-picture of a tropical forest offers to analysing science nothing but matter in motion.

Not here, accordingly, is the second limit of natural knowledge, but at the first appearance of *consciousness*. And it is by no means a question of the human mind in the whole extent of its imaginative and rational powers. "As the most powerful and complicated muscular effort of a man or animal is not essentially more obscure than the simple contraction of a single muscular fibre; as the single secreting-cell conceals the whole problem of secretion, so, too, the loftiest activity of the soul from material conditions is not in the main point more incomprehensible than consciousness in its first stage of sensation. With the first emotion of pleasure or pain that the simplest creature experienced in the beginning of animal life upon earth, this impassable gulf is established, and the world has become henceforth doubly incomprehensible."

Du Bois-Reymond proposes to prove this, independently of all philosophical theories, in a manner that is evident even to the scientific mind. For this purpose he supposes that we have a complete ('astronomical') knowledge of the processes in the brain, and that not of the unconscious processes only, but also of those which, in point of time, coincide always with the intellectual processes, and are therefore, it is probable, necessarily bound up with them. Then, of course, it would be a lofty triumph "if we could say that in a particular intellectual process a particular movement of particular atoms took place in particular ganglionic centres and nervous tubes." The "unveiled insight into the material conditions of intellectual processes" would edify us more than any scientific discovery yet made, but the intellectual processes themselves would be just as incomprehensible to us as now. "The astronomical knowledge of the brain, the highest knowledge we can attain, reveals to us nothing but matter in motion." But if we suppose that from this knowledge certain intellectual processes or dispositions, as memory, the association of ideas, and so on, might become intelligible, that too is delusion; we only learn certain conditions of intellectual life, but do not learn how the intellectual life is itself developed from these conditions.

"What conceivable connection exists between certain movements of certain atoms in my brain on the one hand, and on the other the to me original and not further definable but undeniable facts, 'I feel pain, feel pleasure; I take something sweet, smell roses, hear organ-sounds, see something red,' and the just as immediately resulting certainty, 'therefore I am'? . . . It is impossible to see how from the co-operation of the atoms consciousness can result. Even if I were to attribute consciousness to the atoms, that would neither explain consciousness in general, nor would that in any way help us to understand the unitary consciousness of the individual."

This second limitation of natural knowledge also Du Bois-Reymond calls an absolute one: no conceivable progress in the sciences can ever help us to get over it. But all the less will the man of science be deprived of the right, unconfused by myths, dogmas, and philosophical systems puffed up by their antiquity, to form inductively his own opinion as to the "relations between spirit and matter."

"He sees in a thousand cases that material conditions influence the intellectual life. To his unprejudiced eye there appears no ground to doubt that really the sense-impressions communicate themselves to what is called the soul. He sees the human mind, as it were, grow with the brain. . . . No theological prejudice prevents him from recognising, with Descartes, in the souls of animals the

members of the same order of development successively
less and less perfect, but still related to the soul of man."
He sees how in the vertebrates those portions of the brain
which physiology must regard as bearers of the higher
intellectual functions gradually develop themselves with
the advance of the activities of the soul. "Finally, the
evolution theory in connection with the doctrine of natural
selection forces upon him the idea that the soul has arisen
as the gradual result of certain material combinations, and
perhaps, like other hereditary endowments that are useful
to the individual in the struggle for existence, has advanced and perfected itself through an innumerable series
of generations."

We must almost believe that Materialism might be very
well content. By way of supererogation, Du Bois-Reymond
expressly takes under his protection Vogt's notorious expression, that the thoughts bear the same relation to the
brain as the gall to the liver, or urine to the kidneys.[3]
Physiology knows nothing of æsthetic distinctions. To
it the secretion of the kidneys is an object of the same
dignity as the functions of the nobler organs. "It is
scarcely blameworthy either in Vogt's saying that the
activity of the soul is represented as a product of material
conditions in the brain." The only defect is in the creating
the idea that the activity of the soul may be as intelligibly
explained from the structure of the brain, as the secretion
from the structure of the gland.

But this it is, of course, against which Materialism
revolts. If anything at all remains 'unintelligible,' Materialism may still be an excellent maxim of scientific
research (and that we too agree in thinking it), but it is
no longer philosophy. Other systems, such as Scepticism,
may adopt the unintelligible element, or even make the

---

[3] It may be added here that the
much-discussed 'expression of Vogt'
is substantially already in Cabanis.
The brain produces "la sécrétion de
la pensée": Rapports du Physique et
du Moral de l'Homme, Par. 1844, p.
138. The editor, L. Peisse, remarks
on it: "Cette phrase est restée
célèbre."

unintelligibleness of things their very principle ; but Materialism is essentially a positive philosophy, which asserts its fundamental doctrines with dogmatic certainty, and one of whose most important assertions it is that by means of these doctrines the whole world may easily be understood. And however much our modern Materialists are inclined to sceptical and relativistic fits, however easily they may talk perhaps of the unintelligibleness of the ultimate grounds of all existence, or set up the world of man as the world of inquiry, while giving up the question whether there may be another way of conceiving things, the unintelligibleness of the intellectual element they will not concede, because they find one of the greatest achievements of Materialism in this, that even the activities of the soul in man and animals are thoroughly explained out of the functions of matter.

That in this is involved a serious misunderstanding must have already been made sufficiently clear in our first book. But we are nowhere more directly confronted with it than in the polemic which was directed in the Materialistic interests against Du Bois-Reymond. We may indeed say of his opponents what Kant said of Hume's (cf. *ante* p. 206), that "they always assumed as conceded precisely what he doubted, and, on the contrary, demonstrated with eagerness and often with arrogance what he never thought of disputing."

This is most striking in the case of Dr. Langwieser, a specialist in brain diseases, who has discussed Du Bois-Reymond's 'Limits of Natural Knowledge' in a small pamphlet published at Vienna, 1873. Langwieser had already written in 1871 a 'Versuch einer Mechanik der Psychischen Zustände,' which offers some noteworthy, if somewhat crudely developed, contributions to a future understanding of the functions of the brain. That the author overestimates the range of his explanations is very natural, and that he believes that from his standpoint, through the proof of mechanical brain-functions, he has also explained consciousness, is a feature which he shares with Materialism generally. One would suppose that such a writer, when an inquirer like Du Bois-Reymond comes forward, would at least awake out of "dogmatic slumber," and would see clearly what was the real point at issue; but instead of this we have entire misapprehension. Nor would the misapprehension of an individual writer long detain us, but that we seem to have here, as it were, the classical model of a whole class of similar misapprehensions, and that this very point is of the highest importance for the appreciation of Materialism.

The misapprehension is so gross that Langwieser actually asserts that Du Bois-Reymond contradicts himself in assuming Laplace's principle of the calculation of the future from a perfect formula of the universe. "In order to calculate by means of the mechanism of the atoms events of the past or future in which the human mind has co-operated or will co-operate as an essential factor, the intellectual circumstances of humanity fall also within the province of the knowable atomic mechanism, which is just what Du Bois-Reymond denies." . . . "But if he would answer that Laplace's 'mind' would be cognisant also of the atomic movements of all human brains, and would take them into account, so that it would calculate also the influence of the intellectual processes of man upon material events, only that the understanding of the intellectual processes from these atomic movements would be forbidden him, this again involves a contradiction. For so soon as he can calculate every idea as an atomic movement, with its further consequences and effects, then he knows from its effects also the nature of the thing, as everywhere else, so also in the sphere of intellectual things; for the nature of a thing is nothing more or less than so far (*sic*) as it expresses itself in its effects."

Here, therefore, we have a case in point where the opponent assumes as admitted and obvious just what Du Bois-Reymond doubts; and the remainder of the pamphlet is devoted to proving what the celebrated physiologist has never doubted, and to the elucidation of which he has himself made the most valuable contributions.

An unprejudiced reader of the lecture on the 'Limits of Natural Knowledge,' if he be provided with the necessary knowledge, can never for a moment doubt that the author amongst the atoms includes also the brain-atoms of man, and that for him man, together with his 'voluntary' actions, is to the student of science but a part of the universe, similar in all respects to the other parts. But Du Bois-Reymond would, at the same time, be careful not to speak of this " influence of intellectual processes upon material events," because such an influence, strictly speaking, is scientifically quite inconceivable. Were it possible for a single cerebral atom to be moved by 'thought' only so much as the millionth of a millimetre out of the path assigned to it by the laws of mechanics, the whole 'world-formula' would become inapplicable and unmeaning. But human actions, even, *e.g.*, those of the soldiers destined to plant the cross upon the mosque of Sophia, of their generals, the diplomatists concerned, and so on—all these actions result, scientifically speaking, not from 'thoughts,' but from muscular movements, whether these serve to make a march, to draw a sword or guide a pen, to give utterance to the word of command, or to fix the eye upon a point of attack. The muscular movements are set free by nervous activity; this arises from the functions of the brain, and these are entirely determined by the structure of the brain, by the sensory conductors and by the atomic movements of molecular changes and so on, under the influence of the centripetal nervous activity. We must quite realise that the law of the conservation of energy can undergo no exception in the interior of the brain without becoming wholly meaningless, and we must rise to the conclusion therefore that the whole activity of man, individuals as well as peoples, might go on, as it actually does go on, without the occurring in any single individual of anything resembling a thought or a sensation. The glance of man might be just as 'full of soul,' the sound of his voice just as 'moving,' only that there would be no soul answering to this phrase, and that no one would be 'moved' in any other way than that the unconsciously changing looks would assume a gentler expression, or the mechanism of the cerebral atoms would bring a smile upon the lips or tears into the eyes.   Thus, and in no other way, did Descartes conceive the animal world, and there is not the slightest room to question the scientific admissibility of such a supposition. That it is false we only infer from the similarity in the symptoms of animal sensations with those which we observe in ourselves. But in the same way it is only by an inference from analogy that we attribute consciousness to any other people than ourselves. We find it connected in ourselves with corporeal processes, and we justly conclude that it will be so also in the case of others; but scientifically we can know nothing whatever but the symptoms and 'conditions' of the intellectual element outside us, and not this element itself. We may give the sharpest, and I might say the clearest and most convincing, expression to the view from which Du Bois-Reymond starts, if we suppose two worlds, both occupied by men and their doings, with the same course of history, with the same modes of expression by gesture, the same sounds of voice for him who could *hear* them, *i.e.*, not simply conduct their vibrations through the auditory nerve to the brain, but be conscious of them to himself. The two worlds are therefore to be absolutely alike, with only this difference, that in the one the whole mechanism runs down like that of an automaton, without anything being felt or thought, whilst the other is just *our* world; then the formula for these two worlds would be entirely the same. To the eye of exact research they would be indistinguishable.

That we do not believe in the one of these worlds is nothing but the immediate effect of our peculiar personal consciousness, as each of us knows it in himself alone, and which we attribute also to everything that is externally like ourselves. But the fusion between the apprehension of the external symptoms of mind and their interpretation from our own consciousness is so complete, and so deeply rooted from our birth, that it requires an acute and unprejudiced thinker to separate these two factors.

But it is quite a different question when we come to the causal connection between material processes and the intellectual states combined with them. That in this respect the fullest independence of the intellectual and the physical may be asserted without trespassing beyond the 'limits of natural knowledge' is expressly recognised by Du Bois-Reymond; and so far, then, as the Materialists are concerned merely to get rid of supernatural notions and events, they need not be troubled by the doctrine set forth. Du Bois-Reymond, at the utmost, propounds as possible and even probable what they themselves maintain with dogmatic certainty; nay, Laplace's idea, as Langwiescr has quite rightly discovered, contains more than the mere possibility. However puzzling may seem the way in which the intellectual and the physical are connected, however inexplicable may be the nature of the latter, yet the absolute dependence of the intellectual on the physical must be asserted, so soon as it is shown, on the one hand, that the two sets of phenomena entirely correspond, and, on the other, that the physical events follow strict and immutable laws, which are merely an expression of the functions of matter. What changes a more thorough examination may produce in this view we shall find out further on.

In the same way as the Materialists, so too have their antipodes, the theologians and theologising philosophers, understood the doctrine of the limits of natural knowledge. They look away past the grossly Materialistic character of the views which Du Bois-Reymond develops, and cling to the one great fact, that he sets absolute and impassable limits to scientific research. Force and matter are inexplicable, atomistic knowledge is only a 'substitute' for real knowledge; and therefore Materialism is rejected —rejected by one of our first scientific men. Why, then, may not speculation and theology again cheerfully luxuriate over the abandoned field, and teach with great authority what science does not know? That they do not know it themselves has nothing to do with the question. The celebrated physiologist has declared consciousness—nay, even the simplest sensation—as inaccessible to scientific research; why, then, may not the old metaphysic and the old wise psychology of notions rummage out their dolls again and set them dancing on the vacant field? The old bugbear is gone; the man of science, who only teaches what he knows, has promised to let the game alone; so then we are in merry possession again of our domains! Everything will now go on as if there were no such thing as science. The sphere of mind has nothing to do with science!

That such misapprehensions are possible can only be due partly to the deeply-rooted habit of not clearly defining the idea of knowledge, and of identifying understanding with the investigation of causal connection. Partly, indeed, the fault must rest with the lecturer, although less for what he says than for what he does not say; and finally, with the way in which a fragment from the criticism of all knowledge is torn out, and without sufficient indications of its connection with further questions is flung amongst the public. In this respect, the writer himself may not have fully appreciated the position, although he shows himself otherwise not unversed in the history of philosophy. A deeper indication we find only towards the end of the discourse: Du Bois-Reymond here raises the question whether the two limits of natural knowledge may not perhaps be the same, " *i.e.*, whether, if we understood the nature of matter and force, we should not also understand how the substance underlying them can, under certain conditions, feel, will, and think." This again is quite a Materialistic turn, instead of which the disciple of the Critical Philosophy would rather ask, whether, if we had fully understood the relation of consciousness to the way in which we conceive natural objects, it would not at once be perfectly clear to us, why we must in scientific thought represent the substance of the world as matter and force? That the two problems are identical is, in fact, much more than probable. And in the last result it would come to the same thing, whether the latter is resolved into the former or conversely; and yet the one method of reduction is in its tendency Materialistic, and the other Idealistic. The solution supposed would, of course, if it were at all possible, do away with the antithesis between Materialism and Idealism.

There is a single passage in this carefully thought-out discourse which is not only liable to misunderstanding, but is positively incorrect; we will proceed therefore to make some critical remarks upon it. In the world in motion of Laplace's imaginary Mind, the cerebral atoms also move * " as in dumb play." And then he proceeds: " It surveys their hosts, it penetrates their complications, but it *understands not their gestures;* to it they do not think, and therefore its world remains without qualities."

Let us recollect, in the first place, that this Mind contemplates even human actions as necessary consequences of the movements of the cerebral atoms! Let us recollect that the law of necessity, the keys of which this Mind possesses, rules all, even the subtlest and most significant movements of glance, of look, the modulation of the voice, and that the way in which men associate and affect each other in hate and love, in jest and disputation, in struggle and labour, must at least, from the external aspect, be perfectly intelligible to this Mind. It can predict the slightest shadow of secret envy or tacit intelligence in a

* [S. 28; 4te Aufl., S. 32, where the phrase is altered to meet Lange's criticism.—Tr.]

human glance just as well as a total eclipse of the moon. But let us further recollect that this Mind was supposed to be a mind *related to man*, that it is accordingly itself capable of all these emotions which its formulæ express. *Can it, then, fail to read its own sensations into what it sees externally before itself?* We do just the same thing when we perceive envy, anger, gratitude, or love in our fellow-men. We, too, perceive only the tokens, and interpret them from our own hearts. This Mind, indeed, has primarily only its formulæ, while we have immediate intuition. But we need only lend it a little fancy, a quite intelligible fancy, such as we ourselves possess, and it will at once transform its formulæ into intuition.

Of course, at first, those formulæ only speak to it that express the external phenomenon, which we, too, know from daily life; but if it completely observes the causal connection of this external phenomenon with the motion of the cerebral atoms, it will very soon read in the latter its causes and effects, and it will then understand 'the gestures' of these atoms from their influence upon the external gestures of the man just as much as, *e.g.*, the telegraph-clerk with a little practice works the messages immediately from the rhythm of the clicking lever, without being obliged first to read the signs impressed upon the paper.

If now this Mind, besides all its other magnified human qualities, possessed too a high degree of critical acumen, it would see that it perceives the intellectual life, not by means of objective knowledge, in daily life as little as in science, but that it carries it over from its own internal experience in the one case into formulæ, in the other into intuitions. It would also readily admit that no immediate knowledge of foreign sensations is given it, and that it has no idea at all how sensation and consciousness arise from material movements. In these respects it would calmly join Du Bois-Reymond in his 'Ignorabimus;' but at the same time it be would the *most perfect psychologist* that we can possibly conceive, and psychology, as a science, can never be to us anything but a fragment of the knowledge which this Mind possesses in all its fulness.

But if we look at the matter carefully, it is the same with all sciences without exception, so far as we have not to do with the appearance of knowledge. Everything is, in a certain sense, natural knowledge, for all our knowledge is directed towards *intuition.* It is only in the object that our knowledge takes its bearings through the discovery of fixed laws; it is from the subject that we interpret and give life to the different forms, so far as we refer them to the intellect. Immediate knowledge of the intellectual element we have only in our own self-consciousness; but whoever tries to spin a science out of this alone, without being guided by the object, falls irredeemably a victim to self-delusion.

If, then, this is so, what is the value of the demonstration of the limits of natural knowledge ? However much the methodological character of the so-called 'mental sciences' differs from that of the natural sciences, they are nevertheless all included in Du Bois-Reymond's ideal of the natural sciences, so far, that is, as they rest upon real knowledge, and not upon mere imagination.[4] It might be

---

[4] The distinction between the 'mental' and the 'natural sciences' is very sharply emphasised by Mill in his 'Logic.' He requires for the former, indeed, essentially the same method of inquiry, but, on the other hand, he greatly over-values (hence the standpoint of the English Association-Psychology) the source of subjective observation, which he considers almost exclusively, while he under-estimates the advancement of these sciences by the help of the corresponding phenomenon—the physiological method. Helmholtz appreciates the distinction more correctly in his lecture 'On the Relation of Natural Science to General Science' (Popular Lect., E. T., p. 16 ff.). Hence the distinction which results from the difference of the subject-matter, method and modes of proof, comes to the front. When Helmholtz at the same time demands for the historian, the philologist, the jurist, &c., "a delicately and fully-trained insight into the springs of human action," which rests again upon "a certain warmth of sympathy and an interest in observing the workings of other men's minds," this must be conceded. They are just the means by which we may more finely and rapidly apprehend and more correctly interpret the *signs* in words, writing, gestures, traces and monuments of all kinds *that are open to external observation.* The mind imagined by Laplace, however, needs in this respect not an exceptional but only an ordinary human capacity, in order to possess the fullest insight in the mental sciences too, so far as he can follow them up

supposed that this decided the triumph of Materialism, and that the thanks which its opponents have offered for the bold ' confession ' of the famous physiologist are absolutely objectless.   But if we recall what has been said in the chapter on Kant we shall easily see that this is not so. The ' limits of natural knowledge ' are, ideally speaking, identical with the limits of knowledge in general ; but this very circumstance increases their importance, and the whole inquiry becomes a confirmation from the scientific side of the critical standpoint in the theory of knowledge.

The limit of knowledge is, in truth, no rigid barrier which absolutely opposes itself at a certain point to its natural course of progress.   The mechanical theory of the world has before and behind an infinite task, but as a whole it essentially carries within itself a limit which it will never be able to escape at any point of its course.   Does the physicist explain red light when he shows us the number of vibrations that correspond with it ?   He explains so much of the phenomenon as he can, and the rest he leaves to the physiologist.   The latter, again, explains what he can ; but even if we credit his science with a perfection which it does not at present possess, he too has in fine, like the physicist, nothing but atomic movements at his disposition.[5]   In his case the arch is completed by the

with his feelings ; for he possesses in his knowledge of the external facts a means of controlling and improving the principles of interpretation of signs, and as at the same time he understands every language (for his world-formula contains all the facts of the development and modification of all significant sound), he knows, too, how any human mind, from the ablest to the poorest, interprets the signs of the intellectual facts. A poet, indeed, for all his infinite knowledge, he could not become, unless it were otherwise in him to be so.

[5] The demand made by Kirchmann, Czolbe, Spiller, &c., that the qualities which, since Locke, and at bottom since Demokritos, are regarded as " secondary " and merely subjective, must have an objective reality, rests, indeed, in the first place, upon an inadequate theory of knowledge, and in so far that ' red,' ' sour taste,' ' bell-ringing,' &c., are phenomena in the subject, cannot be shaken. But if natural knowledge gives me, *even in the brain*, only *atomic movements* as the corresponding facts, while sensations are undoubtedly present (have empirical reality), I can very easily base the conjecture that in the vibrating string, too, there is something else, that is not, indeed, like my idea of the sounding, coloured objects, but yet has far more relationship with them than the undulating atom.

resolution of centripetal into centrifugal nervous currents. The rest, then, he cannot hand on any further, and he proclaims the 'limit of natural knowledge.' But is the chasm in this case different from that in the case of the physicist, or have we any guarantee that his vibrations also, like those of the physiologist, are not necessarily combined with a process of an entirely different nature? Is it not a very natural and quite justifiable conclusion from analogy that there is *everywhere* behind these vibrations something concealed? Behind the vibrations in the brain hide our own sensations; we can, therefore, *fix* the 'limit of natural knowledge' at this point; but that it *lies only here*, and not rather in the character of knowledge itself, must, at least on a little reflection, appear very improbable.

And it is not without reason that this is a point from which the most various speculations take their start. Du Bois-Reymond dispels the idea of a 'world-soul' by pointing out that we do not find in the structure of the world any analogy with the structure of a human brain.* The argument is strong enough against anthropomorphic conceptions of such a world-soul, but not against the idea in a more general form. Other conceptions, such as, *e.g.*, Schopenhauer's identification of will and motive impulse, the 'world-æther,' with which Spiller[6] takes the field against Du Bois-Reymond, Ueberweg's sensient matter, and so on, may be easily shown to be transcendental speculations; but the ground from which these speculations spring remains, and negatively we may answer with confidence, that of the dead, dumb, and silent world of the vibrating atoms we know nothing, but that it is to us a necessary conception, in so far as we try to represent scientifically the causal connection of phenomena. As, however, we have seen that this necessary conception ex-

---

* S. 32; 4te Aufl., S. 38.

[6] Spiller, Das Naturerkennen nach seinen angeblichen u. wirklichen Grenzen, Berlin, 1873. This treatise, too, as against Du Bois-Reymond, is full of misapprehensions of the kind denoted in the text.

plains not what is given, namely, our sensations, but only a certain order in their origin and decay, so we must see that this conception, in its whole nature and its necessary principles, is not calculated to reveal to us the ultimate, innermost nature of things.

We reach exactly the same result if we start from matter and force. Here it is easy to show that theoretical physics has, from any point of view, a whole infinity of subtler and ever subtler explanations and mathematical analyses before it, while the difficulty that opposes itself to knowledge always remains the same. So soon, however, as we come back to the atoms, we find everywhere traces of the inadequacy of the mechanical conception. As is well known, Hume tried (cf. *ante*, p. 160) to remove the objections to a Materialistic explanation of thought, by professing to find the same incomprehensibleness in all other cases of a causal relation. In this he was right; but the protection that he thus extends to Materialism in one respect in another serves to its destruction. The contradictions cannot attach to the 'thing in itself;' they must therefore have their root in our modes of thought.

If consciousness and brain-movement coincide, without our being able to understand how the one could act upon the other, we can hardly avoid the old Spinozistic idea, which finds an echo too in Kant, that both are the same thing—projected, as it were, upon different organs of apprehension. Materialism clings so obstinately to the reality of matter and its motion, that a genuine dogmatist of this school does not long hesitate to declare the brain-motion to be the real and objective fact, and the sensation merely a sort of appearance or a delusive reflex of objectivity. But it is not only 'appearance' that 'deceives:' the *idea of appearance* also has often proved deceitful. The ancient philosophers especially were very naïf in their belief that they had disposed of a thing when they explained it to be 'appearance;' as if the notion of appearance were not a relative one! A ray of light, a streak of cloud, *appears* to be a form, but the light and the cloud are still real. If, for instance, motion is explained to be appearance, we may have a reason for regarding the thing in itself as eternally resting; but the apparent motion contradicts this judgment. It is an absolutely given fact, like the light or cloud-streak.

Such must be our judgment of the Materialistic treatment of sensation if the brain-motion is to be exalted to its real essence. This standpoint is very distinctly represented by Langwieser, for instance, in his polemic against Du Bois-Reymond. " Little as our self-consciousness," he says,[*] " teaches us the anatomy of our body, or at least the fibrous structure of our brain, and little therefore as there is *any such thing as self-consciousness in an objective sense,* we are just as little able *subjectively to know our sensations for what they are."*

Here we see how the old naïf view of sense impressions is yet further strengthened by the introduction of the modern ideas of ' objective' and ' subjective.' The subjective is, strictly speaking, nothing; or, in other words, subjective existence is not the true, proper existence, with which alone science is concerned. Our own consciousness —the starting-point of all thought with philosophers since Descartes—is only such a subjective phenomenon. When we know the organs of the brain in which it arises, and the currents stirring in these organs, then only do we know what the thing is : we have observed consciousness ' objectively,' and then everything is done that can reasonably be required.

To these conceptions of a Materialistic natural philosopher who despises philosophy as " Mysticism," we will now oppose the opinion of a philosophically trained scientific man. The astronomer Zöllner shows, in his remarkable and important book ' On the Nature of Comets,' that we only attain to the conception of an object at all through sensation. Sensations are the *material* out of which the

[*] S. 12.

world of external things constructs itself. The very simplest kind of sensations that we can conceive already includes, so soon as we imagine a connection in the changing sensations in an organism, the conception of time and of causality. "From this it seems to me to result," concludes Zöllner, "that the phenomenon of sensation is a much more fundamental fact of observation than the motion of matter, which we are obliged to attribute to it as the most universal quality and condition of the intelligibleness of sensuous changes."[7]

In fact, the notion of atoms and their motion may be derived from sensation, but not conversely sensation from atomic motions. We might then attempt to start *from sensation*, and so break down the barrier of natural knowledge, and thus, as it were, make all natural science the special province of psychology; but such a psychology, as we shall see further on, has not the means within itself to become an exact science. Only when we resolve our sensations and ideas of sensation in abstraction into those simplest elements of extension in space, of resistance and of movement, do we obtain a basis for the operations of science. In so far as in these most abstract representations of sensible things there appears a necessary agreement of all men in virtue of the *a priori* elements of our knowledge, so far indeed these representations are 'objective,' as opposed to the more concrete sensations combined with pain and pleasure which we call 'subjective,' because in these our subject does not find itself in a universal and necessary agreement with all other subjects that experience sensations. At the same time everything is at bottom in the subject, just as 'object' originally means nothing more than the object of our conception. The sensation and the representation of sensation is the universal; the representation of atoms and their vibrations the particular case. The sensation is *actual* and *given;* but in the atoms nothing

[7] Zöllner, Ueber die Natur der Ko-   Theorie d. Erkenntniss, 2 Aufl.,
meten: Beiträge z. Geschichte u.   Leipzig, 1872, S. 320 ff.

is at bottom given except the remains of faded sensations, by means of which we create the image of them. The idea that something external, absolutely independent of our 'subject,' corresponds to this image, may be very natural, but is not absolutely necessary and conclusive; otherwise there could never have existed Idealists like Berkeley.

If, therefore, of the two objects—sensation and atomic movement—one must be taken as reality, the other as mere appearance, there would be much more reason to take sensation and consciousness as real, and the atoms and their movements as mere appearance. That we construct natural science upon this appearance cannot make any difference. Natural knowledge would then be only an analogon of true knowledge—a means of enabling us to find our way, like a map which renders us excellent service, although it is very far removed from being the country itself in which we are travelling in idea.

But such a distinction is neither necessary nor desirable. Sensation and atomic movement are for us just as 'real' as phenomena, although the former is an immediate phenomenon, atomic movement only a mediate one through thought. Because of the strict connection which the assumption of matter and its motion creates in our conceptions, it deserves to be called 'objective;' for only by its means does the manifoldness of objects first become one great comprehensive 'Object,' which we oppose as the permanent 'object' of our thought to the changing content of the Ego. This whole reality, however, is simply empirical reality, harmonising very easily with transcendental ideality.

From the standpoint of the critical philosophy which bases itself on the theory of knowledge, all need disappears of breaking through the 'limits of natural knowledge' we have been discussing, since these limits are not a foreign and hostile power, but are our own peculiar nature. If, however, we would still make another last attempt to get

rid of the appearance of an irreconcilable dualism in a more
popular way, there presents itself the method struck out
by Zöllner, *to attribute sensation to matter in itself,* and to
conceive the mechanical processes as regularly and universally connected with the processes of sensation.   But we
must never forget that the explanation thus attained is
not a scientific, but a speculative one, and that the real
problem, the unintelligible element in the phenomenon, is
not disposed of, but merely postponed.   In order
to possess scientific value, this theory would have to prove
the origin of human sensation from the sense-processes of
the self-moving particles, at least as strictly as the building up of the body out of cells, or the passage of mechanical
motion from the outer world into the condition of our
nervous system.   Two problems would still remain : the
notion of *force and matter* would be burdened with all the
old difficulties, and with a new and greater one besides.
Consciousness, again, would indeed have a link to connect
it with matter, but its *unity* in its relation to the *multiplicity of the constituent sensations* would at bottom still
present the same incomprehensibleness as before did the
relation of consciousness to the vibrations of the atoms of
the brain.

Moreover, it is still very questionable whether, if such
a theory could ever be carried out, it would not end by
dropping the atoms and their vibrations altogether, like a
scaffolding when the building is completed.   The world
of sensation—the only world given—would, in fact, be explained out of its own elements, and would no longer need
the extraneous support.   But if there were any sufficient
reason to retain also the conception of atoms, then the material world would still be a world of representation ; and
the conjecture that behind the two corresponding worlds—
the material world and the world of sensation—there lies
an *unknown third thing* as their common cause, would
carry us deeper than the simple identification of the two.

Thus we see how in fact thorough scientific investigation through its own consequences carries us beyond Materialism. This is however always the case in this one point only, where we are compelled to conceive the universe of science as a phenomenal world, by the side of which the phenomena of mental life, despite their apparent dependence upon matter, remain essentially something foreign and different. We may, starting from other premises, as especially from the physiology of the sense-organs, attain to the same limit of natural knowledge; but we cannot find any point unconnected with the whole mechanical theory of things in which, by pushing material inquiries further, their inaccuracy could be proved. Whatever other reproaches have been made, as it were, from the judgment-seat of scientific thoroughness against the 'dilettantcism' of the Materialists, are either unsound or they touch not the essence of Materialism, but merely some chance expression of one of its adherents.

This applies especially, too, to some of the attacks which Liebig in his 'Chemical Letters' undertakes against the Materialists. Thus, *e.g.*, when he says in his 23d Letter, " *Exact inquiry has proved* that at a certain period the earth possessed a temperature which was incompatible with organic life; for coagulation of the blood takes place at 78° C. *It has proved that organic life upon earth had a beginning.* These are important facts; and if they were the only acquisitions of this century, philosophy would still be under an obligation to the natural sciences."

Well, scientific research has no more proved this than Lyell has proved the eternity of the present condition of the earth! The whole field is only accessible to hypothesis, which is more or less supported by facts. History shows us how great theories come and go, while the individual facts of experience and observation form an abiding and constantly growing treasure of knowledge. Philosophy is positively ungrateful enough to claim the whole of this so-called achievement of the positive sciences as her own property. When Kant shows us that our understand-

ing necessarily seeks for every cause an earlier cause, for
every apparent beginning an earlier beginning, while the
efforts of the reason after unity demand a conclusion, the
anthropomorphic origin of the conflicting theories is laid
completely bare. We may then seek for further proofs,
but must never demand of philosophy that she should not
recognise her own children in the many-coloured coat of
natural science.

The companion-piece to the 'demonstrated' beginning of
organic life is afforded by the contemptuous side-glance with
which Liebig complains that the 'dilettanti,' who propose to
derive all terrestrial life from the simplest organism of the
cell, deal so complacently with an infinite series of years.

It would be interesting to learn any reasonable ground
why, in proposing a hypothesis as to the origin of now
actually existing bodies, we should *not* complacently dispose of an infinite series of years. The hypothesis of
gradual evolution may be attacked on other grounds;
that question must stand on its own merits. But if it is
condemned because it requires an extraordinarily long
series of years, that is to fall into one of the most conspicuous errors of ordinary thought. A few thousand years
are familiar enough to us; we can even rise, at the suggestion of the geologists, to millions. Nay, since astronomers
have taught us to conceive of distances in space to be
reckoned by billions of miles, we may assume billions of
years also for the formation of the earth, although this
seems to us somewhat extravagant, because we are not, as
in the case of astronomy, driven to such assumptions by
actual calculation. Beyond these figures, then, the largest
to which we are accustomed to rise, there comes *infinity—
eternity.* Here we are again in our element; especially
the notion of absolute eternity is from our earliest school-
days very familiar to us, although we have long been
quite clear that we cannot, properly speaking, conceive it.
What lies between a billion or a quadrillion and eternity
seems to us a fabulous realm into which only the most

luxuriant imagination extravagates. And yet the strictest common sense must tell us that, *a priori*, and before experience has passed judgment, the largest number that we can assume for the age of organisms is not in the least more probable than any power of this number. It would not even be a true methodological maxim to suppose the smallest possible number until a larger one is rendered more probable by the facts of experience. Rather the contrary, indeed; since, in the case of very great and very gradual changes, the real problem lies in forming an idea in how *many years natural forces would be adequate to complete them.* The smaller the number we assume, the *more numerous must be our proofs*, since the shorter space is *a priori* the less probable. In a word, the proof must be adduced *for the minimum*, and not, as prejudice assumes, *for the maximum.* The shrinking, therefore, from great numbers is by no means to be confounded with the shrinking from bold or numerous hypotheses. The hypothesis of gradual development may perhaps on other grounds appear bold or unjustifiable; the largeness of the numbers makes it not in the least more hazardous.

Not less uncritical does Liebig become when he categorically asserts, "Chemistry will never succeed in constructing in the laboratory a cell, a muscular fibre, a nerve, or, in short, any one single portion of the organic frame possessed of vital properties." Why not? Because the Materialists have confounded organic matter with organic parts? That is no ground for such an assertion. We may correct the confusion, and the question of the chemical production of the cell still remains an open and not quite an idle question. It was long believed that the substances of organic chemistry could only originate in the organism. This belief is gone. Shall we now believe that the organism itself can originate only from organisms? One article of faith is dead; long live its successor! Shall we not rather conclude that such dogmas have not much scientific value at all?

Strictly considered, scientific research does not produce Materialism; but neither does it refute it, at least not in the sense in which most of its opponents would like to see it refuted. For the 'limits of natural knowledge' in their true sense by no means satisfy the great mass of its opponents. It requires a considerable degree of philosophical training to find here the solution of the question, and to content oneself with this solution.

Nevertheless, in actual life and in the daily interchange of opinions, scientific inquiry by no means occupies so neutral or even negative an attitude towards Materialism as is the case when all consequences are rigidly followed out. It is assuredly no mere chance that it is almost entirely scientific men who have brought about the revival of Materialistic theories in Germany. Nor is it chance that, after all the 'confutations' of Materialism, now more than ever there appear books of popular science and periodical essays which base themselves upon Materialistic views as calmly as if the matter had been settled long ago. The whole phenomenon sufficiently explains itself from what we have already said. For if Materialism can be set aside only by criticism based upon the theory of knowledge, while in the sphere of positive questions it is everywhere in the right, then as long as those great barriers are overlooked, it is easy to foresee that, for the great masses of those occupied with natural science, the Materialistic order of thought lies exclusively within their field of view. There are only two conditions under which this consequence can be avoided. The one lies behind us; it is the *authority of philosophy*, and the deep influence of religion upon men's minds. The other still lies some distance ahead; it is the general spread of *philosophical culture*[8] among all who devote themselves to scientific studies.

[8] We add a few paragraphs from the first edition, which deal particularly with the demand of philosophical training for the man of science, in connection with the address above mentioned of Von Mohl the botanist. [See Note B. at end of chapter.]

Hand in hand with philosophical goes *historical* culture. Next to the contempt of philosophy, a Materialistic trait appears in the lack of historical genius, which is so often combined with our scientific inquiry. Nowadays a historical view is often supposed to mean a conservative one. This results partly from the fact that learning has often allowed itself, for gold and honour, to be misapplied in supporting obsolete powers, and in serving predatory interests, by pointing to departed splendours and the historical acquisition of rights hurtful to the common weal. Natural science cannot easily be misused for such purposes. Perhaps, too, the continual call for renunciation imposed by science has a bracing effect on character. In this aspect the unhistorical sense of men of science could only redound to their glory.

The other aspect of the matter is, that the lack of historical apprehension interrupts the thread of progress as a whole; that trifling points of view control the course of investigations; that the depreciation of the past is accompanied by a Philistine over-estimate of the present condition of science, in which the current hypotheses are regarded as axioms, and blind traditions as the results of investigation.

History and criticism are often the same thing. The numerous medical men who still regard a seven-months' child as more likely to live than a child of eight usually regard it as a fact of experience. When we have discovered the origin of this opinion in astrology,[9] and are sufficiently rational to doubt the fatal influence of Saturn, we doubt also the supposed fact. Any one who is ignorant of history will, amongst our usual remedies, consider salutary all those which have not been expressly proved by modern inquiries not to be so. But any one

[9] According to the rules of astrology, the seventh month is governed by the equivocal moon, the eighth by destruction-bringing Saturn, the ninth by Jupiter, the star of happiness and perfection. Consequently a birth under the influence of Saturn was regarded as much more threatened by dangers than one under the influence of the moon.

who has once seen a prescription of the sixteenth or seventeenth century, and has well considered that, even after these horrible and absurd compositions, people used to 'recover,' will cease to trust vulgar 'experience,' and will, on the contrary, believe only in those strictly defined effects of any medicine or poison which have been established by the most careful and scientific modern investigations.   Ignorance of the history of science was partly the reason that men began some decades ago to regard the 'elements' in modern chemistry as in the main definitely ascertained; while at present it is becoming more and more clear that not only are new ones to be discovered, and others perhaps to be split up, but that the whole idea of an element is a merely provisional necessity.

Many chemists still begin the history of their science with Lavoisier. As in children's histories the dark period of the Middle Ages is often concluded with the words, "Then Luther appeared," so with them Lavoisier appears, in order to banish the phlogistic superstition; upon which, after the delusion is expelled, the science quite spontaneously results from people's common sense. Of course, as *we* regard the matter so must it be regarded! No reasonable man can do otherwise. The right path would long ago have been attained if it had not been for phlogiston! How could old Stahl, too, be so deluded?

On the other hand, he who sees in history the inseparable fusion of error and truth, he who observes how the constant approximation to an infinitely distant goal of perfect knowledge is the result of innumerable stages, he who sees how error itself becomes the bearer of manifold and enduring progress, will not so easily conclude from the undeniable progress of the present age to the incontestableness of our hypotheses. He who has seen that progress is never attained by the sudden dispelling of an erroneous theory, like a cloud before the glance of genius, but that it is only supplanted by a higher theory, which is painfully gained by the most skilful methods of inquiry, will not regard the effort of some inquirer to demonstrate a new and unfamiliar idea with a contemptuous smile, while he will in all fundamental questions put little trust in tradition, much in method, and none at all in the unmethodical understanding.

Through Feuerbach in Germany and Comte in France an opinion has grown up that the scientific understanding is nothing but ordinary common sense asserting its natural rights after the expulsion of hindering fantasies. History shows us no trace of such a sudden advance of common sense upon the mere removal of some disturbing fantasy; it rather shows us everywhere new ideas making their way despite opposing prejudice, coalescing with the very error that they should dispel, or taking some wrong direction with it, so that the entire expulsion of prejudice is as a rule the final completion of the whole process, as it were the cleaning of the completed machine. In fact— to keep for brevity's sake, to our figure—error often appears historically as the mould within which the bell of truth is cast, and which is only broken up when the casting is complete. The relation of chemistry to alchemy, of astronomy to astrology, may illustrate this. That the most important positive results are only attained after the completion of the foundations of a science is natural. We owe to Copernicus, as to details, very little of our present knowledge of the starry sky; Lavoisier, who retained the last relics of the old alchemy in the primitive acid for which he sought, would be a child in our modern chemistry. When the true foundations of a science are secured, a great mass of consequences present themselves with relatively little mental labour: it is easier to strike a bell than it is to cast one. But whenever an important step forward is made in principles, we have nearly always the same spectacle presented; a new idea takes its place despite prejudice—at first, perhaps, even supported by it. Only as it unfolds does it burst asunder the rotten coverings. Where there is not this idea, this positive effort, the dispelling of prejudice does us no good at all. In the Middle Ages many were free from belief in astrology. In all times we find traces of ecclesiastical and secular opposition to this superstition; but it was not from amongst these men, but from the astrologers that astronomy proceeded.

The most important result of historical study is the academic calmness with which our hypotheses or theories are regarded without enmity and without credulity as what they are—as stages in that endless approximation to truth which seems to be the destiny of our intellectual development. This, of course, at once disposes of any system of Materialism, so far as it presupposes at least a belief in the transcendental existence of matter. But as regards progress in the exact sciences, assuredly he will not be most capable of discoveries who despises the theory of yesterday and swears by that of to-day; but he who sees in all theories but a means of approximating to the truth, and of surveying and mastering the facts for our purposes.

This freedom from the dogmatism of theories does not exclude the employing of them. We should deviate just as far on the other side from the true course if we were to suppress in their birth all general ideas on the connection of things, and cling obstinately to mere detail, to the sensibly demonstrable facts. As the mind of man only finds its highest satisfaction—one that transcends the sphere of natural knowledge—iu the ideas which it produces from the imaginative depths of the spirit, so it cannot devote itself successfully to the serious and severe labour of research, without resting, as it were, in the idea of the universal, and drawing fresh energy from it. Classifications and laws serve us on the one hand, as Helmholtz has very rightly shown, as a means of remembering and surveying an otherwise unsurveyable sum of objects and events; but, on the other hand, this embracing as a whole of the manifold in phenomena answers to the synthetic impulse of our mind, which everywhere strives after unity, as well in the great whole of philosophy as in the simplest concepts embracing a plurality of objects. We shall now no longer, as did Plato, ascribe to the universal, as opposed to the individual, a truer reality and an existence independent of our thought; but within our subjectivity it will be to us more than the mere bracket that holds the facts together.

And this subjectivity of ours, too, has its significance for the man of science also, since he is not a discovering-machine, but a man in whom all sides of human nature work in inseparable unison. But here we find Materialism again on the opposite side. The same mental tendency which, on the one hand, leads to our transforming great hypotheses as to the basis of phenomena into a fixed dogma, shows itself, on the other hand, very shy of the collaboration of ideas in scientific research. We have seen how in antiquity Materialism remained sterile because it adhered doggedly to its great dogma of atoms and their motion, and had little sense for new and bold ideas. The Idealistic school, on the contrary, especially the Platonists and Pythagoreans, gave antiquity the richest fruits of scientific knowledge.

In modern times an incomparably more favourable account of Materialism can be given as regards its participation in inventions and discoveries. Atomism, which once only led to speculations as to the possibility of phenomena, has become since Gassendi the basis of physical investigation into the actual! The mechanical theory of the world has since Newton gradually dominated our whole apprehension of nature. Thus, if we only leave out of view the 'limits of natural knowledge,' Materialism is now not only the result, but, strictly speaking, the very presupposition of all scientific study. But, of course, the more clearly and generally this is perceived, so too the critical standpoint of the theory of knowledge, which again destroys Materialism, spreads more and more amongst scientific men; and always first amongst the most important and most far-seeing of them. It does not in the

least stay the triumphal march of scientific research if
the naïve belief in matter disappears, and there opens
behind all nature a new and infinite world, which stands
in the closest connection with the world of the senses,
which is perhaps the same thing merely regarded from
another side, but which is just as familiar to our subject,
to our Ego with all the emotions of its spirit, as the proper
home of its inmost essence, as the world of atoms with their
eternal vibrations stands opposed to it as strange and cold.

Materialism, of course, seeks to make the world of atoms,
too, the true home of the mind. This cannot be without
influence upon its method. It trusts the *senses*. Even its
metaphysic is formed on the analogy of the world of experience. Its atoms are small corpuscles. We cannot
indeed represent them as small as they are, because that
transcends any human conception; but we may represent
them by comparison, as though we saw and felt them.
The whole Materialistic theory of the world is brought
about through the senses and the categories of the understanding. But precisely these organs of our mind are
chiefly real in their nature. They give us *things*, even
though no thing in itself. The deeper philosophy comes
behind, that these things are our conceptions; but it cannot alter the fact that precisely the class of those conceptions which are related to things through understanding
and sensibility has the greatest permanency, certainty,
and regularity, and for that very reason we may conjecture, also the strictest connection with an external world
governed by eternal laws.

Materialism too is imagining, when it represents to
itself the elements of the phenomenal world, but it is
imagining in the naïvest way under the guidance of the
senses. In this constant leaning upon those elements of
our knowledge which have the best regulated function, it
possesses an inexhaustible spring of pure method, a protection against error and fantasy, and a purer feeling for
the language of things.

It has the drawback, moreover, of a comfortable contentment with the world of phenomena, which allows sense-impressions and theories to become fused into an inextricable whole. As the impulse is wanting to go beyond the apparent objectivity of the sensible phenomena, so too the impulse is wanting to charm a new language from things by paradoxical questions, and to undertake experiments which, instead of aiming merely at mere extension in detail, rather destroy previous modes of thought, and bring with them entirely new insight into the sphere of science. Materialism is, in a word, conservative in science. How it happens that it nevertheless becomes, as to the most important departments of life, under certain circumstances a revolutionary ferment will appear farther on.

Idealism is in its very nature metaphysical speculation, although a speculation which may appear to us as the enthusiastic representative of higher unknown truths. The circumstance that an imaginative, creative impulse is contained in our breasts, which in Philosophy, Art, and Religion often comes into direct contradiction with the witness of our senses and understanding, and then again can produce creations which the noblest and soundest of men hold higher than mere knowledge, this circumstance of itself points to the fact that Idealism too is connected with the unknown truth, although in a very different way from Materialism. In the witness of the senses all men agree. Mere judgments of the understanding do not hesitate or err. But ideas are poetic births of the single *person ;* perhaps powerful enough to master whole ages and peoples with their charm, but still never universal, and still less immutable.

Nevertheless the Idealist might go just as safely in the positive sciences as the Materialist, if he would only constantly remember that the phenomenal world—however much it is mere appearance—is yet a connected whole, into which no foreign members may be introduced without

risk of ruining the whole. But the man who once soars
aloft into the world of ideas is continually in danger of
confounding it with the sensible world, and thereby of
falsifying experience or of passing off his speculations as
" true " or " correct " in that prosaic sense in which these
terms belong only to the knowledge of the senses and the
understanding. For apart from the so-called ' inner truth '
of Art and Religion, the criterion of which consists only in
the harmonious satisfaction of the soul, and has absolutely
nothing at all in common with scientific knowledge, we
can only describe as true what *necessarily* appears so to
every being of human organisation, and such an agreement
can only be found in the knowledge of the senses and
understanding.

There exists, however, a connection between our ideas
and this knowledge—a connection in our mind, whose
creations only transcend nature in their object and intention, while, as thoughts and products of human organisation, they are equally members of the phenomenal world,
which we find everywhere cohering by necessary laws.
In a word, *our ideas, our brain-fancies, are products of
the same nature which produces our sense-perceptions and
the judgments of our understanding.* They do not arise
in the mind quite casually, irregularly and unexpectedly,
but they are, properly considered, products of a psychological process, in which our sensible perceptions likewise
play their part. The idea is distinguished from the fancy
by its *value*, not by its *origin*. But what is meant by
value ? A relation to the nature of man, and to his perfect, ideal nature. Thus idea measures itself by idea, and
the roots of this world of intellectual values run back, just
as much as the roots of our sense-conceptions, into the
inmost nature of man, which is withdrawn from our observation. We can psychologically comprehend the idea as
a product of the brain ; as intellectual value we can only
measure it by similar values. The cathedral at Köln we

compare with other cathedrals and other works of art; its stones with other stones.

Ideas are as indispensable for the progress of the sciences as facts. They do not necessarily lead to metaphysic, although they always overstep experience. Springing from the elements of experience unconsciously and rapidly as the shooting of a crystal, the idea may refer back to experience, and seek its confirmation or rejection in experience. The understanding cannot make the idea, but it regulates it and favours it. The scientific idea arises, like the poetical, like the metaphysical idea, from the interaction of all the elements of the individual mind; but it takes a different course, since it submits itself to the judgment of investigation, in which only the senses, the understanding, and the scientific conscience sit as judges. This tribunal demands not absolute truth, otherwise the progress of humanity would be in very doubtful case. Utility, compatibility with the witness of the senses in the experiment challenged by the idea, decided preponderance over the opposite views—this is enough to give the idea the right of citizenship in the realm of science. Childish science constantly confuses idea and fact; science, which has developed and become sure and methodical, shapes the idea, with the help of exact research, into hypothesis and finally into theory.

Even the most one-sided Idealist will never entirely despise the attempt to call experience itself to bear witness to its own insufficiency. If in the facts of the sensible world no trace could be found to show that the senses give us only a coloured and perhaps quite inadequate picture of the real things, it would be anything but well with the conviction of the Idealist. But even the commonest illusions of the senses afford a hold for his view. The discovery of the universal proportion in musical tones followed from an idea of the Pythagoreans, which contradicts original sense appearances; for in sound our ear does not give us the least consciousness of a universal proportion. Yet the senses themselves testified for the senses ; the divided string, the various dimensions of metallic hammers, were sensibly observed in connection with the various tones. So the idea of the vibration theory of light, once rejected, was later again received on the evidence of the senses and of the calculating understanding ; the phenomena of interference could be observed.

From this it follows that the Idealist also may be a scientific inquirer ; but his inquiries will, as a rule, exhibit a revolutionary character, just as the Idealist with regard to the state, to civic life, to conventional morality, is the bearer of revolutionary ideas.

We must not forget, however, that we have to do with degrees of more or less. Apart from the few champions of consequent systems, there are in actual life no more Idealists and Materialists—as definite classes of individuals—than there are phlegmatic and choleric persons. It would be childish to suppose that no man who is in the main a Materialist could have a scientific idea which entirely overturns traditional views. Our scientific men have almost all, especially now, when the tendency of the age is in that direction, Idealism enough, although they chiefly believe what they can see and feel.

In the history of modern scientific inquiry we cannot distinguish so surely as in antiquity the influences of Materialism and Idealism. So long as we do not possess very careful biographies of the chief leaders of scientific progress, which take account of *the whole man*, the ground beneath our feet is very uncertain. The pressure of the Church prevented for the most part the expression of real opinions, and many a noble man speaks to us yet only through the facts of his discoveries, in whom we may well presume fertile speculation, mighty struggles of mind, and a treasure of profound ideas.

Most scientific men of our own day think very little of ideas, hypotheses, and theories. Liebig, on the other hand, in his complaints against Materialism, goes too far, again, when, in his Discourse on Bacon, he entirely rejects empiricism.

"In all investigation Bacon sets great value on experiments. Of their meaning, however, he knows nothing. He looks upon them as a sort of mechanism, which once put in motion brings forth the result of itself. But in science all investigation is deductive or *a priori.* Experiment is but an aid to the process of thought, like a calculation: the thought must always and necessarily precede it if it is to have any meaning.

"An empirical mode of research in the usual sense of the term does not exist. An experiment not preceded by a theory, that is, by an idea, bears the same relation to scientific research as a child's rattle does to music."

Strong words! But in truth empiricism is not in quite such desperate case. Liebig's masterly analysis of Bacon's experiments, for which philosophers and historians must feel grateful to him, has shown us indeed that from Bacon's experiments not only nothing resulted, but also that nothing *could* result. But we find enough to account for this in the unconscientiousness and frivolity of his procedure, in the capricious taking up and abandoning of his object, in the want of concentration and perseverance; especially, in fine, in his superfluity of methodical crotchets and artifices, which overgrow the useful part of the method, and offer refuges to caprice and feebleness, while they are of no practical application whatever. If Bacon had only developed the idea of induction and the by no means unimportant doctrine of negative and prerogative instances, his own method would have compelled him to greater stability. But as it was, he devised the hesitating classifications of the *instantiæ migrantes, solitariæ, clandestinæ,* &c., which throw open the door to every kind of caprice, assuredly in the vague impulse to be able to prove his favourite ideas. That no idea guided him in his inquiries seems to us to be by no means the case; rather the contrary. His doctrine of heat, for instance, which Liebig exposes so unsparingly, looks altogether towards a preconceived opinion.

In the overloading of his theory of proof with useless notions, Bacon betrays the effects of the Scholasticism he is combating; but it was not then empty ideas which hindered the success of his researches, but the entire lack of those qualities which qualify for research in general. Bacon would have been just as little able to edit critically an ancient author as he was to make a proper experiment.[10]

It is a peculiarity of fruitful ideas that they are only developed, as a rule, in the course of thorough and persevering occupation with a definite object; but such an occupation may be fruitful even without guiding theories. Copernicus devoted his whole life to the heavenly bodies; Sanctorius to his scales : the former had a guiding theory, which sprang up in early years from philosophy and observation; but was not Sanctorius too a man of science ?[11]

APPENDIX.

Note A (*See Note* I).

THE old Faculties formed themselves pretty quickly after the rise of the University of Paris, the arrangements of which became the model for Germany. They stand in the closest relation each to a particular practical avocation; for the Philosophical Faculty only became a distinct whole through the separation of the other three. It remained the general faculty as compared with the three special ones, devoted partly to the common preparation for professional studies, partly to free science. All newly arising sciences naturally fell to it, so far as they did not stand in intimate relation to some special pursuit. If the original principle on which the

---

[10] On Bacon's scientific and personal character comp. i. p. 236 and Note 60.

[11] There followed here in the first edition a methodological exposition which went into too much detail for the purpose of the work, from which, however, we retain some passages, the interest of which is not yet over. [See Note C.]

universities were formed had remained a living principle, possibly several new faculties might have been formed of the same character as the existing ones, as, *e.g.*, a cameralistic, a pædagogic, or an agricultural faculty. Nor is there any intrinsic objection to the formation of a new faculty in a new principle; we must only establish that this is so, and then closely examine the new principle. We have before us a regular war of the faculties, in which the philosophers have the worst of it. The medical men first propose the establishing of the scientific faculty; the men of science wish to tear themselves away from the maternal embrace of the *facultas artium.* Their colleagues will not let them go, and there is a regular struggle for emancipation. We can see that the philologist of the schools allows himself to be carried too far by regard for a certain unity in the training of future teachers; but a real philosopher should never meet an actually felt need for such a separation by dogged adherence to the existing state of things. He should rather ask himself what is the foundation of the repulsive force which demands the separation; he should endeavour by his services to make himself indispensable to those whom he wishes to retain. If a university has no men who in such a case stand above the controversy, and above all inquiry into the inner aspect of the matter, then it has no philosopher at all. When Feuerbach declares that it is the specific work of a philosopher to be no professor of philosophy, this is a gross exaggeration; but so much is certain, that at present a bold and independent man will not easily obtain a public chair in Germany. We complain of the neglect of the natural sciences; we might rather complain of the strangling of philosophy. We must not take it ill of the Tübingen men of science if they endeavour to free themselves from a dead body; but we must deny that this separation is determined by the nature of scientific research and of philosophy.

The natural sciences possess, in their clear and luminous method, in the convincing force of their experiments and demonstrations, a powerful safeguard against the corruption of their doctrines by men who work at direct variance to the principles of their investigation; and yet, if philosophy is entirely suppressed and laid aside, the time might come when in scientific faculty a Reichenbach should teach Odyle force, or a Richter controvert Newton's law. In philosophy wantonness of thought is easier to commit and easier to cloak. There is no so sensuously clear and logically certain criterion of the sound and true as in natural science. Meanwhile we will propose a remedy. If the men of science voluntarily come back to philosophy without, therefore, altering a little the strictness of their method— if we begin to recognise that all distinctions in the faculties are superfluous—if philosophy, instead of being an extreme, rather forms a link between the most various sciences, and effects a fruitful interchange of positive results—then we will admit that she is capable once more of the great function of holding up to the age the torch of criticism, of gathering the rays of knowledge into a focus, and of advancing and moderating the revolutions of history.

The neglect of natural science in Germany is due to the same conservative tendency as the depression and corruption of philosophy. Especially there has been a want of money; and it will unhappily be a long time before we have come up with England and France in this respect. (This has, at least as regards France, already ceased to be the case.) Herr von Mohl saw, in the physical museum of a German university, "a fearful instrument which was supposed to represent an air-pump. The academic commission, upon whose approval and direction depended the equipment of the physical professor, had determined, in order that the work might not go to a foreign instrument-maker, that the air-pump should be jobbed out to a fire-engine maker." This affords an opportunity for bemoaning the subjection of the physical professor to the control of the other members of his faculty. But is a decent provision for such requirements at the free disposal of the physical professor not conceivable without a separation of the faculties? And is not even in the present state of things the philosopher, who must be acquainted with scientific methods and the prerequisites of their application, the natural colleague of the physicist?

But no! There is the hitch. Descartes, Spinoza, Leibniz, Kant would be so; but the majority of our present philosophical professors—there Herr von Mohl is quite right; only he should not lay the blame upon Philosophy herself, nay, even attribute it to the very nature of philosophical thought, if nowadays such a co-operation is not easily to be expected.

NOTE B (*See Note 8*).

We demand from the modern scientific inquirer more philosophical culture, but not more inclination to construct original systems themselves. On the contrary, in this respect we are not yet freed from the evils of the period of the philosophy of nature. Materialism is the last offshoot of that epoch, when every botanist or physiologist thought that he must bless the world with a system.

But who, then, ever asked such men as Oken, Nees von Esenbeck, Steffens, and other students of nature to philosophise instead of to inquire? Has any philosopher, even in the most delirious age, seriously proposed to replace exact research by his system? Even Hegel, the most arrogant of modern philosophers, never regarded his system in this sense as the definitive conclusion of scientific knowledge, as it must have been on the view we are controverting. He recognised thoroughly that no philosophy can get beyond the sum of the intellectual influences of its time. It is true that he was so far blinded as to overlook the rich philosophic treasures which the individual sciences bring ready-made to the thinker, and especially to estimate far too lowly the intellectual value of the exact sciences. On the other hand, the men of science in these days prostrated themselves before speculation as before an idol. If their own science had been more strongly based in Germany, it could have better resisted the tempests of the mania for speculation.

(Further on, with reference to Mohl's contention that often a mutual understanding between scientific research and philosophy becomes quite impossible):

Thus the man of science learns from things; the philosopher will know everything from himself, and therefore they do not understand each other.

The misunderstanding can only arise where they both speak of the same things, and thus give different results on different methods. They understand now, or they do not understand, that they are proceeding on different methods. When, for instance, a professor of philosophy will prove to medical men, "in a scientific way," all kinds of metaphysical hocus-pocus, then this professor, and he only, is to blame for this misunderstanding. Even real philosophers will reject such an anthropologist just as sharply as the man of science, perhaps more sharply, because as a student of the two modes of procedure he more quickly sees through the errors of method. An example of such a scientific police was furnished some years ago by Lotze in his Polemic (1857) against the anthropology of the younger Fichte. He only made one mistake, that after he had scientifically quite defeated him he proposed to shake hands and exchange gifts, like the Homeric heroes. The Homeric heroes gave no more presents to the man they had beaten!

The same result may follow when a man of science commits the same error, that is, when he tries to pass off his metaphysical dreamings in the guise of facts. Only in this case the stricken man of science will often exercise the promptest supervision, because he knows most precisely the way in which the supposed facts have been developed.

But when we require higher philosophical culture from the scientific inquirer, it is by no means speculation that we would so pressingly commend to him, but philosophical criticism, which is indispensable to him, just because he himself in his own thinking, despite all the exactness of special researches, will never succeed in wholly suppressing metaphysical speculation. Even in order more correctly to recognise his own transcendental ideas as such, and to distinguish them more surely from what is given by experience, he needs the criticism of ideas.

If, now, a certain judicial function is assigned to philosophy in this respect, this by no means involves any pretension to guardianship. For apart from the fact that every one can be a philosopher in this sense who knows how to handle the universal laws of thought, the sentence never refers to the strictly empirical element, but to the metaphysic mixed up with it, or to the purely logical side of inference and the formation of ideas. What meaning is there, therefore, in the comparison of the relation of the natural sciences to philosophy, to the attitude of philosophy to the dogma of the theologian? If it means to suggest the need of an emancipation, then we have a great anachronism before us. Philosophy no longer needs to demand her freedom from theological dogmas. It is perfectly obvious that she is in no way called upon to govern herself according to these dogmas. But she will, on the other hand, always claim the right to deal with these dogmas, and that as objects of her investigation. The dogma is to the philosopher no scientific principle, but the expression of the faith and the speculative activity of an historic period. He must endeavour to understand the rise and decay of dogmas in connection with the moral and intellectual development of humanity, if he is to perform his task in this department.

Exact research must be every philosopher's daily bread. Though the pride of the empiricist may prefer to retire into a sphere of his own, yet he can never hinder the philosopher from following him. There is no longer any philosophy conceivable at our present standpoint without exact research, and exact research is itself just as much in need of continual clarifying by philosophical criticism. It is not dilettanteism where the philosopher makes himself acquainted with the most important results and the methods of all the natural sciences, for this study is the necessary basis of all his operations.   So, again, it is not dilettanteism if the man of science forms for himself a definite, historically, and critically justifiable view as to the thinking processes of mankind, to which he is inextricably bound despite all the apparent objectivity of his investigations and conclusions.   But we must call it censurable dilettanteism—without, however, denying that favoured minds may really embrace both provinces—when the philosopher, in Bacon's fashion, dabbles in experiments with untrained sense and un-practised hand, and when the man of science, without troubling himself with what has been thought and said before him, by the arbitrary treat-ment of traditional ideas, patches himself together a metaphysical system of his own.

It is none the less true, however, that philosopher and man of science can exert a stimulating influence upon each other, by meeting on the ground which is, and must remain, common to both—the criticism of the materials of exact research in reference to the possible conclusions.   Pre-supposing that a strict and sober logic is employed on each side, here-ditary prejudices are thus subjected to an active cross-fire, and service is done to both sides.

What, then, is the meaning of the theory of mutual *laissez-faire* on account of the utter impossibility of an understanding? It seems to us as though in this very principle we have expressed the extreme one-sidedness of Materialism.   The consequences of a general application of this principle would be that everything would fall into egoistic circles. Philosophy falls a complete prey to the trades-union spirit of the faculties. Religion—and this, too, belongs to ethical Materialism—supports itself in the shape of crass orthodoxy upon the perversions and the political rights of the Church ; industry engages in a soulless chase after the momentary profits of exploitation ; science becomes the shibboleth of an exclusive society ; the State inclines to Cæsarism.

NOTE C (*See Note* 11).

Perhaps we are justified in designating as Materialistic a peculiar feature of modern scientific inquiry, consisting in opposition to the strictness of exact inquiry ; of course not an opposition supporting itself on the liber-tinism of the idea, but an opposition resulting from excessive regard for immediate sensuous conviction.

Not to run out into vague generalities, we will connect our observations with the remarkable instance of this opposition that has occurred in Ger-many in the last few years.   We mean the reaction of some physiologists against an essay of the mathematician Radicke on the Meaning and Value of the Arithmetical Mean.   Radicke published in 1858, in the 'Archiv für phys. Heilkunde,' an extended treatise, the object of which was to subject the excessive accumulation of discoveries in physiological chemistry to a critical sifting. For this purpose he employed an ingenious and independent as well as correct procedure, in order to estimate logically the relation of the arithmetical mean from the series of experiments to the deviations of the individual experiments from this mean. It resulted from the application of the principles developed to many hitherto highly valued investigations, that the series of experiments in these investigations gave no scientific result at all, because the individual observations showed too great variations to allow the arithmetical mean to appear with sufficient probability as the product of the influence under investigation. Against this extremely valuable and mathematically inexpugnable essay opposition was raised by several medical men of note, and this opposition produced the singular judgments which we think it our duty to mention here. Vierordt remarked of the essay, which in general he approved, "that besides the purely formal logic of the calculus of probabilities with its mathematical rigour, there is in many cases a *logic of the facts* themselves, which, rightly applied, possesses for the specialist a less, though it may be a very high, degree of proof." The insidious but yet at bottom very unhappily chosen expression, "logic of facts," found approval with many persons to whom the cutting rigour of mathematical methods might be inconvenient. It was, however, proved by Professor Ueberweg, a logician eminently fitted for the treatment of such questions (Archiv für pathol. Anat. xvi.), to possess a very moderate measure of justification. Ueberweg showed convincingly that what may be designated as "logic of facts" may in many cases have a certain value as the preliminary of a stricter investigation, "much as an estimate by the eye so long as a mathematical measurement is impossible;" but that when the calculation has been correctly carried out, there can be no question of a different result obtained through the logic of facts. In fact, that immediate consciousness which comes to the specialist during his experiments is just as much liable to error as any other prejudice. We neither have any reason to doubt that such convictions form themselves during experimentation, nor to suppose that more value may be ascribed to them than generally to the formation of convictions in non-scientific fashion. The really probative element in the exact sciences is not the material fact, the experiment in its immediate influence on the senses, but the ideal colligation of the results. There undoubtedly exists, however, amongst many inquirers, and especially amongst physiologists, an inclination to regard the experiment itself, and not its logical and mathematical interpretation, as the essential part of the investigation. From this there easily follows a relapse into the utmost caprice in theories and hypotheses; for the Materialistic idea of an undisturbed communion between the objects and our senses is inconsistent with human nature, which everywhere, even into the apparently most immediate activity of the senses, manages to introduce the effects of prejudice. That these effects are eliminated is indeed the great secret of all method in the exact sciences, and it is a matter of complete indifference whether we have to do with cases in which we work with *average values*, or with cases where even the *single* experiment is of importance. The average value serves primarily only to eliminate objective deviations; but in order to avoid subjective errors also, the first condition is to determine the probable error in the mean value itself, which also exactly denotes the limits of unjustifiable interpretations. Only if the probable error is sufficiently small to let us regard one result as trustworthy does the series of observations as a whole stand upon the same logical ground as a single experiment in fields where the elimination of objective deviations by a sure mean value is not required. If, *e.g.*, the object of an experiment is to test the behaviour of a newly-discovered metal towards the magnet, if we take all the usual precautions and have good apparatus, the *single experiment* will be enough, since the phenomenon in question can easily be *repeated*, without the small irregularities in the strength of the effect, which will always be present, at all affecting the principle which is to be proved.

These considerations will also determine our judgment of the somewhat more cautious polemic of Voit against Radicke in his 'Untersuchungen über den Einfluss des Kochsalzes, des Kaffees und der Muskelbewegungen' (München, 1860). He often finds in his own investigations differences between individual observations, which must be regarded *not* as casual variations, but rather as differences determined by the nature of the organism and uniformly appearing; as, *e.g.*, the dog under experiment with precisely the same flesh diet now excretes a greater and now a less quantity of urine, and conversely in the case of fasting. But where there is reason to suppose such differences in the very nature of things, it is so obvious that we do not operate with mean values, that it is hard to understand how such a case could be employed at all against Radicke. But whether now, as Voigt requires, in that case we must ascribe to every single trial the value of an experiment entirely depends, as in every experiment, upon the possibility of its repetition under like circumstances; and only when it is repeated can it be seen whether what is to be established is made sufficiently clear in any single trial, or whether we must institute a differently combined series of trials from which to deduce the mean values.

If, that is, in the first series of trials, we have the values a, b, c, d, . . . which show not mere variations, but a distinct progress; then in order to confirm this first trial we require a second, which may give us the values a_1, b_1, c_1, d_1, . . . If the progress is again quite clear, and our only object is to establish this progress generally, there the matter rests. But if we want numerically exact results, and the correspondence is not complete, there is nothing left but to proceed with a third series, a_2, b_2, c_2, d_2, . . . and so on to a_n, b_n, c_n, d_n, . . . when it becomes obvious that we must now combine the values a_1, a_2, a_3 . . . a_n, and, again, b_1, b_2, b_3 . . . b_n. But to these combinations the full force of the method proposed by Radicke must now apply.

CHAPTER II.

"THE world consists of atoms and empty space." In this principle the Materialistic systems of antiquity and of modern days are in harmony, whatever differences may have gradually developed themselves in the notion of the atom, and however different are the theories as to the origin of the rich and varied universe from such simple elements.

One of the most naïf expressions of our modern Materialism has escaped from Büchner, when he calls the atoms of modern times "discoveries of natural science," while those of the ancients are said to have been "arbitrary speculative conceptions."[12] In point of fact, the atomic doctrine to-day is still what it was in the time of Demokritos. It has still not lost its metaphysical character; and already in antiquity it served also as a scientific hypothesis for the explanation of the observed facts of nature. As the connection of our atomism with that of the ancients is historically established, so too all the enormous progress in the present view of the atoms has been gradually developed from the interaction of philosophy and experience. It is indeed the main principle of modern science, the *critical* principle, which has, by its combination with Atomism, brought about this fruitful development.

Robert Boyle, "the first chemist whose exertions were

---

[12] Büchner, Natur u. Geist, S. 102: "Die Atome der Alten waren philosophische Kategorien oder Erfindungen; die der Neuen sind Entdeckungen der Naturforschung."

directed only by the noble impulse to investigate nature,"
travelled over the Continent as a means of culture in his
earlier years, precisely at the time when the scientific
controversy between Gassendi and Descartes burst out.
When he settled at Oxford in 1654, in order to devote his
life henceforth to science, Atomism as a metaphysical
theory had already succeeded in establishing itself. But
the very science to which Boyle had devoted himself was
the last to free itself from the fetters of medieval mysticism and Aristotelian conceptions. It was Boyle who
introduced the atoms into that science which has since
made the most extensive use of this theory; but it is also
Boyle who, by the very title of his 'Chemista Scepticus,'
1661, announces that he has trodden the path of exact
science, in which the atoms can no more form an article
of faith than the philosopher's stone.

Boyle's atoms are still very much those of Epikuros, as
they had again been introduced into science by Gassendi.
They still have various shapes, and this shape has an
influence upon the stability or laxity of the combinations.
By violent motion at one time cohering atoms are torn
asunder, at another others are brought together, and, just
as in the ancient Atomism, they fasten on one another
with their rough surfaces by projections and teeth.[13]

[13] Kopp, Gesch. der Chemie, ii.
307 ff., unjustly ascribes to Boyle a
theory of "attraction" of the atoms.
"This chemist," says he, "already
favoured the view that all bodies
consist of smallest particles, upon
whose *attraction to each other* the
phenomena of combination and decomposition depend. The more *affinity* two bodies have for each other,
the more strongly do their smallest
particles attract each other, the more
nearly do they lie together in combination." Of this account only the
last words are at bottom true. Even
in the example quoted by Kopp there
is nothing about affinity and attraction. The terms "coalition," "associate," &c., are always to be referred
to the connection in the case of
contact. Boyle's real view appears
very clearly from the section 'De
Generatione, Corruptione et Altera-
tione,' pp. 21–30, in the treatise 'De
Origine Qualitatum et Formarum:'
Genevæ, 1688. He speaks everywhere of an adhering or tearing
asunder of the atoms, and the cause
of change is (§ 4) "motus quacunque
causa ortus," that is, that continual
rapid motion of the atoms which had
been assumed by the ancients also,
the origin of which they derive from
the universal and everlasting down-
ward motion. This derivation, of
course, Boyle could not employ, but

When a change takes place in the chemical combination, the smallest particles of a third body force themselves into the pores which exist in the combination of the two others. They can thus combine with one of them, because of the constitution of their surfaces, better than it was combined with the other, and the violent movement of the atoms will then carry away the particles of the latter. In this respect, however, Boyle's Atomism differed from the ancient, in that he assumes with Descartes a shivering of the atoms by the motion, and that he either leaves the origin of their motion in obscurity, or ascribes it to the immediate interference of God.

This form of Atomism must, above all in England, necessarily fall to pieces as soon as Newton's law of gravitation was accepted. We have seen in the First Book how rapidly the purely mathematical assumption of Newton became transformed into a new theory, entirely opposed to all previous ideas. With the *attraction* of the smallest particles of matter, the rough surfaces and manifold forms of the atoms became superfluous. There was now another bond which held them together without any contact, viz., attraction. The impact of the particles on each other lost its importance; even for the imponderables, from whose activity Newton still tried to derive gravitation, an analogous principle was found—that of *repulsive forces.*

The whole history of the modifications in the notion of the atoms is extremely clear so soon as we confine ourself to England and the ideas there developed by physicists and philosophers. Let it only be recollected that Hobbes, whose influence was so important, made the idea of atoms a *relative* one. There were, according to him, as it were, atoms of *different order*, just as mathematicians distinguish

he is very far from substituting for it attraction and repulsion—notions which only developed themselves some decades later in consequence of Newton's theory of gravitation. Rather does Boyle attribute, when he engages in speculation, the origin of atomic motion to the activity of God; but in ordinary scientific contemplation he simply leaves it dark, and contents himself with assuming the existence of such a motion.

different orders of the infinitely little.   An application of
this theory was the assumption of imponderable atoms,
which are found in the interspaces of gravitating matter,
and which, in relation to the corporeal atoms, are conceived
as infinitely little.   So long, then, as the mechanism of
impact was retained, it was these atoms of the second
order which, by their motion, produced on the one hand
the phenomena of light, but on the other hand produced
also the gravitation of the atoms of the first order.   As
soon, however, as the idea of *actio in distans* had gained a
place, it was consistently applied also to the imponderable
atoms, and they now exerted their repulsive influence
without any actual impact.   But with this the idea of the
constitution of matter, as Dalton found it, was fundamentally complete; for the fact that in Dalton's time
there was assumed, not atoms of the second order, but a
continuous covering of light and heat about the ponderable
atoms, is not a very essential innovation.   Even Descartes
and Hobbes assumed, in fact, a permanent filling of space,
since they conceived all the interstices between greater
particles as occupied by smaller and ever smaller particles.
At all events, Dalton found this view too in existence
when he was, towards the end of the eighteenth century,
conducted to the ideas which have given his name a lasting place in the history of science.

Starting from an observation on the different states of
bodies, he says, "These observations have *tacitly* led to the
conclusion, *which seems universally adopted*, that all bodies
of sensible magnitude, whether liquid or solid, are constituted of a vast number of extremely small particles, or
atoms of matter, bound together by a force of attraction,
which is more or less powerful according to circumstances,
and which, as it endeavours to prevent their separation, is
very properly called in that view 'attraction of adhesion;'
but as it collects them from a dispersed state (as from
steam into water), it is called 'attraction of aggregation,'
or more simply 'affinity.'   Whatever names it may go by,

they still signify one and the same power. . . . Besides the force of attraction, which, in one character or another, belongs universally to ponderable bodies, we find another force that is likewise universal, or acts upon all matter which comes under our cognisance, namely, a force of repulsion. This is now generally, and I think properly, ascribed to the agency of heat. An atmosphere of this subtile fluid constantly surrounds the atoms of all bodies, and prevents them from being drawn into actual contact."[14]

If we reflect that the physical conception of attraction only became recognised through the disciples of Newton in the first decades of the eighteenth century, it will seem that a period of about fifty years was enough so entirely to re-model the ancient notion of atoms, that Dalton could find the result as a universally accepted fact. Even the likeness of the smallest particles of every like substance, a point which it is one of Dalton's peculiar services to have strongly maintained, is at bottom only a consequence of the same great revolution in physical principles ; for if the atoms no longer had immediate contact with each other, there was no longer any reason for assuming different shapes laying hold of each other by their teeth and projections.

'Affinity,' which is with Dalton nothing more than the general force of attraction in its particular chemical manifestation, was originally a genuine scholastic quality which formed part of the favourite apparatus of the alchemists.[15]

---

[14] Dalton, New System of Chemical Philosophy, vol. i., 2d ed., Lond., 1842, p. 141 ff., 143 ff.   Comp. Kopp, Gesch. d. Wissensch. in Deutschland : Entwickel. der Chemie, München, 1873, S. 286, where, however, it is not sufficiently observed that as to the middle portion of the longer passage, viz., the assertion of the likeness of the particles in homogeneous bodies, the remark that this is universally adopted does not hold good.   Weihrich, An-

sichten der neueren Chemie, S. 7, says that the view as to the likeness of the atoms in the same body, and their variety in different bodies, seems to come from Baron von Holbach, though it is originally due to Anaxagoras ; but, in fact, there is not sufficient agreement between Holbach and Anaxagoras, or Dalton and Holbach, to allow us to recognise the thread of tradition here.

[15] Kopp, Gesch. d. Chemie, ii. 286 ff., disposes of the opinion that the

It must therefore have been simply laid aside by the spread
of the mechanical cosmology, like other such notions, if
the transcendental turn taken by the theory of gravitation
had not come to its aid.[16]   Newton assumed attractive
forces even for the smallest particles of ponderable matter;
of course, with the reservation of a future explanation of
this attraction from the motion of imponderable matter.
He only declares himself against the identity of chemical
action and gravitation, because he conjectures a different
relation for the dependence of force upon distance in the
two cases.   In the beginning of the eighteenth century
clear water had already been reached.   Buffon regarded
chemical attraction and gravitation as identical.   Boerhave,
one of the clearest heads of the century, returned to the
φιλία of Empedokles, and maintained expressly that the
chemical changes were produced, not by *mechanical impact*,
but by a *combining impulse*, as he explains the expression
' amicitia.'   Under these circumstances, even the 'affinitas'
of the scholastics might again venture out.   Only, of course,
the etymological meaning of the expression had to be
given up.   The 'relationship' remained a mere name; for
instead of an inclination resting upon likeness, there appeared rather an effort towards union which seemed to
rest upon *opposites*.

   " At the beginning of the eighteenth century," says
Kopp, " there arose much opposition to this term, especially among the physicists of that time, who feared that

term 'affinitas' was first introduced
into chemistry in 1696 by Barchusen.
He shows partly that it occurs in
various authors from 1648 (Glauber),
but also that it occurs in Albertus
Magnus (in the 'De Rebus Metallicis,'
printed 1518).   We may mention
further that the term 'affinis,' in the
chemical sense, occurs also in Alsted's
Encyklopädie (1630), p. 2276, and
therefore, at least, in the authorities
employed by this compiler.   As to

the alchemistical origin of the notion
there can be no doubt.
   [16] We may here rely upon the case
of Boyle, who in his older writings,
as in the 'Chemista Scepticus,' still
employs the notion of affinity (cp.
Kopp, Gesch. d. Chemie, ii. 288),
while in the treatise quoted above
(n. 13) on the origin of qualities and
forms, where he has appropriated the
theory of Gassendi (cp. Hist. of Materialism, i. 266, and notes), he avoids
the expression.

its use might involve the recognition of a new ' vis occulta.' In France especially there then predominated a repugnance to the term ' affinity,' and St. F. Geoffroy, at that time (1718 and onwards) one of the chief authorities on chemical relationship, avoided its use. Instead of saying, Two united substances are decomposed if a third is added to them which has more relationship to one of the two bodies than they have to each other, he says, If it has more *rapport* to one of them." [17]   Thus a word comes in very conveniently, not only where ideas are wanting, but even where there are too many. As a matter of fact, there is nothing more in either expression than an hypostatising of the mere process. The paler expression calls up fewer disturbing associations than the coloured one. This might contribute to the avoiding of errors if ideas and names were, in fact, so dangerous in regard to methodical science. The experience of the history of science as to the notion of affinity shows that· the danger is not so great if the objective investigation keeps strictly to its course. The ' vis occulta ' loses its mystic charm, and sinks of itself into a mere comprehensive notion for a class of accurately observed and rigidly defined phenomena.

Hitherto, then, the whole transformation of the ancient idea of atoms is nothing but a single broad consequence of the transformation of the principles of mechanism due to the law of gravitation ; and even the notion of affinity attaches itself to the service of this new circle of ideas without introducing any really new principle as to the nature of force and matter. Chemical experience only directly touches the conception of the nature of matter when Dalton propounds his theory of atomic weights.

The train of thought by which Dalton was led to the fruitful conception of atomic weights is uncommonly clear and simple. He saw himself led by his studies, like

[17] Gesch. d. Chemie, ii. 290.

the German chemist Richter,[18] to the supposition that chemical combinations take place in definite and very simple numerical proportions. While, however, Richter sprang at once from his observation to the most general expression of the idea, viz., that all natural processes are under the control of quantity, number, and weight, Dalton tried hard to secure a picturable conception upon which these simple numbers of the combining weights might be based, and here it was that Atomism came half-way to meet him. And therefore he says himself incidentally, that in order to explain chemical phenomena, all we require is to draw the *right consequences* from the universally adopted Atomism. If Atomism is true, then we cannot intelligibly represent this striking regularity in the combining weights except by a corresponding grouping of the atoms. If we conceive chemical combination in this way, that one atom of the one substance always unites with one, or two, &c., of the other, then the regularity in the combining weights is completely explained and made intelligible. But then it immediately results that the cause of the *variety in the weights* of the combining masses must lie in the *individua atoms*. If we could determine the absolute weight of an atom, we should have the weight of a definite quantum of the body in question by multiplying the atomic weight by the number of atoms ; or, conversely, we could determine, from the weight of the atom and the weight of the given body, the number of the atoms contained in this body by simple division.

In respect of method as well as of the theory of knowledge, it is of interest to see how Dalton's *strictly sensuous* mode of conception forthwith made its way, while the more speculative idea of Richter rather hindered the spread of his extremely important discoveries. It is nowhere so

---

[18] Full details as to Richter and his discoveries are given by Kopp, Entwickel. d. Chemie, in the Gesch. d. Wissensch. in Deutschl., München, 1873, S. 252 ff.

clear as in the history of modern chemistry how sensuous intuition, as an indispensable necessity for the taking of our bearings in phenomena, ever afresh reasserts itself, and almost always attains brilliant results, often as it may have been shown, too, that all these modes of conception are merely helps to the constant establishing of causal connection, and that every attempt to find in them a definitive knowledge of the constitution of matter immediately breaks to pieces on new demands which compel us to reconstruct from its foundations the edifice of these views.

Very soon after the decisive victory of the atomic theory of Dalton, the ground was prepared by new discoveries and speculations for an important modification of the view, which, however, was only able to assert itself generally after a long period of non-recognition. Gay-Lussac's discovery in 1808 that the various gases under equal pressures and equal temperatures combine in *simple volumetric proportions*, and that the volume of such a combination stands in a very simple relation to the volume of its constituents, must have been a fresh challenge to the acumen of theorists, just as had been previously the discovery of the regularity in atomic weights. And just in the same way as Dalton had then been led, namely, by seeking for a sensuously picturable mode of conceiving the cause of this relation, so Avogadro reached his important *molecular theory*. He found (1811) that the similarity in the relations of all gases towards pressure and temperature and in chemical combination cannot be explained, except by the supposition that the *number of smallest particles* in an equal volume of different gases (under equal pressures and temperatures) is the *same*. But in order to carry out this view consistently he had not only to suppose for compound gases a union of several atoms in their smallest particles, but the smallest particles also of the *simple* gases must, at least partially, be regarded as combinations of several atoms.[19] Thus the *molecules* in many respects occupied the position of atoms; only that they were not simple, but were compounded of the atoms. The smallest particles of a chemical body, then, were molecules; the smallest particles of matter generally were atoms. Only in chemical combinations and separations the atoms come forward, as it were, independently, changing their place and grouping themselves into molecules of altered composition.

Avogadro's hypothesis could not make way beside the immense impulse which was being given meanwhile to the knowledge of chemical facts. Berzelius had accepted Dalton's theory, and supplemented it by supposing that the reason of their various affinities must be sought in the *electrical* relations of the atoms. This theory might for a long time be found satisfactory, and all the zeal of inquirers turned towards analysis. With rapid march the young science conquered the respect of scientific men and the reverence of manufacturers. It had become a power while its foundations were still so doubtful that eminent chemists could doubt whether they were quite justified in claiming for their field of activity the name of a science.

The first discoveries of importance in point of principle were not able to shatter the growing dogmatism of the electro-chemical theory. Dulong and Petit found in 1819 that for simple bodies the specific heat is inversely proportional to the atomic weight—a discovery the fortunes of which exhibit the model of the transformations of an empirical law which has never yet been raised to the rank of a true law of nature. Contradictions, maintenance of the too striking core which no chance could explain, modifications and desperate hypotheses of all kinds gathered around this theory, without the gaining of any adequate

[19] For Avogadro's hypothesis compare Lothar Meyer, Die Modernen Theorien der Chemie und ihre Bedeutung für die chemische Statik, 2 Aufl., Breslau, 1872, S. 20 ff. And besides Weihrich, Ansichten der neueren Chemie, Mainz, 1872, S. 8 ff.

insight into the inner reason of the rare but significant connection. The circumstance that the atomic weights here for the first time became more than mere matters of fact, and were brought into any kind of relation with other qualities of matter, was little regarded so long as no serious defect was felt in the prevailing theory. Mitscherlich's discovery of *isomorphism* in 1819 seemed to afford a glance into the local relations of the atoms; it was, however, in the main only regarded as a wished-for confirmation of the universally accepted atomistic theory. When it was next further discovered that substances of like constituents appear in very different crystalline forms (dimorphism), when it was found that there are bodies which differ in all their chemical and physical properties, even in the specific weight of the gases, whilst they still consist of like quantities of like elements (isomerism), then people saw themselves compelled to have recourse to transpositions and various groupings of the atoms, without as yet possessing any definite principle for these combinations. The rapid development of organic chemistry soon led to such an accumulation of these bold combinations that sober men of science became very uncomfortable.

To all this there was added the fact that the untenableness of the electro-chemical theory became with the progress of science every day more clear. A period of doubt and hesitation was inevitable. The *type-theory*, which in its improved shape had led to the ideas as to the grouping of the atoms in the molecules, being brought at last into a sure path, began by rejecting all speculations as to the constitution of matter, and by simply keeping to the fact that in a body of a certain type of composition *substitutions* of one element for another may occur in accordance with certain rules. Liebig declared in an 'Essay on the Constitution of Organic Acids' (1838) that "we know nothing as to the condition in which the elements of two compound bodies are, so soon as they have united in a chemical combination, and the way in which we conceive these elements as grouped in the combination rests merely upon a convention which has been consecrated by habit under the prevailing theory."[20]   Schönbein expressed himself still more sceptically in an essay in the 'Album of Combe-Varin:' "When ideas are wanting, a word comes in very conveniently, and assuredly in chemistry since Descartes a gross misuse has been made of molecules and their grouping, under the delusion that by such playings of the imagination we can explain absolutely obscure phenomena and deceive the understanding."

In fact, these "playings of the imagination" certainly do not seem to deceive the understanding, but rather to lead it to the maxim which has its foundation deep in the theory of knowledge, that only the rigid carrying out of sensuous picturability can protect our knowledge against the much more dangerous playing with words.   A rigidly carried out intuition, even if it is false in itself, often serves to a great extent as a picture and temporary substitute for the true intuition, and it is always by the laws of our sensibility itself, which are not without relation to the laws of the objective world of phenomena, kept within certain bounds.   But so soon as we operate with words to which there are no clear notions, to say nothing of intuitions to correspond, it is over with all sound knowledge, and opinions are produced which have no value whatever, even as steps towards the truth, but will have to be absolutely set aside.

The employing of the imagination to arrange our thoughts as to material processes is, therefore, in fact, more than mere play, even when, as in this period of chemistry, a general hesitation and groping produces the impression of uncertainty.   On the other hand, indeed, even if this groping about ceases, if a sure and generally trodden, and for the present safe enough, path has been found, it is still very far from affording us a guarantee that our assumptions correspond with facts.

[20] Kopp, Entwickel. d. Chemie, S. 597.

With admirable clearness Kekulé attempted, in his 'Lehrbuch der Organischen Chemie,' 1861, to recall the chemists to consciousness of the borders between hypothesis and fact. He shows that the proportional numbers of combining weights have the value of *fact*, and that the symbols of chemical formulas may be regarded as the simple expression of this fact. "If to the symbols in these formulas another meaning is assigned, if they are regarded as denoting the atoms and the atomic weights of the elements, as is now most common, the question arises, What is the (relative) size or weight of the atoms? Since the atoms can be neither measured nor weighed, it is obvious that we can only be led by reflection and speculation to the hypothetical assumption of determinate atomic weights."

Before we see now what the latest period of chemistry (which again, full of confidence, follows a highly developed theory) proposes to do with matter, it is time to take a glance at the views of the mathematicians and physicists.

That modern physics also must rest upon the Atomic theory is an obvious consequence of the historical development. Gassendi, Descartes, Hobbes, and Newton all started from a physical view of the world; and with Boyle, and even Dalton, physical and chemical research go hand in hand. Yet the paths of physics and of chemistry separated from each other in the same measure as mathematical analysis could make itself master of physics, while the facts of chemistry for a time remained inaccessible to it.

Almost simultaneously with Dalton's chemical atomic theory, the long unrecognised undulation theory made a way for itself in optics—with difficulty enough, because of the prejudices which maintained the emission theory of light. Young's demonstration of the number of vibrations for the different colours belongs to the year 1801. Fresnel received in 1819 the prize of the Academy at Paris for his labours on the refraction of light. After this the theory of light became more and more a mechanism of the æther-atoms; but the idea of the atom had to submit patiently to all the modifications brought about by the necessities of calculation. The strongest of these modifications—although at bottom only the last consequence of the transcendental theory of gravitation—was the denial of any and every kind of extension in the atoms. As early as the middle of the eighteenth century this idea had occurred to the Jesuit Boscovich.[21] He found contradictions in the doctrine of the impact of the atoms, which could only be solved by supposing that the effects which are usually ascribed to the resilience of material particles are due to repulsive forces acting from a point situated in space, but without extension. These points are regarded as the elementary constituents of matter. The physicists who belong to this school describe them as 'simple atoms.'

However well Boscovich had already carried out this theory, it was only in our own century that it found wider approval amongst the French physicists, who occupied themselves with the mechanism of atoms. The rigid logical sense of the French scientific men must, in fact, speedily have discovered that in the world of modern mechanical philosophy the atom, as an extended particle, plays a very superfluous part. As soon as the atoms no longer, as with Gassendi and Boyle, acted immediately upon each other by their bodily mass, but by forces of attraction and repulsion, which stretched through empty space, as between the stars, the atom itself had become a mere bearer of these forces, in which there was nothing essential—a bare substantiality excepted—that would not have found its complete expression in these very forces. Was not all influence, even the influence upon our senses, brought about by the unsensuous forces constructed in empty space? The tiny particle had become an empty tradition. It was still retained, indeed, merely because of its similarity to the great bodies which we can see and touch. This palpable character seemed to afford, moreover, a guarantee

---

[21] Fechner, Atomenlehre, 2 Aufl., S. 229 ff., Leipzig, 1864.

of the sensuous element, such as it exists in really sensible things. But when clearly regarded, even this seizing and handling, to say nothing of seeing and hearing, according to the mechanical philosophy based upon the theory of gravitation, is no longer brought about by direct material contact, but simply by means of these entirely unsensuous forces. Our Materialists hold fast to the sensible particle just *because* they *want* to have a sensuous substratum to the unsensuous force. With such cravings of the mind the French physicists could not trouble themselves. There seemed no longer to be scientific grounds for the extendedness of the atoms; why, then, further hamper ourselves with the useless conception?

Gay-Lussac conceived the atoms, on the analogy of the vanishing magnitude of the differential, as infinitely small in comparison with the bodies compounded from them. Ampère and Cauchy regarded the atoms as in the strictest sense unextended. A similar view was expressed by Seguin, and Moigno concurs with him, and would only prefer, with Faraday, simple force-centres, instead of extensionless bodies.

Thus, then, we should have found our way by the mere development of Atomism into the dynamical conception of nature, and that not by means of speculative philosophy, but of the exact sciences.

It has a peculiar charm for the quiet observer to see how the talented natural philosopher and physicist, to whom we are indebted for these notices of Ampère, Cauchy, Seguin, and Moigno,[22] is himself situated towards Atomism. Fechner, the sometime disciple of Schelling, the editor of the mystical and mythical Zend-Avesta, Fechner, who is himself a living proof that even an enthusiastic philosophy does not always corrupt the spirit of true research, has actually employed his atomic theory to indite a challenge to philosophy, by the side of which even

---

· [22] Fechner, Atomenl., S. 231 ff.

Büchner's utterances may seem somewhat flattering. He obviously, indeed, confounds philosophy in general with that kind of philosophy through which he himself has passed. All the ingenious applications of Fechner, the numerous imaginative images and similes, the acute arguments, come at last merely to this, that Fechner looks for every philosopher at the fireside he once haunted himself.

In fact, the whole controversy between philosophy and physics, as Fechner conceives it, is properly an anachronism. Where should we look in these days for the philosophy which could make any serious pretension to forbid physicists their atomism ? We leave here entirely out of account the fact that Fechner's " simple " atoms are at bottom no longer atoms ; that a construction of the universe out of force-centres without any extension must, strictly considered, be reckoned with *dynamical* views. Even to that dynamism, which starts from the denial of empty space, Fechner makes such concessions, that it savours, not of philosophy, but shortsighted self-sufficiency, not to be able quietly to conclude peace, so far as regards merely the relation of philosophy to physics.

Fechner gives up not only the indivisibility of the atoms, and ultimately even their extension, but he observes also quite correctly that the physicist cannot venture to assert " that the space between his atoms is absolutely empty ; that a fine continuous essence does not rather extend between them, which merely has no further influence upon the phenomena that he can judge of." " The physicist does not speak of such possibilities as are indifferent to him, only because they do not help him. But if they can help the philosopher in any way, then it is his business to regard them. And it were a sufficient service to him if they put him in a position to conclude a treaty with the exact sciences. The physicist only uses atoms primarily, not ultimately. If the philosopher concedes his atoms to the physicist primarily, the latter can readily concede to him his full space ultimately. The two things are not contradictory." [23]

Of course not. So long as we thus rigidly sunder the two provinces, he must be a curious philosopher (though we may always possess a few such in Germany) who would contest with the physicist the *primary*, *i.e.*, the *technical* use of Atomism. Such a contest would have, indeed, no logical —and therefore, it may be hoped also, no philosophical— meaning, except in so far as the philosopher himself becomes a physicist, and by special employment of experiment and equations shows how it might be better done. The bare assertion, it must be so, because it is rational, despite the pretensions it contains, does not go so far as to contest the primary use of Atomism; for the philosopher who should postulate a system of physics on his own principles, can still not deny that the way in which things are realised is sometimes a different one; and this way has its justification only in its success. One must be able to do things better, or quietly look on and see how they are done; for the specialist, who remains consistently at Fechner's standpoint, cannot deny, too, that his task may perhaps some day be regulated just as well, if not better, on other principles. But with this possibility he does not trouble himself, so long as nothing crops up on his successful course that compels him objectively to turn into another path.

But does Fechner himself in his Atomism keep to the standpoint of the physicist? By no means. The passage just cited is taken from the first part of his work, in which he sets forth the physical theory of atoms, just as it is taught in the exact sciences. His own view of the 'simple' atoms, on the other hand, he himself reckons as belonging to 'philosophical' Atomism. The advantage of his standpoint he sees only in this, that here the Atomism of the Physicists tapers, as it were, into philosophy, and in its extreme consequences contains a philosophical conception,

[23] Atomenl., S. 76, 77.

while the view of the " philosophers " combated by him is in contradiction with empirical inquiry. We have, then, exactly as in the case of Büchner, a theory of things sprung up on the soil of natural inquiry, which declares war upon all "philosophy," while it nevertheless gives itself out as philosophy. The enigma is solved if we assume that it is the philosophy of the *professor of physics* which here asserts itself against that of the *professor of metaphysics*—a controversy which cannot any longer concern us, as we do not recognise any such guild of philosophers, and, so far as they try to assert themselves in our own day, must deny them any scientific importance.

The philosopher Fechner comes to terms with the physicist Fechner, when the latter requires extended particles, very simply ; the extended particles are then, just like the molecules of the chemists, themselves again compounded bodies. In fact, there are, too, in physics, as in chemistry, other empirical reasons which do not admit of our referring such visible bodies without any middle terms directly to unextended force-centres. Redtenbacher, who has done admirable service in the mathematical theory of molecular movements, constructs his molecules from " dynamids." By these he understands corporeal, gravitating, and extended atoms, which are surrounded by an atmosphere of discrete æther particles, endued with repulsive force. In relation to these, therefore, the corporeal atom is not only extended, but must, in fact, be conceived as extraordinarily large. The reason that determines him to reject Cauchy's punctual atoms lies in the necessity of supposing for the vibrations of corporeal atoms in various directions a varying elasticity in them.

" As we presuppose a system of dynamids with axes of elasticity, we must necessarily regard the atoms as tiny particles of definite if unknown form, for only if the atoms possess axial form, and are not mere points or spheres, can there exist in a state of equilibrium an unlike elasticity in different directions ? Cauchy bases his investigations upon a medium consisting of corporeal points, but at the same time supposes that the elasticity about each point is different in different directions. This is a contradiction, an impossibility, and hence a weak side of Cauchy's theory." [24]

But if now we wish to avoid the assumption—one little agreeable to our understanding—that there are bodies which, in relation to others (the æther particles), are infinitely large and yet utterly indivisible, we find a simple way out of it by regarding the corporeal atom, which forms the core of the dynamid, merely as *relatively* indivisible, that is to say, as indivisible so far as our experience and our calculations require. It may then possess axial form, and again be composed of infinite, infinitely smaller, under-atoms of similar form. This assumption may, without demanding any serious change, run through all Redtenbacher's calculations. It is harmless metaphysic, and can neither bring about nor prevent any discovery. And if, for the convenience of the physicist, we agree to treat the relatively empty space as absolutely empty, the relatively indivisible body as absolutely indivisible, everything remains as it was. The mathematician, in particular, who is accustomed to leave out of his calculation the higher powers of an infinitely small magnitude, can have no reason to demur.

But the thing must still stop somewhere, says ordinary common sense. Good; but it is just the same as in all dealing with infinity. Science leads us to the idea of the infinite; our natural feelings struggle against it. Upon what this struggle is based it is hard to say. Kant would attribute it to the efforts of the reason after unity, which come into conflict with the understanding. But these are merely names for an unexplained fact. Man has not two different organs, understanding and reason, related to each other like eye and ear. It is, however, certain that judgment and inference lead us on from one step to another,

[24] Redtenbacher, Das Dynamidensystem, Grundzüge einer mechanischen Physik, Mannh., 1857, S. 95 ff.

VOL. II.   2 A

and bring us at last to the infinite, while we feel need of some conclusion—a need which comes into conflict with these endless inferences.

Büchner, in his work 'Ueber Natur und Geist,' makes the philosophical Wilhelm—who is, of course, a simpleton —advocate the idea of infinite divisibility. But Augustus, who understands something of natural science, answers him with the following oracular utterance :—

"You trouble yourself with difficulties which are more speculative than practical." (Observe, this is a discussion which is wholly and entirely speculative.) "Though we are not in a position to place ourselves in thought at the farthest point, at which matter is no more divisible, yet there must somewhere be a limit to it." There is, indeed, nothing like a vigorous faith! "To suppose an infinite divisibility is absurd; it means to assume nothing, and to throw doubt upon the existence of matter at all—an existence which no unprejudiced person can successfully deny."

It cannot be our duty to defend Ampère against Büchner, especially as Büchner himself in 'Force and Matter' declares atom to be a mere expression, and admits infinite smallness. We must rather ask ourselves how it comes to pass that, in the light of our contemporary physics, such an idea of matter as Büchner's 'Augustus' regards as necessary can still exist? A professed physicist, even if he assumes extended atoms, will not easily fall into the mistake of making the *existence* of what we in daily life and in science call matter dependent upon the existence of extended particles. Redtenbacher, for instance, asserts against Cauchy merely his axes of elasticity, but not the reality of matter. On the other hand, we must not blink the fact that Büchner's 'Augustus,' as the author probably intended, expresses the views of almost all unscientific persons who have more or less concerned themselves with these questions. But the reason of this may lie in the fact that they cannot sufficiently free themselves from the sensuous idea of compound, apparently compact, bodies, such as our touch and eye present them to us. The professed physicist, at least the mathematical physicist, cannot make the least step in his science without freeing himself from such ideas. Everything as it appears to him is an effect of forces, and matter forms a subject for these forces, which is in itself quite empty. But force cannot be at all adequately represented in forms of sense : we help ourselves by pictures, such as the lines of the figures in the doctrines of mathematics, without ever confounding these pictures with the notion of force. How this constant habituation to an abstract mental conception of force easily passes over with the specialist, into the notion of matter, may be shown us by the example of a physicist whose name reflects special glory upon German science.

W. Weber, in a letter to Fechner,[25] writes thus :—" What is required is, with regard to the causes of motion, to eliminate such a constant part that the remainder is indeed variable, but its variations may be conceived as solely dependent on measurable relations of space and time. In this way we attain to an idea of mass to which the notion of spatial extension is not necessarily attached. Consequently then the magnitude too of the atoms in atomistic modes of conception is measured not at all according to spatial extension, but according to their mass, *i.e.*, according to the relation constant in every atom, in which in this atom the force always stands to its rapidity. The idea of mass (as in the case of the atoms also) is thus no more crude and materialistic than the idea of force, but is entirely equal to it in delicacy and intellectual clearness."

Well, of course, with these speculations, which refine away the nature of mass and of the atom into an hypostasised notion, the latest *doctrines of chemistry,* which have obtained so thorough a success, stand in peculiar opposition. We shall not venture to begin by depreciating these doctrines if we reflect that it is not a mere question of a

[25] Fechner, Atomenl., S. 88 ff.

scientific fashion, but that chemistry, by means of its now ruling views, is just placed in a position to *predict* the existence of as yet undiscovered bodies, according to the requirements of the theory, and thus to a certain extent to proceed deductively.[26]   The decisive idea of this new doctrine is that of the atomicity or " quantivalence " of the atoms.

From the development of the type theory, and the observations on the volumetric combination of the elements in the gaseous state, it was collected that there is a class of elements whose atoms only combine with one atom of another element (type hydrochloric acid) ; another class whose atoms always form a combination with two atoms of another element (type water) ; a third (type ammonia) whose atoms attach to themselves three other atoms.[27]   The atoms in question were called, according to this property, mon-, di-, and tri-atomic, and this classification was found to afford a very valuable starting-point for investigation, since it had been shown that the *substitutions,* that is, the replacing of one atom in a molecule by another, or by a so to say fixed combination of others, might be ordered on the principle of quantivalence, and their possibility predetermined.   Thus from simple combinations it was possible, in accordance with a rule, to infer compound and ever more complex ones; and a quantity of organic substances of very complex structure

---

[26] From the principle of the success in substitution of an atom of methyl in place of an atom of hydrogen, Kolbe inferred the existence and the chemical relations of yet undiscovered combinations, and his predictions were brilliantly justified by subsequent investigations (Weihrich, Ansichten d. neueren Chemie, S. 44). That Kolbe at that time was strongly opposed to the theory of types is here indifferent, as his substitution doctrine was later fused with the corrected theory of types.   Lothar Meyer, Die modernen Theorieen der Chemie

(2 Aufl., 1872), discusses, *inter alia,* in §§ 181 and 182, far-reaching speculations on the existence and the properties of yet undiscovered *elements,* and deals in the Conclusion to his second edition (esp. S. 360 ff.) with the possibility, but at the same time the difficulties, of a deductive procedure in chemistry.

[27] Cp. the extremely lucid and generally intelligible development of what we can here only briefly indicate in Hofmann's Einleit. in d. moderne Chemie, 5 Aufl., Braunschw., 1871.

has been discovered through taking as the clue the law of quantivalence and the resulting concatenation of atoms.

While before it was only the fact of isomerism that had led to the view that the properties of bodies was not absolutely dependent upon the number and character of the elements appearing in them, but that a difference in the disposition of the atoms must also have some influence, now the mode in which the atoms were combined in the molecules became the main principle of inquiry and of explanation; especially when in carbon yet another element was found with tetratomic atoms (type olefiant gas), to which were speedily added, at least hypothetically, atoms combining by fives and sixes.

With reference to methodology and the theory of knowledge, it is of interest to observe here the curious halting of the chemists between a concretely sensuous and an abstract conception of quantivalence. On the one hand, they hesitate to introduce into this dark sphere fanciful ideas, the agreement of which with the reality could hardly pass even for problematical; while, on the other hand, they are guided by a proper inclination to assume nothing that cannot be clearly represented in one way, or even in various ways, in the forms of sense. And thus they talk of the 'points of affinity' in the atoms, of 'attaching' to them, of 'occupied' and still free points, just as if they saw before them, in the extended and crystal-like body of the atom, such points, *e.g.*, as poles of a magnetically working force; but, at the same time, they protect themselves against the acceptation of such sensuous conceptions, and declare the 'points of affinity' to be a mere phrase for the purpose of embracing the facts. Nay, Kekulé has even attempted to reduce the quantivalence of the atoms, with an entire surrender of the 'points of affinity,' to the "relative number of the impacts which one atom receives from another atom in a unit of time."[28]

This hypothesis has not as yet met with approval, but

[28] Cp. Weihrich, Ans. d. n. Chemie, S. 38 f.

for all that the atoms do receive *impacts.* Here the recent theory of heat shows a striking agreement with chemistry. According to Clausius,[29] the molecules of the gases are engaged in a graduated motion, whose living force is proportional to the temperature. In the fluid state of bodies there exists a motion of the molecules increasing with the temperature, which is strong enough to overcome the attraction of two neighbouring particles, but not strong enough to outweigh the attraction of the whole mass; in the solid state the attraction of the neighbouring particles at length outweighs the impulse of heat, so that the molecules can only change their relative position within narrow limits. This theory, which has grown out of the doctrine of the conversion of heat into active force and back again, no longer needs any æther in order to give a satisfactory solution of all the problems of the theory of heat. It explains in the simplest way the changes in the physical conditions under the influence of heat; but it leaves the condition of solid bodies still rather obscure, sheds a half light upon the condition of fluids, and only as to the condition of perfect gases gives so clear a picture that apparently little more can be desired.

Here again, therefore, the latest theories of chemists and of physicists coincide in starting from the gaseous condition of matter as the most intelligible, and attempting to advance from this point.[30]   But here, in the case of the

[29] Clausius, Abhandl. über die mechanische Wärmetheorie (orig. in Poggend. Ann.), Braunschw., 1854 and 1867; Abh. xiv. (ii. 229 ff.); Ueber die Art der Bewegung welche wir Wärme nennen. Clausius there mentions as his immediate predecessor Krönig, who, in his 'Grundzüge einer Theorie der Gase,' started with essentially similar views. He traces, however, in a note the general idea of the increasing motion of the gas-molecules through Dan. Bernoulli and Le Sage back to Boyle, Gassendi, and Lucretius. Clausius himself hit upon his notion without any historical suggestion; but otherwise the co-operation of tradition in this series is unmistakable.

[30] The most noteworthy attempt to turn chemistry in this way into a *mechanism of atoms* is in Naumann, Grundriss der Thermochemie, Braunschw., 1869. In this very clearly written treatise the most essential principles of Clausius' theory may be found in a simplified shape, which avoids the application of the higher mathematics.

perfect gases, the old *mechanism of impact* is, as it were, developed in fresh brilliancy. The universal attraction of matter, together with the other molecular forces which act only at close quarters, are regarded as disappearing, as compared with the gradually increasing heat motion, and this goes on continually until the molecules strike upon other molecules, or upon fixed barriers. The laws of elastic impact here dominate, and the molecules are for simplicity's sake treated as spherical, which, it is true, seems not quite consistent with the requirements of chemistry.

We pass over the numerous advantages which the new theory possesses in offering a natural solution, *e.g.*, for the irregularities of Mariotte's law, for the apparent exceptions to Avogadro's rule, and many similar difficulties. We are chiefly concerned to regard somewhat more closely the principle which here again comes up of the mechanical impact of the molecules and atoms with reference to the question of force and matter.

Here, then, that *picturability* which had disappeared from mechanics since Newton is apparently re-established; and we might, if anything were gained by it, entertain a bold hope that even such cases of *actio in distans* as are still retained by the theory will sooner or later disappear, and be referred to sensuously picturable impact, in the same way as has been done in the case of heat. But, of course, only elastic impact can satisfy the requirements of physics, and this case has its own special difficulties. It cannot, indeed, be denied that the old atomists too, in their theory of the impact of the atoms, must have chiefly had in their minds the notion of elastic bodies; but the conditions under which these passed on their motions to one another were unknown to them, and the distinction between the impact of elastic and unelastic bodies was veiled in darkness to them. As now, their atoms were absolutely *unchangeable;* they could not be elastic either, so that more exact physics stumbled against a contradiction on the very threshold of the system. This contradiction was, indeed, not so obvious as it will appear to us nowadays; for even in the seventeenth century physicists of the first order were very seriously experimenting to find out whether or not an elastic ball, upon impact, suffers a flattening, and therefore a compression.[31]

At present we know that no elasticity is conceivable without dislocation of the *relative positions of the particles* in the elastic body. But from this it unavoidably follows that every elastic body is not only changeable, but also consists of *discrete particles*. The latter proposition can, at most, only be controverted by the same reasons with which Atomism in general is controverted. Exactly the same reasons which from the first have led us to resolve bodies into atoms must also show that the atoms, if they are elastic themselves, again consist of discrete particles, and therefore of sub-atoms. And these sub-atoms? They either resolve themselves into mere force-centres, or if in them again elastic impact has to play any part, they must in turn consist of sub-atoms; and we should again have that process running on to infinity, in which the understanding no more finds satisfaction than the process itself can give way to the understanding.

Accordingly there is already contained in Atomism itself, while it seems to establish Materialism, the prin-

---

[31] Huyghens discusses, in his treatise De Lumine, Opp. Amstelod., 1728, i. p. 10 sq., the necessity of time for the transmission of the motion of one elastic body to another, and observes: "Nam inveni, quod ubi impuleram globum ex vitro vel achate in frustum aliquod densum et grande ejusdem materiæ, cujus superficies plana esset et halitu meo aut alio modo obscurata paululum, quædam maculæ rotundæ supererant, majores aut minores, prout major aut minor ictus fuerat, unde manifestum est, corpora illa pauxillum cedere deindeque se restituere; cui tempus impendant necesse est." The treatise 'De Lumine' dates from the year 1690, while Huyghens possessed the principles of his law of elastic impulse as early as 1668 (cp. Dühring, Princ. d. Mechanik, S. 163). It is, therefore, not at all improbable that Huyghens deduced his laws of impact from general phoronomical principles *before* he had instituted the experiments here mentioned. This agrees also completely with the mode of establishing the laws of impact (as described by Dühring), which is based, not upon experiment, but upon general considerations.

ciples which break up all matter, and thus must cut away the ground from Materialism also.

Our Materialists have, indeed, made the attempt to secure to matter its rank and dignity, by endeavouring to make the notion of force strictly subordinate to that of matter; but we need only look a little more closely into this attempt to see at once how little is thus gained for the absolute substantiality of matter.

In Moleschott's 'Kreislauf des Lebens,' a long chapter bears the title of 'Force and Matter.' The chapter contains a polemic against the Aristotelian notion of force, against teleology, against the assumption of a supersensuous vital force, and other pretty things; but not a syllable as to the relation of a simple form of attraction or repulsion between two atoms to the atoms themselves, which are conceived as the bearers of this force. We hear that force is not a striking god, but we do not hear how it proceeds in order to produce from one particle of matter, on through empty space, a movement in another. At bottom we only get one myth for another.

"Just that property of matter which makes its movement possible we call force.　　　Primary matter exhibits its properties only in relation to other matter. If this is not in the required proximity, under suitable conditions, then it produces neither repulsion nor attraction. *Obviously here the form is not wanting;* but it withdraws itself from our senses, because the opportunity of motion is wanting.　　　*Wherever, at any time, oxygen may happen to be, it has a relationship to potassium.*"

Here we find Moleschott deep in Scholasticism; his "relationship" is the prettiest *qualitas occulta* that can be wished for. It sits in the oxygen like a man with hands. If potassium comes anywhere near, it is laid hold of; if none comes, at least the hands are there, and the wish to get hold of potassium.

Büchner goes still less than Moleschott into the relation of Force and Matter, although his best-known work has these words for its title. Just in passing we may mention the proposition: "A force which does not express itself cannot exist." This is at least a healthy view as compared with Moleschott's incarnation of a human abstraction. The best thing that Moleschott gives us about Force and Matter is a long extract from Du Bois-Reymond's Preface to his ' Untersuchungen über thierische Elektricität;' but just the clearest and most important part of it Moleschott has omitted.

In the course of a thorough analysis of the vague conceptions of a so-called vital force, Du Bois-Reymond happens to ask what we represent to ourselves by 'force.' He finds that there are at bottom neither forces nor matter; that both are rather abstractions from things, only regarded from different points of view.

"Force (so far as it is conceived as the cause of motion) is nothing but a more recondite product of the irresistible tendency to personification which is impressed upon us; a rhetorical artifice, as it were, of our brain, which snatches at a figurative term, because it is destitute of any conception clear enough to be literally expressed. In the notions of Force and Matter we find recurring the same dualism which presents itself in the notions of God and the World, of Soul and Body, the same want which once impelled men to people bush and fountain, rock, air, and sea with creatures of their imagination. What do we gain by saying it is reciprocal attraction whereby two particles of matter approach each other? Not the shadow of an insight into the nature of the fact. But, strangely enough, our inherent quest of causes is in a manner satisfied by the involuntary image tracing itself before our inner eye, of a hand which gently draws the inert matter to it, or of invisible tentacles with which the particles of matter clasp each other, try to draw each other close, and at last twine together into a knot." [32]

However much truth these words contain, yet they

[32] Du Bois-Reymond, l.c., Berl., 1848, i. S. xl. ff.

overlook the fact that the progress of the sciences has led us more and more to put force in the place of matter, and that the increasing exactness of research more and more resolves matter into force. The two ideas therefore do not stand so simply as abstractions beside each other, but the one is by abstraction and inquiry resolved into the other, yet so that there is always something left. If we abstract from the motion of a meteoric stone, the body that moved itself remains over. I can take away its form by removing the cohesive force of its particles; then I still have the matter. I can analyse this matter into its elements by setting force against force. Finally, I can break up in thought the elementary substances into their atoms, and then the unitary matter and everything else is force. If now, with Ampère, we resolve the atom too into a *point* without extension, and the forces which group themselves about it, the *point*, "the nothing," must be matter. If I do not go so far in the process of abstraction, then a certain whole remains simply matter, which otherwise appears to me as a combination of material particles through innumerable forces. In a word, the misunderstood or unintelligible remainder from our analysis is always the matter, however far we choose to carry it. What we here understood of the nature of a body we call the *properties* of matter, and the properties we resolve back into "forces." From this it results that the matter is invariably what we cannot or will not further resolve into forces. Our "tendency to personification," or, if we use Kant's phrase, what comes to the same thing, the *category of substance*, compels us always to conceive one of these ideas as subject, the other as predicate. As we analyse the things step by step, the as yet unanalysed remainder always remains as matter, the true representative of the thing. To it therefore we ascribe the properties we have discovered. Thus the great truth, 'No matter without force, no force without matter,' reveals itself as a mere consequence of the principle, 'No subject without predicate, no predicate without subject;' in other words, we cannot see otherwise than as our eye permits, not speak otherwise than as our mouth is formed, not conceive otherwise than the primary ideas of our understanding determine.

Although, accordingly, the personification lies strictly in the notion of matter, yet the constant personification of force also is involved in the notion of its being an outflow of matter, as it were its tool. It is true, indeed, that no one in a physical investigation seriously imagines force as a hand moving in the air : the tentacles would be more suitable, with which one particle embraces another. What is anthropomorphic in the notion of force still belongs at bottom to the notion of matter, to which, as to every subject, we transfer a part of our *ego*. " We recognise the existence of forces," says Redtenbacher,* " by the manifold effects which they produce, and especially through the feeling and consciousness of our own forces." Through the latter element, however, we give to merely mathematical knowledge only the colouring of feeling, and thus at the same time run the risk of making out of force something that it is not. Precisely that assumption of " supersensuous force " which the Materialists, strictly speaking, prefer to combat, always comes to this, that beside the matter that acts upon other matter, force, we think, moreover, of an invisible person, and so bring a false factor into the calculation. This is, however, never the result of too abstract, but rather of too sensuous a mode of thought. The supersensuous element of the mathematician is exactly the opposite of the supersensuous element with the natural man. When the latter brings in supersensuous forces there is a god, a ghost, or some personal being behind, and therefore a being conceived as sensuously as possible. Personified matter is to the natural man of itself far too abstract, and therefore he pictures in imagination a " supersensuous " person besides. The mathematician may, before he has established his equation, represent the forces pretty much like human

* S. 12.

forces, but he will not therefore incur the risk of bringing a false factor into the calculation. But so soon as we have the equation, then every sensuous conception ceases to play any part. Force is no longer the cause of motion, and matter is no longer the cause of force; there is then only a body in motion, and force is a function of motion.

Thus at least we may bring order and a comprehensive survey into these ideas, even if we can have no perfect explanation what force and matter are. Enough if we can show that our categories have something to do with them. Nobody must ask to see his own retina!

Thus, then, it is intelligible, too, that Du Bois-Reymond does not get beyond the antithesis of force and matter, and we will therefore add the passage omitted by Moleschott, in order to show how advantageously the great inquirer is distinguished from the dogmatic confidence of the Materialists.

" If we ask, What, then, is there left if neither force nor matter possesses reality ? those who range themselves with me at this standpoint answer as follows :—It is simply not granted to the human mind in these things to get beyond a final contradiction. We prefer, therefore, instead of revolving in a circle of fruitless speculations, or hewing the knot asunder with the sword of self-delusion, to hold to the intuition of things as they are, to content ourselves, to use the poet's phrase, with the ' Wunder dessen, was da ist.' For we cannot bring ourselves, because a true explanation is forbidden us in one direction, to shut our eyes to the defects of another, for the sole reason that no third explanation seems possible. And we have renunciation enough to accept the idea that in the end the one goal appointed to all science may be, not to comprehend the nature of things, but to make us comprehend that it is incomprehensible. Thus it has finally turned out to be the task of mathematics, not to square the circle, but to show that it cannot be squared; and that of mechanics, not to establish a *Perpetuum Mobile,* but to demonstrate the fruitlessness of such exertions." To this we add, " And the task of philosophy, not to gather metaphysical knowledge, but to show that we cannot get beyond the circle of experience."

So with the advance of science we become ever more certain in our knowledge of the *relations* of things, and ever more uncertain as to the subject of these relations. Everything remains clear and intelligible so long as we can keep to bodies as they appear immediately to our senses, or so long as we can represent to ourselves the hypothetical elements in them, on the analogy of what appeals to our senses. But theory is always carrying us beyond this, and in explaining the given facts scientifically, in carrying our insight into the connection of things so far as to be able to predict phenomena, we are treading the path of an analysis which carries us on to infinity as much as our conceptions of space and time.

We must not marvel, therefore, that to our physicists and chemists the molecules become ever better known, while the atoms at the same time become ever more uncertain; for the molecules are a complex of hypothetical atoms, which we may conceive without any harm entirely in the fashion of sensible things. If science, which here, indeed, seems to offer us objective knowledge, should ever advance so far as to bring the constituents of the molecules as near to us as the molecules at present are, then these constituents cease to be atoms at all, but are also something composite and variable, as they are already often regarded.

As to the molecules of gases, we already know partly with tolerable certainty, partly at least with great probability, the rapidity with which they move, the mean distance they pass through between every two collisions, the number of collisions in a second, and, finally, even their diameter and absolute weight.[33] That these magnitudes,

[33] Cp. the report of a lecture by the English physicist Maxwell in 'Der Naturforscher,' 1873, No. 45, where at S. 421 is given a table of the figures in question for four different gases.

though subject to many corrections, are not built merely in the air, may be shown by the fact that Maxwell has succeeded in deducing from the same formulæ upon which these estimates rest inferences as to the heat-conducting power of various bodies, which have been brilliantly confirmed by experiment.[34] The molecules are these small masses of matter which we may represent to ourselves on the analogy of visible bodies, and with whose properties we are already partly acquainted by means of scientific inquiry. But they are thus removed from that obscure region in which the true elements of things are hidden. We may maintain that 'Atomism' is proved, if by this we understand nothing more than that our scientific explanation of nature, in fact, presupposes discrete particles which move in at least comparatively empty space. But in this view all the philosophical questions as to the constitution of matter are not solved, but only put aside.

And yet even this separation of matter into discrete particles is by no means demonstrated to the extent that these triumphs of science might lead us to suppose; for in all these theories it is already presupposed, and therefore, of course, appears again in our results. The confirmation of Atomism in this weakened sense can at most be viewed in the same light as perhaps the confirmation of Newton's theory by the discovery of Neptune. The discovery of Neptune, on the basis of a calculation on the Newtonian principles, has rightly been regarded as a highly important, and, in many respects, decisive fact; but nobody will therefore maintain that this confirmation of the system also decides the question whether attraction is an action at a distance or whether it takes place through some medium. Even the question whether Newton's law is absolutely valid or only so within certain limits, whether, *e.g.*, it is modified by a very close approximation of particles or

[34] Cp. Maxwell's lecture just cited, ii. Bd., Köln u. Leipz., 1874, S. 119 and Klein's Viertoljahrs-Revue der ff. Fortschr. d. Naturwissenschaften,

by extremely wide removal of them, is not affected by the discovery of Neptune. Recently an attempt has been made to treat Newton's law as a mere special case of the much more general Weber's formula for electric attraction. Neptune throws no light on this point. Whether gravitation acts instantaneously, or whether it requires some time, however infinitesimally small, to convey its effects from one heavenly body to another, is again a question which is not touched by the most brilliant corroboration of this kind. In all these questions, however, lies the true notion of gravitation, and the generally accepted assumption that it is a rigid and unconditional law of nature, acting instantaneously at all distances, is, in the light of our science of to-day, not even a probable hypothesis.

Thus, even in the modern chemico-physical theory of gases, strictly speaking only *relations* have been demonstrated, not the original *position*. On the principles of the hypothetical deductive method, we can say with Clausius and Maxwell, *if* matter consists of discrete particles, they *must* possess the following properties. If now the necessary consequence of this theory is established by experiment, this by no means amounts to a logical proof of the presupposition. We conclude in the *modus ponens* from the condition to the conditioned, not conversely. If we take the converse proposition, then there is always the possibility left that the same consequences may result from very different presuppositions. The theory which rightly explains, and even predicts, the facts, may, indeed, thus gain so much probability, that for our subjective conviction it comes very near to certainty; but still always only supposing that there can be no other theory which will do the same.

That this can by no means be taken for granted in the mechanical theory of heat, so far as the molecules, at least, are concerned, Clausius has carefully borne in mind, when he expressly observes, in the preface to his famous essays, that the most essential features of his mathematical theory are *independent* of the conceptions he has formed as to molecular movements.

Helmholtz goes still farther in his 'Rede zum Gedächtniss an Gustav Magnus' (Berlin, 1871). Here he says (S. 12), "As to the atoms in theoretical physics, Sir W. Thomson says very pointedly that their assumption can explain no property of bodies that has not previously been attributed to the atoms themselves." (This applies, of course, to the molecules also.) "In giving my assent to this expression I by no means wish to declare myself against the existence of the atoms, but only against the efforts to derive the foundations of theoretical physics from purely hypothetical assumptions as to the atomic structure of natural bodies. We know now that many of these hypotheses, which in their time found much approval, shot very wide of the truth. Even mathematical physics has assumed a different character in the hands of Gauss, of F. E. Neumann, and their disciples in Germany, as well as of those mathematicians who attached themselves to Faraday in England, Stokes, W. Thomson, and Clerk Maxwell. It has been seen that even mathematical physics is a pure science of experience ; that it has to follow the same principles as experimental physics. In our immediate experience we find before us only extended bodies of very various form and composition ; and only on such bodies can we make our observations and experiments. Their effects are compounded of the effects which all their parts contribute to the sum of the whole, and if therefore we wish to learn the simplest and most general laws of the masses and matter found in nature, and especially if we wish to free these laws from the accidents of the form, size, and position of the co-operating bodies, we must go back to the laws of the smallest volumes, or, as mathematicians call it, atomic combination. But these are not, like the atoms, disparate and heterogeneous, but continuous and homogeneous."

We pass by the question whether this procedure,

apart from the mathematical treatment for which it must, according to the principles of the differential and integral calculus, be better suited than Atomism, would give us the like or even greater results for the guidance of the mind in the world of phenomena than we owe to Atomism. Atomism owes its successes to the picturability of its assumptions, and so far from therefore depreciating it we might even raise the question, whether the necessity of our atomistic conception might not be deduced from the principles of Kant's theory of knowledge; though this would not forbid the mathematicians, who nowadays love to travel in transcendental ways, to seek their fortune in other paths. That Kant himself, on the contrary, is regarded as the father of 'Dynamism,' by which is meant the dynamism of the continuity theory, need very little affect us, since, however much his Epigoni may have insisted on this continuity-theory, its necessity from the standpoint of the critical philosophy has very little evidence for it, and, as we have said, we might almost try the opposite way with more prospect of success; for the operation of the category in its fusion with intuition always aims at synthesis in an *isolated* object, that is to say, an object which is dissociated in our conception from the infinite links that bind it to everything else. If we bring Atomism under this point of view the isolation of the particles would appear as a necessary physical conception, the validity of which would extend to the whole complex of the world of phenomena, while it would yet be only the reflex of our organisation; the atom would be a creation of the Ego, but for that very reason a necessary basis of all natural science.

We observed above that in our physical and chemical inquiry, the atom becomes the more obscure as clearer light is thrown upon the molecule. This, of course, refers only to the atom in the narrower sense of the word, to the supposed *ultimate* constituent of matter. They always vanish into the inconceivable as the light of research comes nearer to them. Thus, for instance, Lothar Meyer shows that the number of the atoms contained in a molecule while it is within certain limits uncertain must yet not be estimated too high : even the dimensions of the atoms must not be supposed to be infinitesimal as compared with the molecules. The atoms produce lively motions, &c., within the molecules. But immediately upon this twilight knowledge stands the remark, that these atoms probably " are particles of a higher order than the molecules, but still not the ultimate smallest particles."

" It seems rather that as the masses of greater, and therefore more easily perceptible, extension are composed of molecules—the molecules or particles of the first order of atoms or particles of the second order—so too the atoms in turn consist of combinations of particles of a third higher order.

" To this view we are led by the consideration that, if the atoms were invariable, indivisible magnitudes, we must assume just as many kinds of entirely different elementary matters as we know chemical elements. The existence of some sixty, or even more, fundamentally different kinds of matter is, however, in itself not very probable. It is made more improbable still through the knowledge of certain properties of the atoms, amongst which the mutual relations which the atomic weights of different elements exhibit to each other, especially deserve attention." [35]

It is extremely probable that even the atoms of the third order, although they would be atoms of the unitary primitive matter, would, on a closer inspection, resolve themselves into atoms of a fourth order. But all such processes, which run on *ad infinitum*, show that in these questions we have to do merely with the necessary conditions of our knowledge, and not with the question what things may be in themselves, and without any reference to our knowledge..

If in place of this infinite series we substitute anywhere

[35] Lothar Meyer, Die Modernen Theorieen der Chemie, 2 Aufl., §§ 154, 155.

extensionless force-centres, we give up the principle of picturability.[36] It is a transcendental conception, like action at a distance, and the question whether and how far such conceptions are admissible can nowadays, when such quantities of them meet us, hardly any longer be disposed of by a simple reference to the Kantian principles of the theory of knowledge. We must let those who need such modes of conception have their way, and observe what comes of it. If, as the physicist Mach[37] thinks possible, the hypothesis of a space of more than three dimensions should give us a thoroughly simple explanation of actual phenomena, or if we must conclude, with Zöllner,[38] from the darkness of the heavens and other actual phenomena that our space is non-Euklidean, then the whole theory of knowledge must be subjected to an entire revision. For this there are as yet no peremptory reasons;

[36] Completely futile is the objection of Büchner's Augustus (Natur. u. Geist, s. 86), that it is utterly impossible to understand how from unextended incorporeal elements there can result matter and bodies filling space, or how matter can come from force. It is not even necessary that matter should *come* if force is in a position to produce upon our senses—that is, upon the force-centres which finally take up our sense-impressions, such an impress as to result in the conception of bodies. That this conception is something different from its cause, and that we have extended and homogeneous bodies at all merely *in this conception*, must indeed be admitted also by the atomist, who resolves bodies into atoms which are no way contained in our notion of bodies. That the bodies in themselves also, independently of our conception, may consist of simple atoms, Fechner tries to show: Atomenl. 2 Aufl. S. 153. Here appears, however, as in Fechner's whole conception, and essentially even in Demokritos, a new principle which makes things and their properties result from atoms—that of constellation in a whole. But this very principle a deeper-going criticism must regard as being primarily based merely in the subject.

[37] Cp. Mach, Die Geschichte und Die Wurzel des Satzes von der Erhaltung der Arbeit: Prag, 1872. On p. 36 he says, "The reason why no one has hitherto succeeded in establishing a satisfactory theory of electricity lies, perhaps, in the fact that all have sought to explain electrical phenomena in every case by molecular processes in a space of three dimensions." And again, on p. 55, "My attempts to explain mechanically the spectra of chemical elements, and the fact that this theory was contradicted by experience, confirmed me in the view that chemical elements should not be represented in a space of three dimensions."

[38] Zöllner, Die Natur d. Kometen, S. 299 ff.

but even the theory of knowledge must not become dog-matic. Let every one take care how he proceeds! He who holds fast to picturability falls into the process *ad infinitum;* he who abandons it leaves the sure ground from which hitherto all the progress of science has been developed. Between this Scylla and Charybdis we can hardly find a safe path.

Of essential influence upon our judgment as to the rela-tion of force and matter is the law, which has in recent times become so conspicuous and important, of the persist-ence of force. We may conceive it in various ways. We may assume that the chemical elementary substances have certain invariable qualities, with which the general mecha-nism of the atoms co-operates in order to produce pheno-mena; but, again, we may suppose that even the qualities of the elements are only certain forms which, under like circumstances occur in like manner, of the universal and essentially unitary motion of matter. So soon, for instance, as we regard the elements as mere modifications of a homo-geneous primary matter, this latter view becomes a matter of course. Of course, in this strictest and most consequent sense the law of the persistence of force is anything but proved. It is only an 'ideal of the reason,' which, how-ever, cannot well be dispensed with as the ultimate aim of all empirical investigation. Nay, we may assert that just in this widest sense it may claim, too, an axiomatic validity. But then the very last remnant of the independence and dominance of matter would be gone.

Why is the law of the persistence of force in this sense so incomparably more important than the law of the per-sistence of matter, which Demokritos enunciated as an axiom, and which, as the 'indestructibility of matter,' plays so important a part with our modern Materialists?

The explanation is, that in the present state of the natural sciences matter is everywhere the unknown, force the known, element. If instead of force we rather talk of a 'property of matter,' we must beware of a logical circle!

A 'thing' is known to us through its properties; a subject is determined by its predicates. But the 'thing' is, in fact, only the resting-place demanded by our thought. We know nothing but properties and their concurrence in an unknown something, the assumption of which is *a figment of our mind*, though, as it seems, an assumption made necessary and imperative by our organisation.

Dubois's famous 'iron-particle,' which is assuredly the same 'thing,' "whether it traverses the universe in an aërolite, dashes along the metals in an engine-wheel, or runs in a blood-cell through the temples of a poet," is only "the same thing" in all these cases, because we leave out of view the peculiarity of its position towards other particles and the resulting reactions; and, on the other hand, regard as constant other phenomena, which we yet know only as forces of the iron-particle, because we know that in accordance with fixed laws we can always reproduce them. We must first have solved for us the enigma of the parallelogram of forces, if we are to believe in the persistent thing. Or is a force, which moves with the intensity x in the direction $a - b$ also certainly the same thing, if its effect has coalesced with another force into a resultant force of the intensity y and the direction $a - d$? Yes, certainly, the original force is still preserved in the resultant form, and it continues to be preserved even if, in the everlasting vortex of mechanical reactions, the original intensity x and the direction $a - b$ never appear again. From the resultant force I can again take out as it were the original force, if I destroy the second composing force by an equally great one in an opposite direction. Here, then, I know precisely what I must understand by the persistence of force, and what I must not understand. I know, and I must know, that the notion of *persistence* is only a convenient mode of conception. Everything persists, and nothing persists, just as I regard the facts. The actual facts lie only in the equivalents of force which I make to persist through calculation and observation. The equivalents are, as we have seen, also the only real actual fact in chemistry; they are expressed, discovered, calculated by weights, that is, by forces.

Our modern Materialists do not love to deal with the law of the persistence of force. It comes to us from a quarter to which they have not much turned their attention. Although the German public, when the Materialistic controversy broke out, had been acquainted for many years with this important theory, we find scarcely a syllable about it in the most important controversial writings. The fact that Büchner later certainly took up the law, and devoted a special chapter to it in the Fifth Edition of his "Force and Matter," is only a new proof of the activity and many-sidedness of this critic; but it will be in vain to look in him for entire clearness as to the range of this law, and as to its relation to the doctrine of the indestructibility of matter. As to the dogmatic Materialists, who, however, in our time are everywhere and nowhere, by this doctrine of the persistence of force the very ground is cut from beneath their feet.

The true element in Materialism—the exclusion of the miraculous and arbitrary from the nature of things—is by this law established in a higher and more general way than they can establish it from their standpoint; the untrue element—the erection of matter into the principle of all that exists—is by it entirely, and as it would seem definitively, set aside.

It is therefore not to be wondered at, although at the same time not to be entirely approved, that one of those who have best handled the doctrine of the persistence of force almost comes back again to the Aristotelian notion of matter. Helmholtz says, in his ' Abhandlung über die Erhaltung der Kraft,' literally as follows :—

"Science regards the objects of the external world according to abstractions of two kinds : according to their mere existence, apart from their effects on other objects or our senses as such it calls them matter. The existence of matter in itself, therefore, is peaceful and inoperative; we distinguish in it distribution in space and quantity which is treated as eternally invariable. Qualitative distinctions we must not attribute to matter in itself; for if we speak of different kinds of matter, we always assign their difference merely to the difference of their effects, that is, to their forces. Matter in itself, therefore, cannot admit of any other change than one in space, that is, motion. The objects of nature, however, are not inoperative; indeed, we attain to the knowledge of them at all only through their effects, which exhibit themselves on our sense-organs, while we conclude from these effects to a cause of the effects. If, then, we wish to apply the notion of matter in reality, we may only do this by again attributing to it by a second abstraction " (more correctly by a necessary act of imagination, a personification forced upon us psychologically) " what we just before wished to abstract from it, namely, the power to exercise effects, that is, by attributing to it forces. It is obvious that the ideas of matter and force, as applied to nature, *can never be separated.* Pure matter would be indifferent to the rest of nature, because it could never determine any change in nature or in our sense-organs; pure force would be something that must *be (dasein)*, and yet again not *be, because we call the existent matter—weil wir das daseiende Materie nennen.* It is just as inaccurate to try and explain matter as something real, and force as a mere notion to which nothing real corresponds; both are rather abstractions from the real, formed in exactly the same way. We can perceive matter only through its forces, never in itself."[39]

[39] Helmholtz, Ueber die Erhalt. der Kraft, eine physikal. Abhandl., vorgetr. in der Sitzung d. physikal. Gesellsch. zu Berlin, 23 Juli 1847. This strictly scientific essay, after the works of Mayer the first treatment of the principle of the persistence of force that appeared in Germany, must not be confounded with the popular essay with the same title in the Second Part of the " Popular Lectures " of Helmholtz. The passage in question is at S. 3, 4.

Ueberweg, who loved to indicate his dissent in marginal annotations, has in every copy of this essay, opposite to the words, " weil wir das daseiende Materie nennen," quite rightly observed, *"vielmehr Substanz"—rather substance.* In fact, the reason why we cannot suppose a pure force is only to be sought in the psychological necessity by which our observations appear to us under the category of substance. We perceive only forces, but we demand a permanent representative of these changing phenomena, a substance. The Materialists naïvely assume the unknown matter as the only substance; Helmholtz, on the other hand, is quite conscious that we have to do here merely with an *assumption* which is demanded by the nature of our thought, without being valid for absolute reality. It makes little difference, therefore, that in this assumption he puts matter instead of the substance, which he presupposes, however, to be without qualities. His standpoint is essentially that of Kant; but so far as the passive and inoperative nature of matter is concerned, this relapse into the Aristotelian definition might be avoided by adopting a relative idea of matter. This involves also a relative idea of force; and we may be permitted, as the conclusion of this inquiry, to submit here a trio of correlative definitions.

Thing we call a connected group of phenomena, which we conceive as a unity by abstracting their wider relations and internal changes.

Forces we name those properties of the thing which we have discovered by definite effects upon other things.

Matter (Stoff) we call that element in a thing which we cannot or will not further analyse into forces, and which we hypostasise as the origin and bearer of the observed forces.

But have we not, after all, adopted a vicious circle in these explanations? Forces are properties, not of a self-existent matter, but of ' the thing,' and therefore of an abstraction. Do we not, therefore, put into the most concrete, the matter, something that is only the abstraction of an abstraction? And if now we take force in the *strictly physical sense*, is it not a function of the mass, and therefore of matter?

To this we must reply, in the first place, that the notion of mass in mathematical physics is nothing more than a number. If I express the work that a force can accomplish in foot-pounds, the co-efficient, which denotes the height to which anything is raised, is combined with a co-efficient which denotes the weight. But what else is weight than an effect of gravity? We conceive the weight of the whole body as analysed into the weights of a number of hypothetical points, and the sum of these weights is the mass. There is nothing more involved in this notion, and can be nothing more involved. We have therefore only resolved the given force into a sum of hypothetical forces, as to the bearers of which everything applies that we have said above of the atoms. With the assumption of these bearers, which we can neither dispense with nor understand, we have reached the *limit of natural knowledge* that we discussed in the previous chapter.

Fechner[40] has attempted to give matter a meaning independently of force, by explaining it to be what makes itself known to the feeling of touch as the 'palpable,' against the somewhat obvious objection that this palpability rests merely upon the force of resistance (we may in strictly mechanical sense describe it as work done); he appeals to the fact that resistance would be first inferred from relations of touch and other sensations, and is therefore not an empirical (that is, *one* given in *immediate experience*) basis of the idea of matter. But in this immediate experience of the individual sensation, from which Fechner starts, even the scientific notion of matter is not yet to be found. We have nothing but the subjective side of the sensation, which is a mere modification of our condition, and the objective which we can describe quite

[40] Cp. Atomenl., cap. xv. and xvi., especially S. 105 f., and with reference to the notion of force, S. 120.

generally as relation to an object. But this 'object' is in the natural psychological development primarily but a *thing*, and only by reflexion on the apparently changing properties of one and the same thing can the conception arise of matter that persists in all changes. But the same process of necessity develops also the conception of the forces of this matter. And thus even in the psychological solution of the notion of matter we can find no safe anchorage, leaving aside the fact that the decision of the question does not lie here, but in the attempts to discover what still remains of our traditional notions, when they are analysed by the keenest methods of scientific thought.

There is more solidity in Fechner's attack upon the notion of force. The only object of physics, he shows, is the visible and palpable in space, and the laws of its motion. "Force is in physics nothing more than an expression to represent the laws of equilibrium and motion, and every clear apprehension of physical force resolves itself into this. We speak of the laws of force; yet, if we look closer, they are only the laws of equilibrium and motion, which are valid when matter is compared with matter." If here we put things again instead of matter, there is little to object to in this. In fact, it never at all occurs to us to hypostasise force itself instead of matter, and to draw the conclusion—because all that we know in things may be expressed in terms of force, and matter is only a contradictory residue of our analysis, we assume that force has an independent existence. It is enough for us to know that force is a mere 'expression' of absolute applicability, compared with which, so far as our analysis extends, the 'expression' matter retreats into the infinite or the incomprehensible.

If we try to define force as the 'explanation of movement,' this is only to substitute one expression for another. There is no 'explanation' of movement beyond the equivalents of vital and elastic forces, and these equivalents denote a mere relation of phenomena. According to

Fechner, the explanation of movements lies in the law; but is not the law ultimately but an 'expression' for the totality of the relations amongst a group of phenomena?

That the notion of matter even to its incomprehensible residue can not only be reduced to that of force, but that it must also arise again synthetically from these elements, is shown by an interesting example in Zöllner. The question is whether a modification of Newton's laws of motion, in the sense of Weber's law of electricity, cannot be deduced from the assumption that the effects do not pass from one point to another instantaneously, but with a certain expenditure of time; and it is remarked that Gauss had already made an attempt at a 'translatable conception' of such a propagation of force through space, without, however, succeeding. Recently, again, the mathematician C. Neumann has endeavoured to solve this problem by very simply making the potential values, and therefore the mathematical expression for pure quantities of force, transmit themselves through space. This is obviously to cut asunder with the sword the Gordian knot of the 'translatableness' of the conception. We have a supplementary force, the bearer of which is no longer matter, but the mere formula, as if we were to say motion is what moves itself in space. But Zöllner shows quite justly that the mere fact of the hypostasising of this independently moving potential value comes absolutely to the same thing, as if we should make material particles move from one body to another. In fact, we need only attribute to the abstract ideas of force and motion an independent existence, and we turn them at once into *substance,* and substance in the scientific view completely coincides in this case with ' matter.' [41]

We cannot ask a clearer proof that the whole problem of force and matter runs into a problem of the theory of knowledge, and that the natural sciences can only find

[41] Zöllner, Die Natur der Kometen, S. 334-337.

sure ground in *relations*, while certain bearers of these relations (as, for instance, atoms) may be hypothetically introduced and treated as actual realities; always, of course, supposing that we do not erect these 'realities' into a dogma, and that we leave the unsolved problems of speculation to stand where they stand, and as what they really are, that is to say, *problems of the theory of knowledge.*

END OF VOL. II.

PRINTED BY BALLANTYNE, HANSON AND CO
EDINBURGH AND LONDON